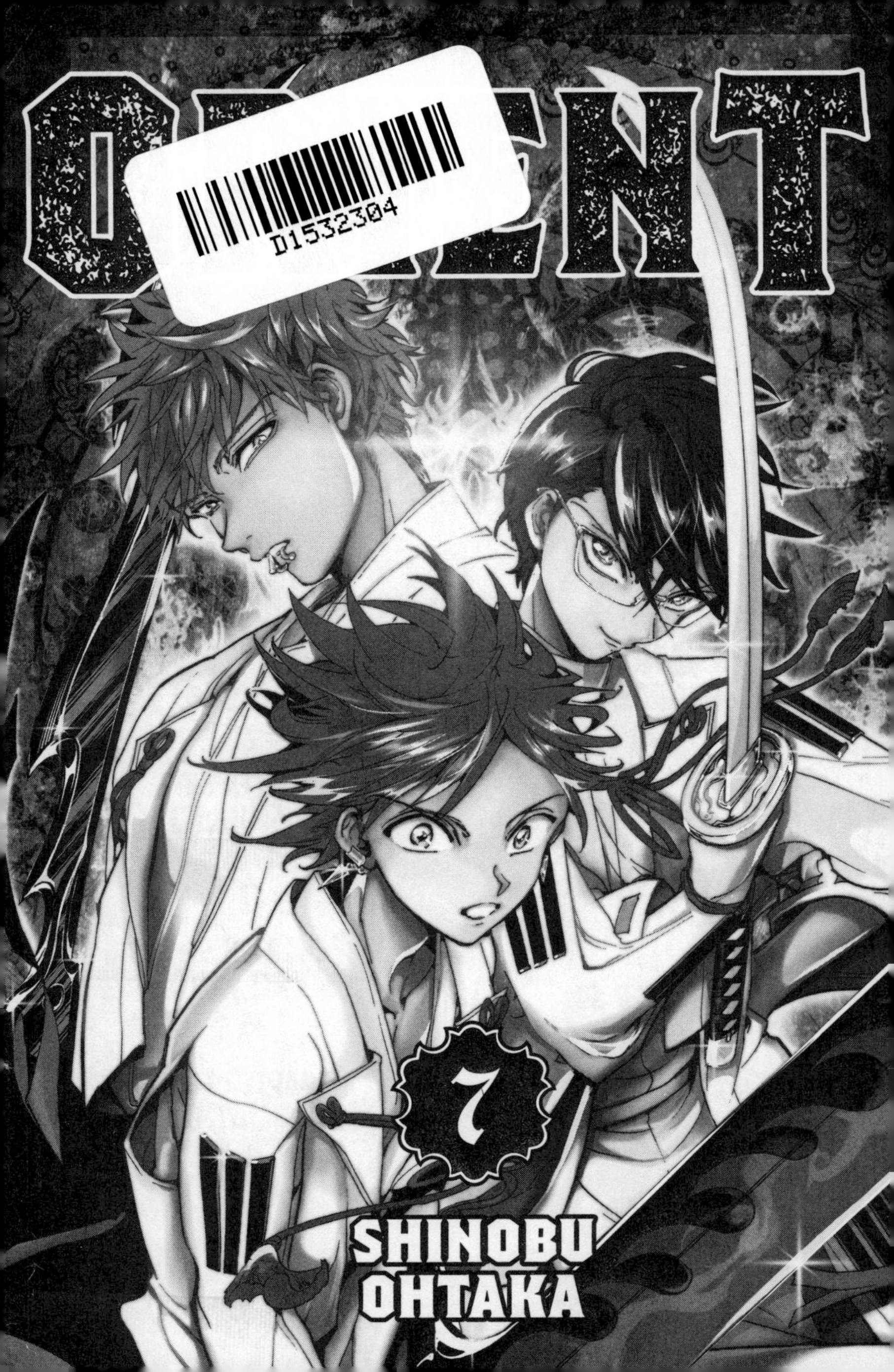
7
SHINOBU
OHTAKA

ORIENT

7

SHINOBU OHTAKA

CONTENTS

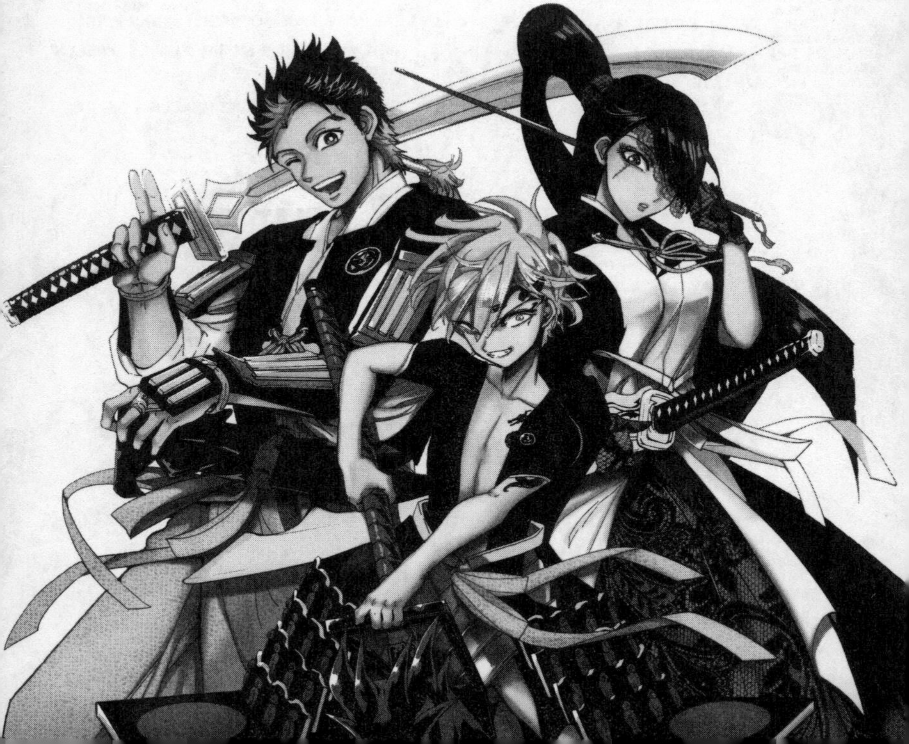

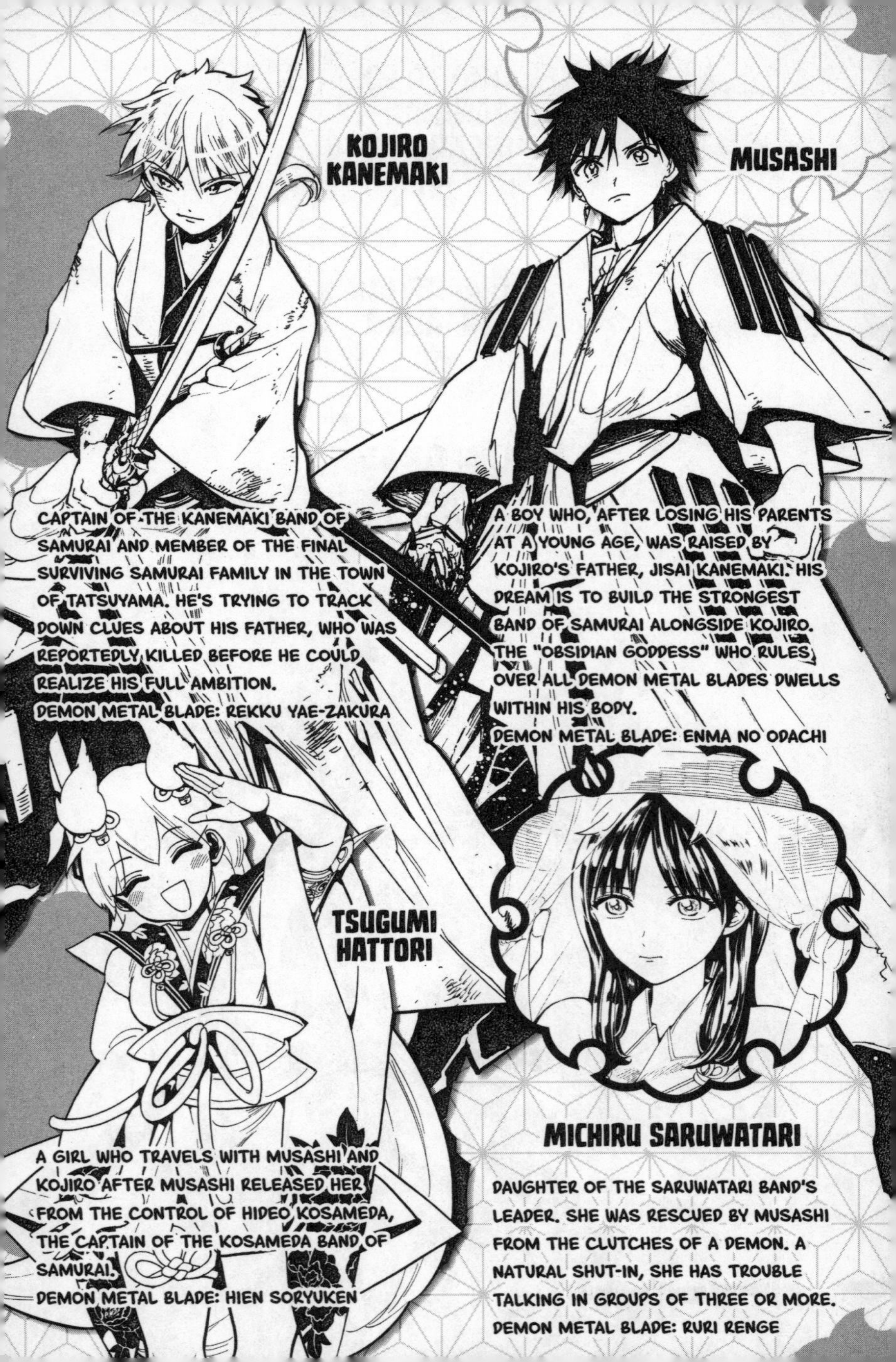
MUSASHI
A BOY WHO, AFTER LOSING HIS PARENTS AT A YOUNG AGE, WAS RAISED BY KOJIRO'S FATHER, JISAI KANEMAKI. HIS DREAM IS TO BUILD THE STRONGEST BAND OF SAMURAI ALONGSIDE KOJIRO. THE "OBSIDIAN GODDESS" WHO RULES OVER ALL DEMON METAL BLADES DWELLS WITHIN HIS BODY.
DEMON METAL BLADE: ENMA NO ODACHI
KOJIRO KANEMAKI
CAPTAIN OF THE KANEMAKI BAND OF SAMURAI AND MEMBER OF THE FINAL SURVIVING SAMURAI FAMILY IN THE TOWN OF TATSUYAMA. HE'S TRYING TO TRACK DOWN CLUES ABOUT HIS FATHER, WHO WAS REPORTEDLY KILLED BEFORE HE COULD REALIZE HIS FULL AMBITION.
DEMON METAL BLADE: REKKU YAE-ZAKURA
MICHIRU SARUWATARI
DAUGHTER OF THE SARUWATARI BAND'S LEADER. SHE WAS RESCUED BY MUSASHI FROM THE CLUTCHES OF A DEMON. A NATURAL SHUT-IN, SHE HAS TROUBLE TALKING IN GROUPS OF THREE OR MORE.
DEMON METAL BLADE: RURI RENGE
TSUGUMI HATTORI
A GIRL WHO TRAVELS WITH MUSASHI AND KOJIRO AFTER MUSASHI RELEASED HER FROM THE CONTROL OF HIDEO KOSAMEDA, THE CAPTAIN OF THE KOSAMEDA BAND OF SAMURAI.
DEMON METAL BLADE: HIEN SORYUKEN

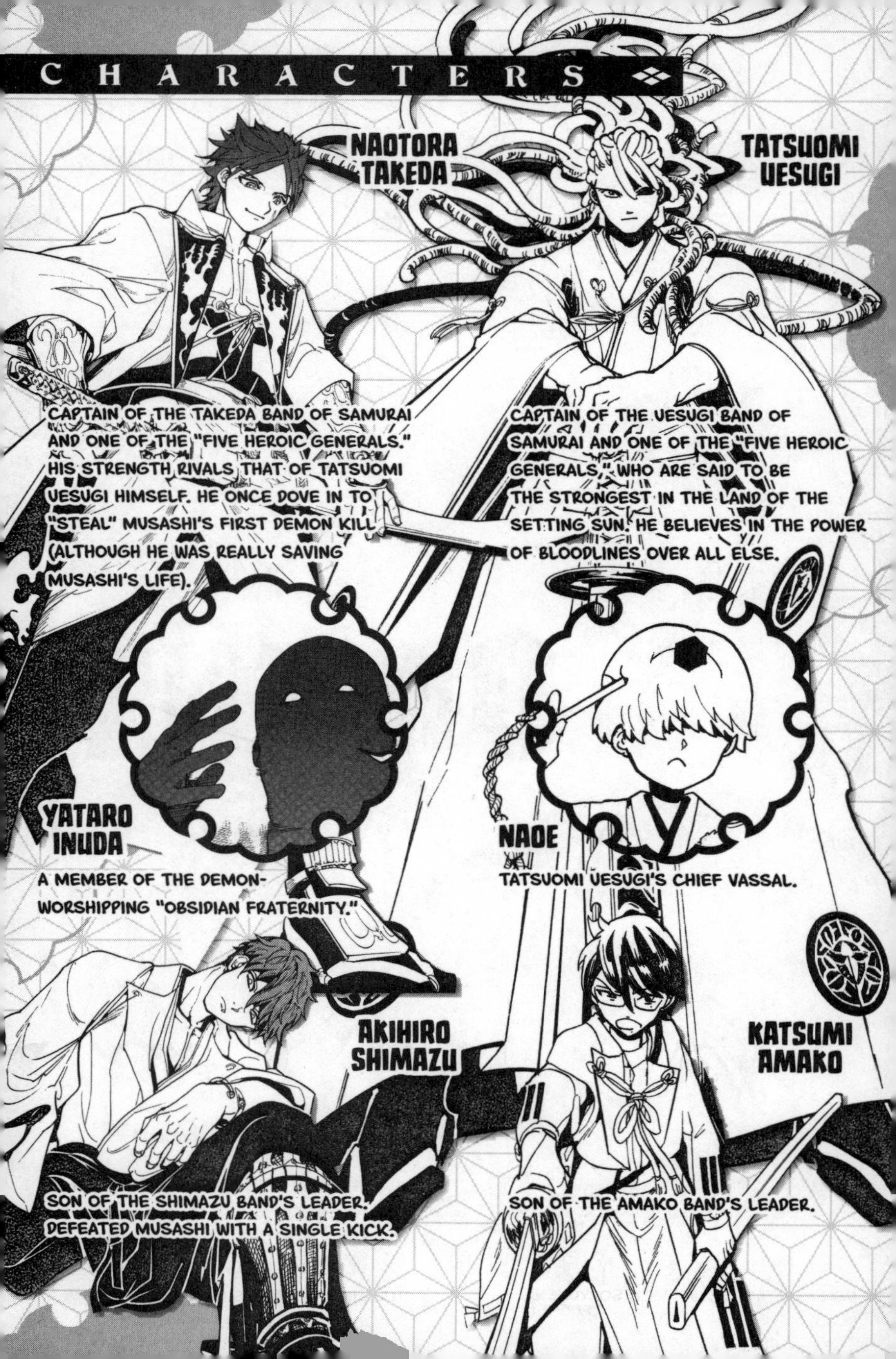
CHARACTERS
TATSUOMI UESUGI
CAPTAIN OF THE UESUGI BAND OF SAMURAI AND ONE OF THE "FIVE HEROIC GENERALS," WHO ARE SAID TO BE THE STRONGEST IN THE LAND OF THE SETTING SUN. HE BELIEVES IN THE POWER OF BLOODLINES OVER ALL ELSE.
NAOTORA TAKEDA
CAPTAIN OF THE TAKEDA BAND OF SAMURAI AND ONE OF THE "FIVE HEROIC GENERALS." HIS STRENGTH RIVALS THAT OF TATSUOMI UESUGI HIMSELF. HE ONCE DOVE IN TO "STEAL" MUSASHI'S FIRST DEMON KILL (ALTHOUGH HE WAS REALLY SAVING MUSASHI'S LIFE).
NAOE
TATSUOMI UESUGI'S CHIEF VASSAL.
YATARO INUDA
A MEMBER OF THE DEMON-WORSHIPPING "OBSIDIAN FRATERNITY."
KATSUMI AMAKO
SON OF THE AMAKO BAND'S LEADER.
AKIHIRO SHIMAZU
SON OF THE SHIMAZU BAND'S LEADER. DEFEATED MUSASHI WITH A SINGLE KICK.

ORIENT

CHAPTER 53: SHIMAZU'S SWORD SKILLS

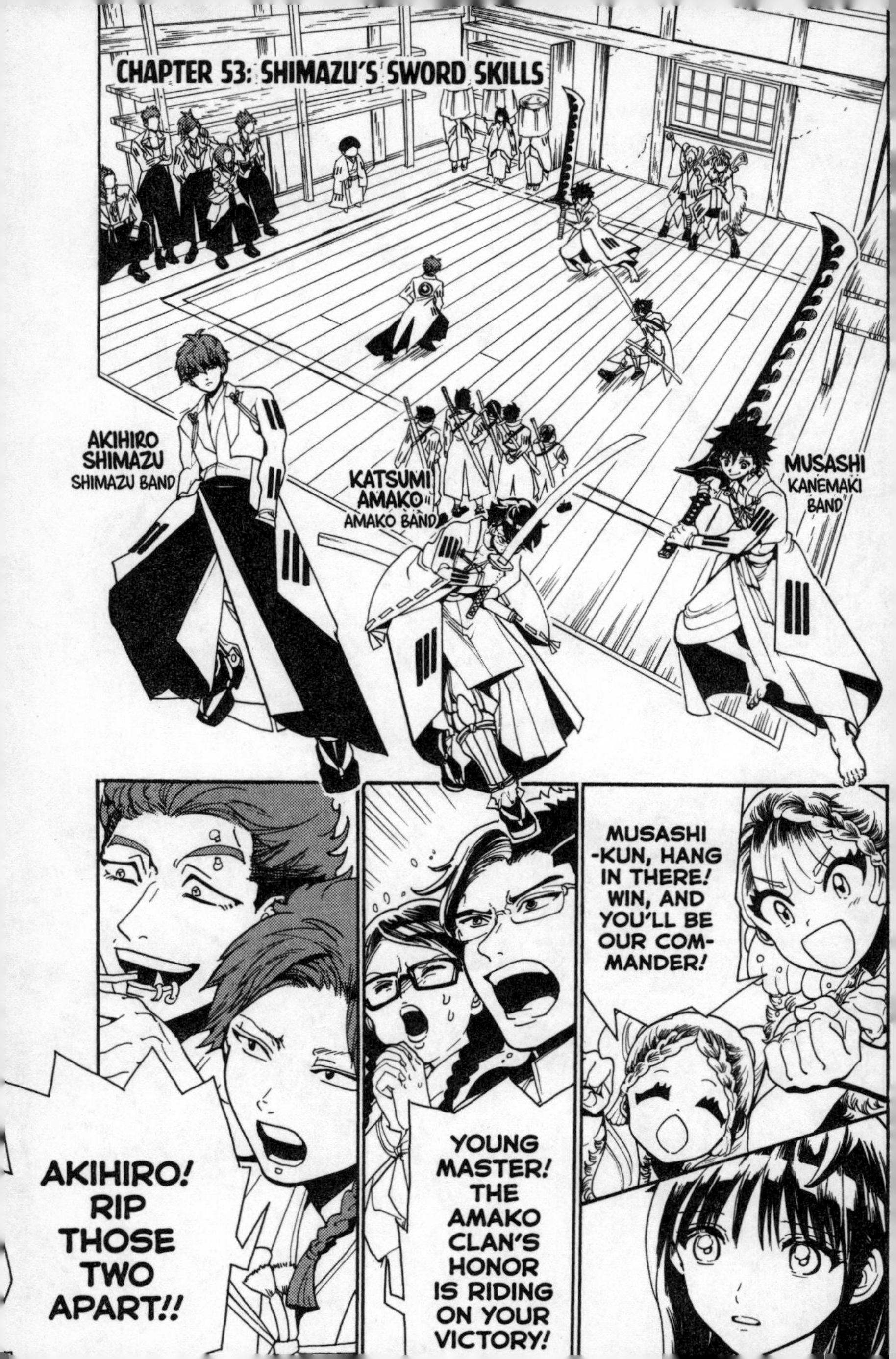
MUSASHI
KANEMAKI BAND
KATSUMI AMAKO
AMAKO BAND
AKIHIRO SHIMAZU
SHIMAZU BAND
MUSASHI-KUN, HANG IN THERE! WIN, AND YOU'LL BE OUR COMMANDER!
YOUNG MASTER! THE AMAKO CLAN'S HONOR IS RIDING ON YOUR VICTORY!
AKIHIRO! RIP THOSE TWO APART!!

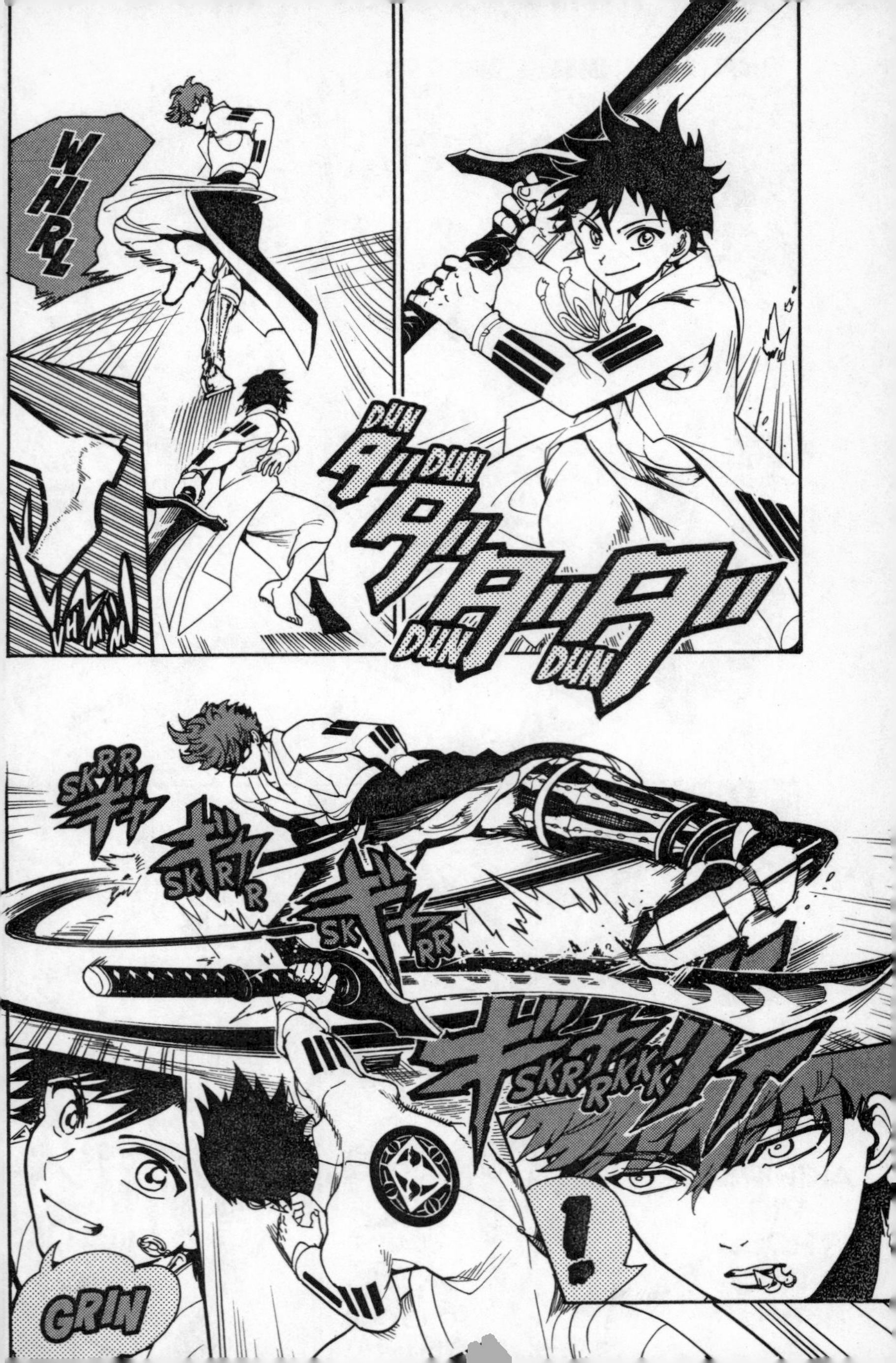
DUN DUN DUN DUN
WHIRL
VHMMM
SKRR
SKRR
SKRR
SKRRRKKK
!
GRIN

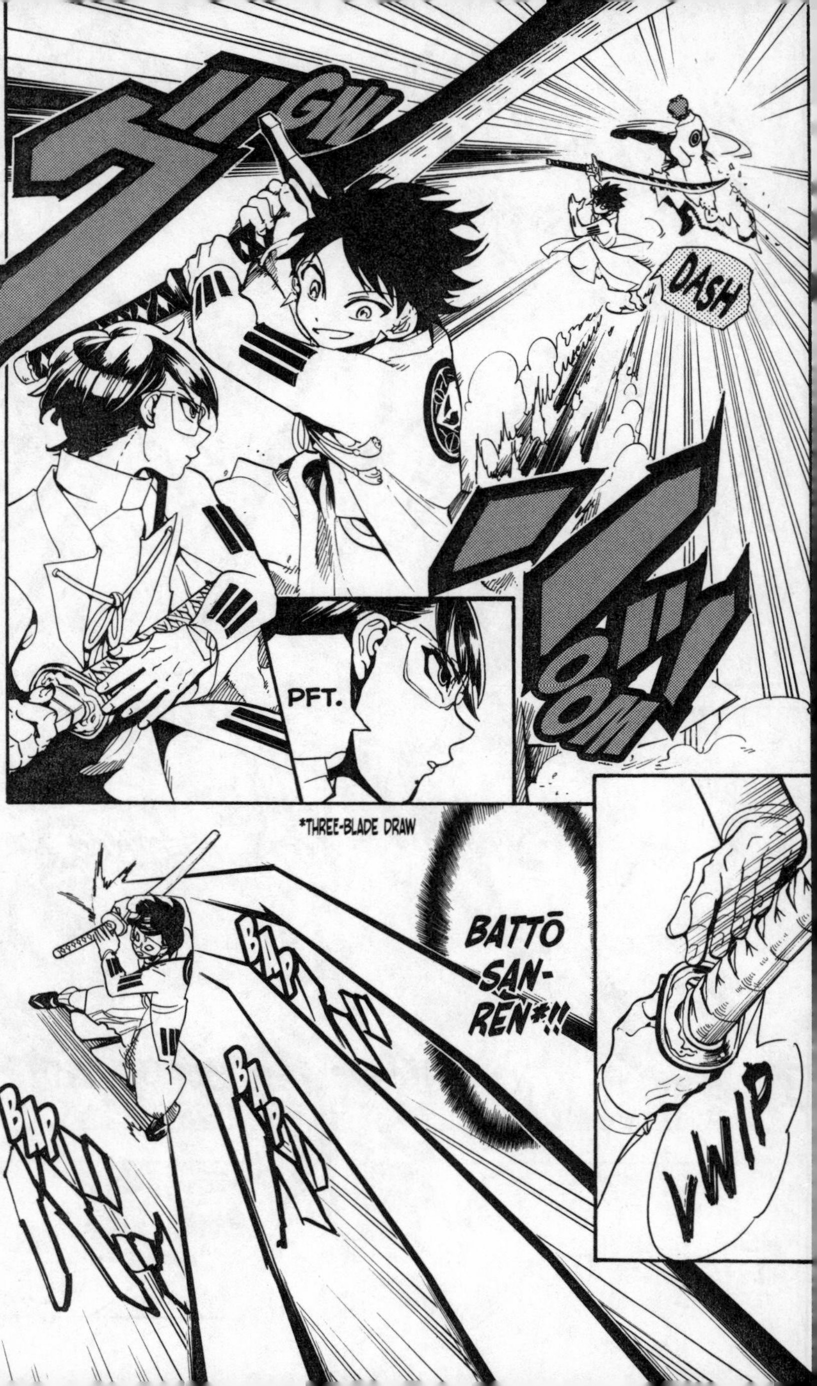
DASH
PFT.
VWIP
BATTŌ SAN-REN*!!
BAP
BAP
BAP
*THREE-BLADE DRAW

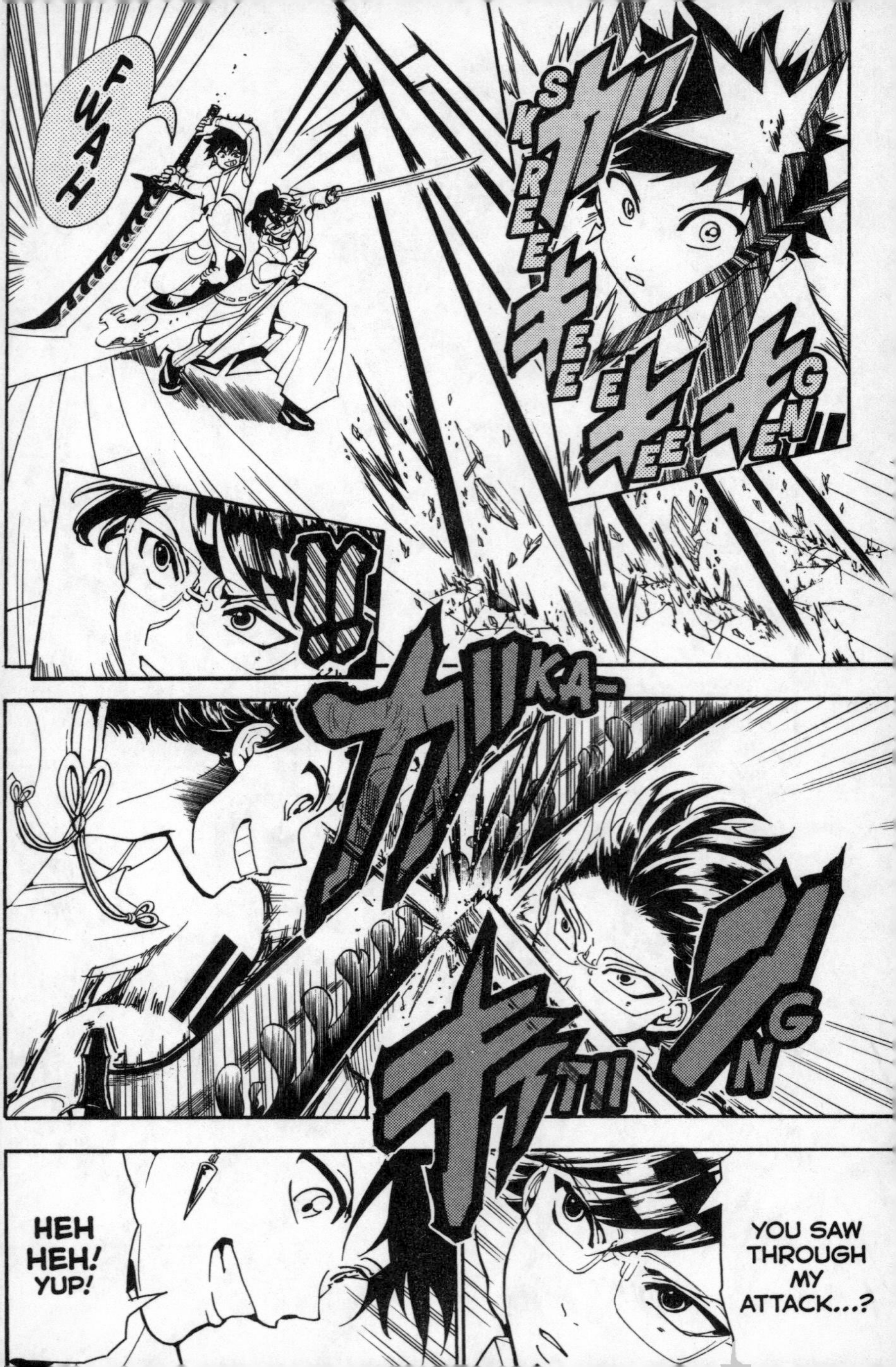
SKREEEEEEEEENG...
FWAH
!!
KA-
TIIING
YOU SAW THROUGH MY ATTACK...?
HEH HEH! YUP!

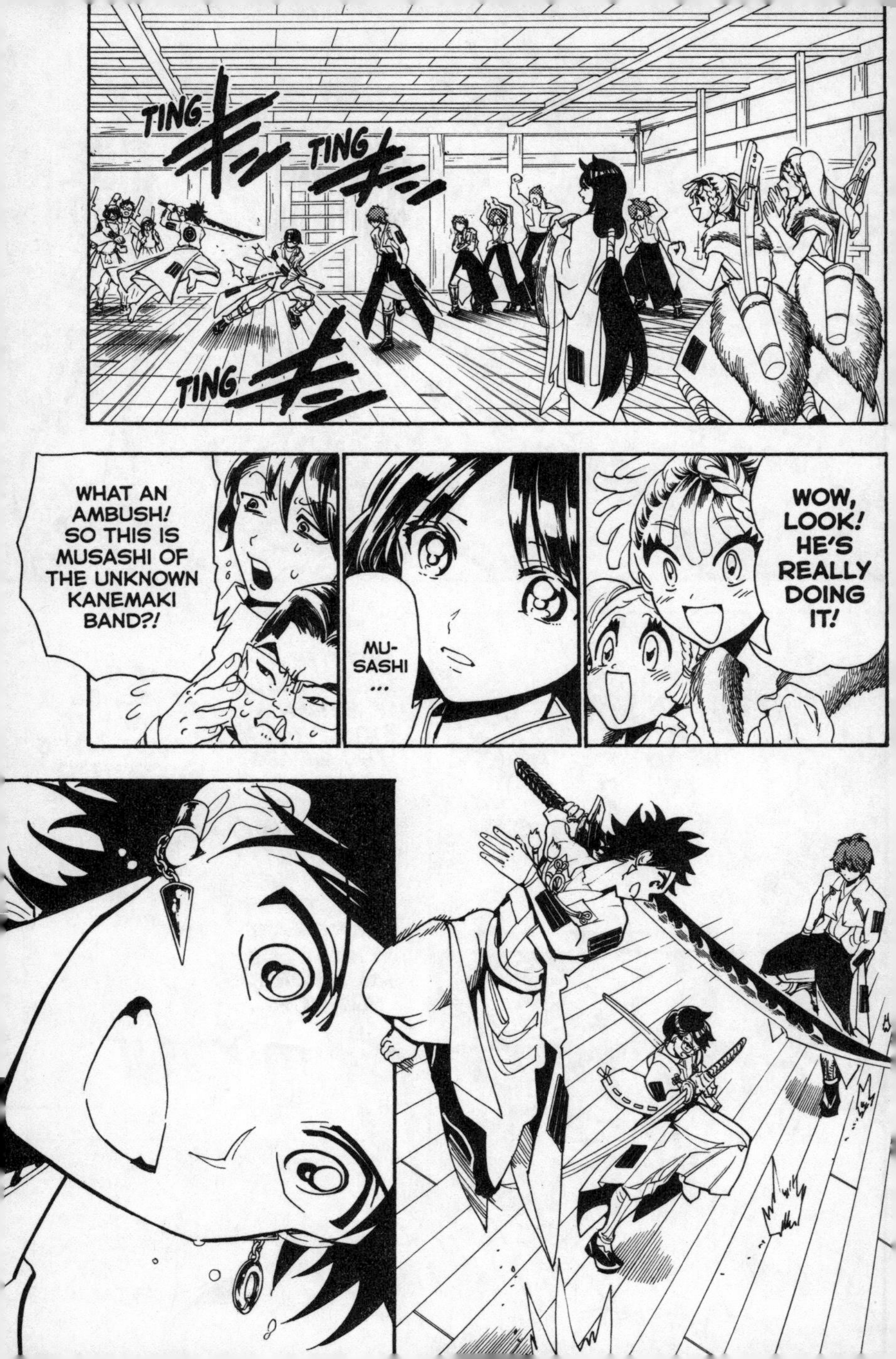
TING
TING
TING
WOW, LOOK! HE'S REALLY DOING IT!
MU-SASHI...
WHAT AN AMBUSH! SO THIS IS MUSASHI OF THE UNKNOWN KANEMAKI BAND?!

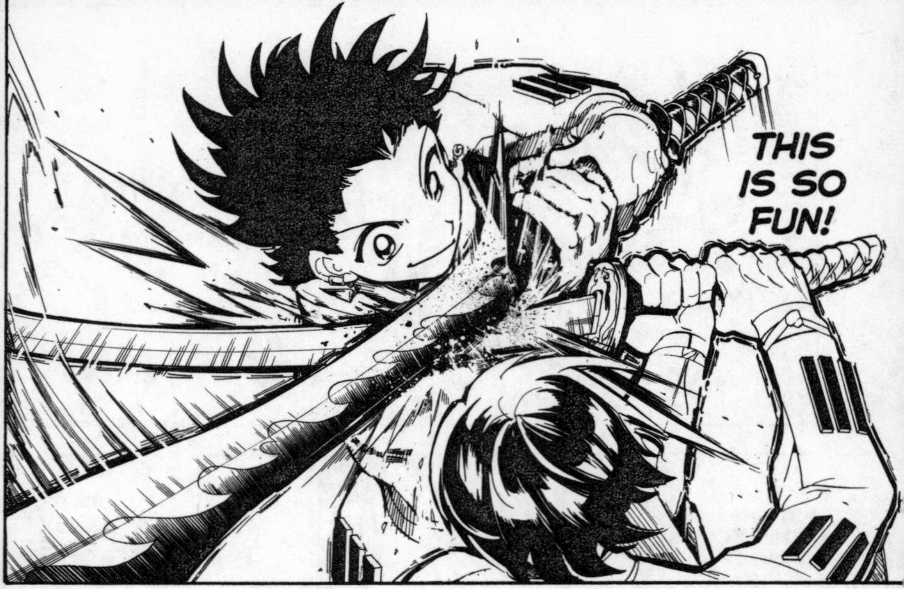
THIS IS SO FUN!

UNTIL NOW, I HAD NO IDEA WHETHER MY SKILLS MADE THE GRADE, 'CAUSE ALL I'D BEEN FIGHTING AGAINST WERE FIRE-BREATHING GIANTS AND WEIRD GLOWING SWORDS! BUT NOW...

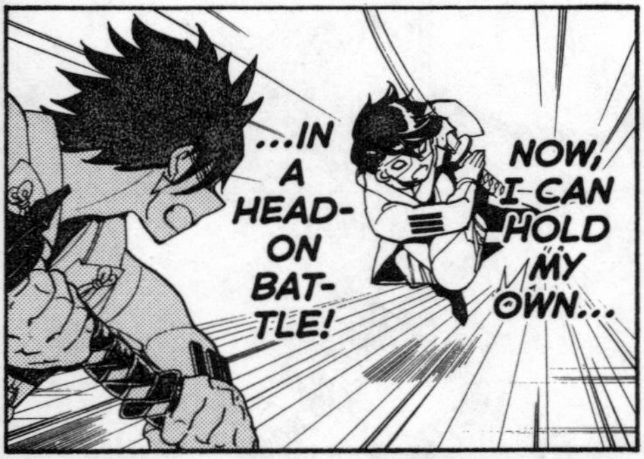
NOW, I CAN HOLD MY OWN...
...IN A HEAD-ON BATTLE!

I CAN SLASH AWAY TO MY HEART'S CONTENT USING THE SWORD SKILLS KOJIRO'S DAD TAUGHT ME...

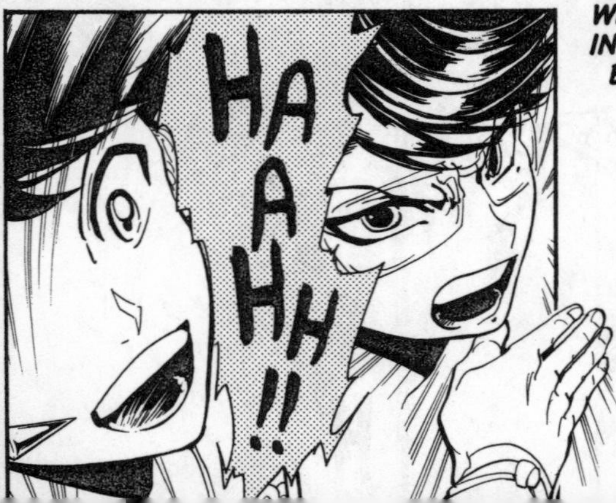
HAAHH!!

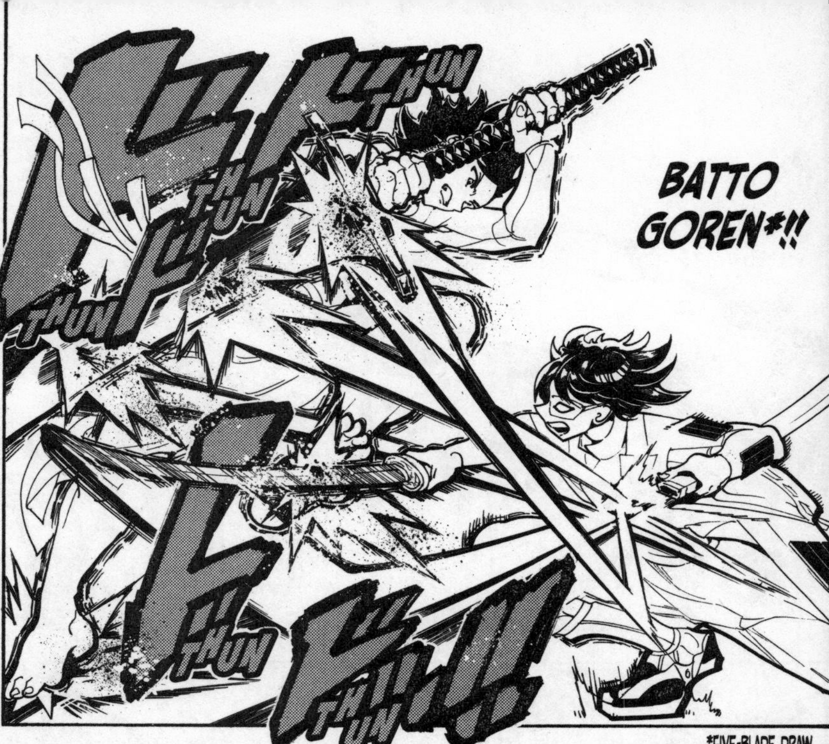
THUN THUN THUN THUN THUNK!!
BATTO GOREN*!!

*FIVE-BLADE DRAW

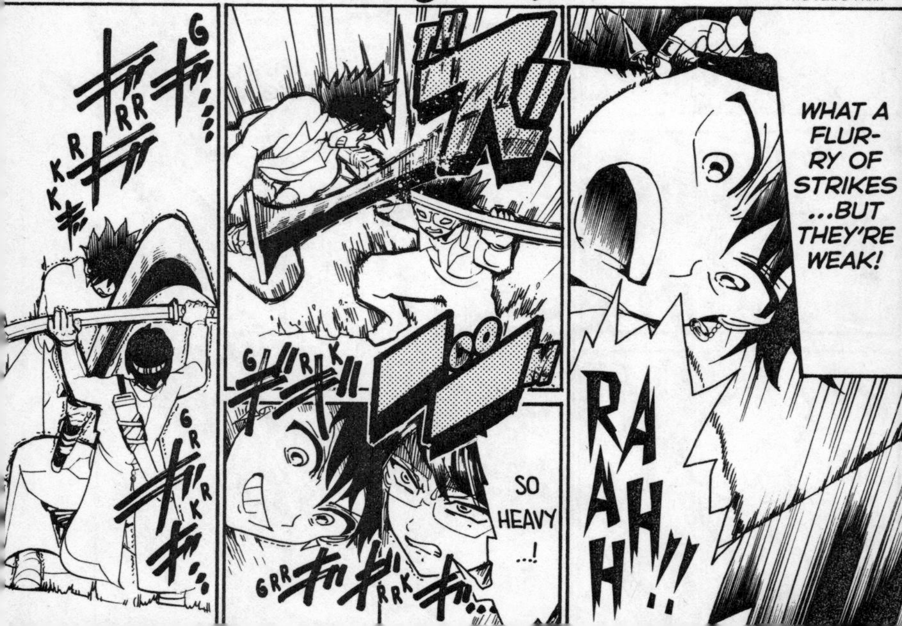
WHAT A FLURRY OF STRIKES ...BUT THEY'RE WEAK!
RAAHH!!
GRRK
SO HEAVY...!
GRRK
GRRRK
GRRK

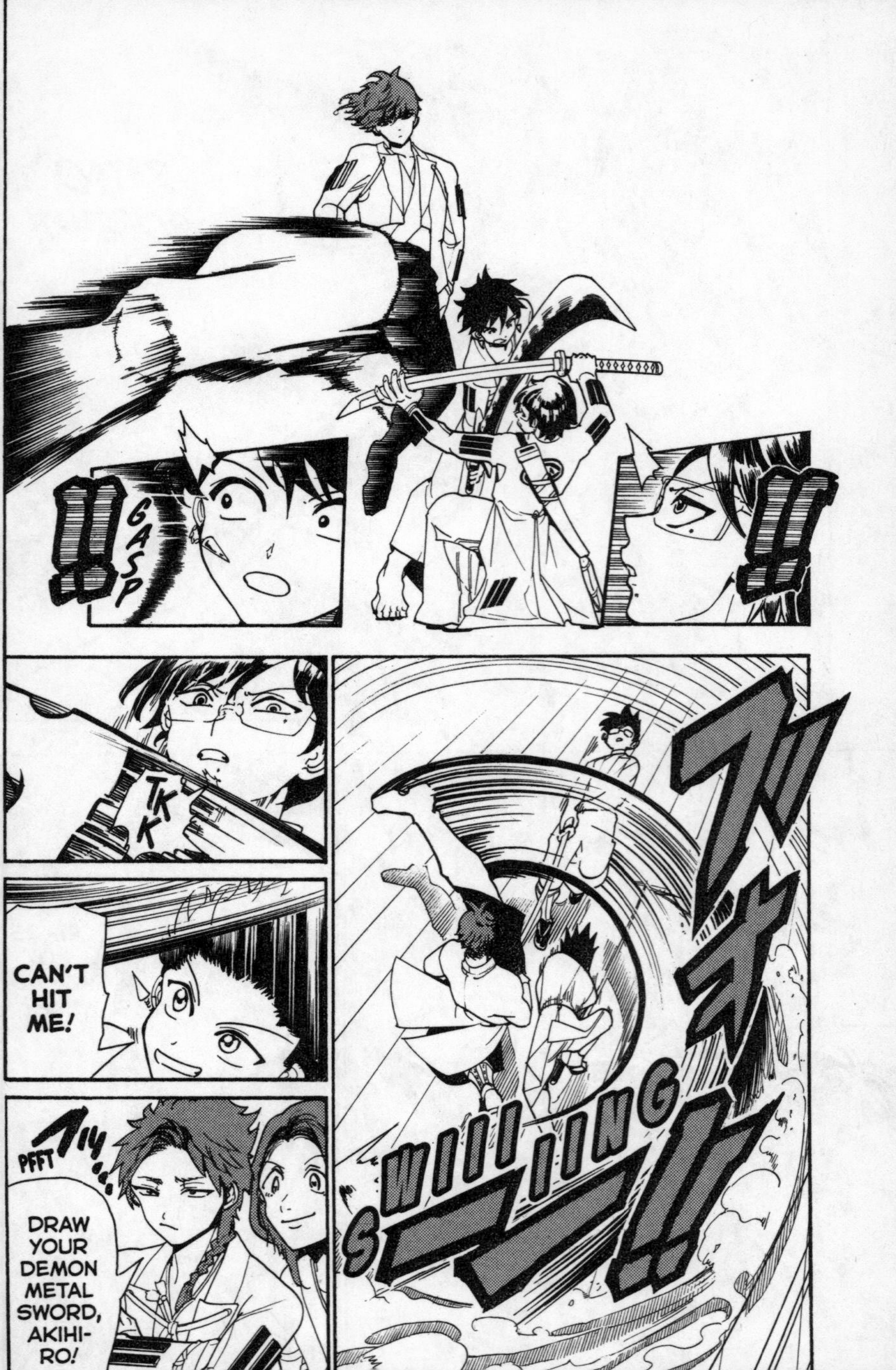
!!
!!
GASP
SWIIIIIING
TKK
CAN'T HIT ME!
PFFT
DRAW YOUR DEMON METAL SWORD, AKIHIRO!

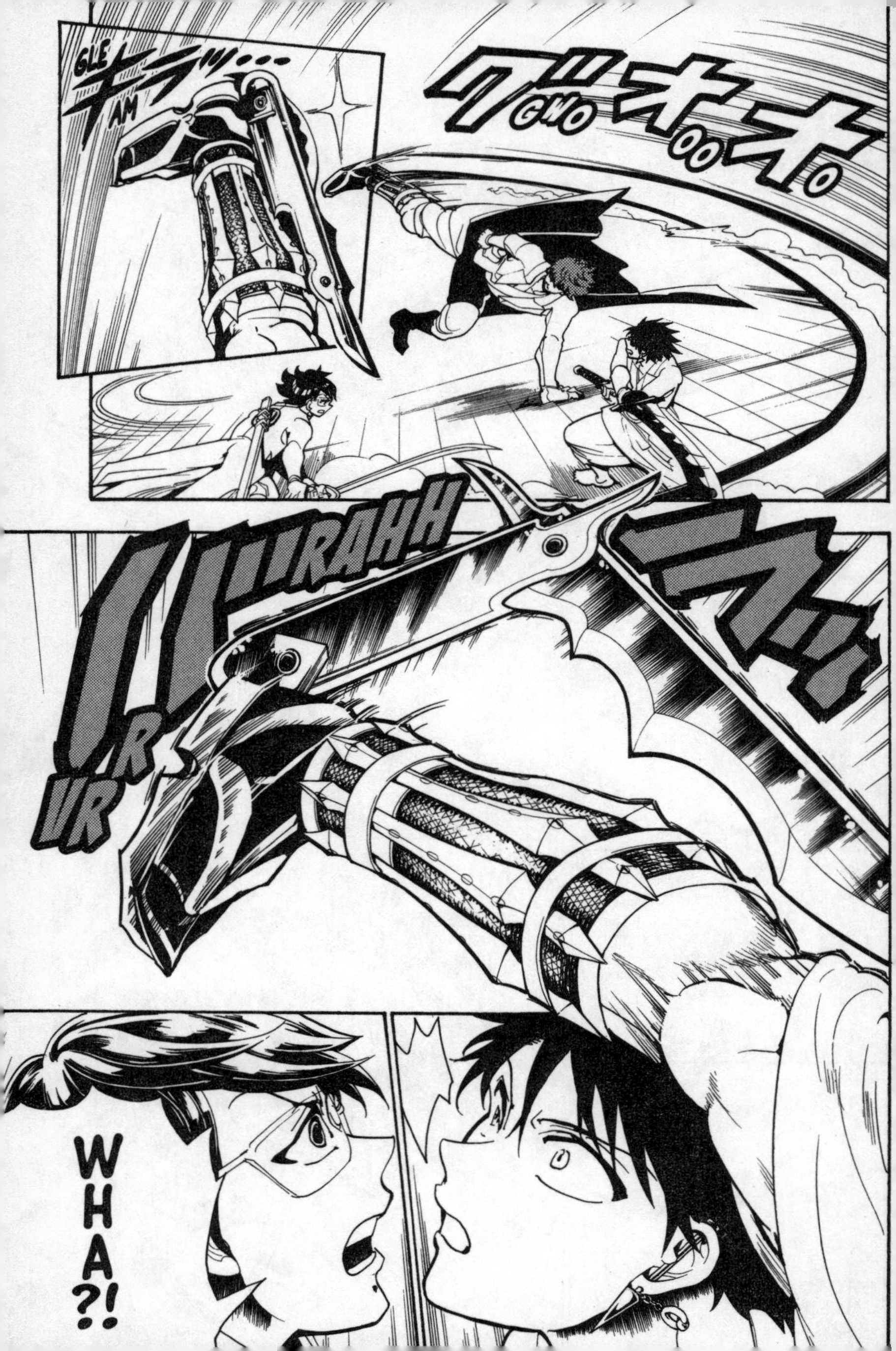
GWO OO O
GLE AM
VR R URAHH
WHA?!

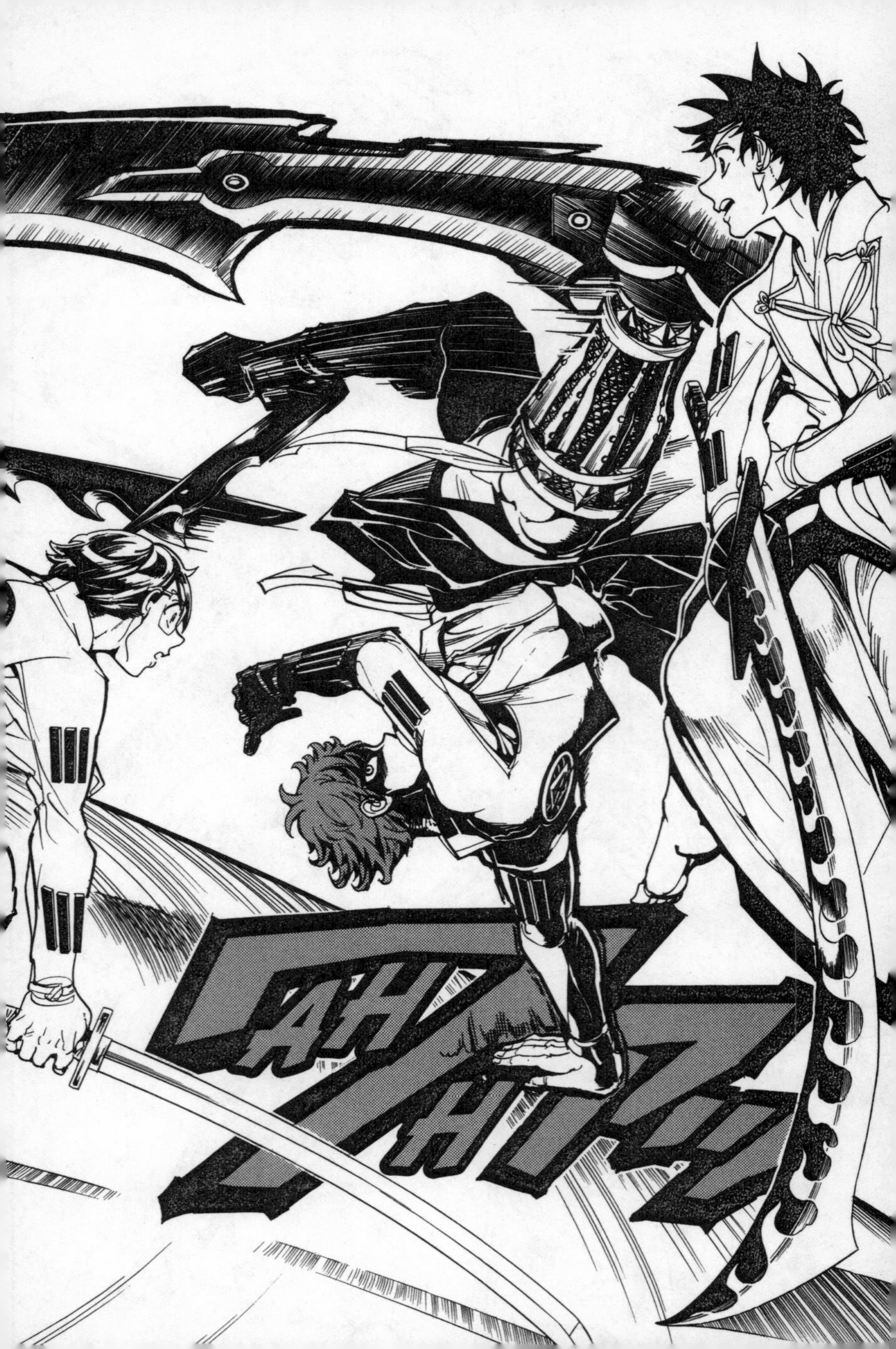
AH

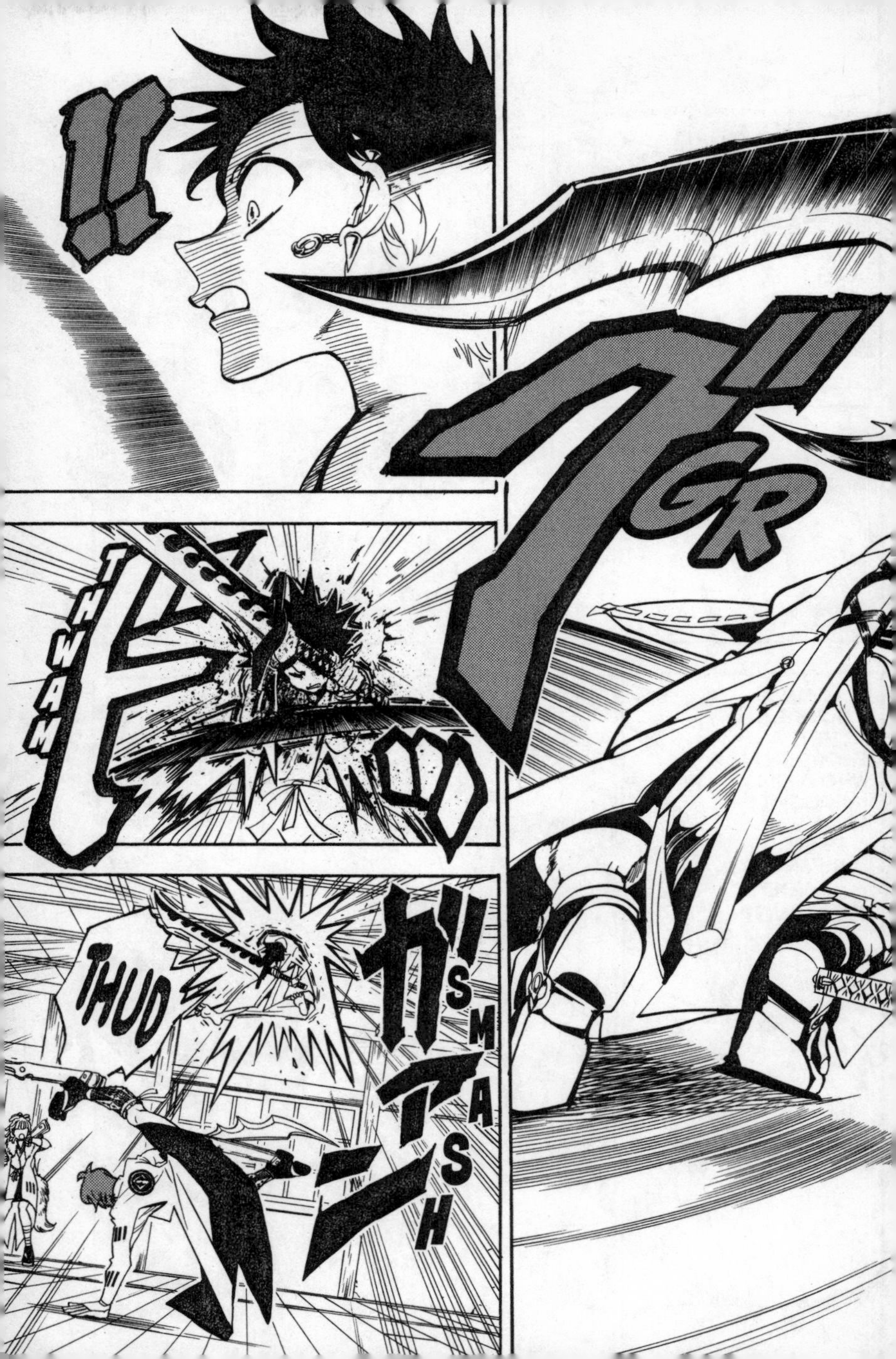

GR
!!
THWAM
SMASH
THUD

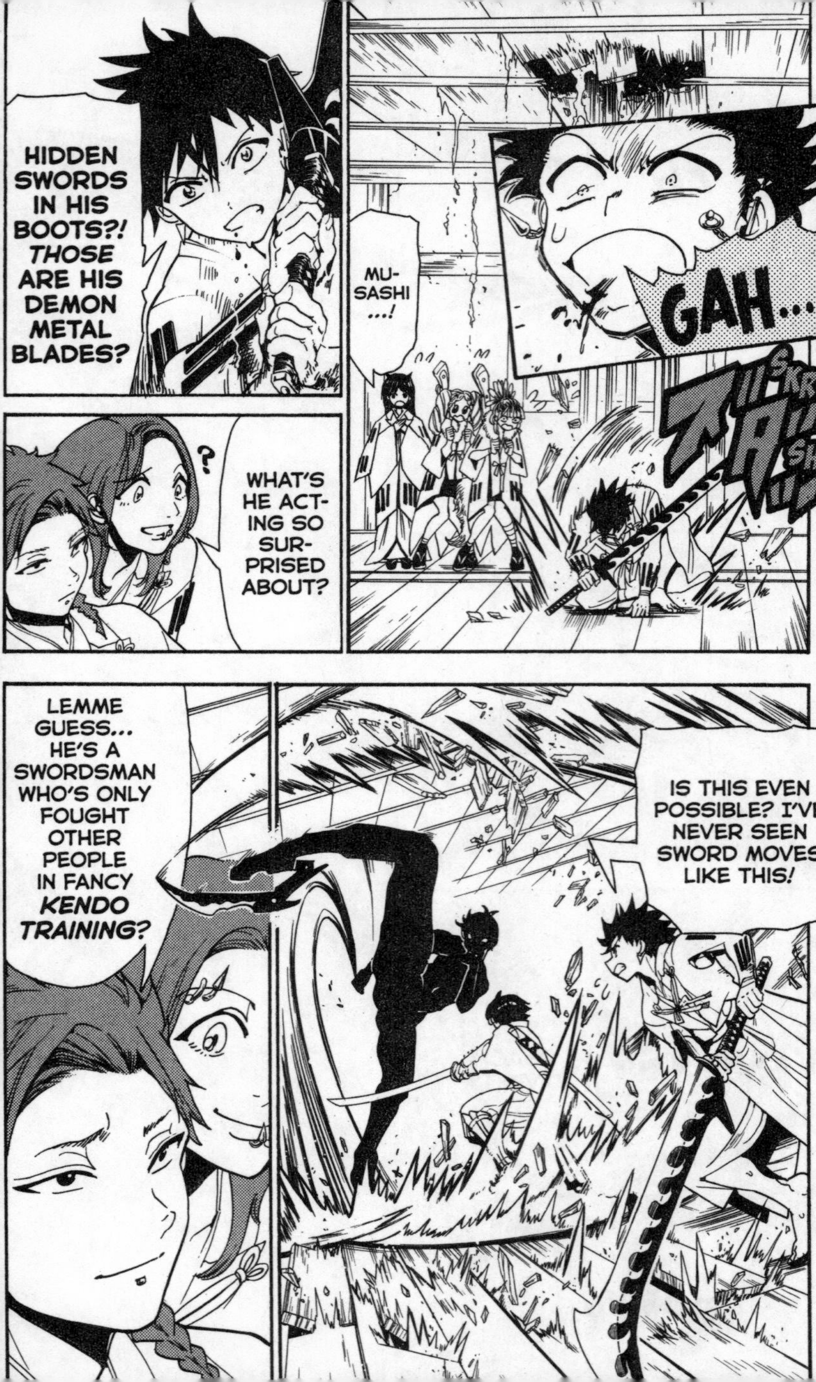
GAH...
MU-SASHI ...!
SKRASH
HIDDEN SWORDS IN HIS BOOTS?! *THOSE* ARE HIS DEMON METAL BLADES?
WHAT'S HE ACTING SO SURPRISED ABOUT?
IS THIS EVEN POSSIBLE? I'VE NEVER SEEN SWORD MOVES LIKE THIS!
LEMME GUESS... HE'S A SWORDSMAN WHO'S ONLY FOUGHT OTHER PEOPLE IN FANCY *KENDO TRAINING?*

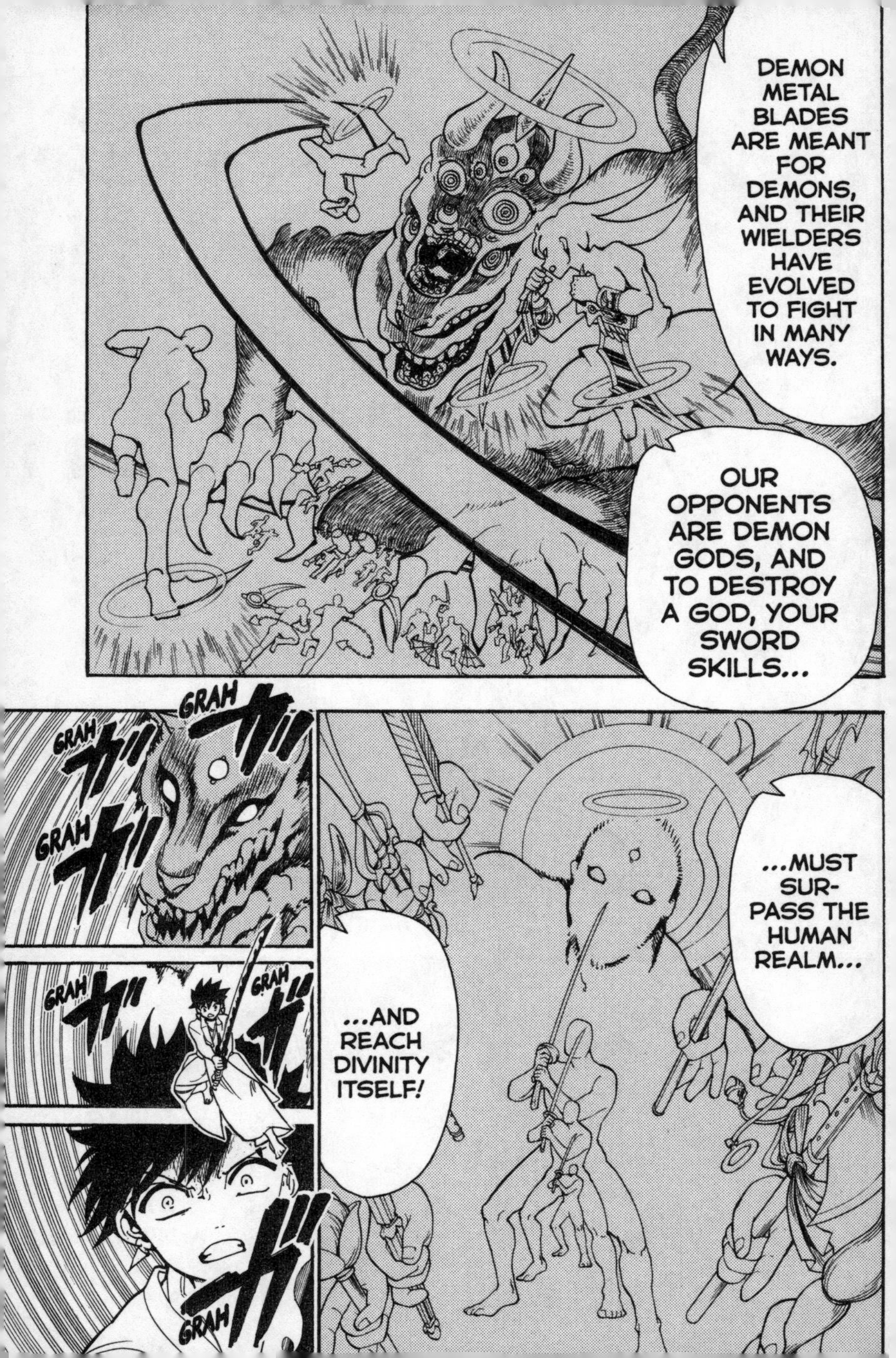
DEMON METAL BLADES ARE MEANT FOR DEMONS, AND THEIR WIELDERS HAVE EVOLVED TO FIGHT IN MANY WAYS.
OUR OPPONENTS ARE DEMON GODS, AND TO DESTROY A GOD, YOUR SWORD SKILLS...
...MUST SUR-PASS THE HUMAN REALM...
...AND REACH DIVINITY ITSELF!
GRAH
GRAH
GRAH
GRAH
GRAH
GRAH

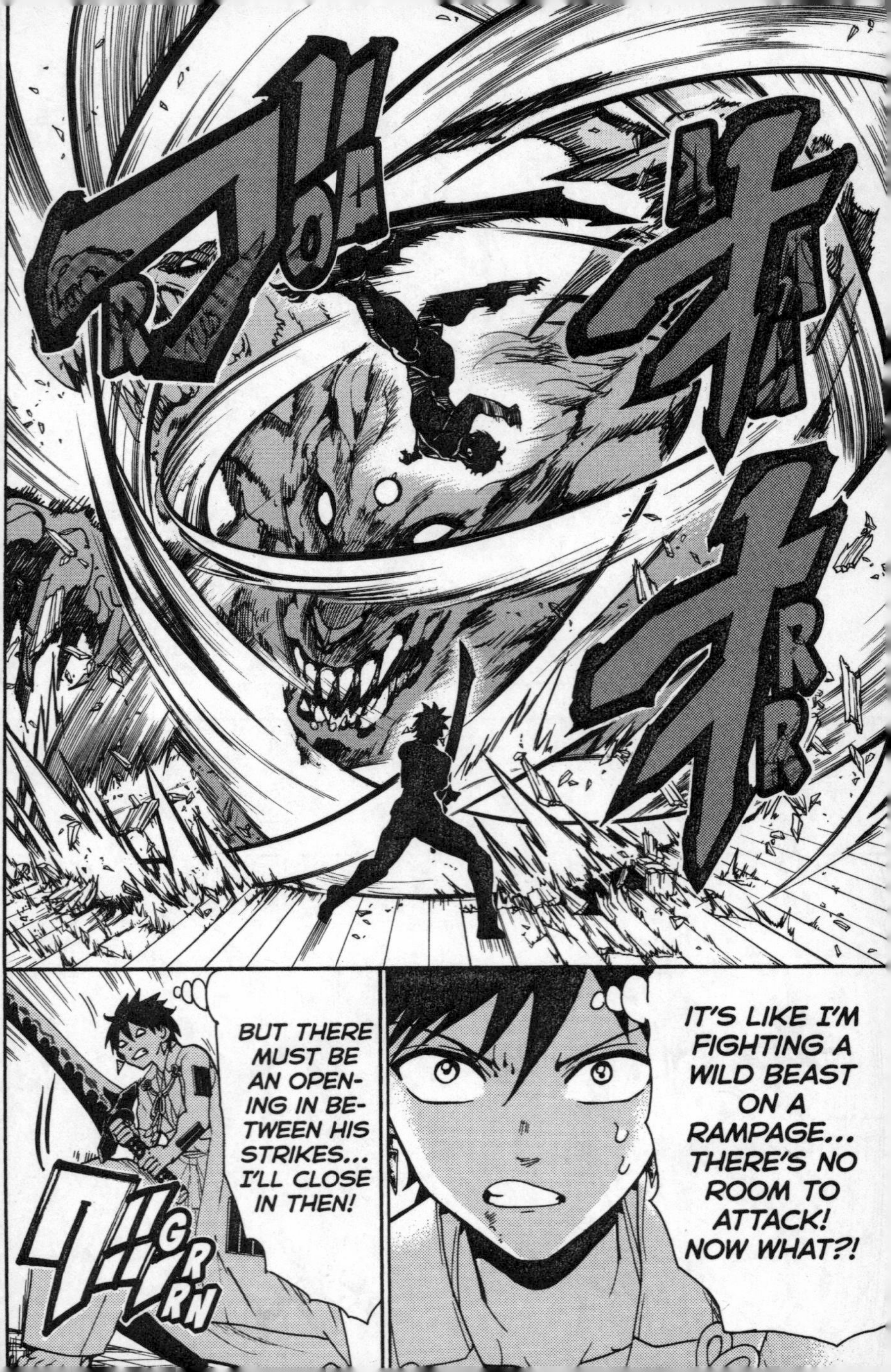
IT'S LIKE I'M FIGHTING A WILD BEAST ON A RAMPAGE... THERE'S NO ROOM TO ATTACK! NOW WHAT?!
BUT THERE MUST BE AN OPENING IN BETWEEN HIS STRIKES... I'LL CLOSE IN THEN!
GRRN

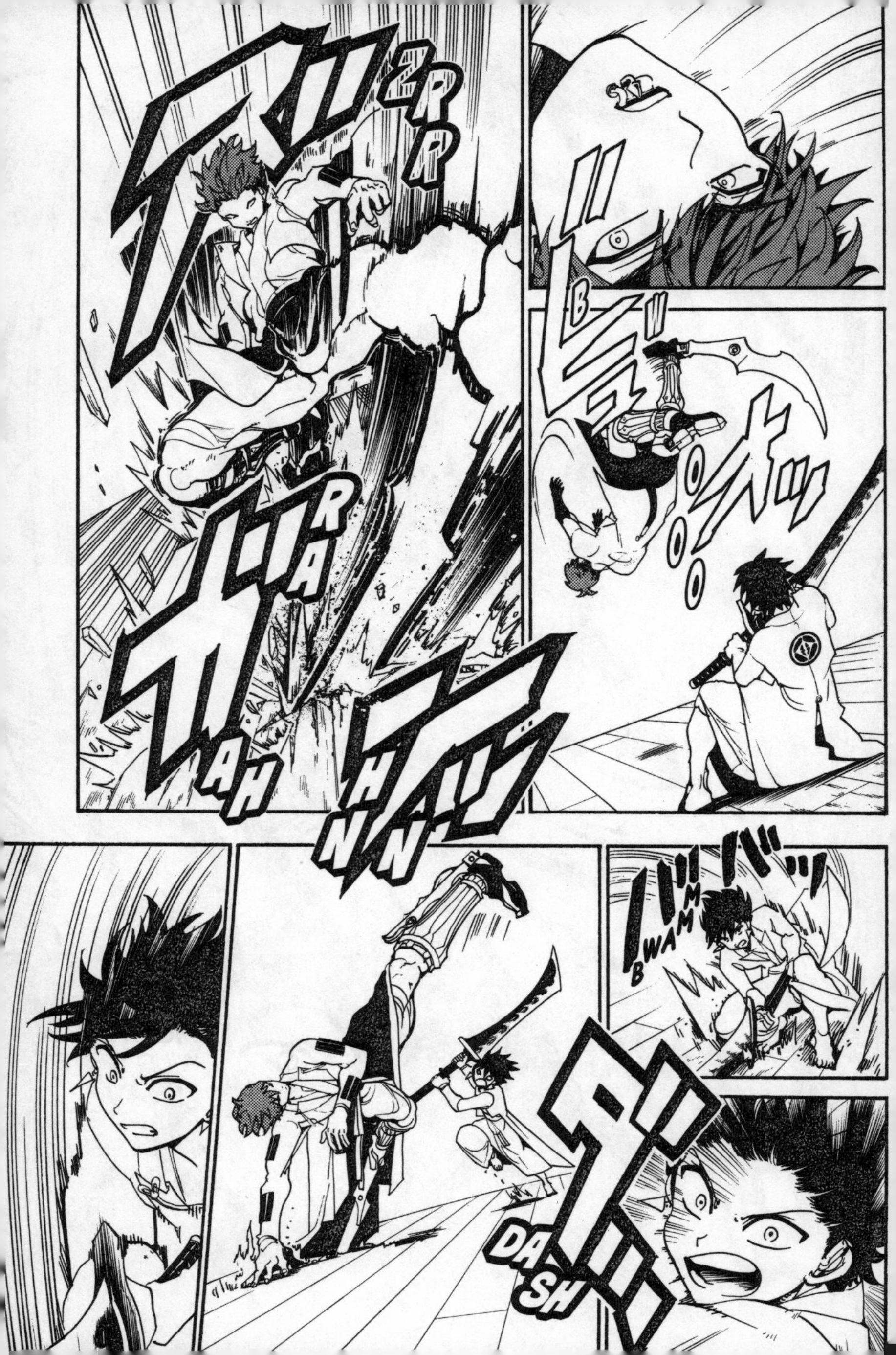

BWOOOO
ZRR
RAAH
HNN
BWAM
DASH

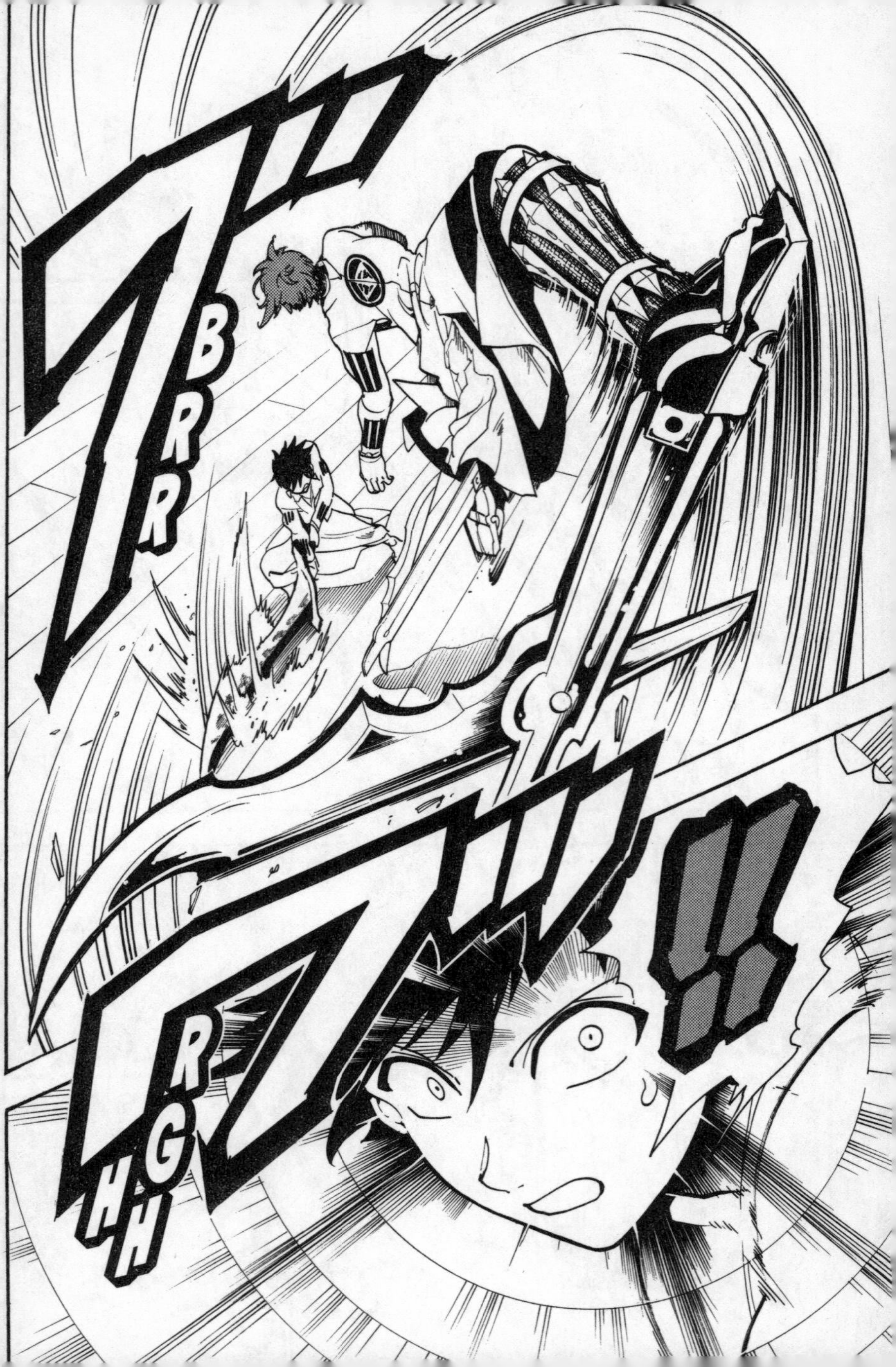
BRRR
RRGHH

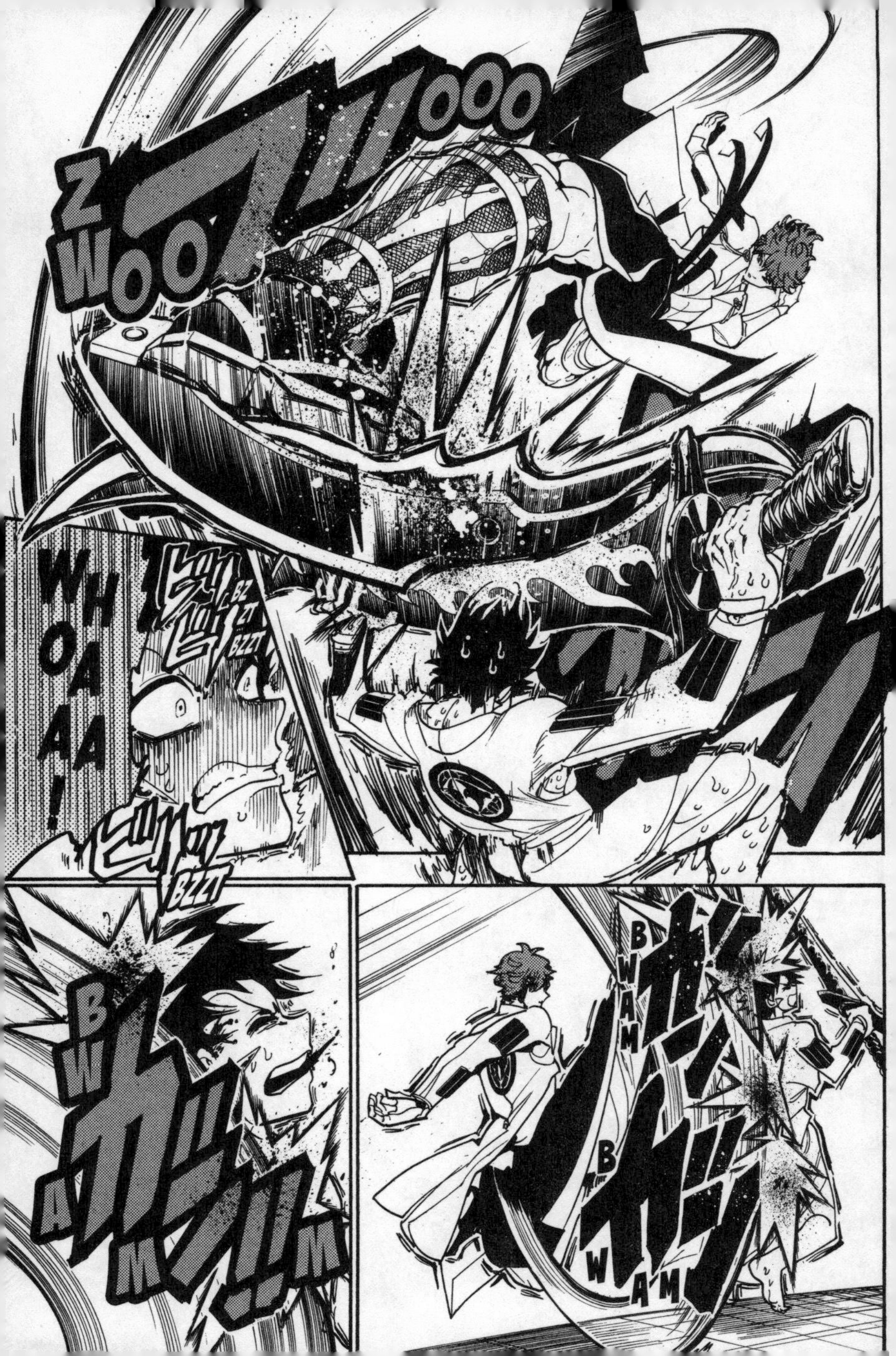
ZWOOOOO
WHOAAAA!
BZ ZT BZZT
BZZT
BWAM
BWAM
BWAM

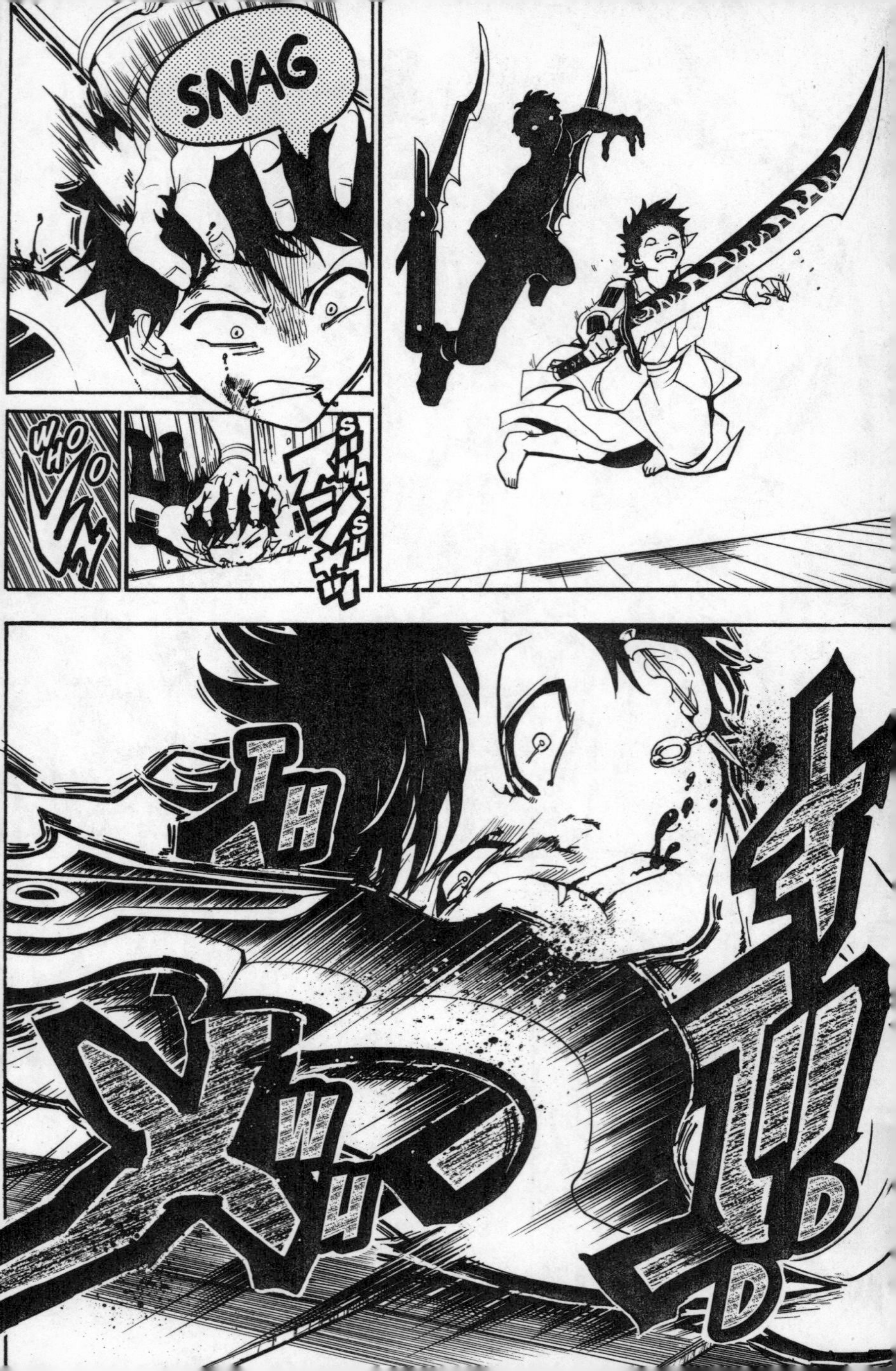

SNAG
SMASH
WHOOM
TH
WH
DD

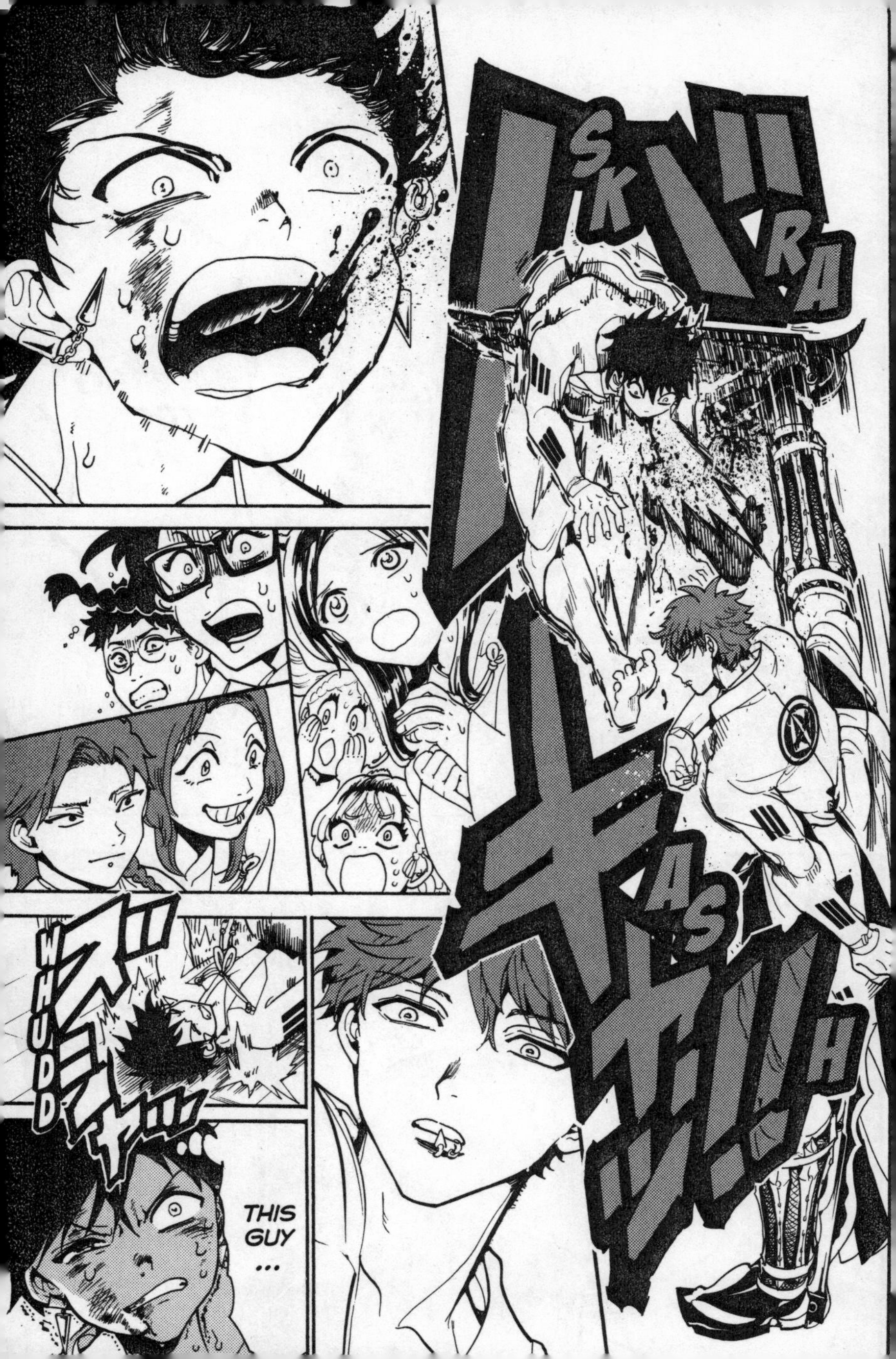
SKRA
ASH
WHUDD
THIS GUY ...

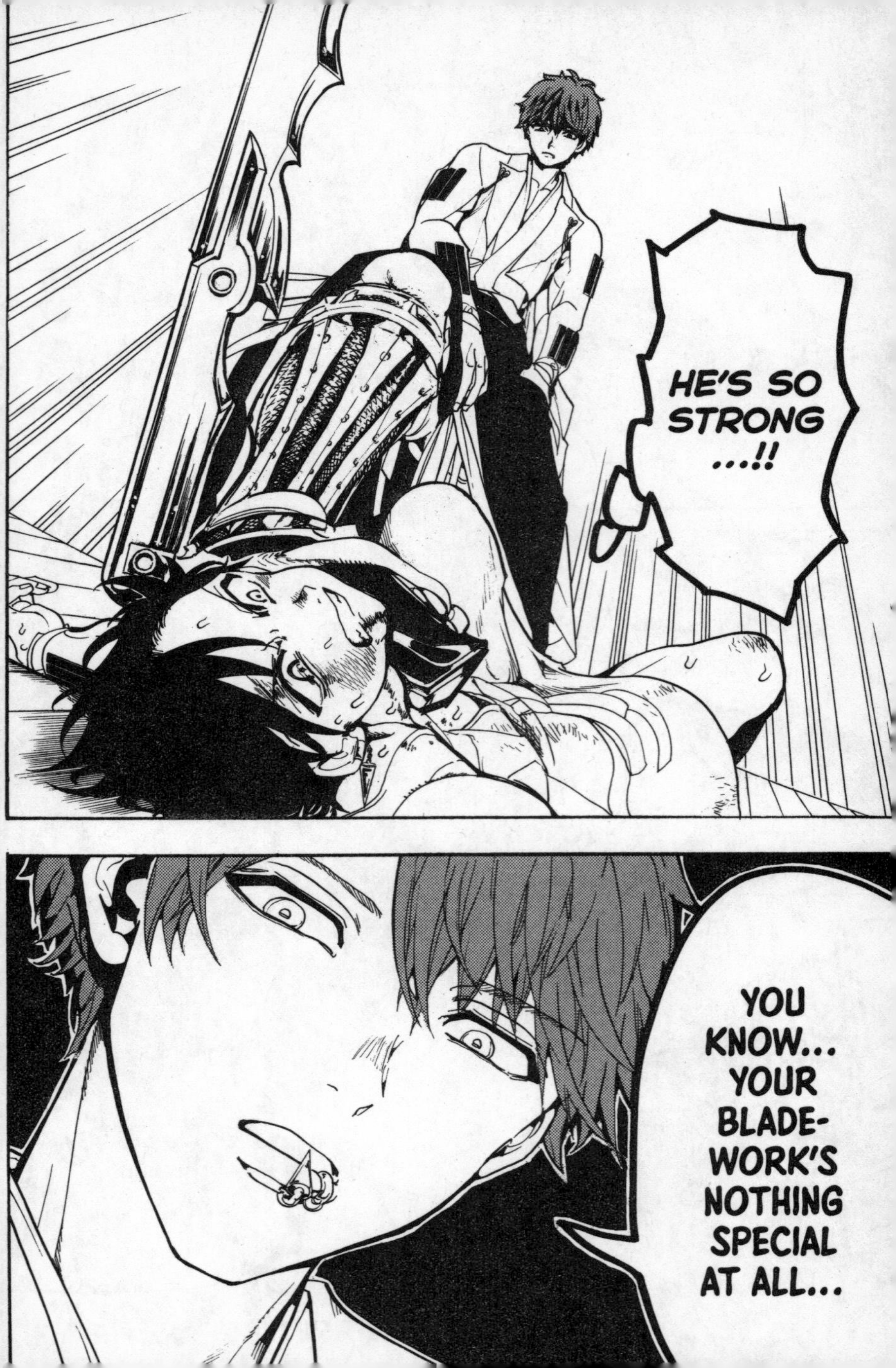
HE'S SO STRONG ...!!
YOU KNOW... YOUR BLADE-WORK'S NOTHING SPECIAL AT ALL...

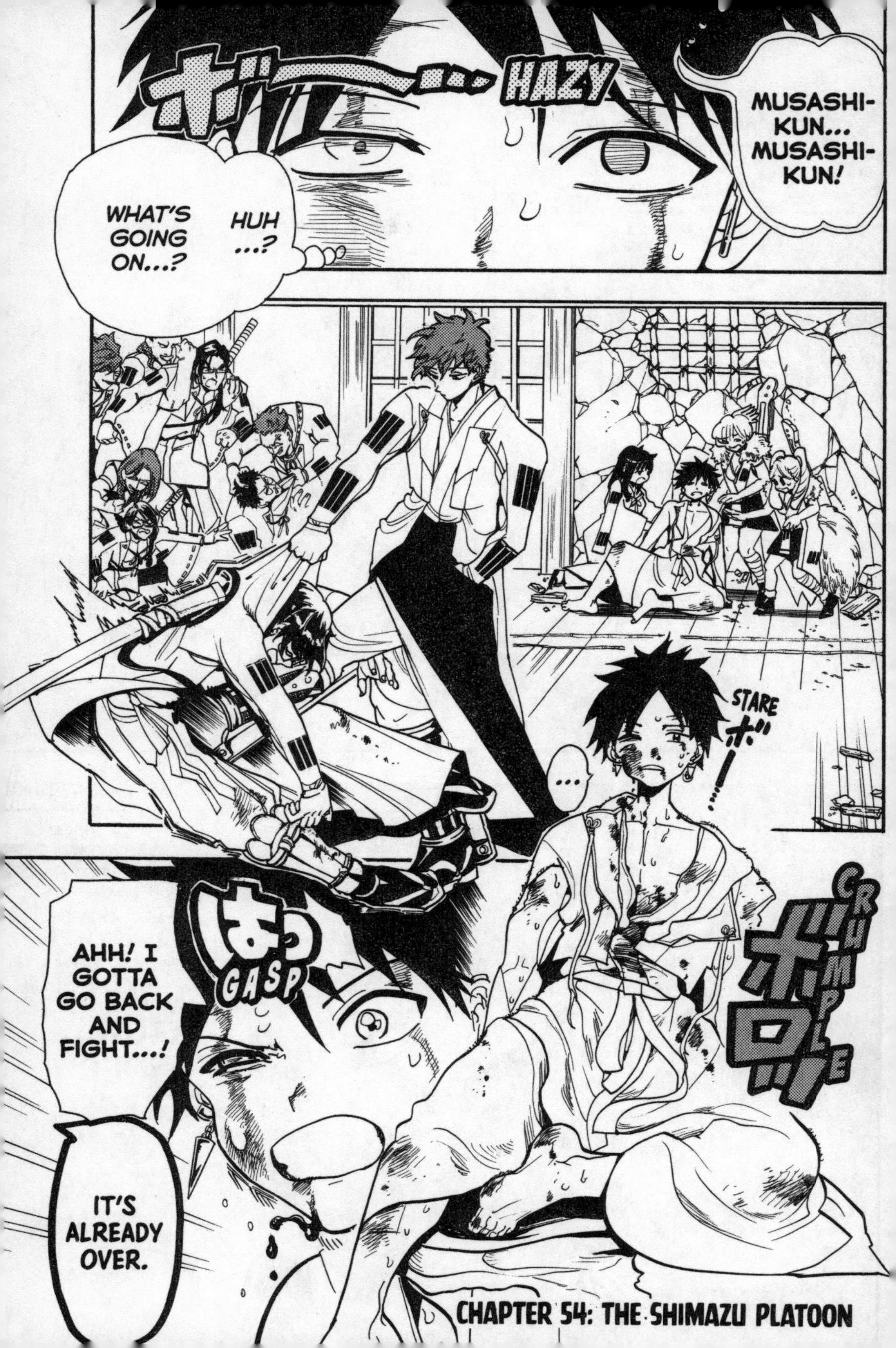
MUSASHI-KUN... MUSASHI-KUN!
HAZY
HUH...?
WHAT'S GOING ON...?
...
STARE
CRUMPLE
GASP
AHH! I GOTTA GO BACK AND FIGHT...!
IT'S ALREADY OVER.

CHAPTER 54: THE SHIMAZU PLATOON

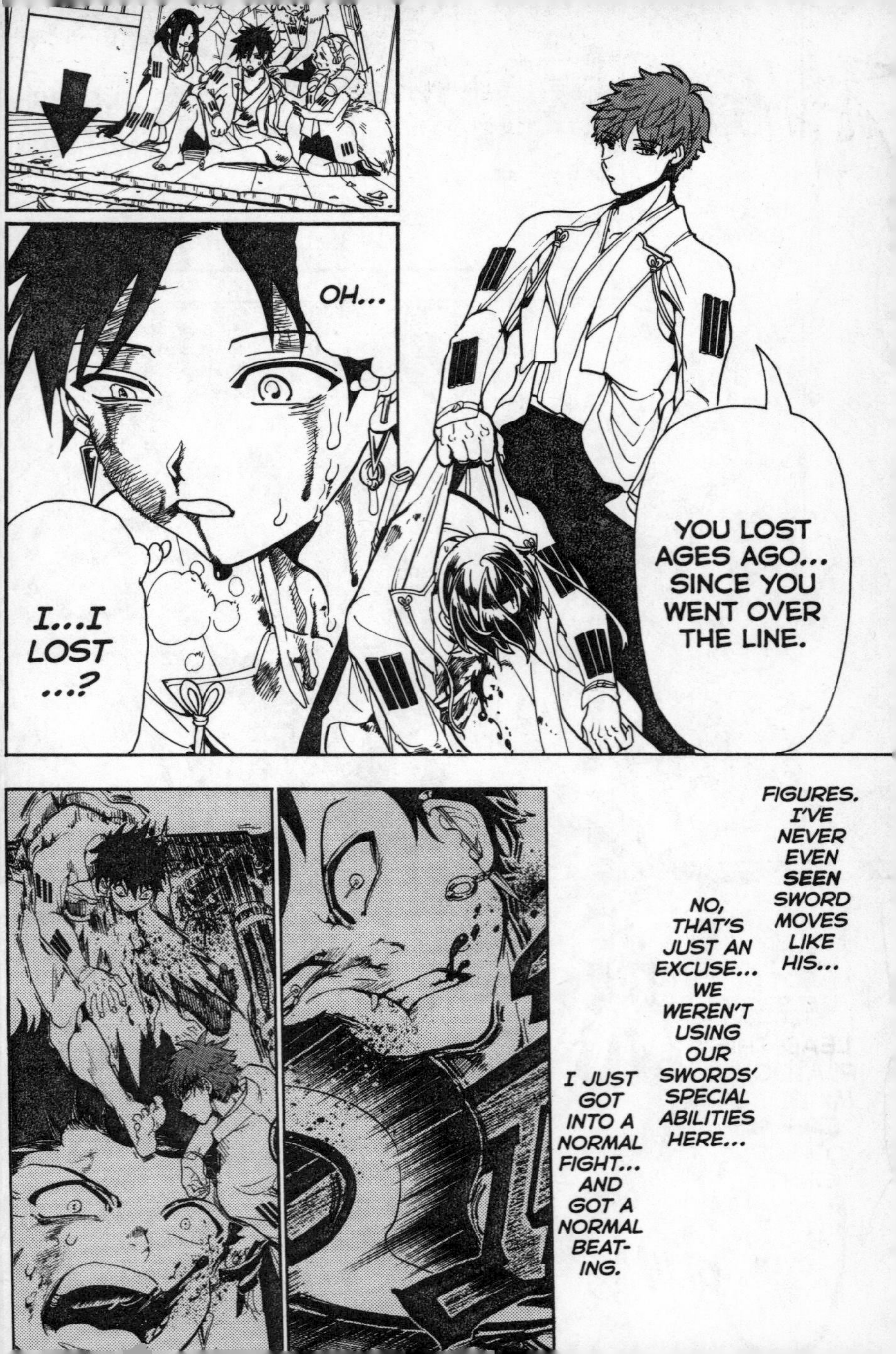
YOU LOST AGES AGO... SINCE YOU WENT OVER THE LINE.
OH...
I...I LOST ...?
FIGURES. I'VE NEVER EVEN SEEN SWORD MOVES LIKE HIS...
NO, THAT'S JUST AN EXCUSE... WE WEREN'T USING OUR SWORDS' SPECIAL ABILITIES HERE...
I JUST GOT INTO A NORMAL FIGHT... AND GOT A NORMAL BEAT-ING.

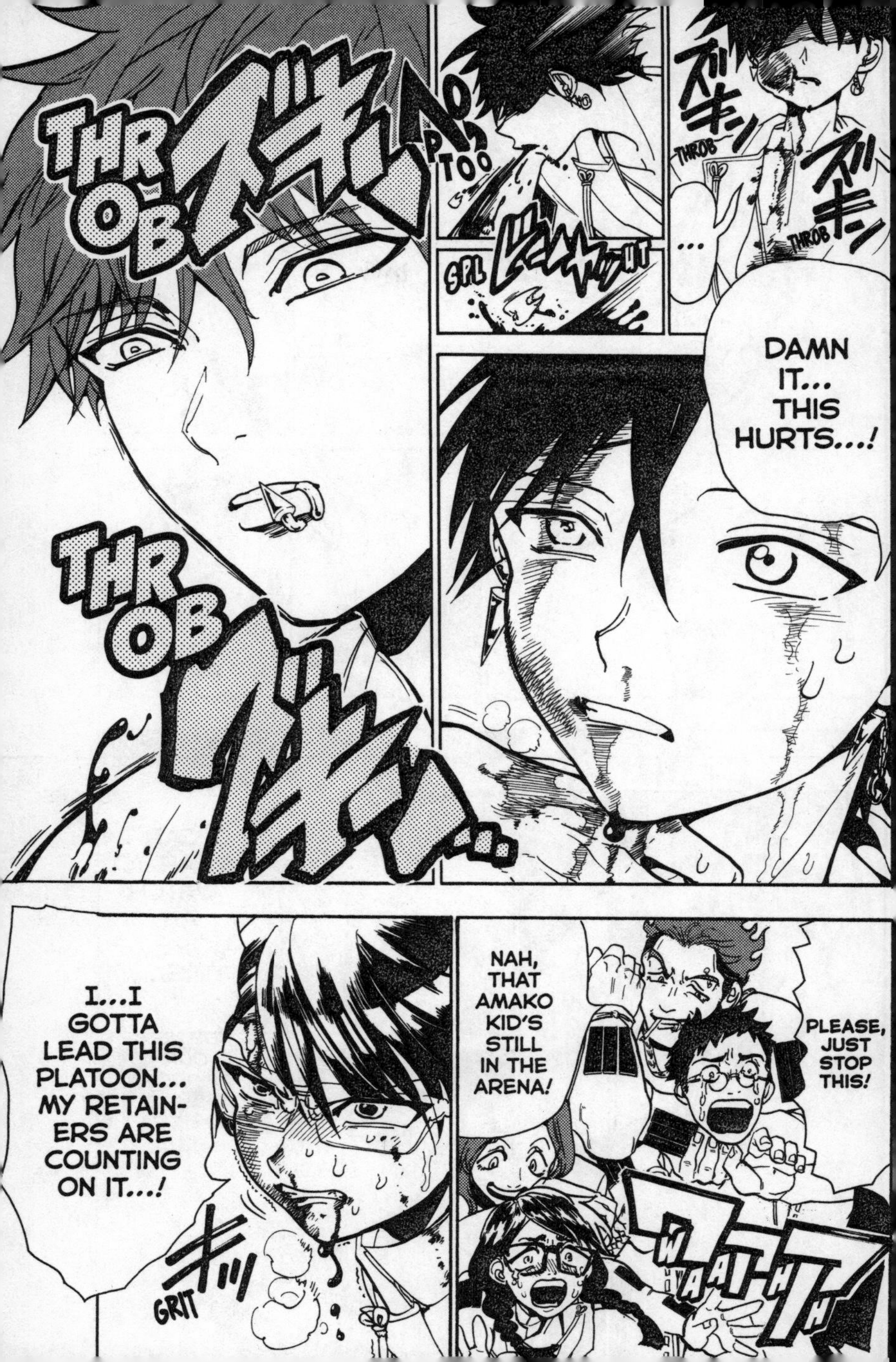
THROB
THROB
...
PTOO
SPL
HT
DAMN IT... THIS HURTS...!
THROB
THROB
NAH, THAT AMAKO KID'S STILL IN THE ARENA!
PLEASE, JUST STOP THIS!
WAAHHH
I...I GOTTA LEAD THIS PLATOON... MY RETAINERS ARE COUNTING ON IT...!
GRIT

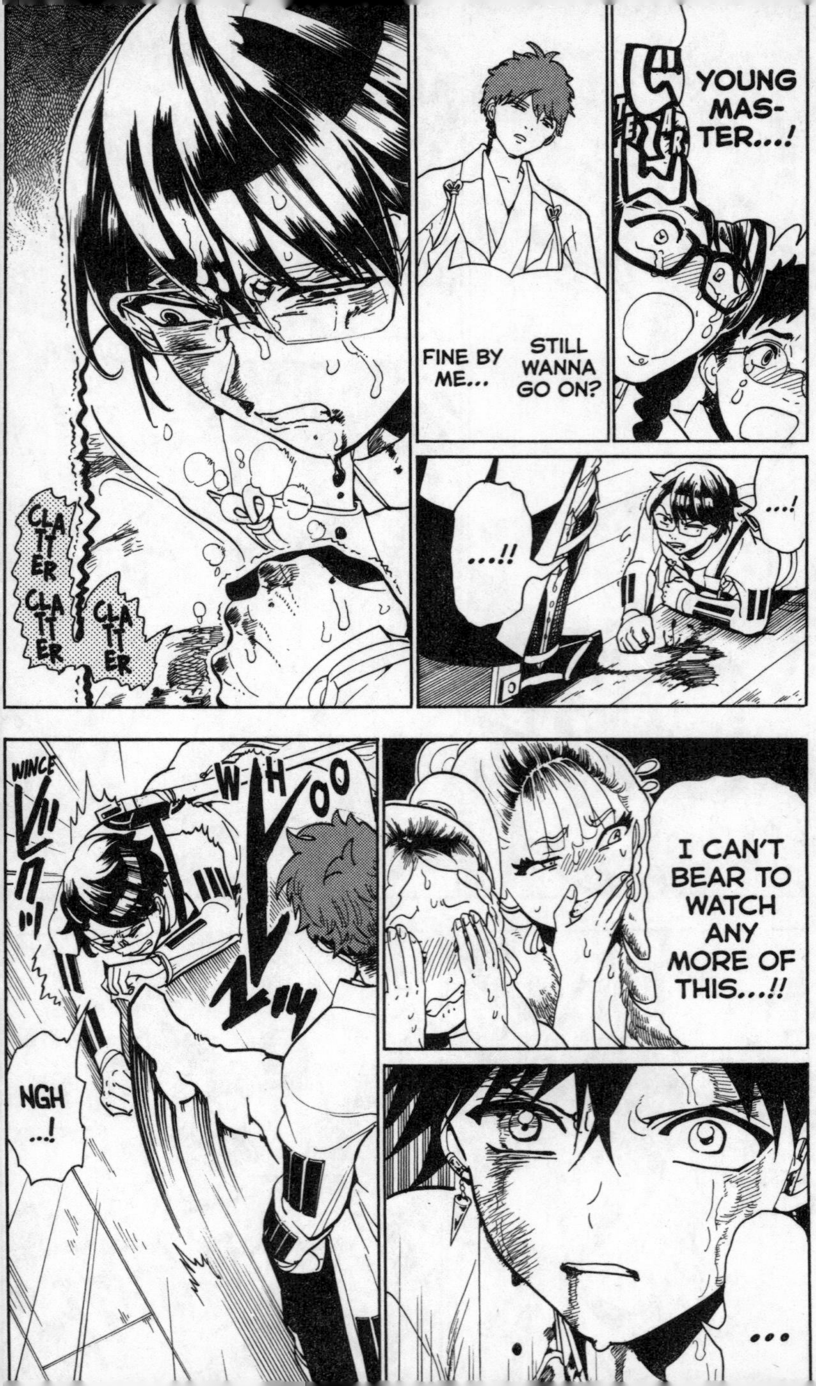
YOUNG MAS- TER...!
STILL WANNA GO ON?
FINE BY ME...
...!
...!!
CLATTER
CLATTER
CLATTER
I CAN'T BEAR TO WATCH ANY MORE OF THIS...!!
...
WINCE
NGH ...!

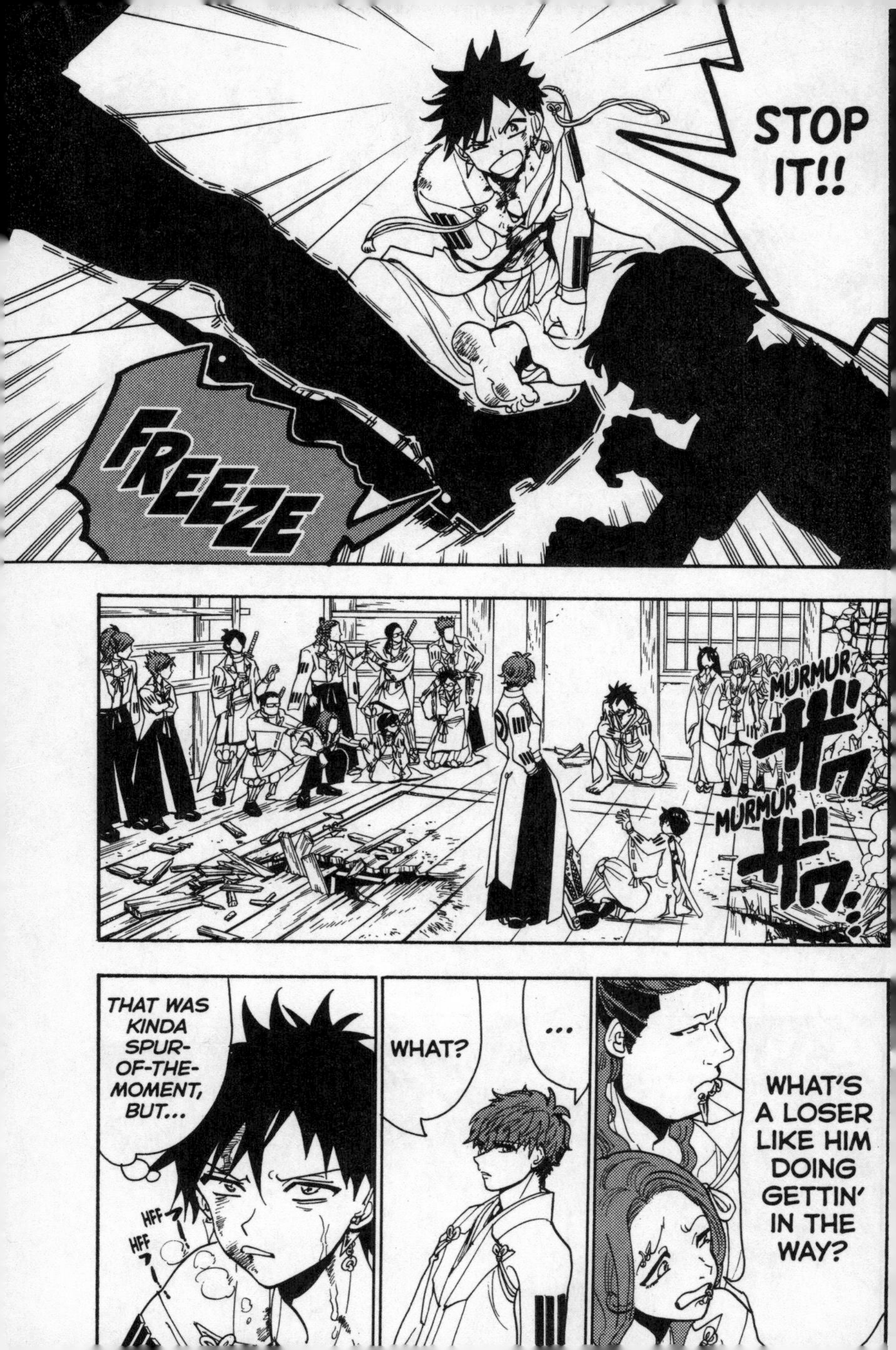
STOP IT!!
FREEZE
MURMUR
ザワ
MURMUR
ザワ…
WHAT'S A LOSER LIKE HIM DOING GETTIN' IN THE WAY?
...
WHAT?
THAT WAS KINDA SPUR-OF-THE-MOMENT, BUT...
HFF
HFF

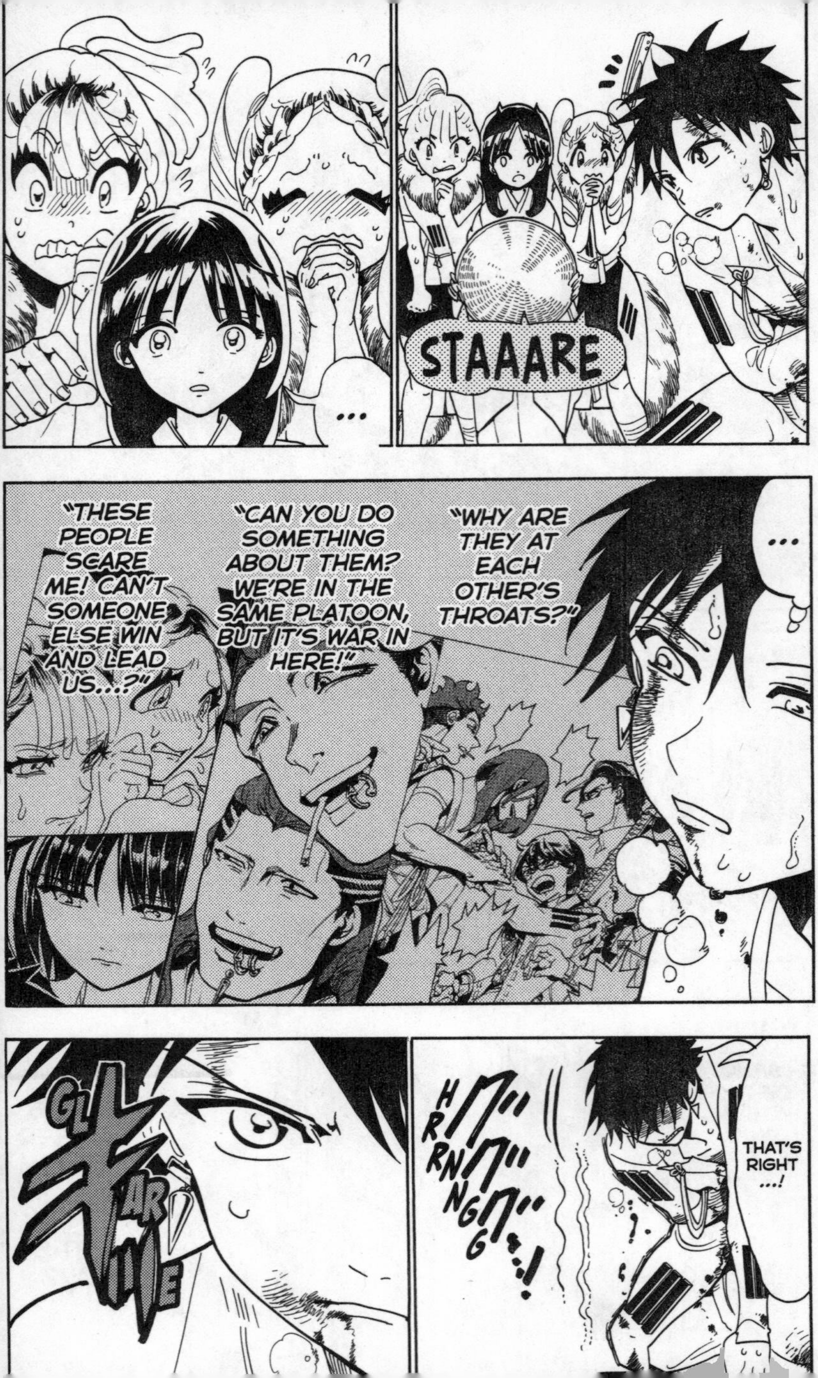
STAAARE
...
...
"WHY ARE THEY AT EACH OTHER'S THROATS?"
"CAN YOU DO SOMETHING ABOUT THEM? WE'RE IN THE SAME PLATOON, BUT IT'S WAR IN HERE!"
"THESE PEOPLE SCARE ME! CAN'T SOMEONE ELSE WIN AND LEAD US...?"
THAT'S RIGHT ...!
HRRNNGG

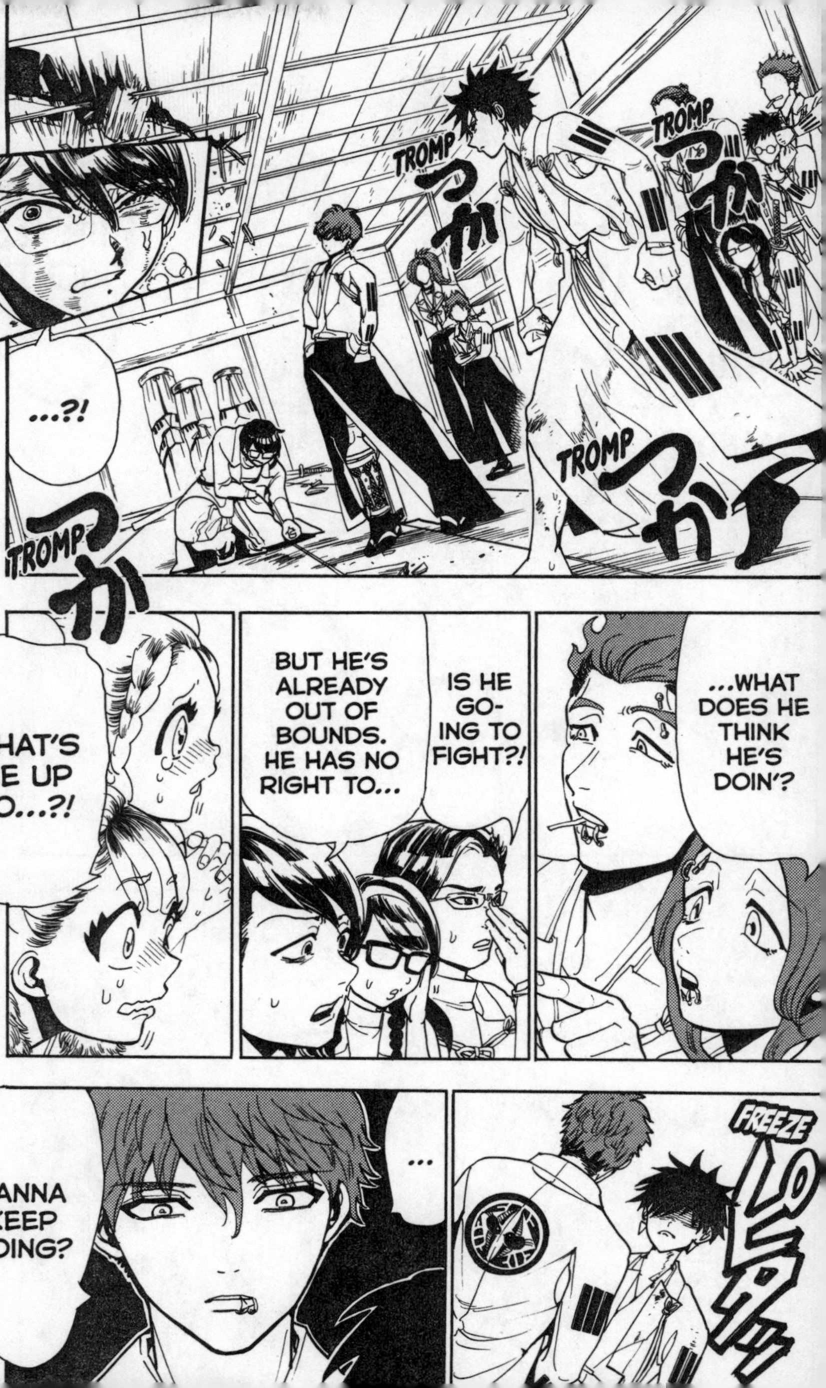

TROMP
つか
TROMP
つか
TROMP
つか
...?!
TROMP
つか
...WHAT DOES HE THINK HE'S DOIN'?
IS HE GO-ING TO FIGHT?!
BUT HE'S ALREADY OUT OF BOUNDS. HE HAS NO RIGHT TO...
WHAT'S HE UP TO...?!
FREEZE
...
WANNA KEEP GOING?

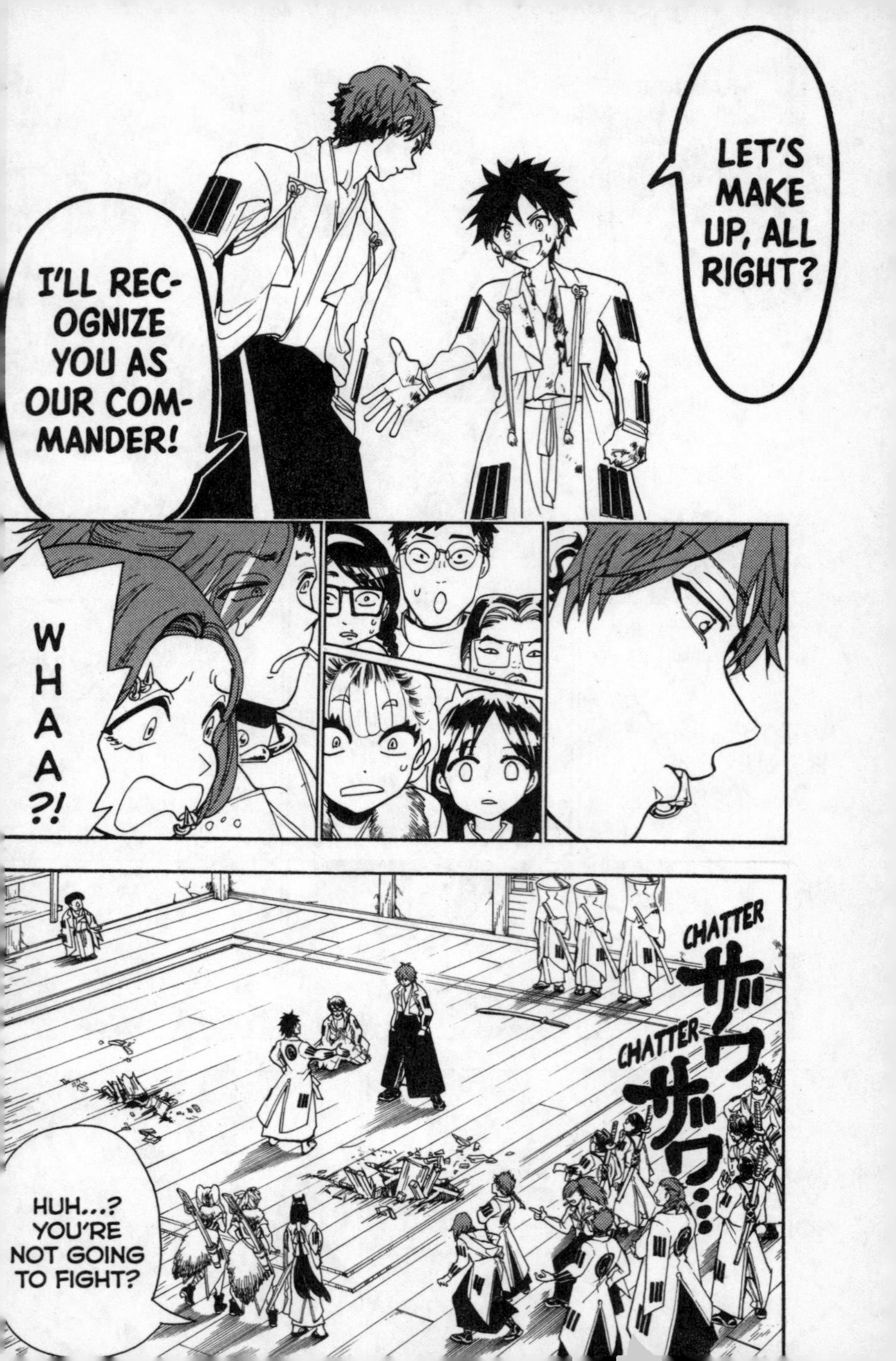
LET'S MAKE UP, ALL RIGHT?
I'LL REC- OGNIZE YOU AS OUR COM- MANDER!
WHAA?!
CHATTER
ザワ
CHATTER
ザワ…
HUH...? YOU'RE NOT GOING TO FIGHT?

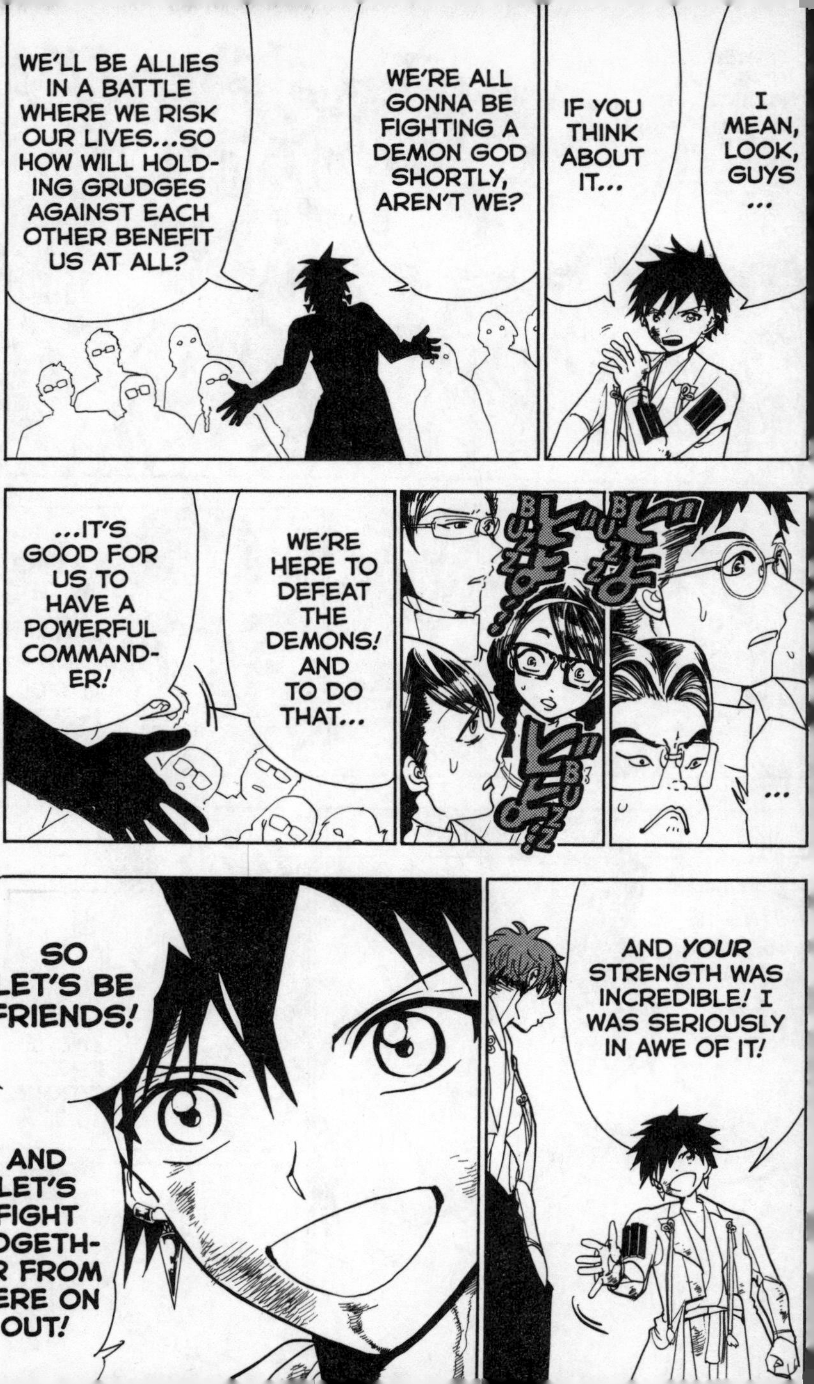
I MEAN, LOOK, GUYS...
IF YOU THINK ABOUT IT...
WE'RE ALL GONNA BE FIGHTING A DEMON GOD SHORTLY, AREN'T WE?
WE'LL BE ALLIES IN A BATTLE WHERE WE RISK OUR LIVES...SO HOW WILL HOLDING GRUDGES AGAINST EACH OTHER BENEFIT US AT ALL?
...
BUZZ
BUZZ
BUZZ
WE'RE HERE TO DEFEAT THE DEMONS! AND TO DO THAT...
...IT'S GOOD FOR US TO HAVE A POWERFUL COMMANDER!
AND YOUR STRENGTH WAS INCREDIBLE! I WAS SERIOUSLY IN AWE OF IT!
SO LET'S BE FRIENDS!
AND LET'S FIGHT TOGETHER FROM HERE ON OUT!

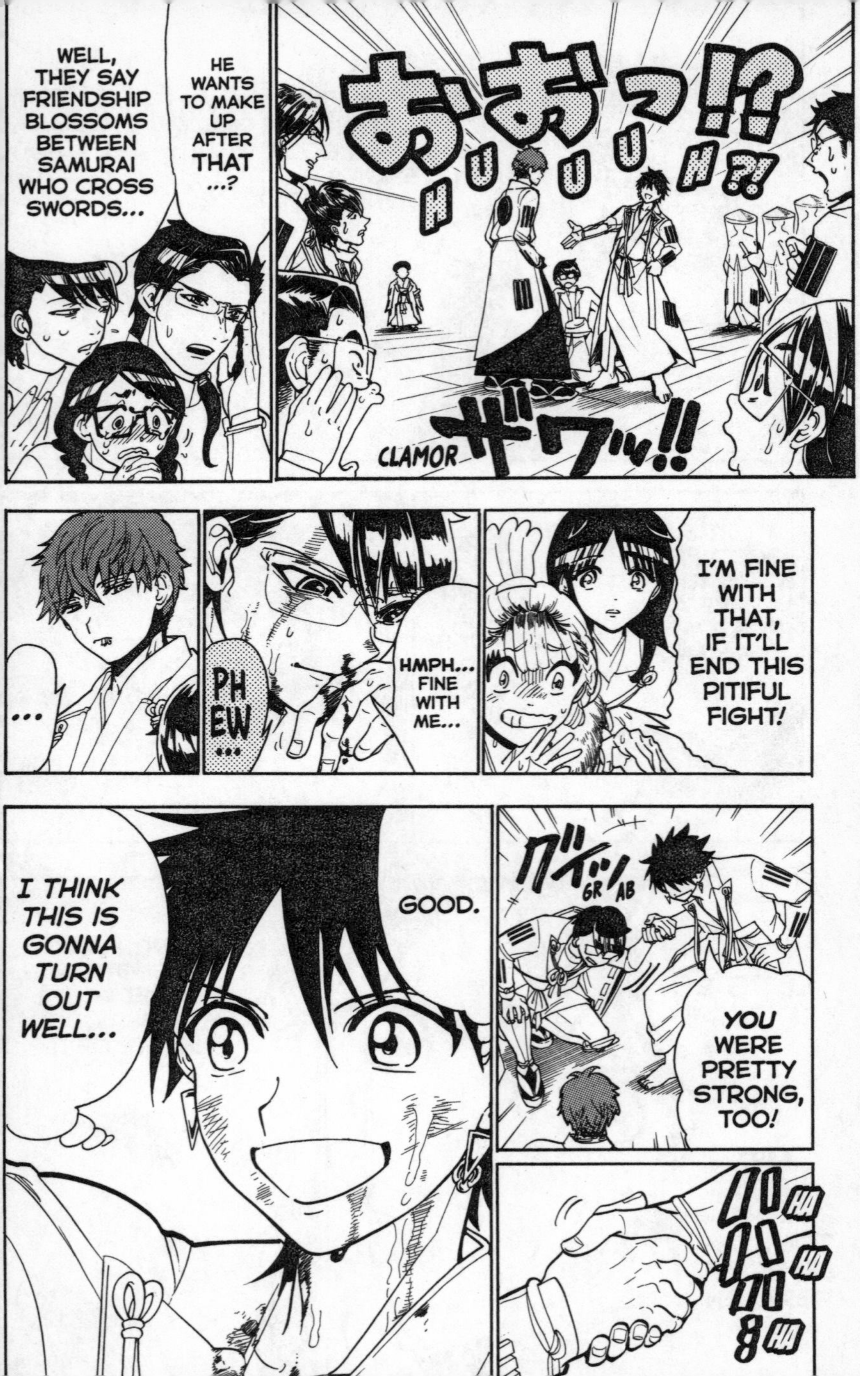

おおっ!?
HUUUUH?!
CLAMOR
ザワッ!!
HE WANTS TO MAKE UP AFTER THAT...?
WELL, THEY SAY FRIENDSHIP BLOSSOMS BETWEEN SAMURAI WHO CROSS SWORDS...
I'M FINE WITH THAT, IF IT'LL END THIS PITIFUL FIGHT!
HMPH... FINE WITH ME...
PHEW...
...
グイッ
GRAB
YOU WERE PRETTY STRONG, TOO!
ハハハ
HA HA HA HA
GOOD.
I THINK THIS IS GONNA TURN OUT WELL...

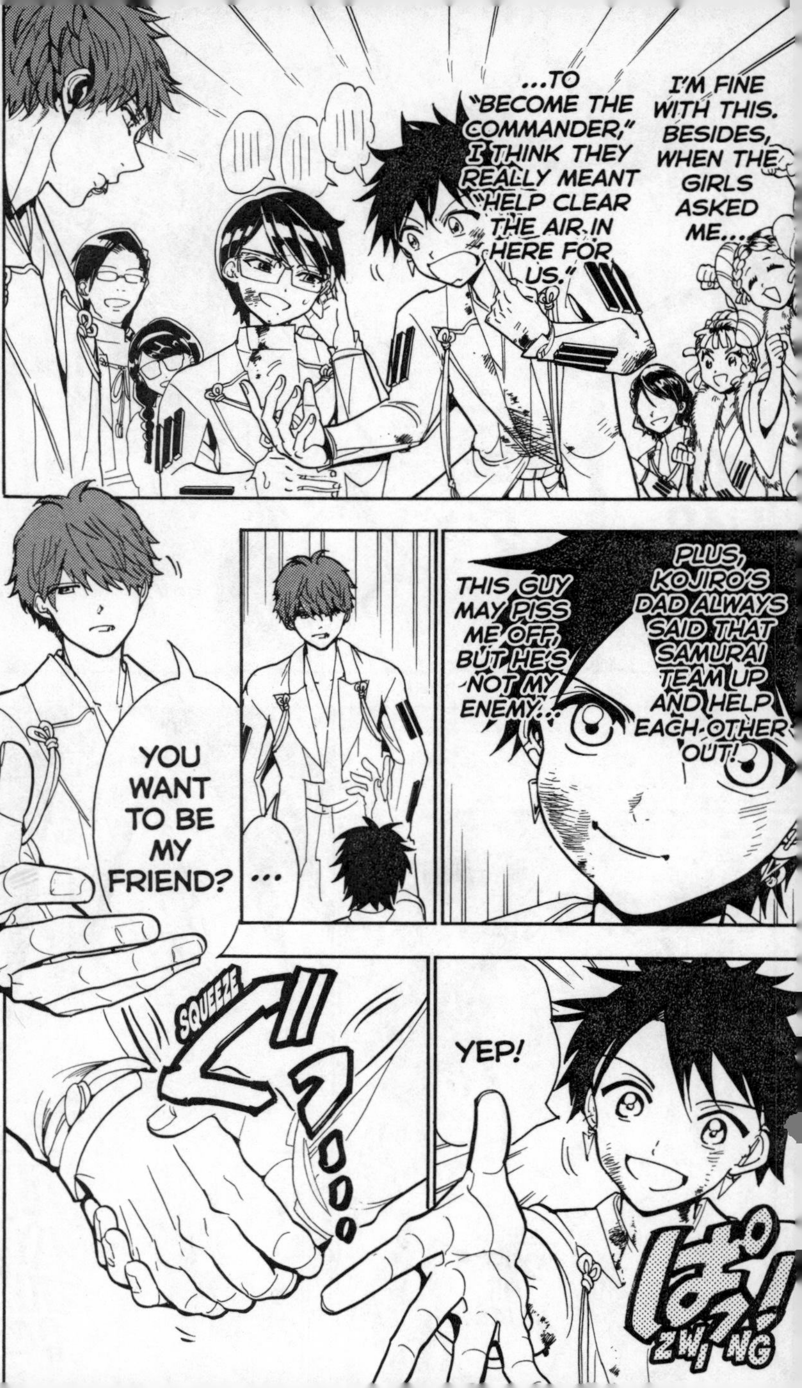
I'M FINE WITH THIS. BESIDES, WHEN THE GIRLS ASKED ME...
...TO "BECOME THE COMMANDER," I THINK THEY REALLY MEANT "HELP CLEAR THE AIR IN HERE FOR US."
PLUS, KOJIRO'S DAD ALWAYS SAID THAT SAMURAI TEAM UP AND HELP EACH OTHER OUT!
THIS GUY MAY PISS ME OFF, BUT HE'S NOT MY ENEMY...
...
YOU WANT TO BE MY FRIEND?
YEP!
ZWING
SQUEEZE

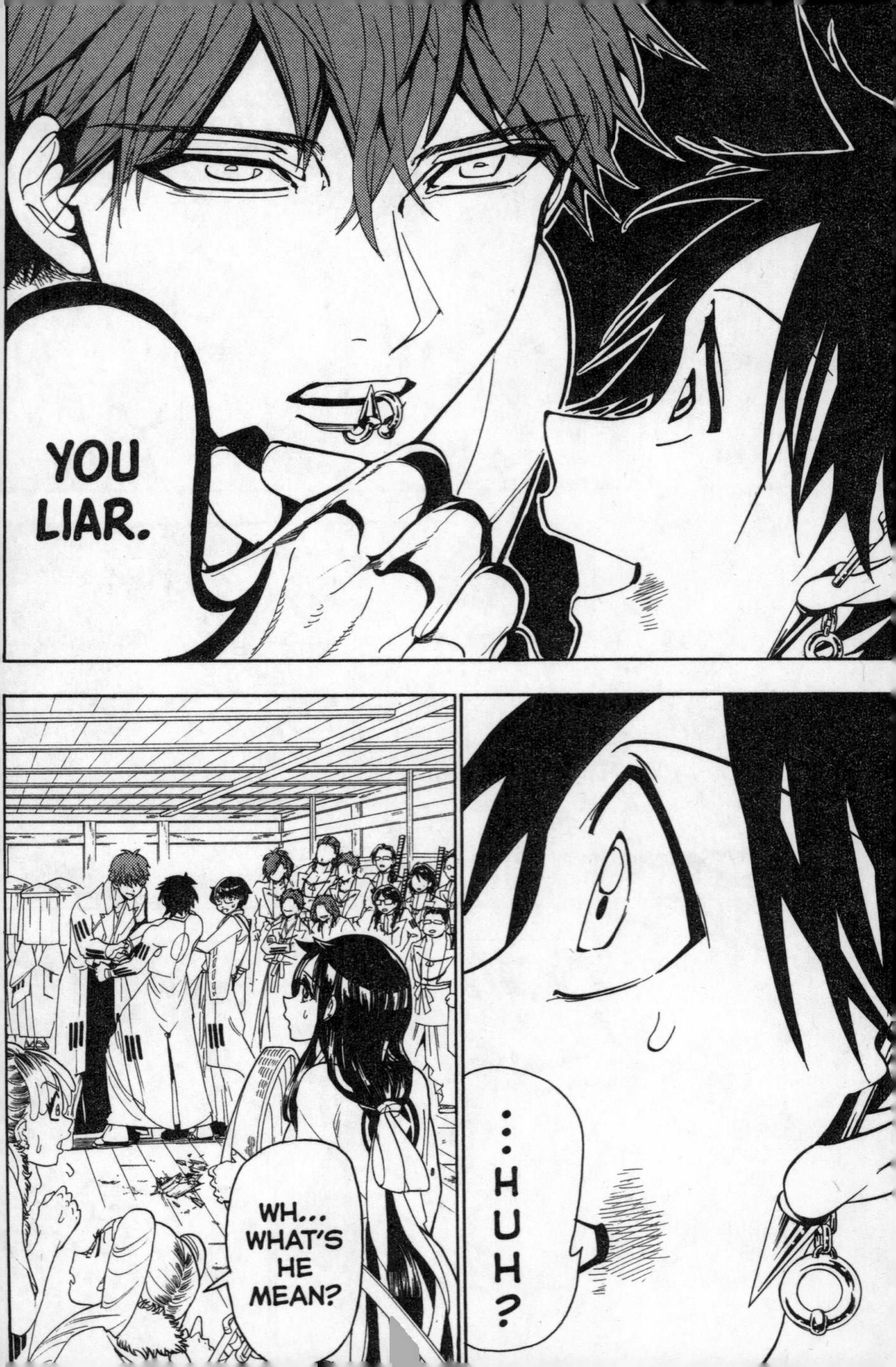
YOU LIAR.
...HUH?
WH... WHAT'S HE MEAN?

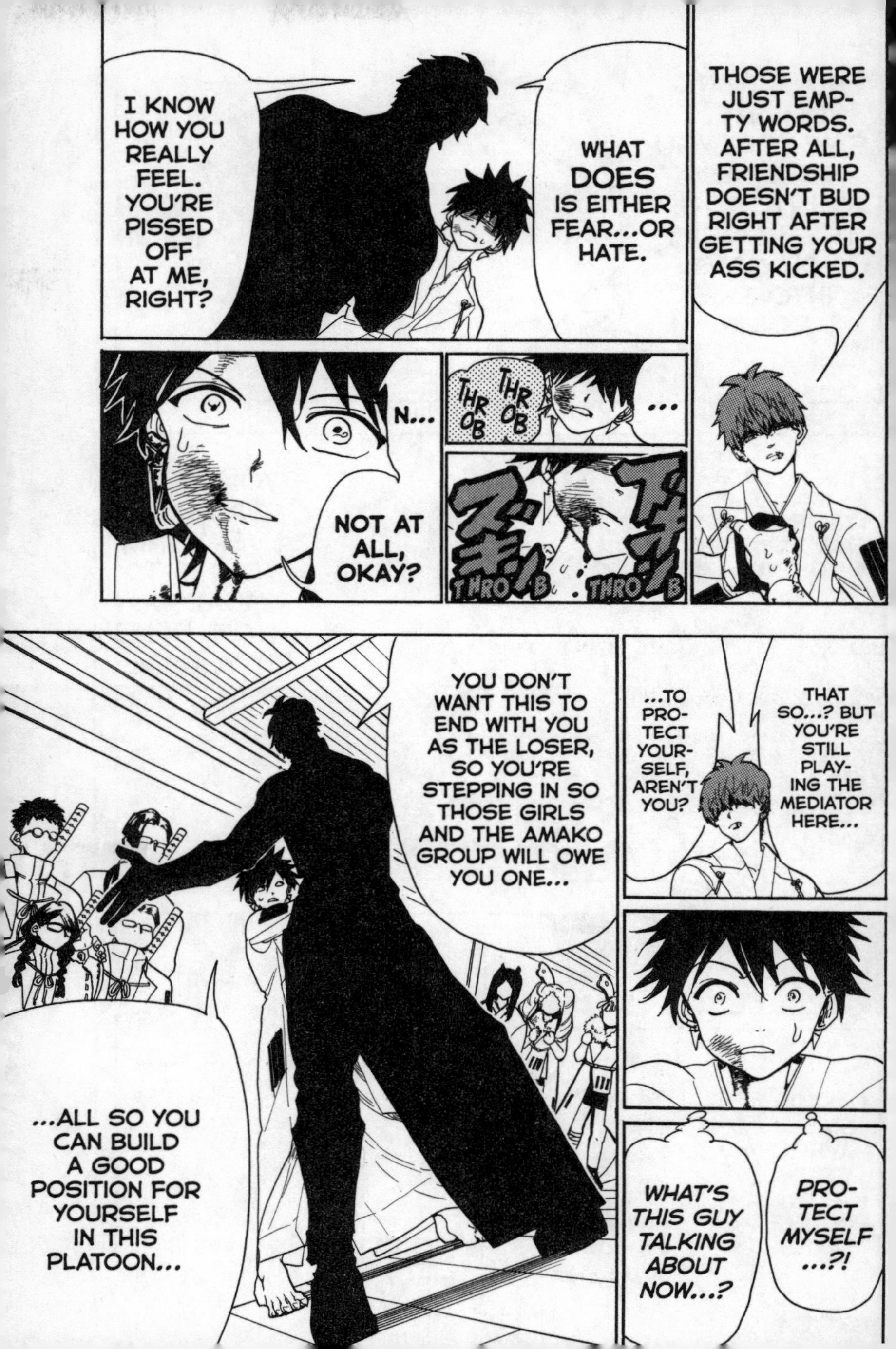
THOSE WERE JUST EMPTY WORDS. AFTER ALL, FRIENDSHIP DOESN'T BUD RIGHT AFTER GETTING YOUR ASS KICKED.
WHAT DOES IS EITHER FEAR...OR HATE.
I KNOW HOW YOU REALLY FEEL. YOU'RE PISSED OFF AT ME, RIGHT?
...
THROB THROB
THROB THROB
N...
NOT AT ALL, OKAY?
THAT SO...? BUT YOU'RE STILL PLAYING THE MEDIATOR HERE...
...TO PROTECT YOURSELF, AREN'T YOU?
PROTECT MYSELF...?!
WHAT'S THIS GUY TALKING ABOUT NOW...?
YOU DON'T WANT THIS TO END WITH YOU AS THE LOSER, SO YOU'RE STEPPING IN SO THOSE GIRLS AND THE AMAKO GROUP WILL OWE YOU ONE...
...ALL SO YOU CAN BUILD A GOOD POSITION FOR YOURSELF IN THIS PLATOON...

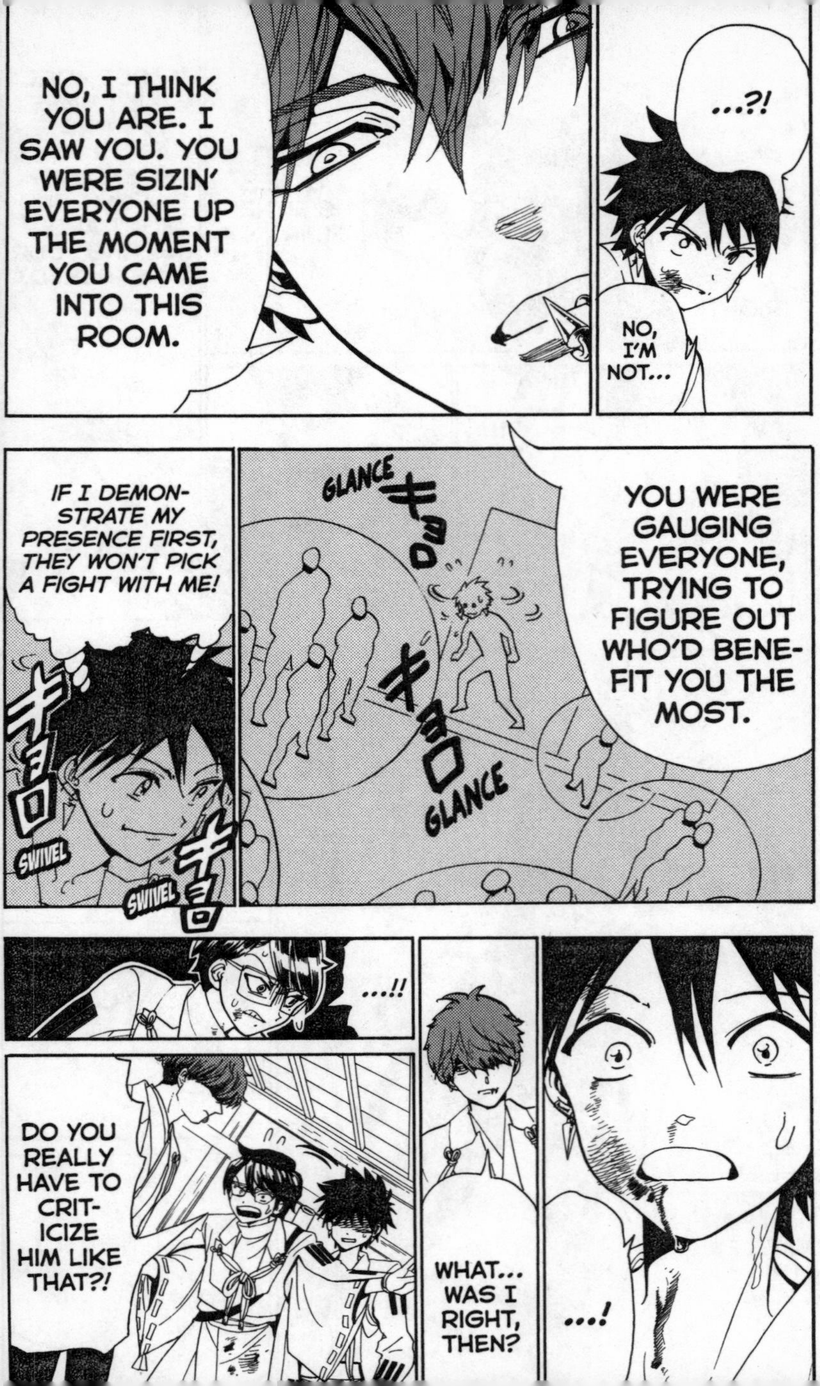
...?!
NO, I'M NOT...
NO, I THINK YOU ARE. I SAW YOU. YOU WERE SIZIN' EVERYONE UP THE MOMENT YOU CAME INTO THIS ROOM.
YOU WERE GAUGING EVERYONE, TRYING TO FIGURE OUT WHO'D BENE-FIT YOU THE MOST.
GLANCE
GLANCE
IF I DEMON-STRATE MY PRESENCE FIRST, THEY WON'T PICK A FIGHT WITH ME!
SWIVEL
SWIVEL
...!
WHAT... WAS I RIGHT, THEN?
...!!
DO YOU REALLY HAVE TO CRIT-ICIZE HIM LIKE THAT?!

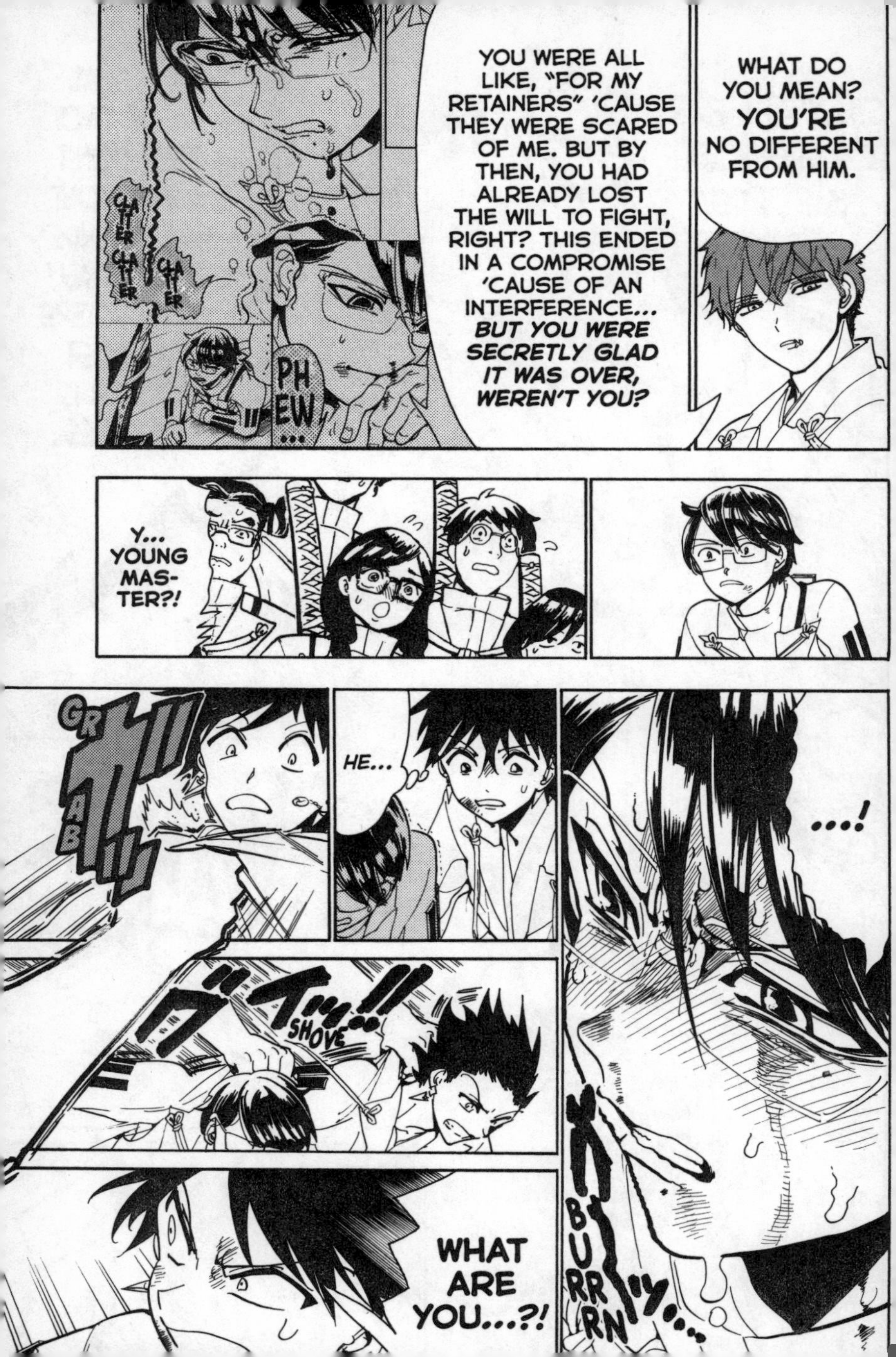
WHAT DO YOU MEAN? YOU'RE NO DIFFERENT FROM HIM.
YOU WERE ALL LIKE, "FOR MY RETAINERS" 'CAUSE THEY WERE SCARED OF ME. BUT BY THEN, YOU HAD ALREADY LOST THE WILL TO FIGHT, RIGHT? THIS ENDED IN A COMPROMISE 'CAUSE OF AN INTERFERENCE... *BUT YOU WERE SECRETLY GLAD IT WAS OVER, WEREN'T YOU?*
CLATTER
CLATTER
CLATTER
PHEW...
Y... YOUNG MASTER?!
...!
BURRRRN
HE...
GRAB
SHOVE
WHAT ARE YOU...?!

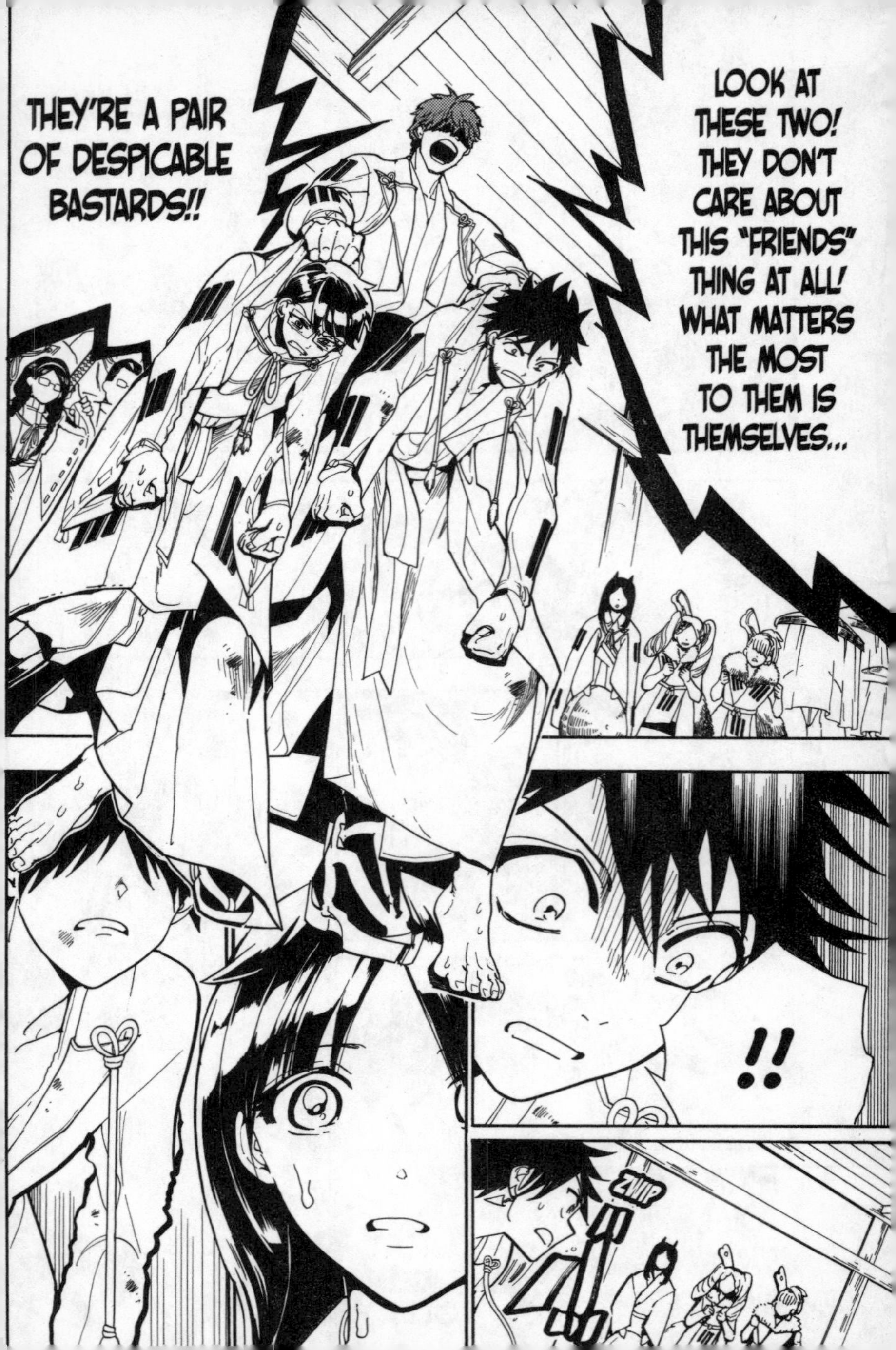
LOOK AT THESE TWO! THEY DON'T CARE ABOUT THIS "FRIENDS" THING AT ALL! WHAT MATTERS THE MOST TO THEM IS THEMSELVES...
THEY'RE A PAIR OF DESPICABLE BASTARDS!!
!!
ZWIP

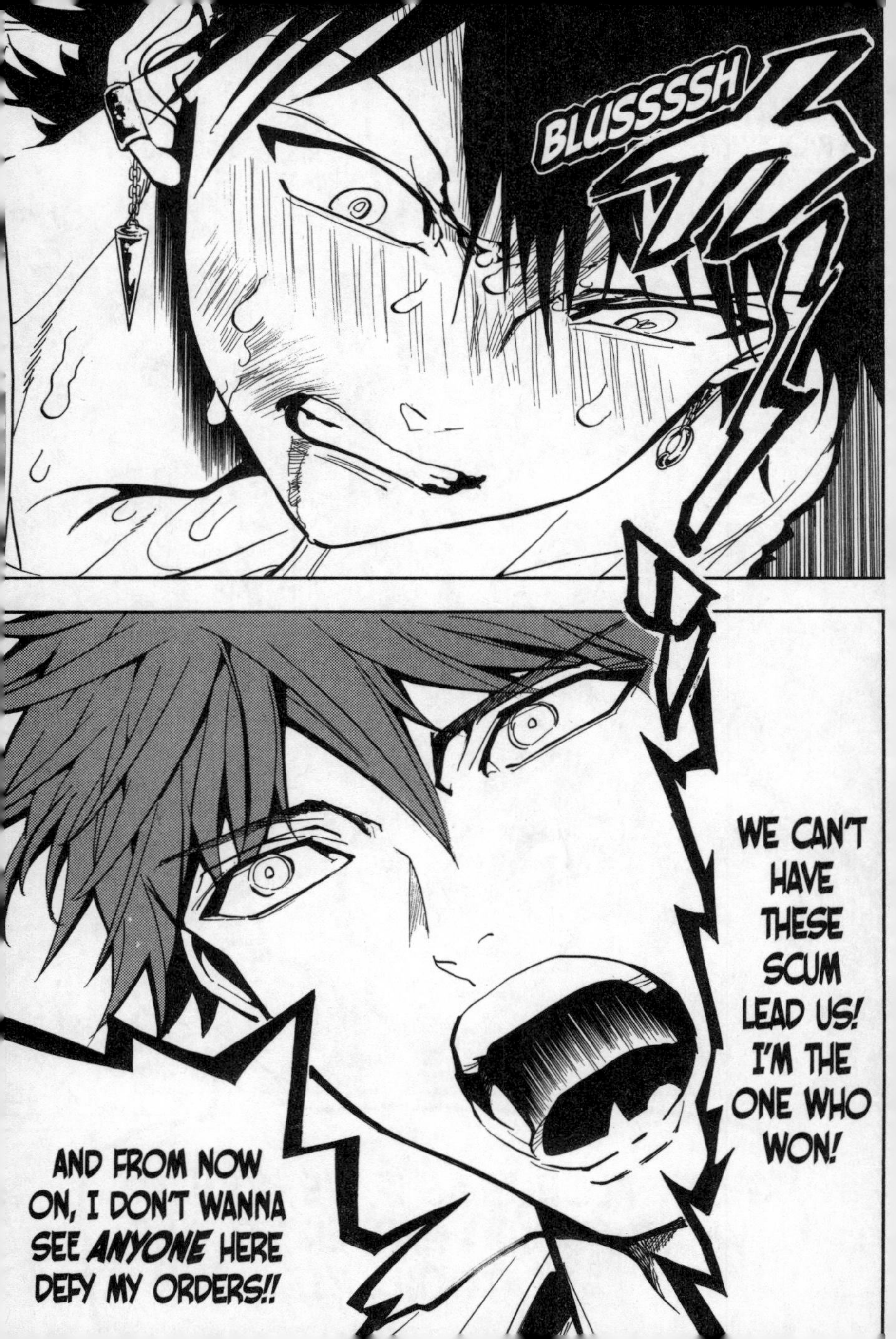
BLUSSSSH
WE CAN'T HAVE THESE SCUM LEAD US! I'M THE ONE WHO WON!
AND FROM NOW ON, I DON'T WANNA SEE *ANYONE* HERE DEFY MY ORDERS!!

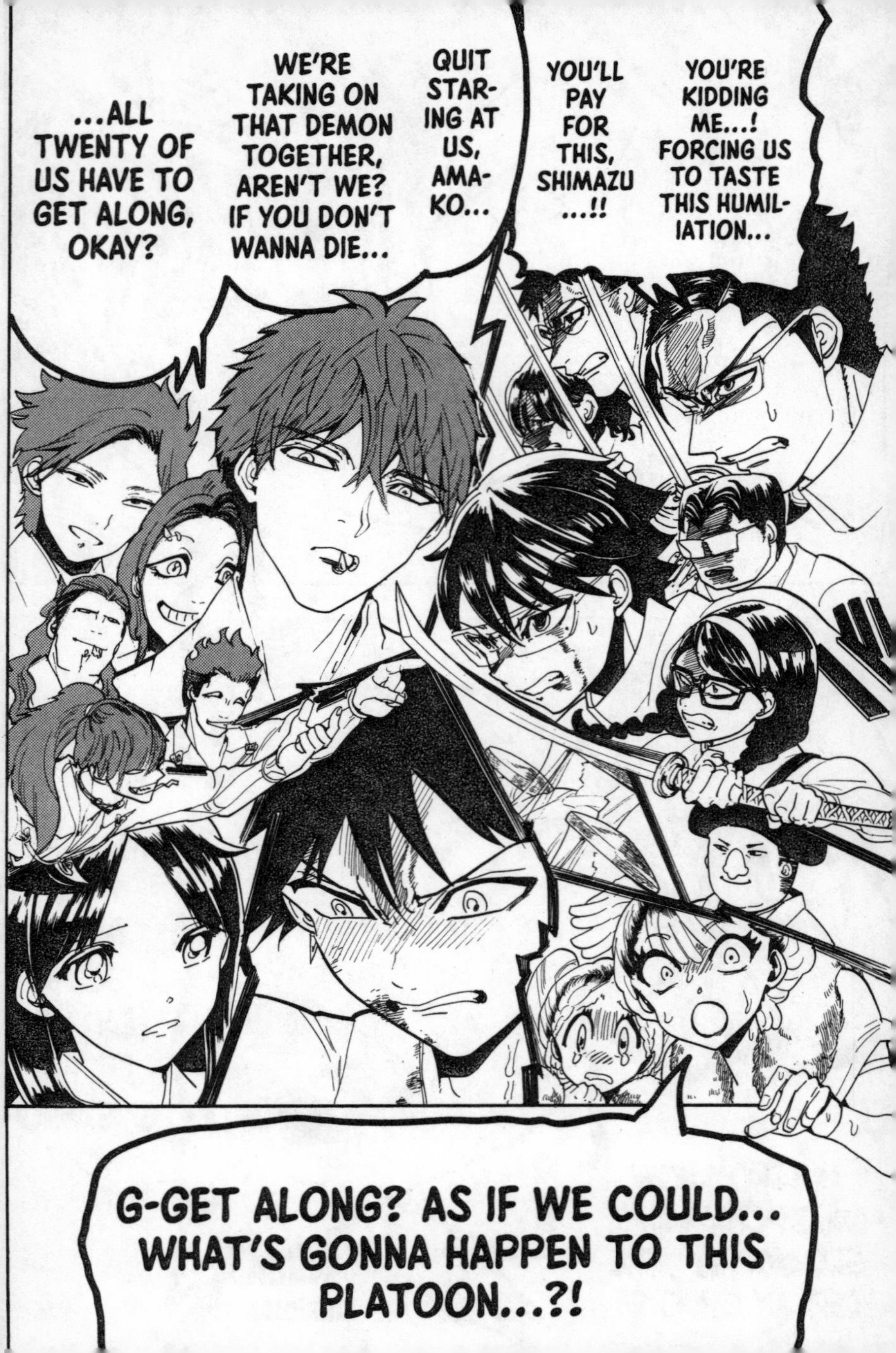
YOU'RE KIDDING ME...! FORCING US TO TASTE THIS HUMILIATION...
YOU'LL PAY FOR THIS, SHIMAZU...!!
QUIT STARING AT US, AMAKO...
WE'RE TAKING ON THAT DEMON TOGETHER, AREN'T WE? IF YOU DON'T WANNA DIE...
...ALL TWENTY OF US HAVE TO GET ALONG, OKAY?
G-GET ALONG? AS IF WE COULD... WHAT'S GONNA HAPPEN TO THIS PLATOON...?!

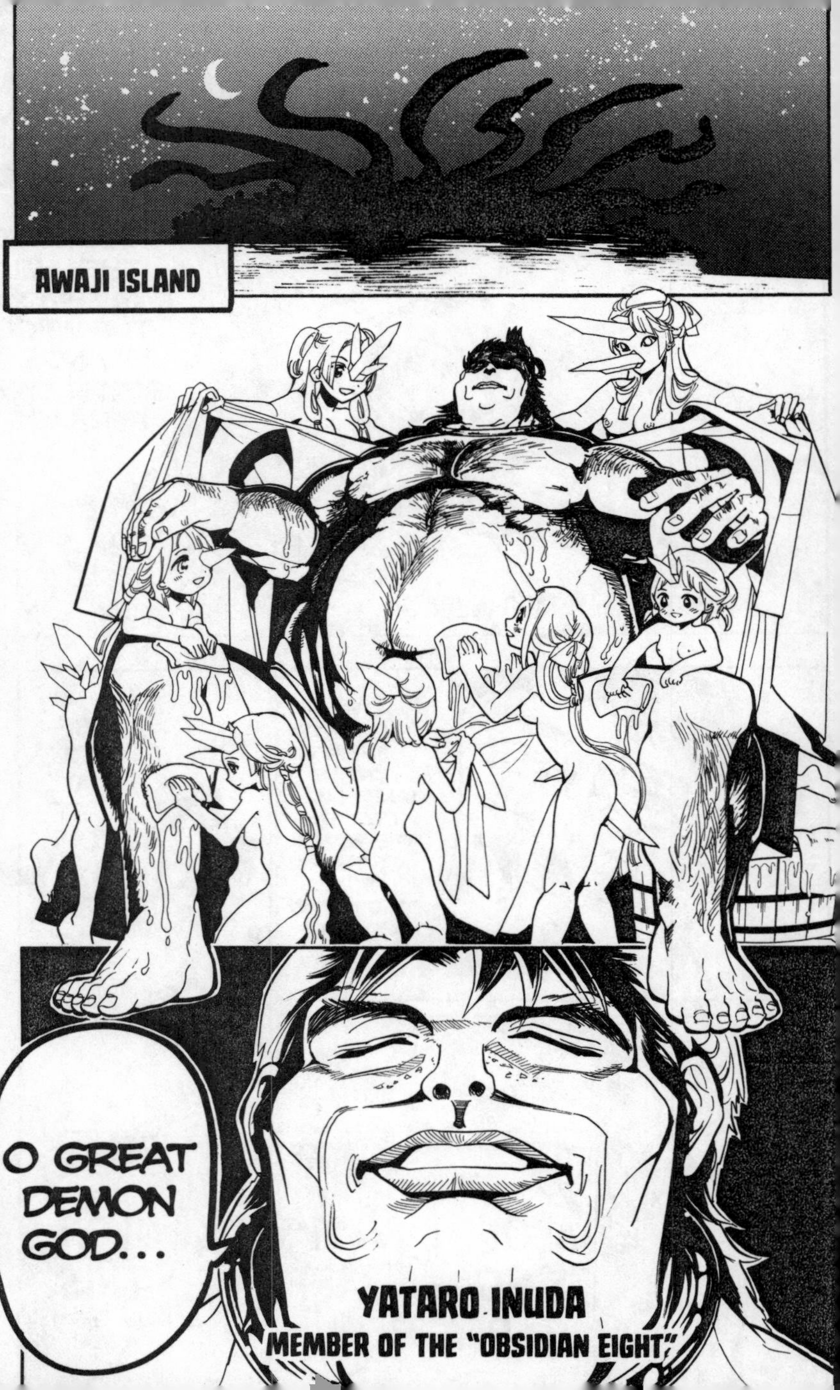
AWAJI ISLAND
O GREAT DEMON GOD...
YATARO INUDA
MEMBER OF THE "OBSIDIAN EIGHT"

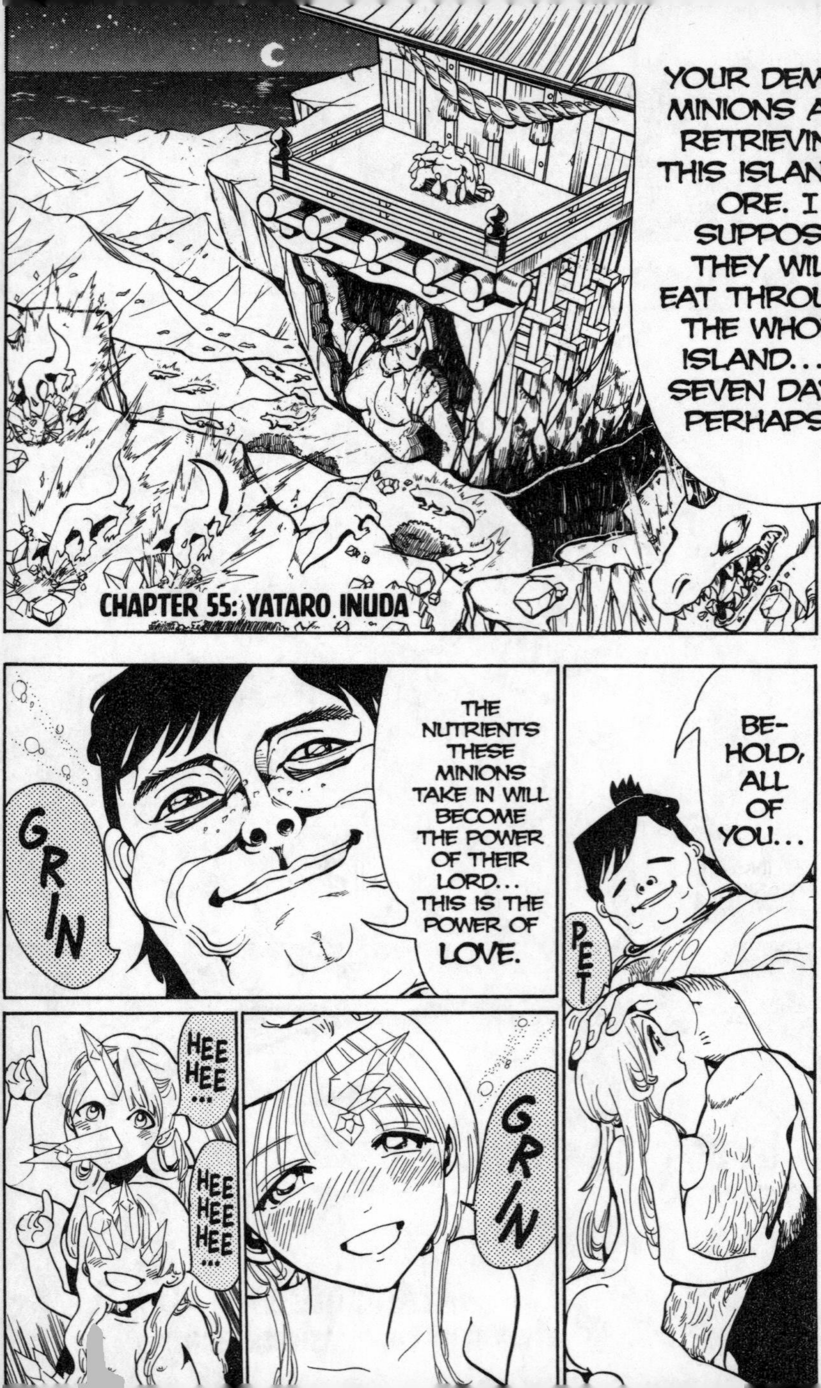
YOUR DEMON MINIONS ARE RETRIEVING THIS ISLAND'S ORE. I SUPPOSE THEY WILL EAT THROUGH THE WHOLE ISLAND...IN SEVEN DAYS, PERHAPS?
CHAPTER 55: YATARO INUDA
BE-HOLD, ALL OF YOU...
PET
THE NUTRIENTS THESE MINIONS TAKE IN WILL BECOME THE POWER OF THEIR LORD... THIS IS THE POWER OF LOVE.
GRIN
GRIN
HEE HEE...
HEE HEE HEE...

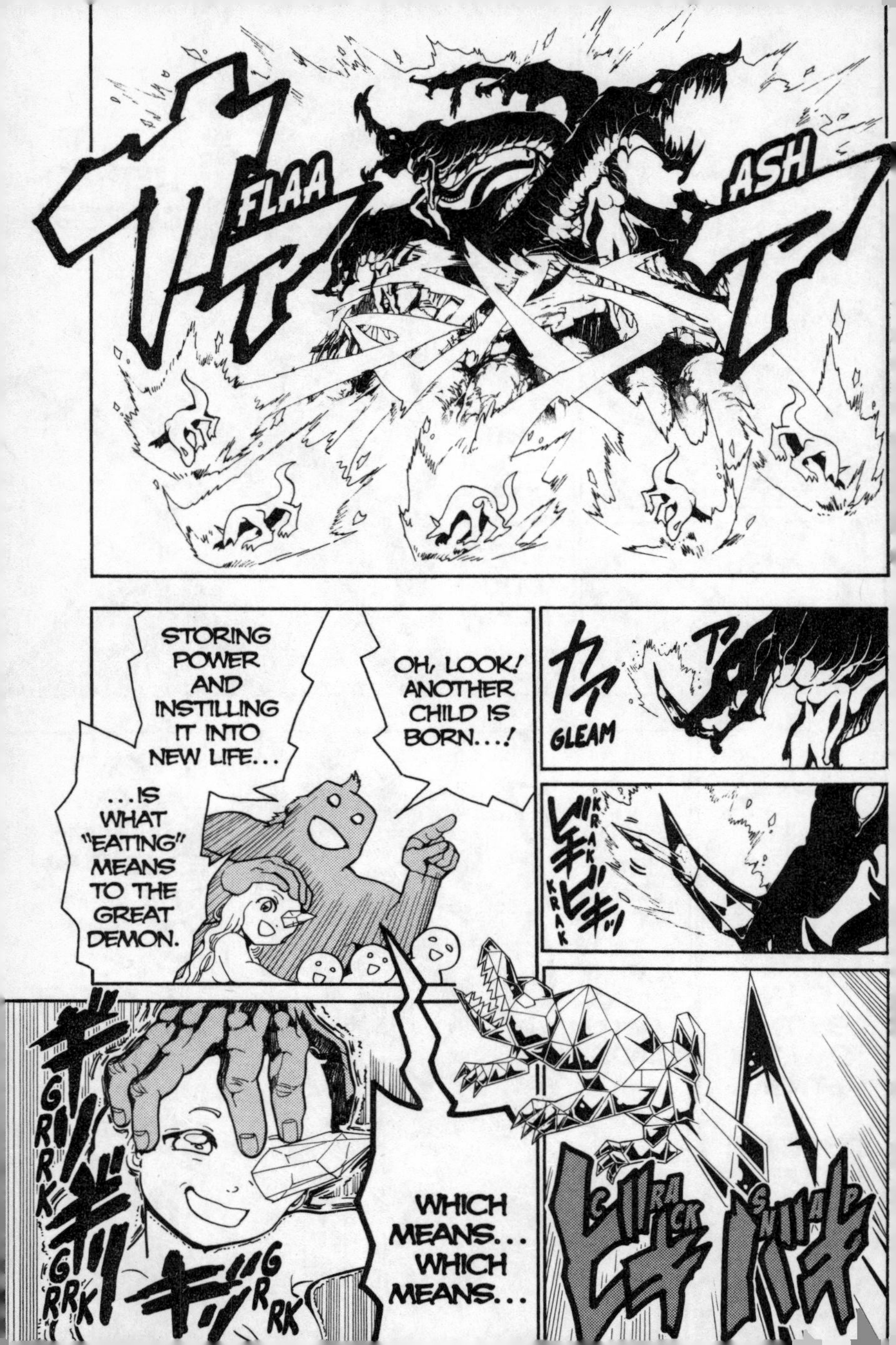
FLAA ASH
GLEAM
KRAK KRAK
OH, LOOK! ANOTHER CHILD IS BORN...!
STORING POWER AND INSTILLING IT INTO NEW LIFE...
...IS WHAT "EATING" MEANS TO THE GREAT DEMON.
CRACK
SNAP
WHICH MEANS... WHICH MEANS...
GRRK
GRRK
GRRK

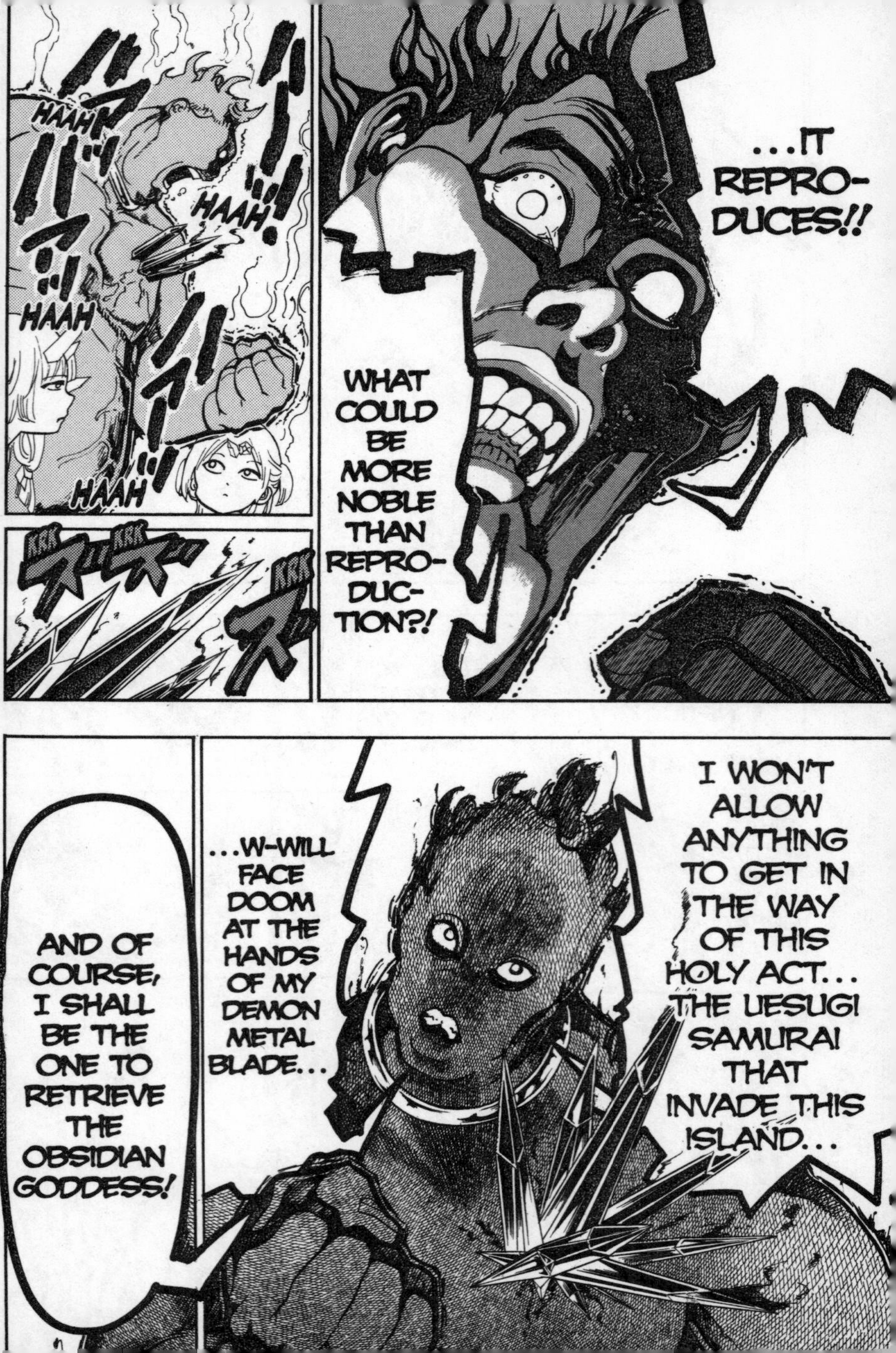

...IT REPRODUCES!!
WHAT COULD BE MORE NOBLE THAN REPRODUCTION?!
HAAH
HAAH!
HAAH
HAAH
KRK
KRK
KRK
I WON'T ALLOW ANYTHING TO GET IN THE WAY OF THIS HOLY ACT... THE UESUGI SAMURAI THAT INVADE THIS ISLAND...
...W-WILL FACE DOOM AT THE HANDS OF MY DEMON METAL BLADE...
AND OF COURSE, I SHALL BE THE ONE TO RETRIEVE THE OBSIDIAN GODDESS!

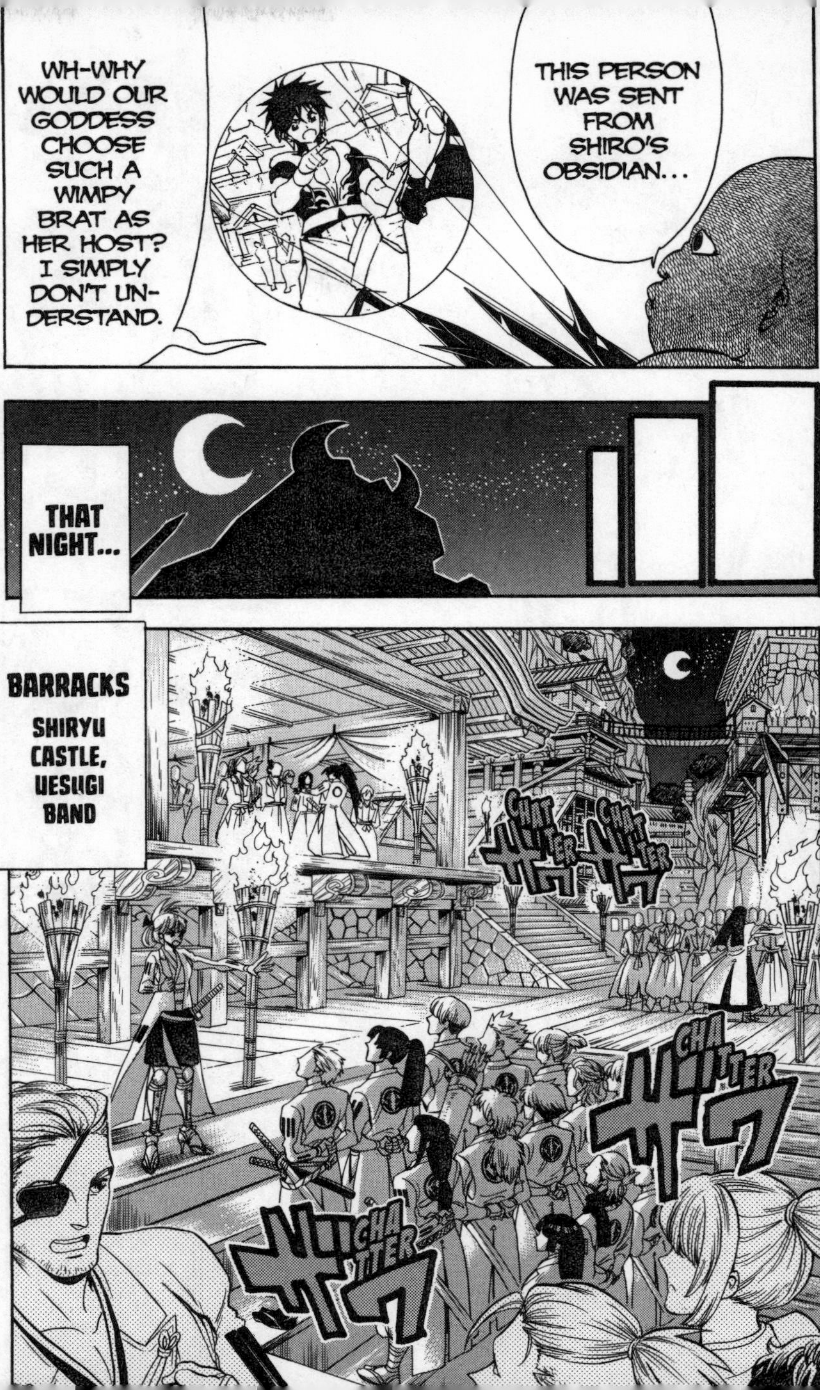
THIS PERSON WAS SENT FROM SHIRO'S OBSIDIAN...
WH-WHY WOULD OUR GODDESS CHOOSE SUCH A WIMPY BRAT AS HER HOST? I SIMPLY DON'T UN-DERSTAND.
THAT NIGHT...
BARRACKS
SHIRYU CASTLE, UESUGI BAND
CHATTER
CHATTER
CHATTER
CHATTER

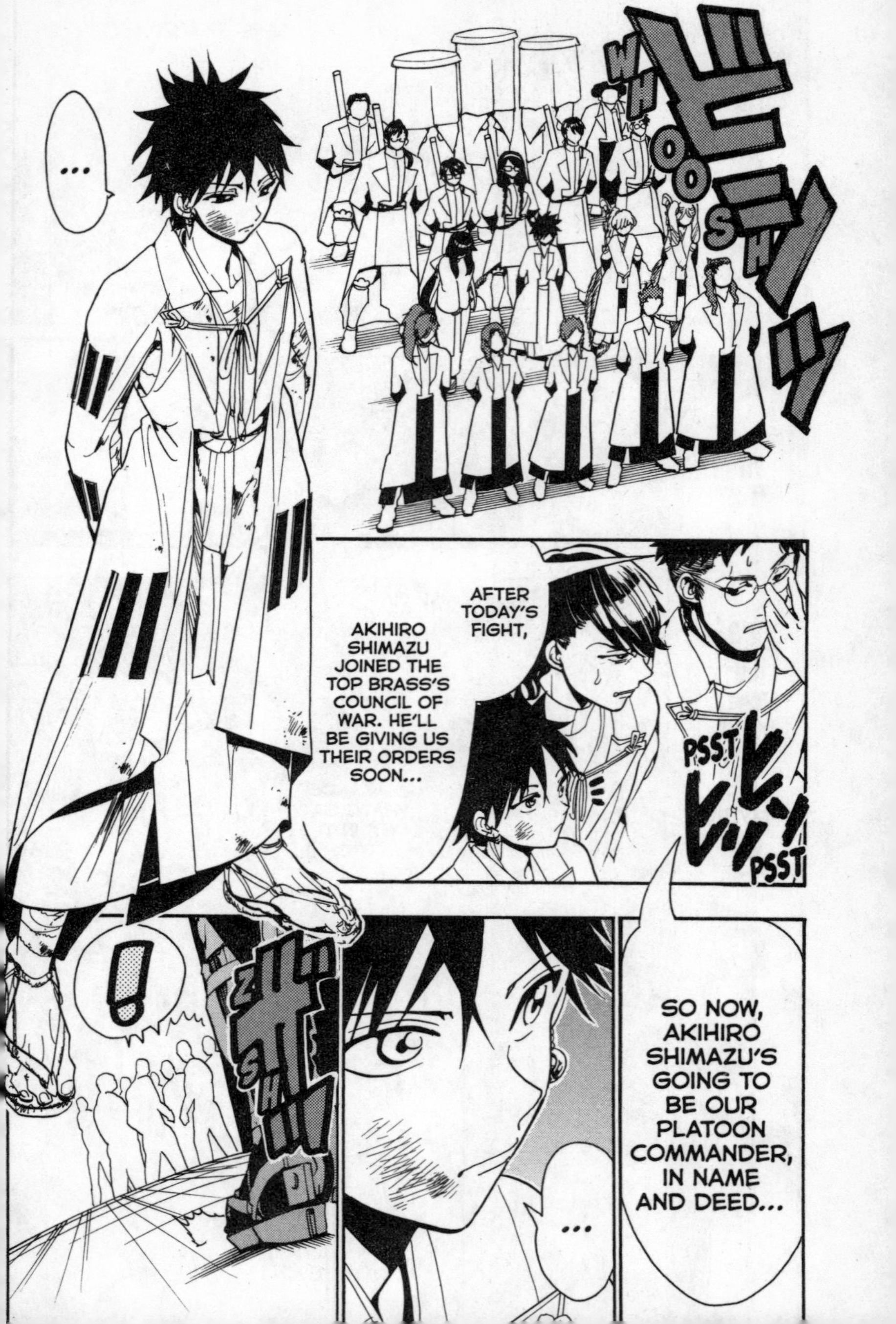
WHOOSH
AFTER TODAY'S FIGHT,
AKIHIRO SHIMAZU JOINED THE TOP BRASS'S COUNCIL OF WAR. HE'LL BE GIVING US THEIR ORDERS SOON...
PSST
PSST
...
SO NOW, AKIHIRO SHIMAZU'S GOING TO BE OUR PLATOON COMMANDER, IN NAME AND DEED...
...
!
ZSH

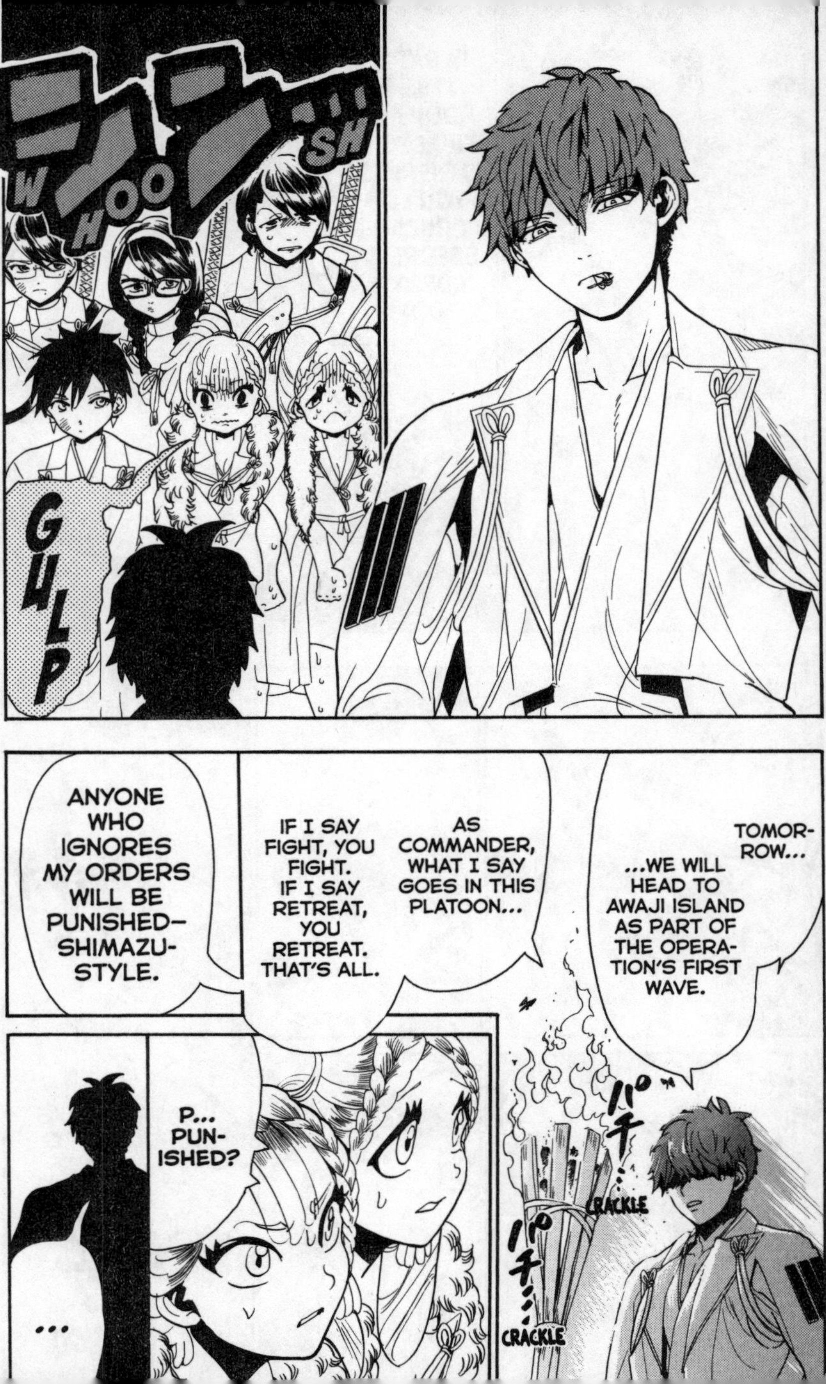
WHOOSH
GULP
TOMORROW...
...WE WILL HEAD TO AWAJI ISLAND AS PART OF THE OPERATION'S FIRST WAVE.
AS COMMANDER, WHAT I SAY GOES IN THIS PLATOON...
IF I SAY FIGHT, YOU FIGHT. IF I SAY RETREAT, YOU RETREAT. THAT'S ALL.
ANYONE WHO IGNORES MY ORDERS WILL BE PUNISHED—SHIMAZU-STYLE.
パチ
CRACKLE
パチ
CRACKLE
P... PUNISHED?
...

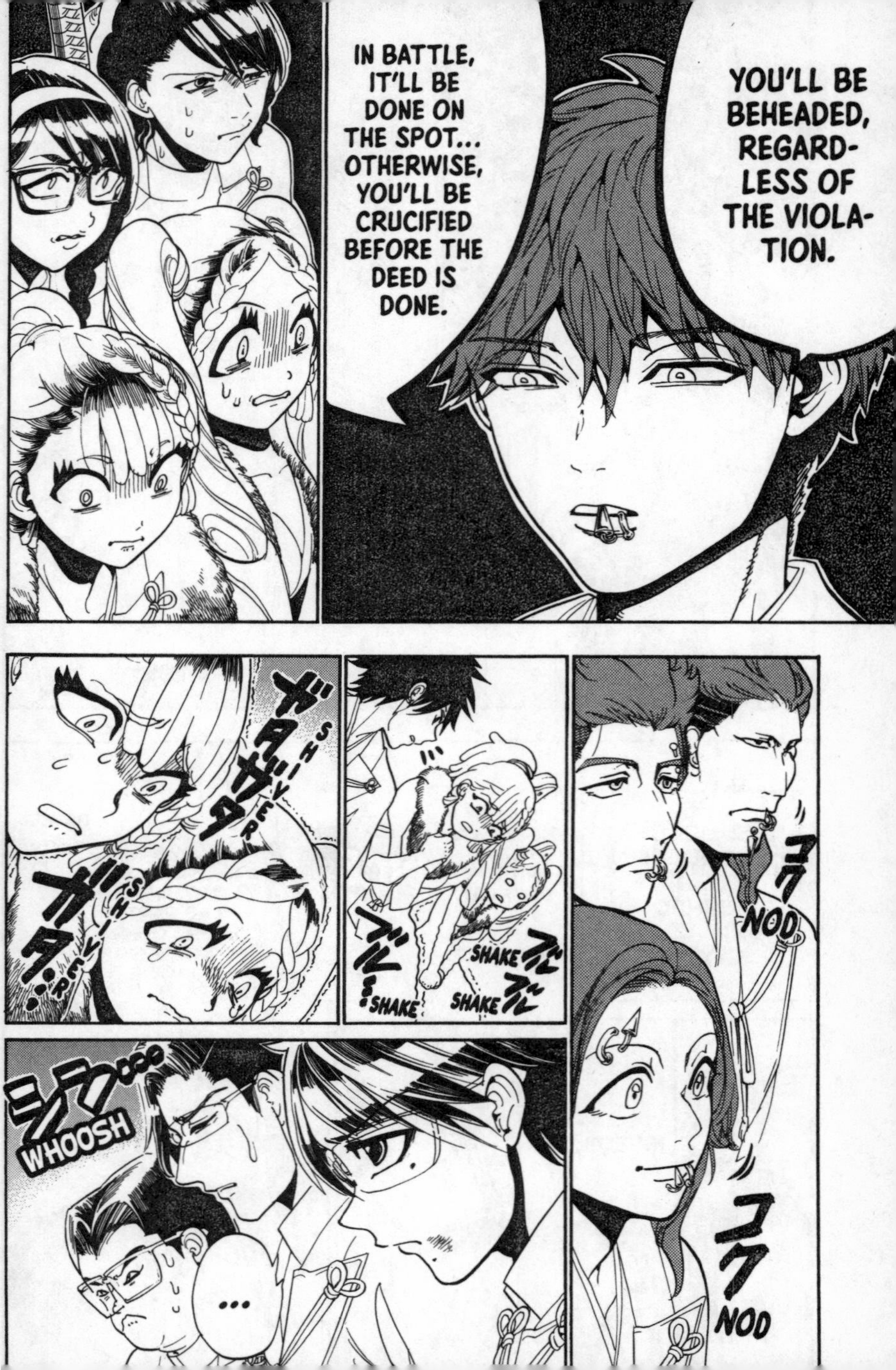
YOU'LL BE BEHEADED, REGARDLESS OF THE VIOLATION.
IN BATTLE, IT'LL BE DONE ON THE SPOT... OTHERWISE, YOU'LL BE CRUCIFIED BEFORE THE DEED IS DONE.
コク NOD
コク NOD
ブル SHAKE
ブル SHAKE
ブル SHAKE
SHIVER
SHIVER
WHOOSH
...

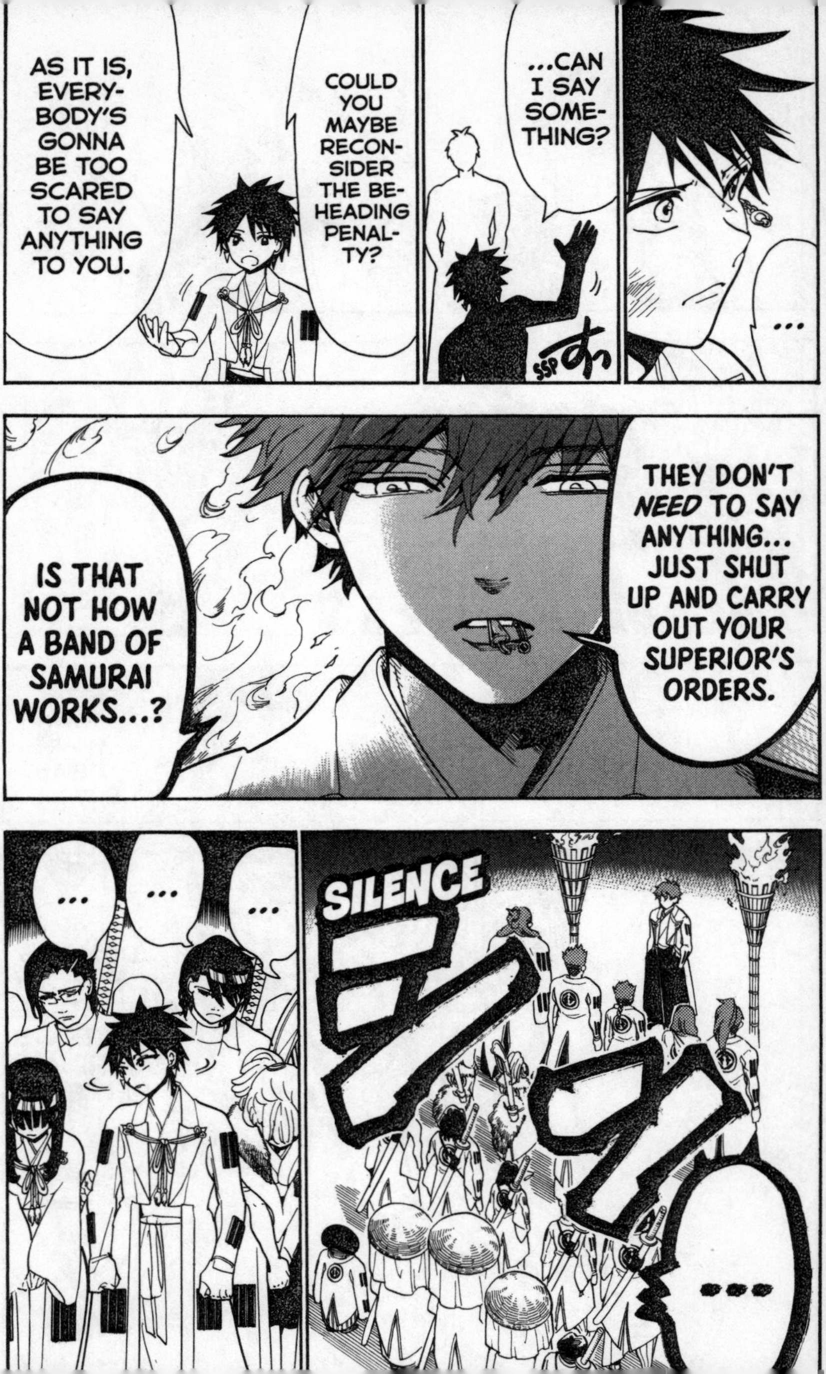
...
...CAN I SAY SOMETHING?
SSP すっ
COULD YOU MAYBE RECONSIDER THE BEHEADING PENALTY?
AS IT IS, EVERYBODY'S GONNA BE TOO SCARED TO SAY ANYTHING TO YOU.
THEY DON'T *NEED* TO SAY ANYTHING... JUST SHUT UP AND CARRY OUT YOUR SUPERIOR'S ORDERS.
IS THAT NOT HOW A BAND OF SAMURAI WORKS...?
SILENCE
...
...
...
...

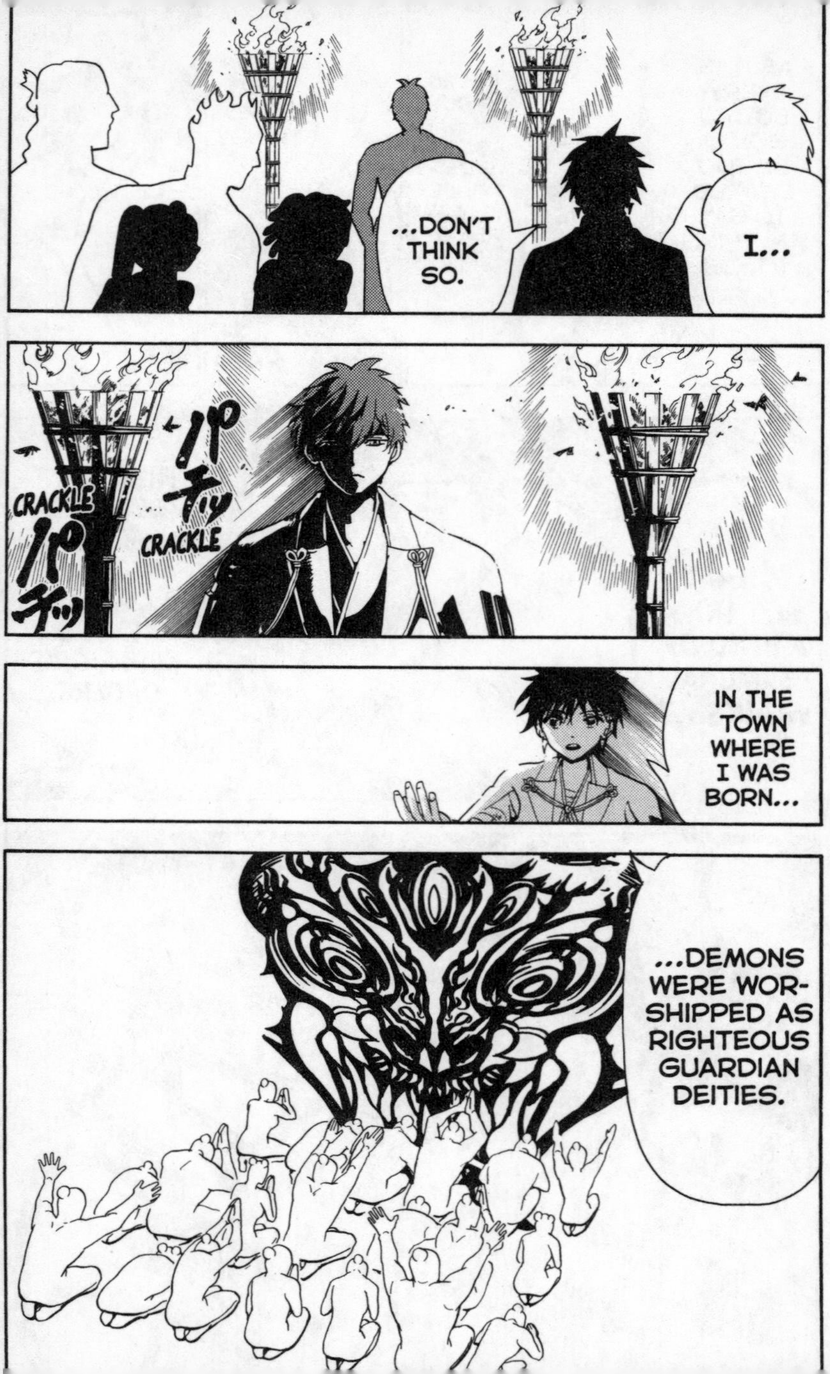
I...
...DON'T THINK SO.
パチッ
CRACKLE
CRACKLE
パチッ
IN THE TOWN WHERE I WAS BORN...
...DEMONS WERE WOR-SHIPPED AS RIGHTEOUS GUARDIAN DEITIES.

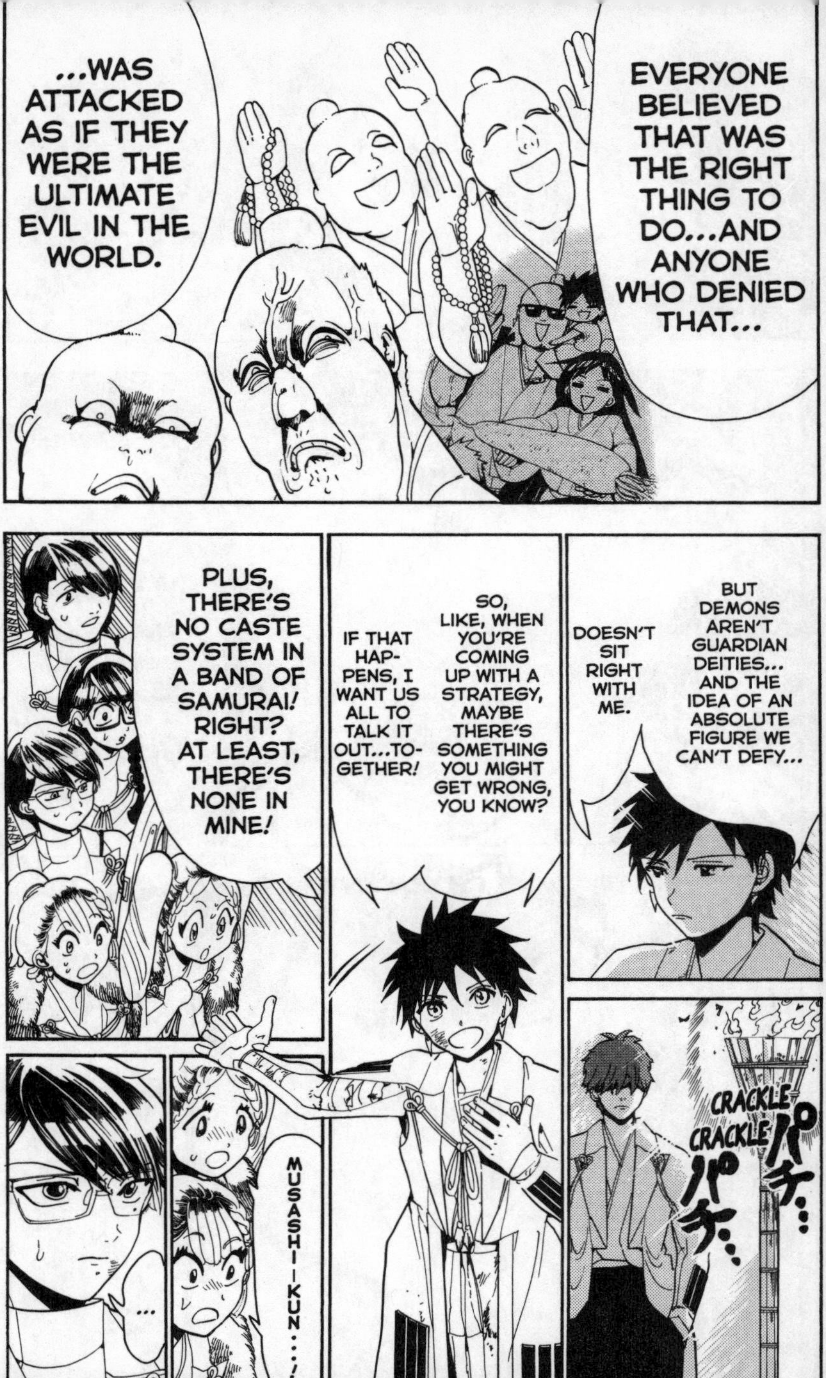
EVERYONE BELIEVED THAT WAS THE RIGHT THING TO DO...AND ANYONE WHO DENIED THAT...
...WAS ATTACKED AS IF THEY WERE THE ULTIMATE EVIL IN THE WORLD.
BUT DEMONS AREN'T GUARDIAN DEITIES... AND THE IDEA OF AN ABSOLUTE FIGURE WE CAN'T DEFY...
DOESN'T SIT RIGHT WITH ME.
CRACKLE
CRACKLE
パチ...
パチ...
SO, LIKE, WHEN YOU'RE COMING UP WITH A STRATEGY, MAYBE THERE'S SOMETHING YOU MIGHT GET WRONG, YOU KNOW?
IF THAT HAP-PENS, I WANT US ALL TO TALK IT OUT...TO-GETHER!
PLUS, THERE'S NO CASTE SYSTEM IN A BAND OF SAMURAI! RIGHT? AT LEAST, THERE'S NONE IN MINE!
MUSASHI-KUN...!
...

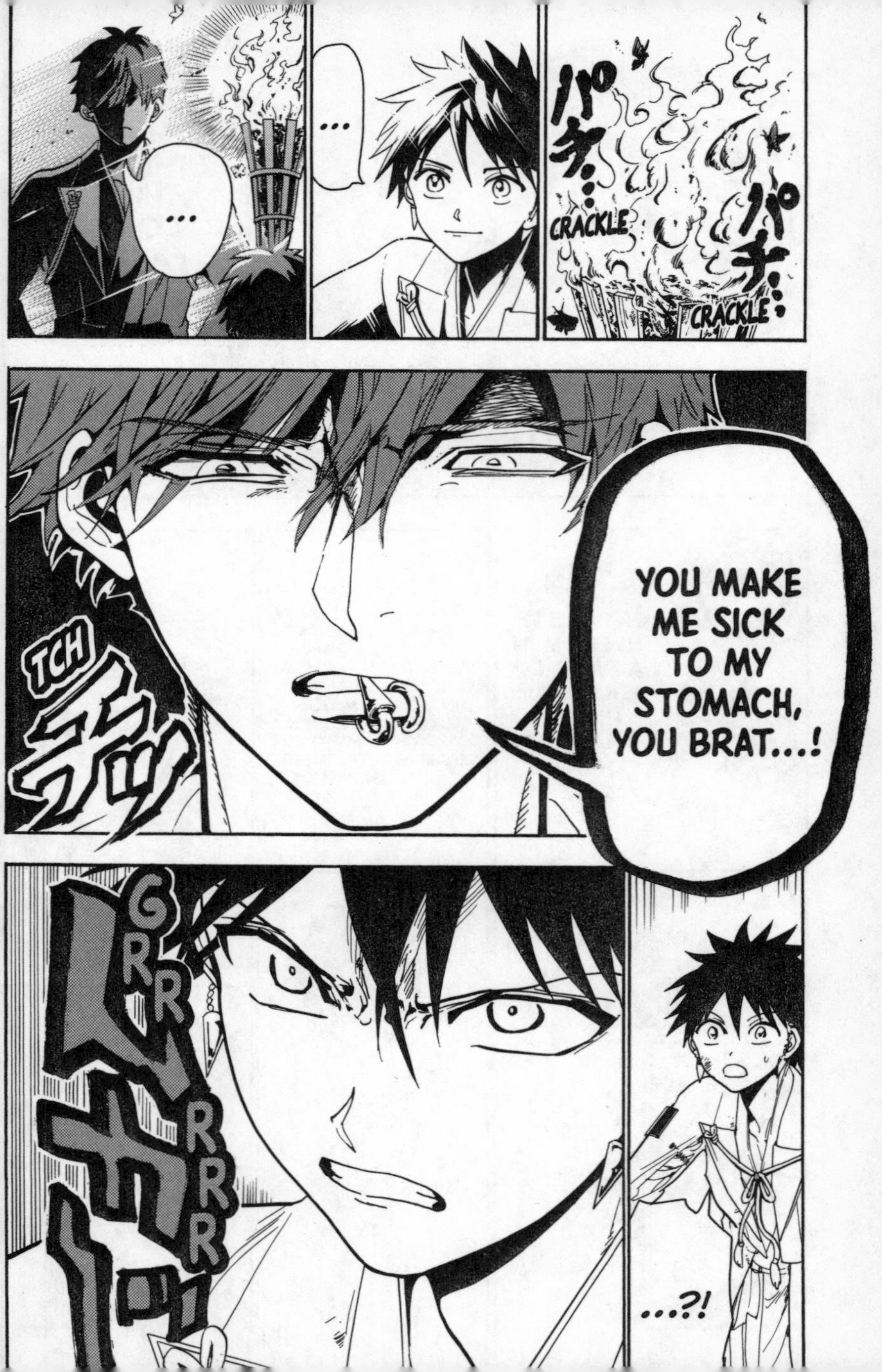

パチ…
CRACKLE
パチ…
CRACKLE
...
...
YOU MAKE ME SICK TO MY STOMACH, YOU BRAT...!
TCH
...?!
GRRRRRR

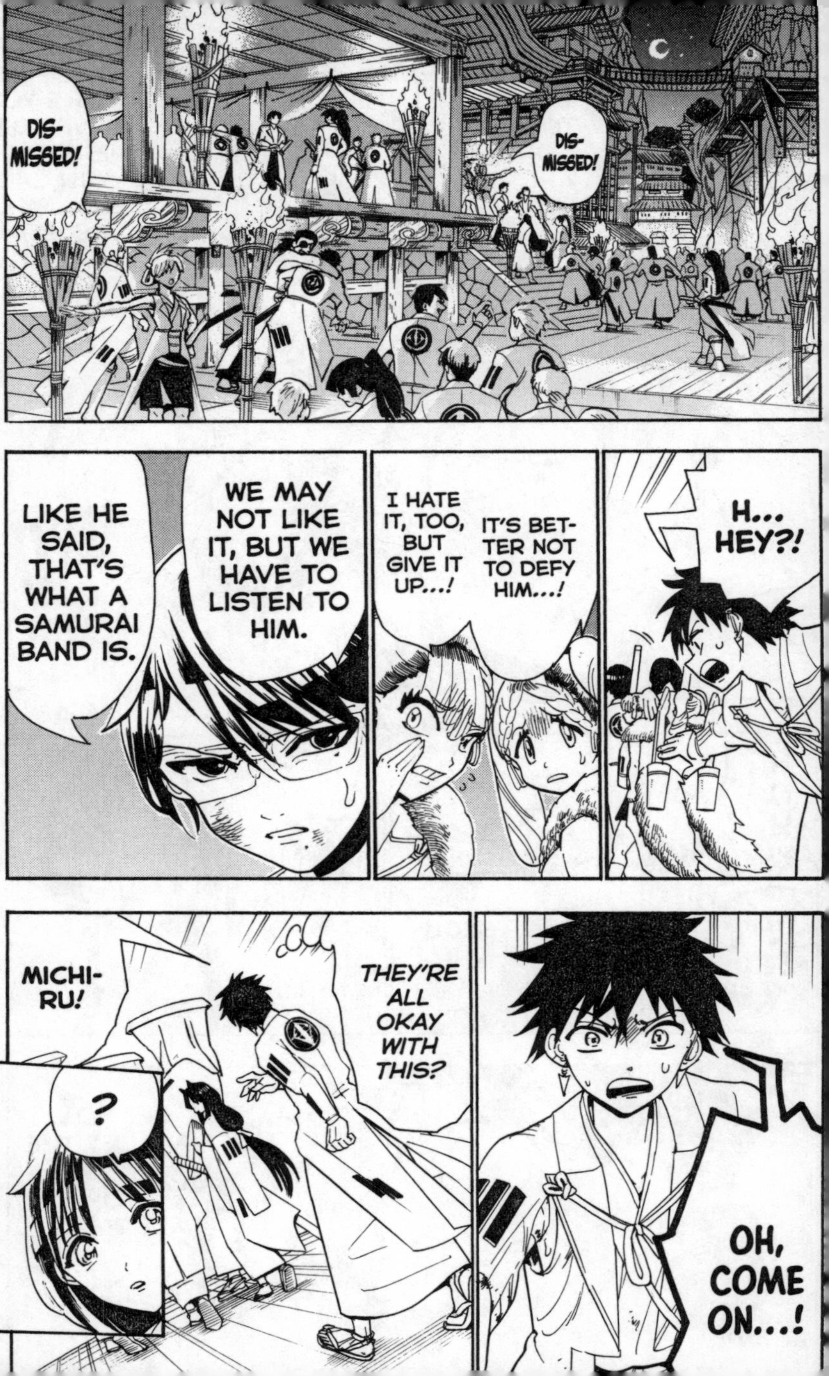
DIS-MISSED!
DIS-MISSED!
H... HEY?!
IT'S BET-TER NOT TO DEFY HIM...!
I HATE IT, TOO, BUT GIVE IT UP...!
WE MAY NOT LIKE IT, BUT WE HAVE TO LISTEN TO HIM.
LIKE HE SAID, THAT'S WHAT A SAMURAI BAND IS.
OH, COME ON...!
THEY'RE ALL OKAY WITH THIS?
MICHI-RU!
?

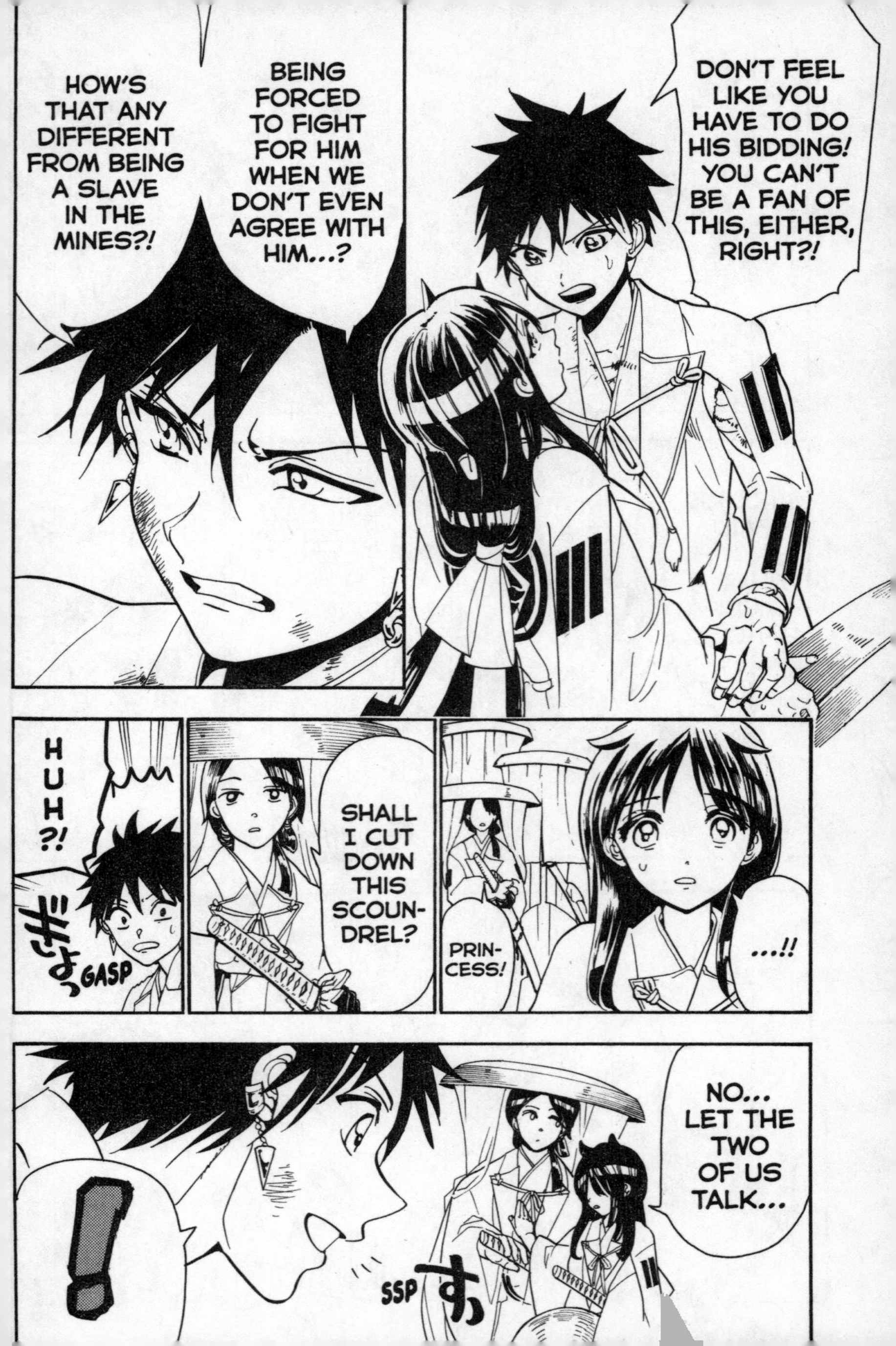
DON'T FEEL LIKE YOU HAVE TO DO HIS BIDDING! YOU CAN'T BE A FAN OF THIS, EITHER, RIGHT?!
BEING FORCED TO FIGHT FOR HIM WHEN WE DON'T EVEN AGREE WITH HIM...?
HOW'S THAT ANY DIFFERENT FROM BEING A SLAVE IN THE MINES?!
...!!
PRIN-CESS!
SHALL I CUT DOWN THIS SCOUN-DREL?
HUH?!
GASP
NO... LET THE TWO OF US TALK...
SSP

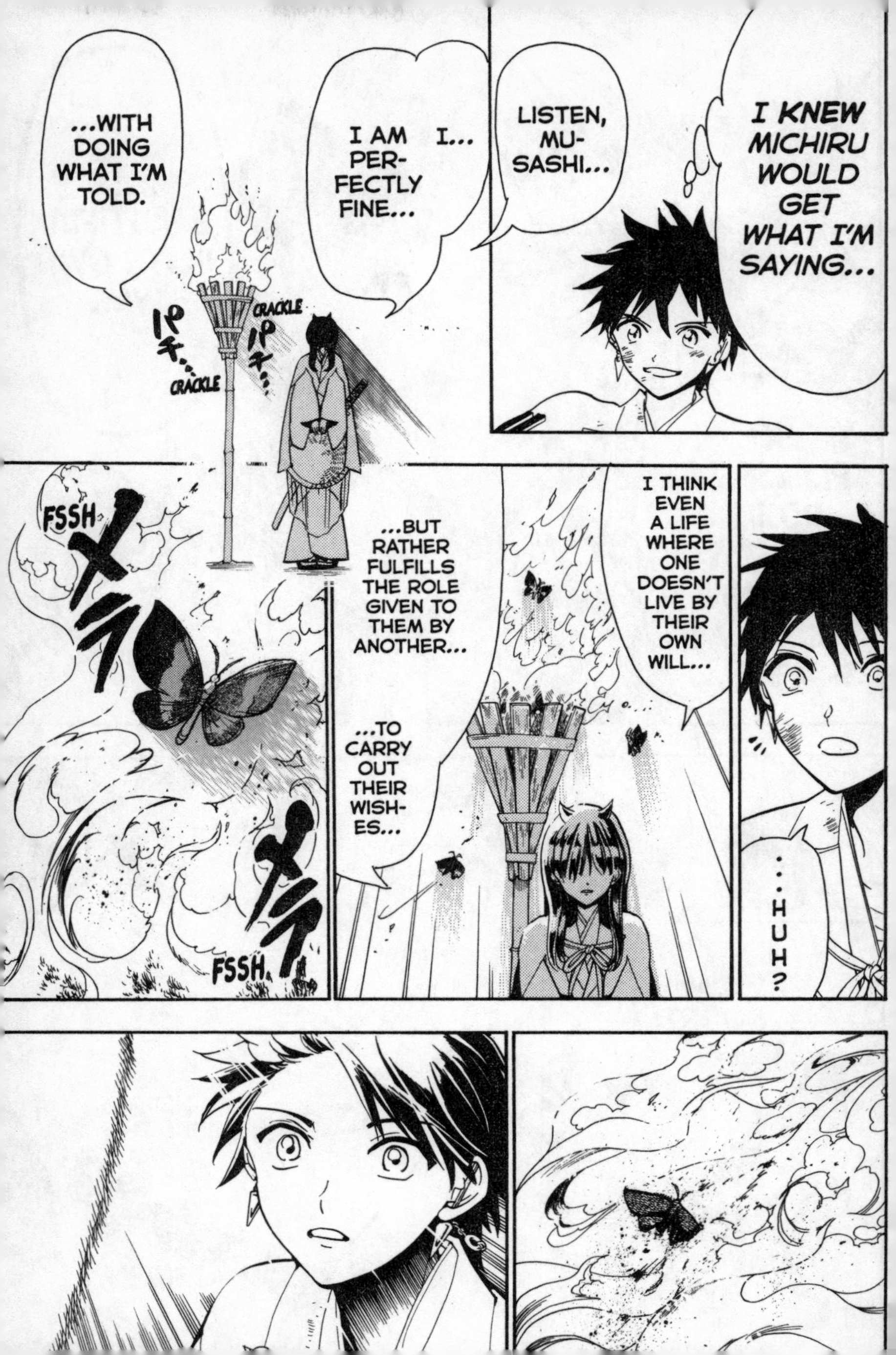
I KNEW MICHIRU WOULD GET WHAT I'M SAYING...
LISTEN, MU-SASHI...
I...
I AM PER-FECTLY FINE...
...WITH DOING WHAT I'M TOLD.
パチ... CRACKLE
パチ... CRACKLE
...HUH?
I THINK EVEN A LIFE WHERE ONE DOESN'T LIVE BY THEIR OWN WILL...
...BUT RATHER FULFILLS THE ROLE GIVEN TO THEM BY ANOTHER...
...TO CARRY OUT THEIR WISH-ES...
メラ FSSH
メラ FSSH

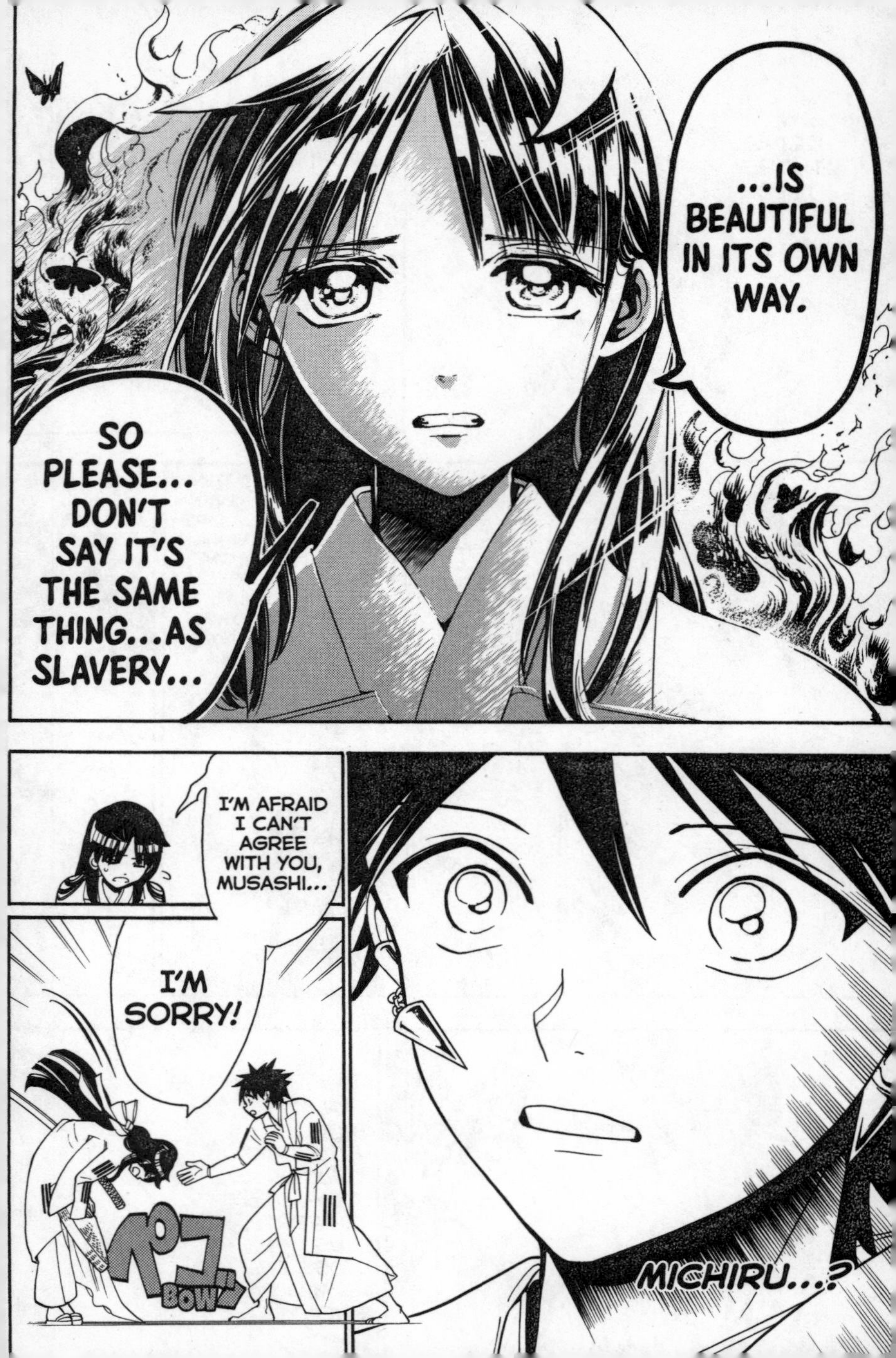
...IS BEAUTIFUL IN ITS OWN WAY.
SO PLEASE... DON'T SAY IT'S THE SAME THING...AS SLAVERY...
MICHIRU...?
I'M AFRAID I CAN'T AGREE WITH YOU, MUSASHI...
I'M SORRY!
BOW

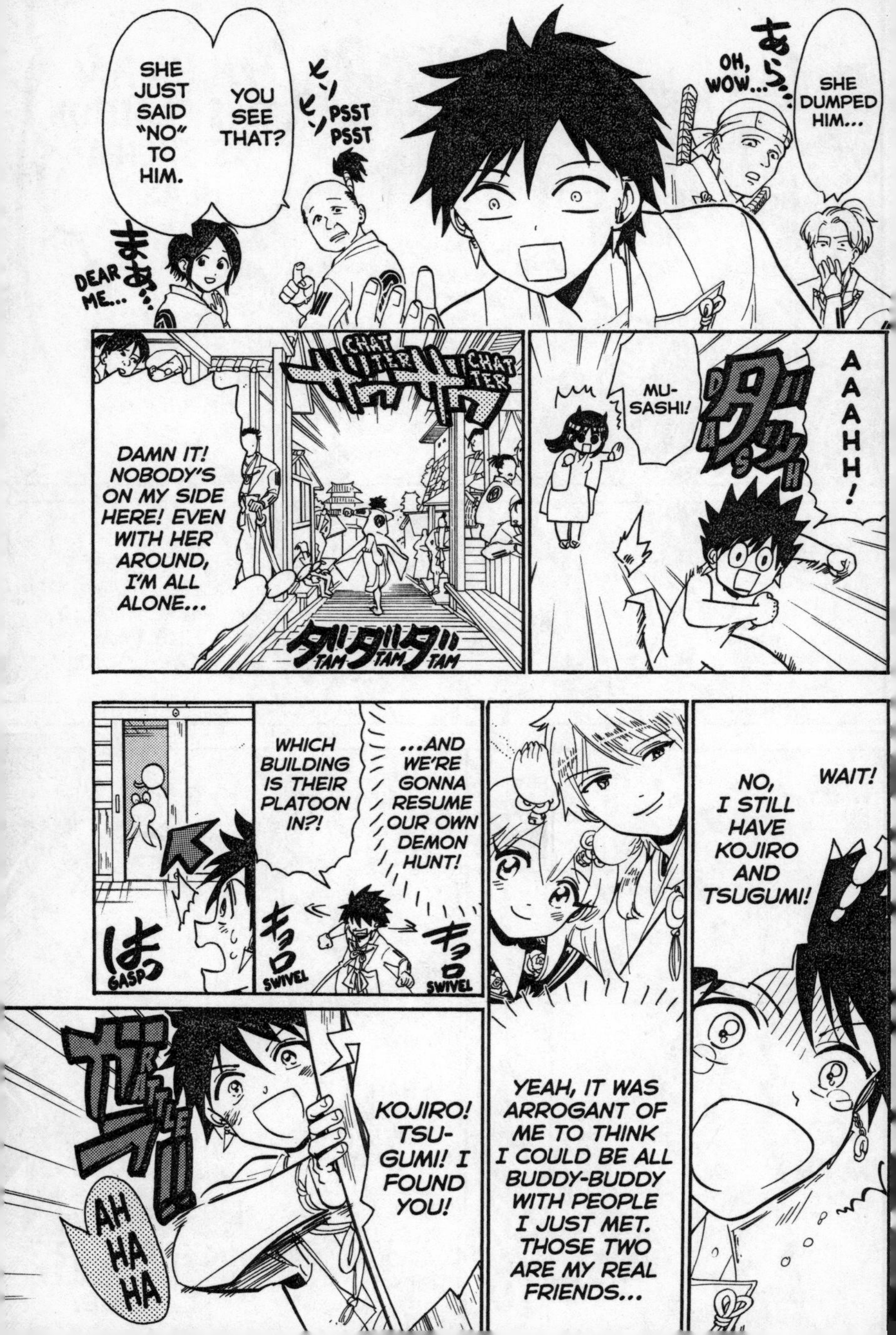
あら
OH, WOW...
SHE DUMPED HIM...
ヒソヒソ
PSST PSST
YOU SEE THAT?
SHE JUST SAID "NO" TO HIM.
まあ
DEAR ME...
AAAAHH!
MU-SASHI!
CHATTER CHATTER
DAMN IT! NOBODY'S ON MY SIDE HERE! EVEN WITH HER AROUND, I'M ALL ALONE...
TAM TAM TAM
WAIT!
NO, I STILL HAVE KOJIRO AND TSUGUMI!
YEAH, IT WAS ARROGANT OF ME TO THINK I COULD BE ALL BUDDY-BUDDY WITH PEOPLE I JUST MET. THOSE TWO ARE MY REAL FRIENDS...
...AND WE'RE GONNA RESUME OUR OWN DEMON HUNT!
WHICH BUILDING IS THEIR PLATOON IN?!
SWIVEL
SWIVEL
GASP
KOJIRO! TSU-GUMI! I FOUND YOU!
AH HA HA HA

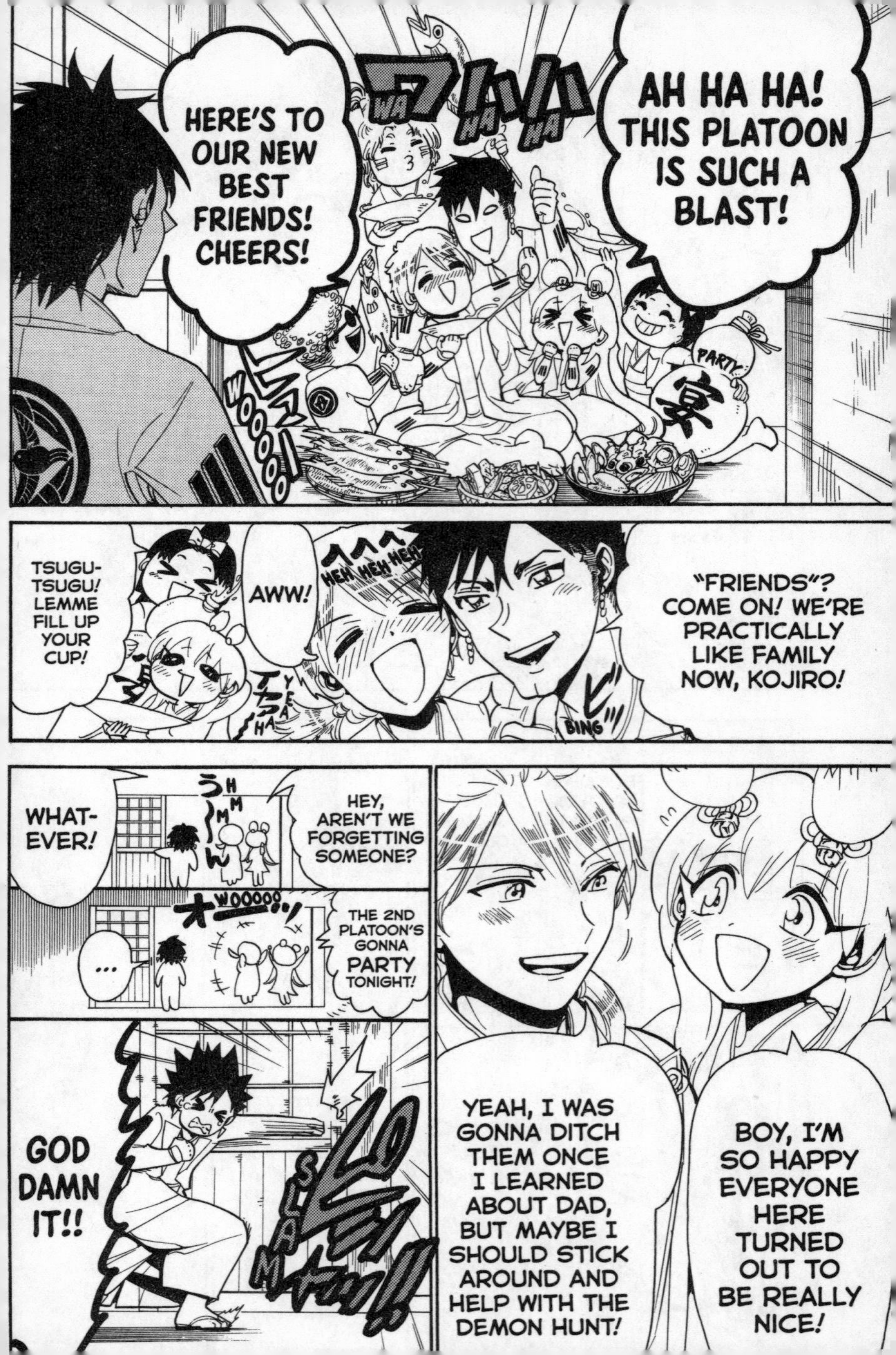
AH HA HA! THIS PLATOON IS SUCH A BLAST!
WA HA HA HA
HERE'S TO OUR NEW BEST FRIENDS! CHEERS!
WOOOOOO
"FRIENDS"? COME ON! WE'RE PRACTICALLY LIKE FAMILY NOW, KOJIRO!
BING
HEH HEH HEH
AWW!
TSUGU-TSUGU! LEMME FILL UP YOUR CUP!
BOY, I'M SO HAPPY EVERYONE HERE TURNED OUT TO BE REALLY NICE!
YEAH, I WAS GONNA DITCH THEM ONCE I LEARNED ABOUT DAD, BUT MAYBE I SHOULD STICK AROUND AND HELP WITH THE DEMON HUNT!
HEY, AREN'T WE FORGETTING SOMEONE?
HMM
WHAT-EVER!
THE 2ND PLATOON'S GONNA PARTY TONIGHT!
WOOOOO!!
...
SLAM
GOD DAMN IT!!

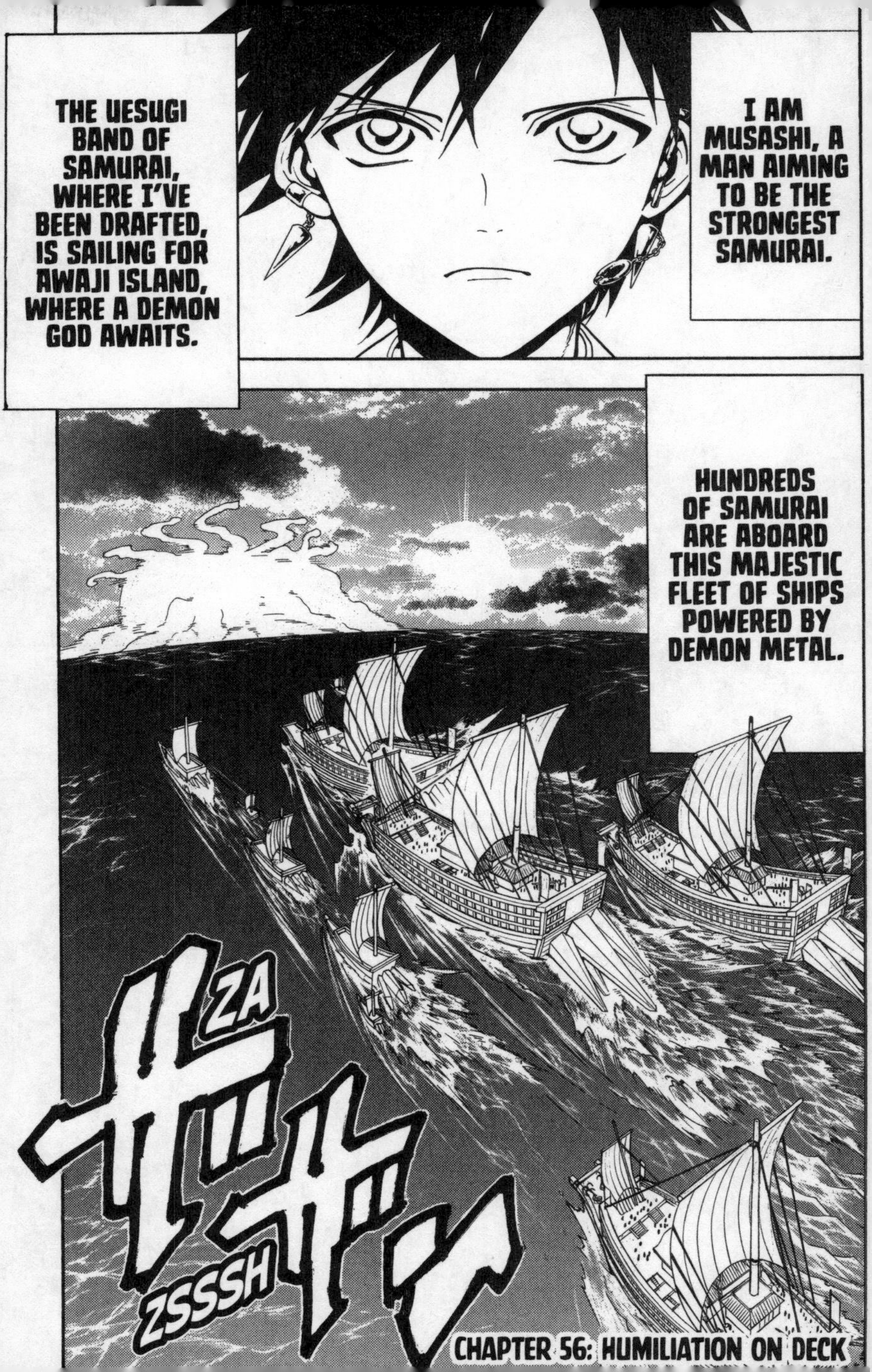
I AM MUSASHI, A MAN AIMING TO BE THE STRONGEST SAMURAI.
THE UESUGI BAND OF SAMURAI, WHERE I'VE BEEN DRAFTED, IS SAILING FOR AWAJI ISLAND, WHERE A DEMON GOD AWAITS.
HUNDREDS OF SAMURAI ARE ABOARD THIS MAJESTIC FLEET OF SHIPS POWERED BY DEMON METAL.
ZA
ZSSSH
CHAPTER 56: HUMILIATION ON DECK

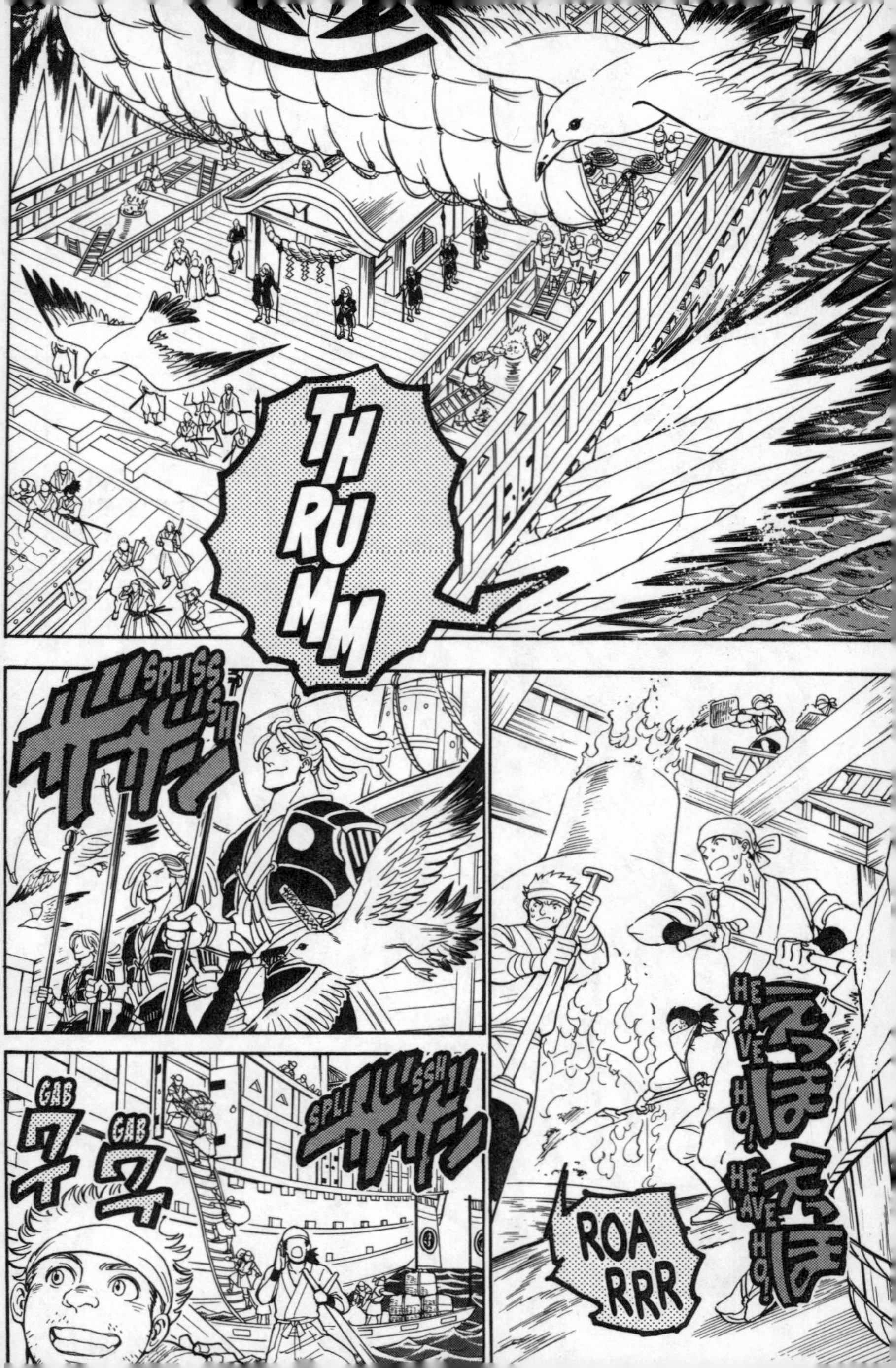

THRUMM
HEAVE HO! HEAVE HO!
ROARRR
SPLISSH
SPLISSSH!!
GAB GAB

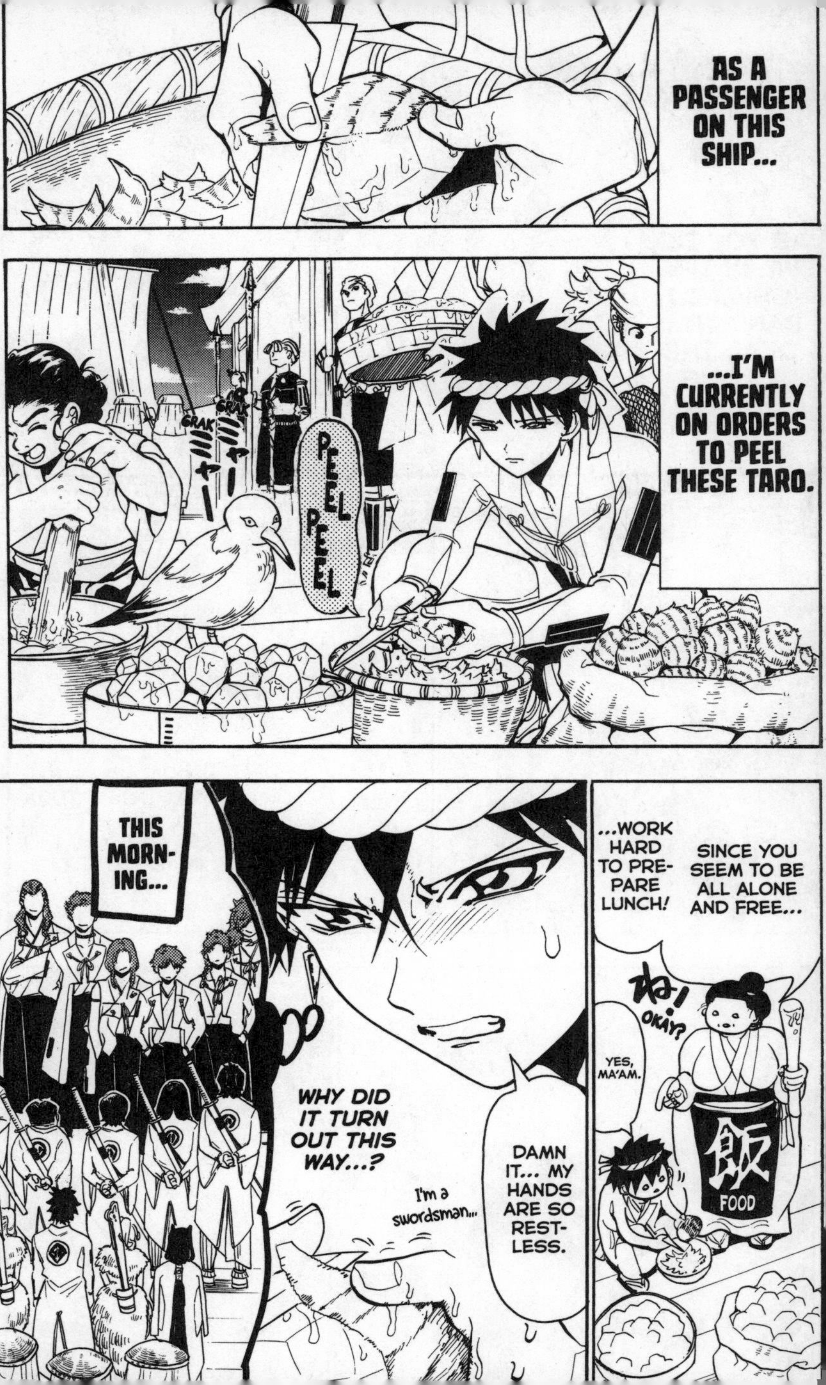
AS A PASSENGER ON THIS SHIP...
...I'M CURRENTLY ON ORDERS TO PEEL THESE TARO.
PEEL PEEL
GRAK
GRAK
SINCE YOU SEEM TO BE ALL ALONE AND FREE...
...WORK HARD TO PREPARE LUNCH!
ね! OKAY?
YES, MA'AM.
飯
FOOD
THIS MORNING...
DAMN IT... MY HANDS ARE SO RESTLESS.
I'm a swordsman...
WHY DID IT TURN OUT THIS WAY...?

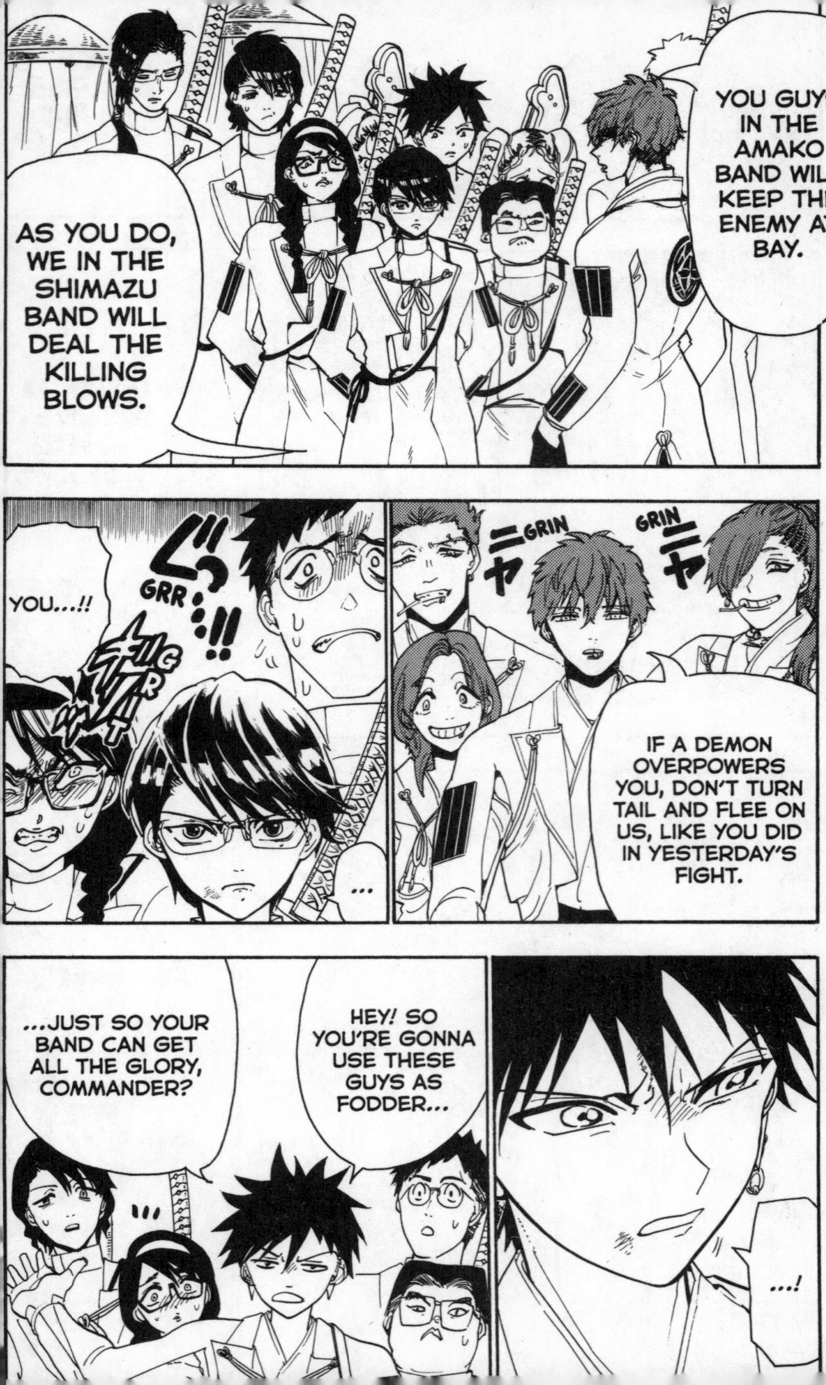
YOU GUYS IN THE AMAKO BAND WILL KEEP THE ENEMY AT BAY.
AS YOU DO, WE IN THE SHIMAZU BAND WILL DEAL THE KILLING BLOWS.
GRIN
GRIN
IF A DEMON OVERPOWERS YOU, DON'T TURN TAIL AND FLEE ON US, LIKE YOU DID IN YESTERDAY'S FIGHT.
GRR
YOU...!!
GRIT
...
...!
HEY! SO YOU'RE GONNA USE THESE GUYS AS FODDER...
...JUST SO YOUR BAND CAN GET ALL THE GLORY, COMMANDER?

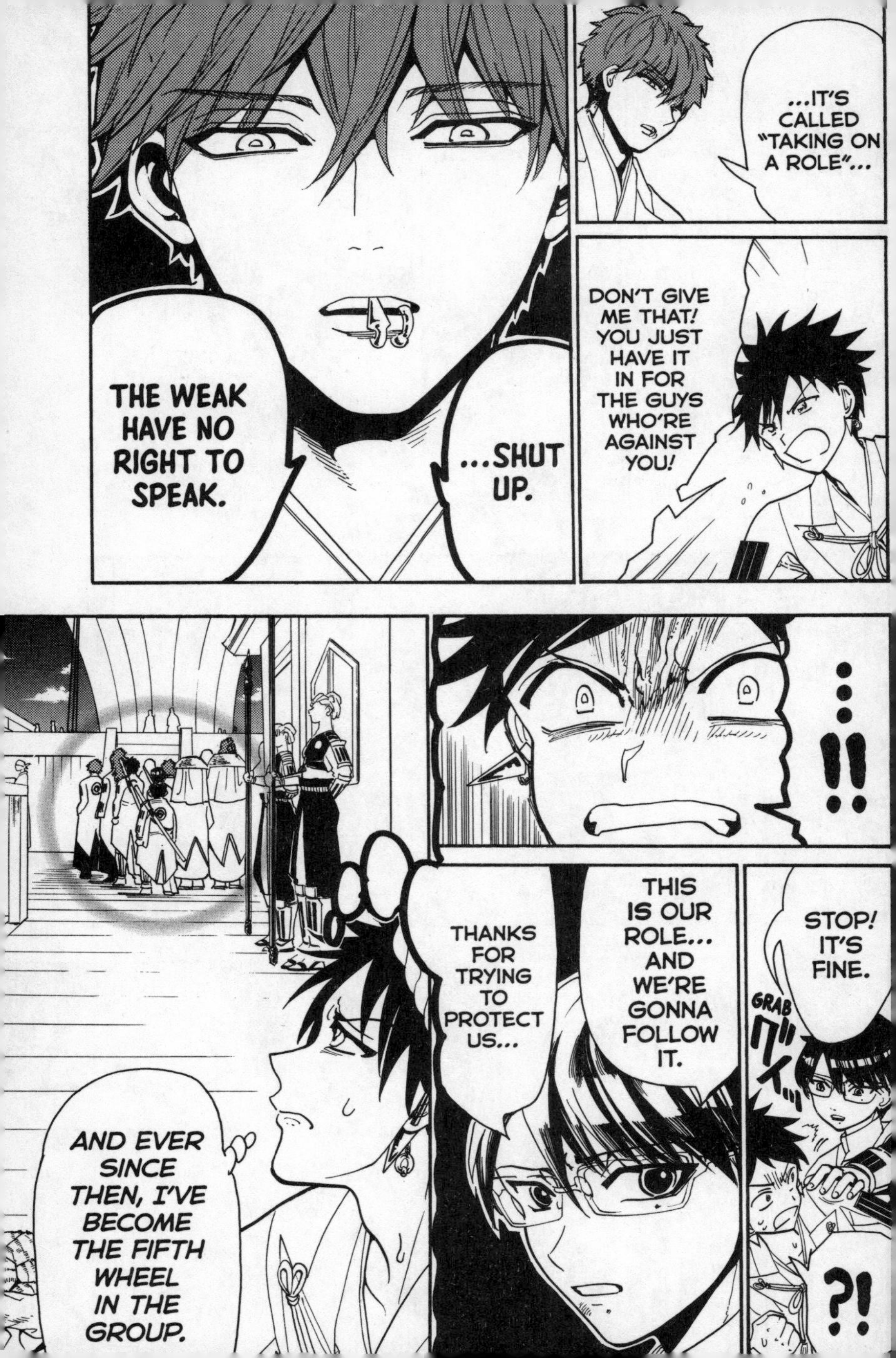
...IT'S CALLED "TAKING ON A ROLE"...
DON'T GIVE ME THAT! YOU JUST HAVE IT IN FOR THE GUYS WHO'RE AGAINST YOU!
...SHUT UP.
THE WEAK HAVE NO RIGHT TO SPEAK.
...!!
STOP! IT'S FINE.
GRAB
?!
THIS IS OUR ROLE... AND WE'RE GONNA FOLLOW IT.
THANKS FOR TRYING TO PROTECT US...
AND EVER SINCE THEN, I'VE BECOME THE FIFTH WHEEL IN THE GROUP.

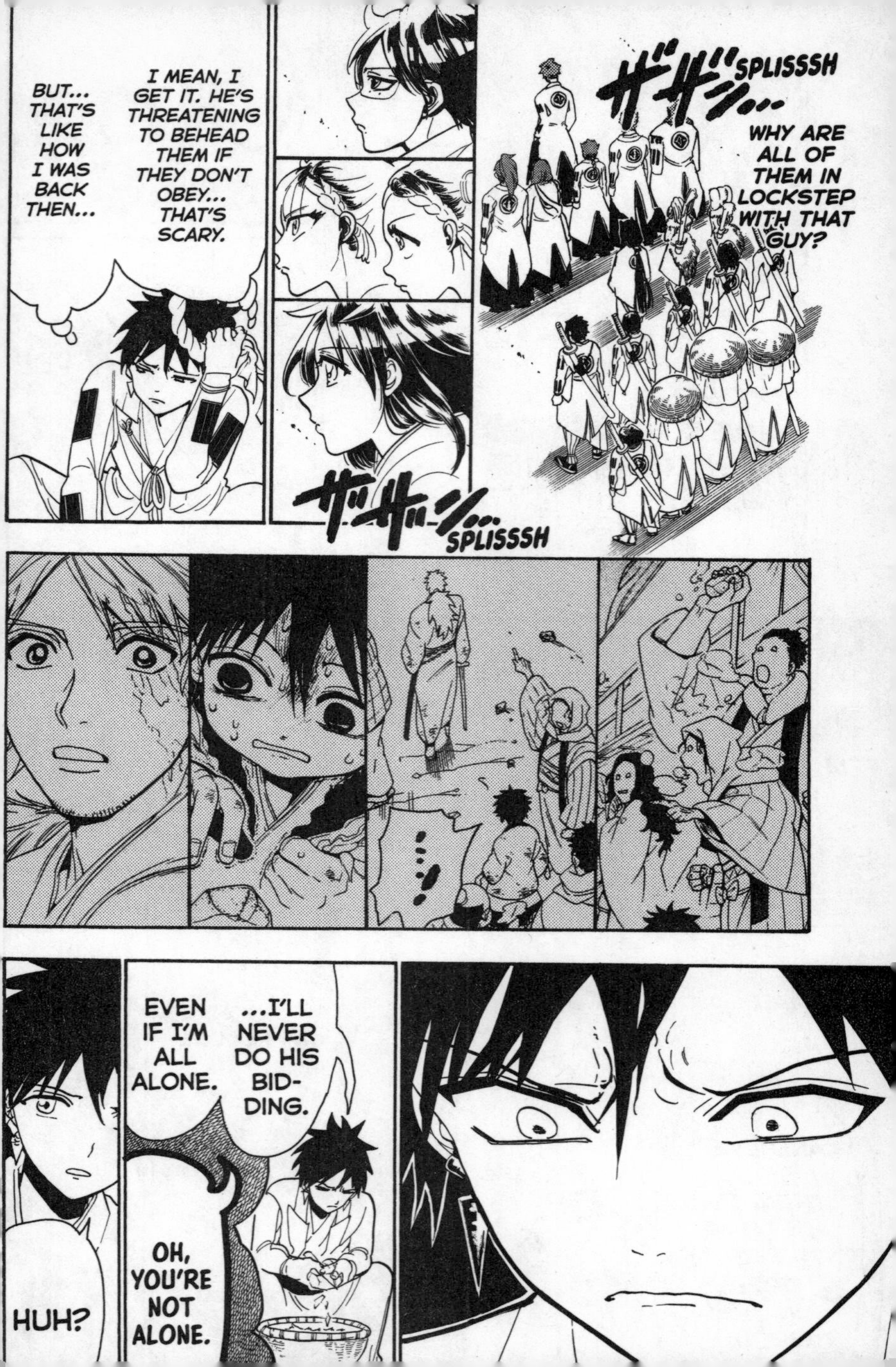
SPLISSSH
WHY ARE ALL OF THEM IN LOCKSTEP WITH THAT GUY?
SPLISSSH
I MEAN, I GET IT. HE'S THREATENING TO BEHEAD THEM IF THEY DON'T OBEY... THAT'S SCARY.
BUT... THAT'S LIKE HOW I WAS BACK THEN...
...!
...I'LL NEVER DO HIS BID-DING.
EVEN IF I'M ALL ALONE.
OH, YOU'RE NOT ALONE.
HUH?

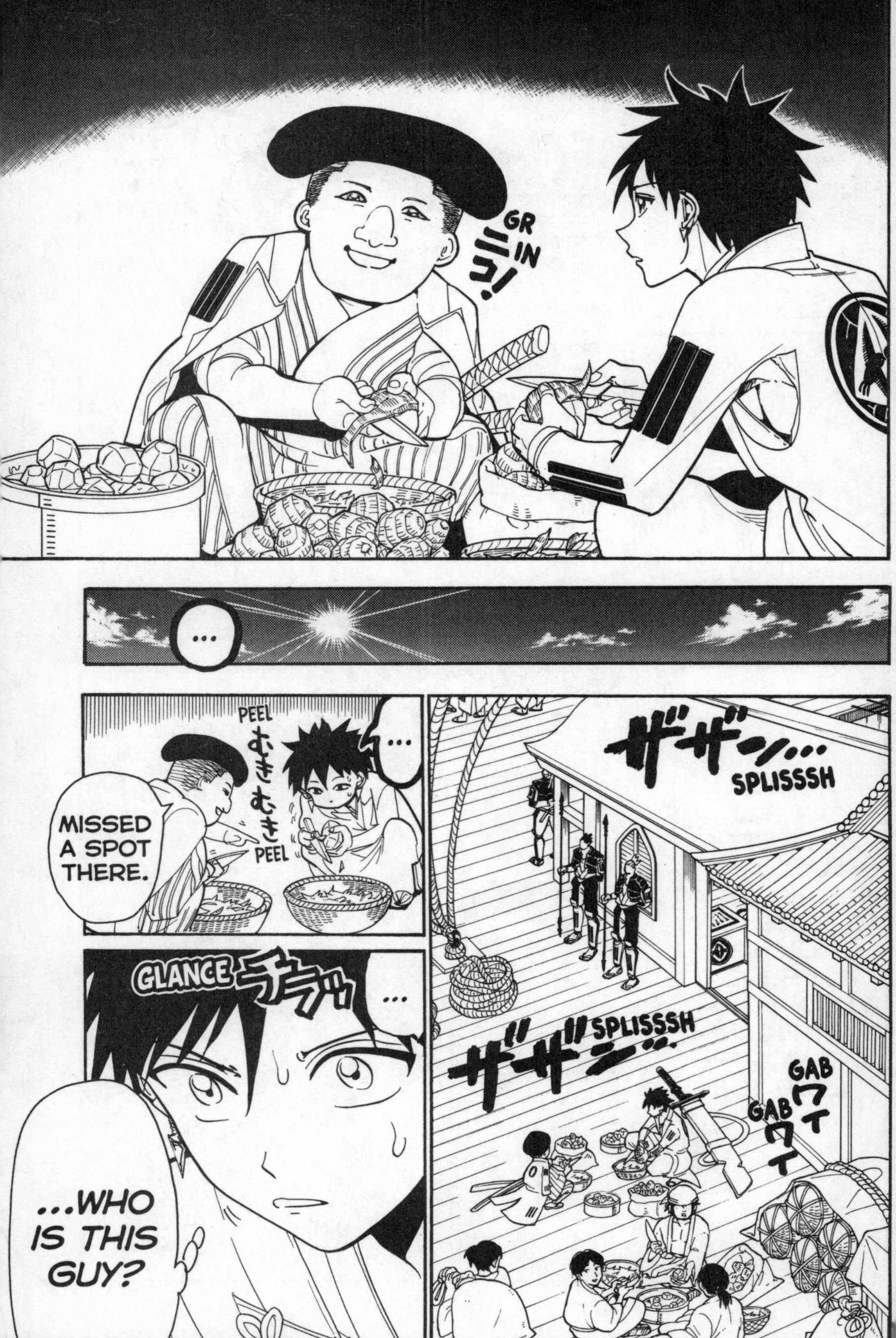
GR IN ニコ!
...
ザザン… SPLISSSH
ザザーン SPLISSSH
GAB ワイ GAB ワイ
...
PEEL むきむき PEEL
MISSED A SPOT THERE.
GLANCE チラッ
...
...WHO IS THIS GUY?

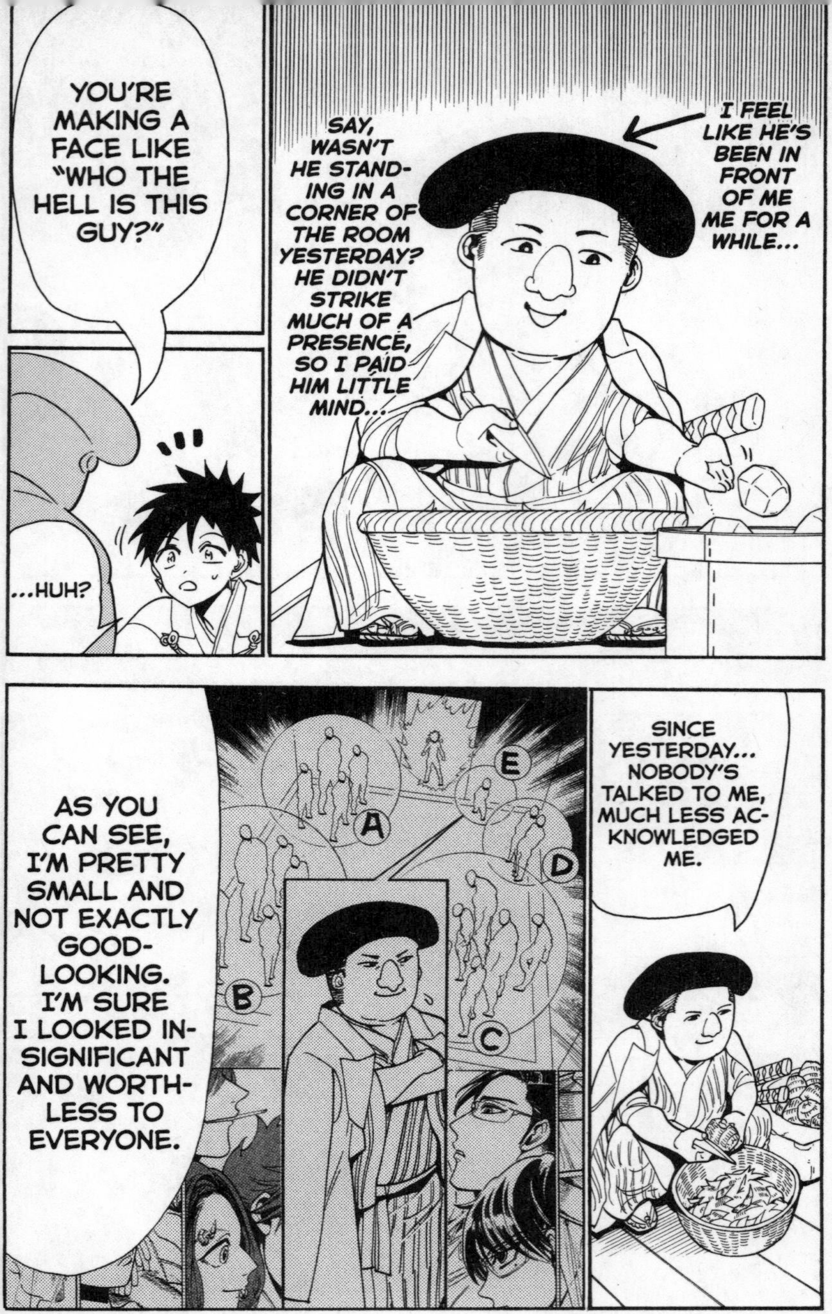
I FEEL LIKE HE'S BEEN IN FRONT OF ME ME FOR A WHILE...
SAY, WASN'T HE STANDING IN A CORNER OF THE ROOM YESTERDAY? HE DIDN'T STRIKE MUCH OF A PRESENCE, SO I PAID HIM LITTLE MIND...
YOU'RE MAKING A FACE LIKE "WHO THE HELL IS THIS GUY?"
...HUH?
SINCE YESTERDAY... NOBODY'S TALKED TO ME, MUCH LESS ACKNOWLEDGED ME.
AS YOU CAN SEE, I'M PRETTY SMALL AND NOT EXACTLY GOOD-LOOKING. I'M SURE I LOOKED INSIGNIFICANT AND WORTHLESS TO EVERYONE.
E
A
D
B
C

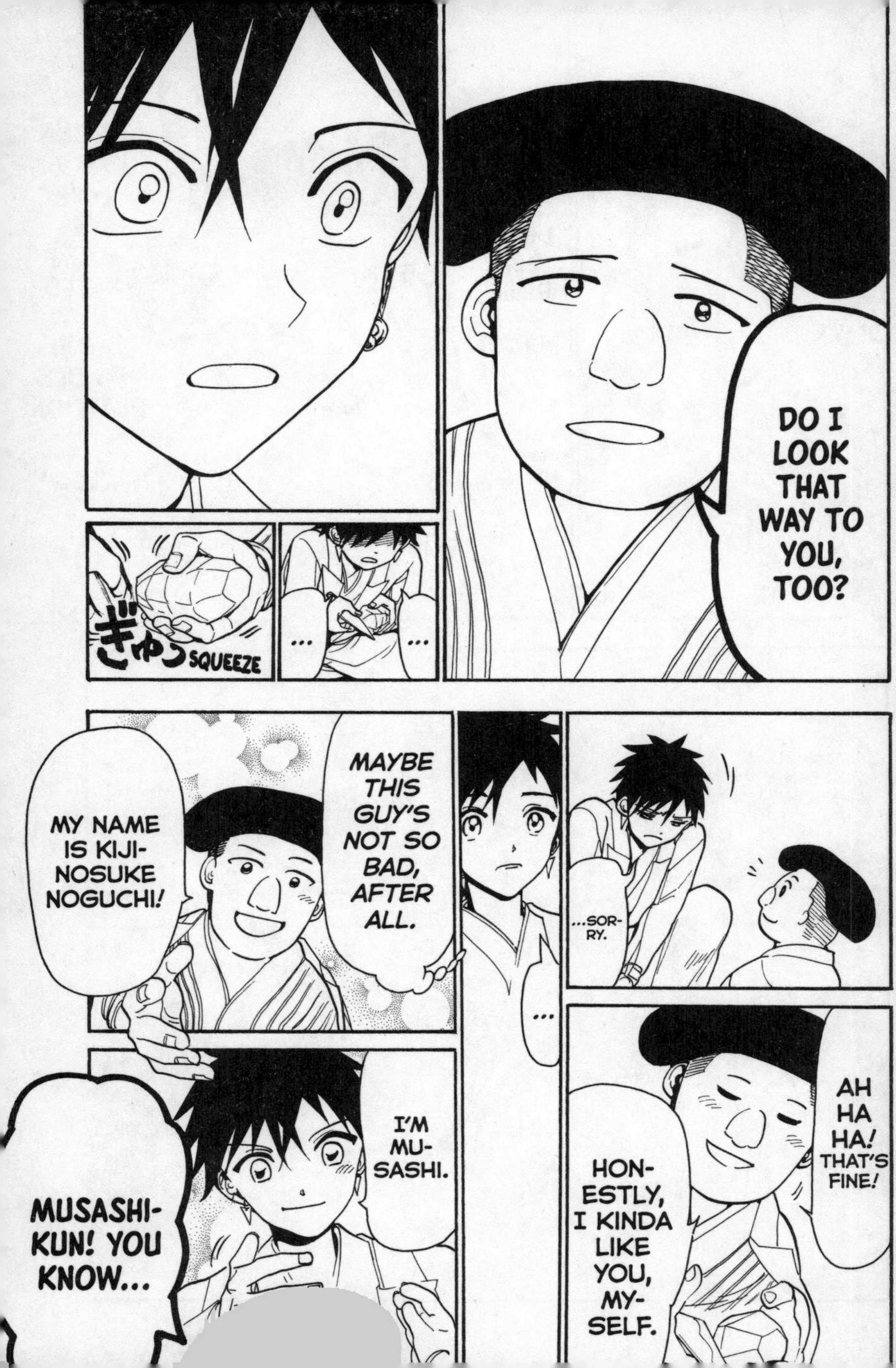
DO I LOOK THAT WAY TO YOU, TOO?
...
...
ぎゅっ SQUEEZE
...SOR-RY.
...
AH HA HA! THAT'S FINE!
HON-ESTLY, I KINDA LIKE YOU, MY-SELF.
MAYBE THIS GUY'S NOT SO BAD, AFTER ALL.
MY NAME IS KIJI-NOSUKE NOGUCHI!
I'M MU-SASHI.
MUSASHI-KUN! YOU KNOW...

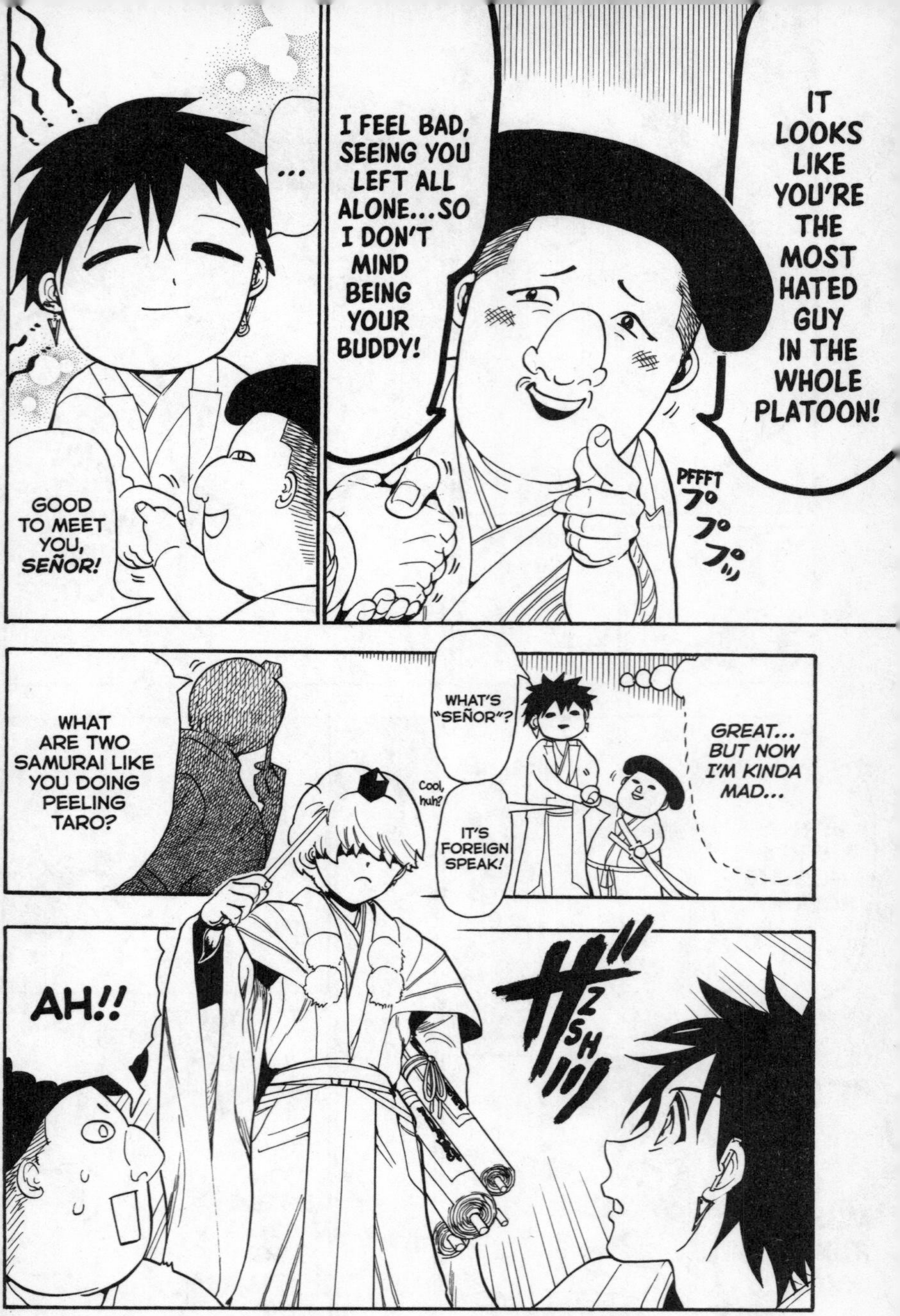
IT LOOKS LIKE YOU'RE THE MOST HATED GUY IN THE WHOLE PLATOON!
I FEEL BAD, SEEING YOU LEFT ALL ALONE...SO I DON'T MIND BEING YOUR BUDDY!
PFFFT
プ プ プッ
...
GOOD TO MEET YOU, SEÑOR!
GREAT... BUT NOW I'M KINDA MAD...
WHAT'S "SEÑOR"?
Cool, huh?
IT'S FOREIGN SPEAK!
WHAT ARE TWO SAMURAI LIKE YOU DOING PEELING TARO?
ZSH
AH!!

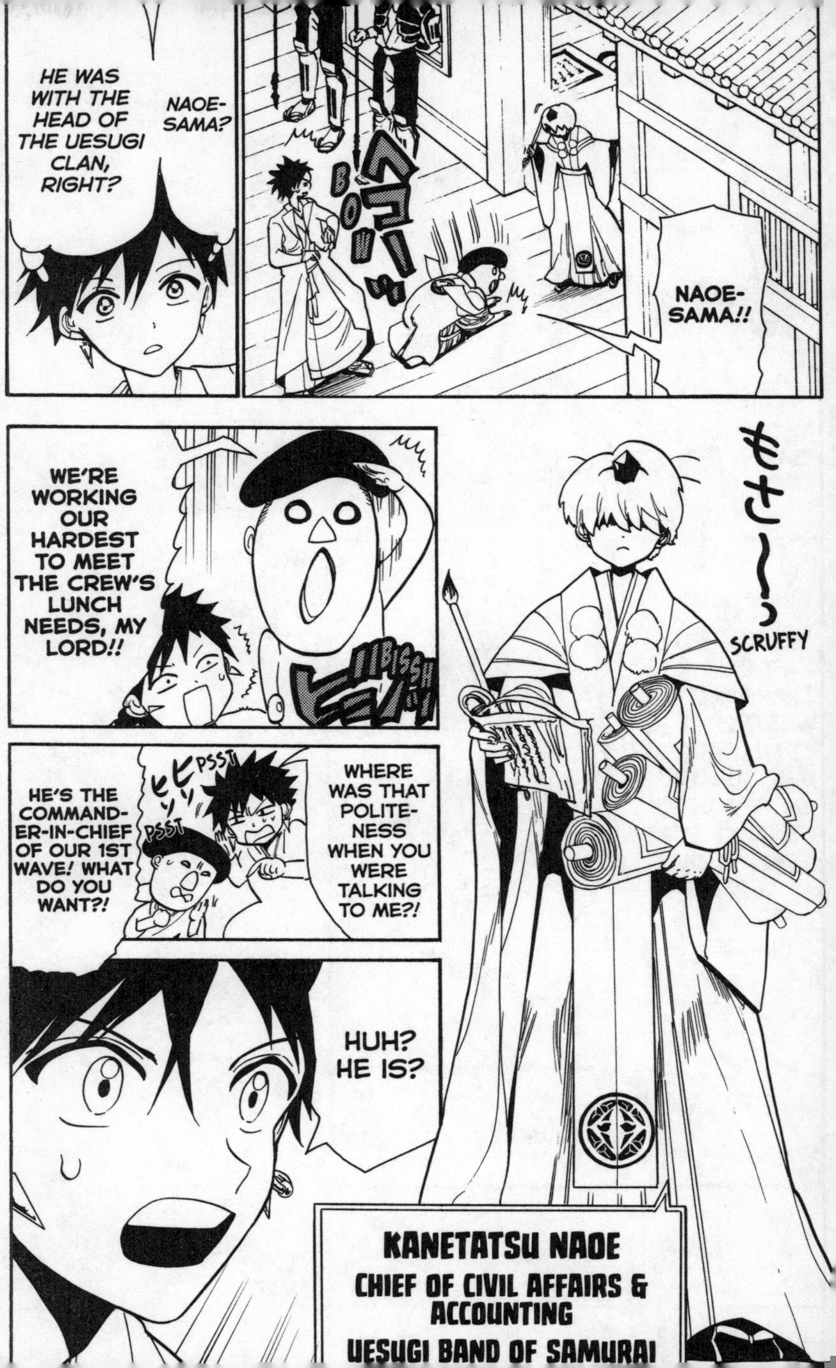
NAOE-SAMA!!
BOW
NAOE-SAMA?
HE WAS WITH THE HEAD OF THE UESUGI CLAN, RIGHT?
もさ～っ
SCRUFFY
KANETATSU NAOE
CHIEF OF CIVIL AFFAIRS & ACCOUNTING
UESUGI BAND OF SAMURAI
WE'RE WORKING OUR HARDEST TO MEET THE CREW'S LUNCH NEEDS, MY LORD!!
BISSH
WHERE WAS THAT POLITENESS WHEN YOU WERE TALKING TO ME?!
PSST
PSST
HE'S THE COMMANDER-IN-CHIEF OF OUR 1ST WAVE! WHAT DO YOU WANT?!
HUH? HE IS?

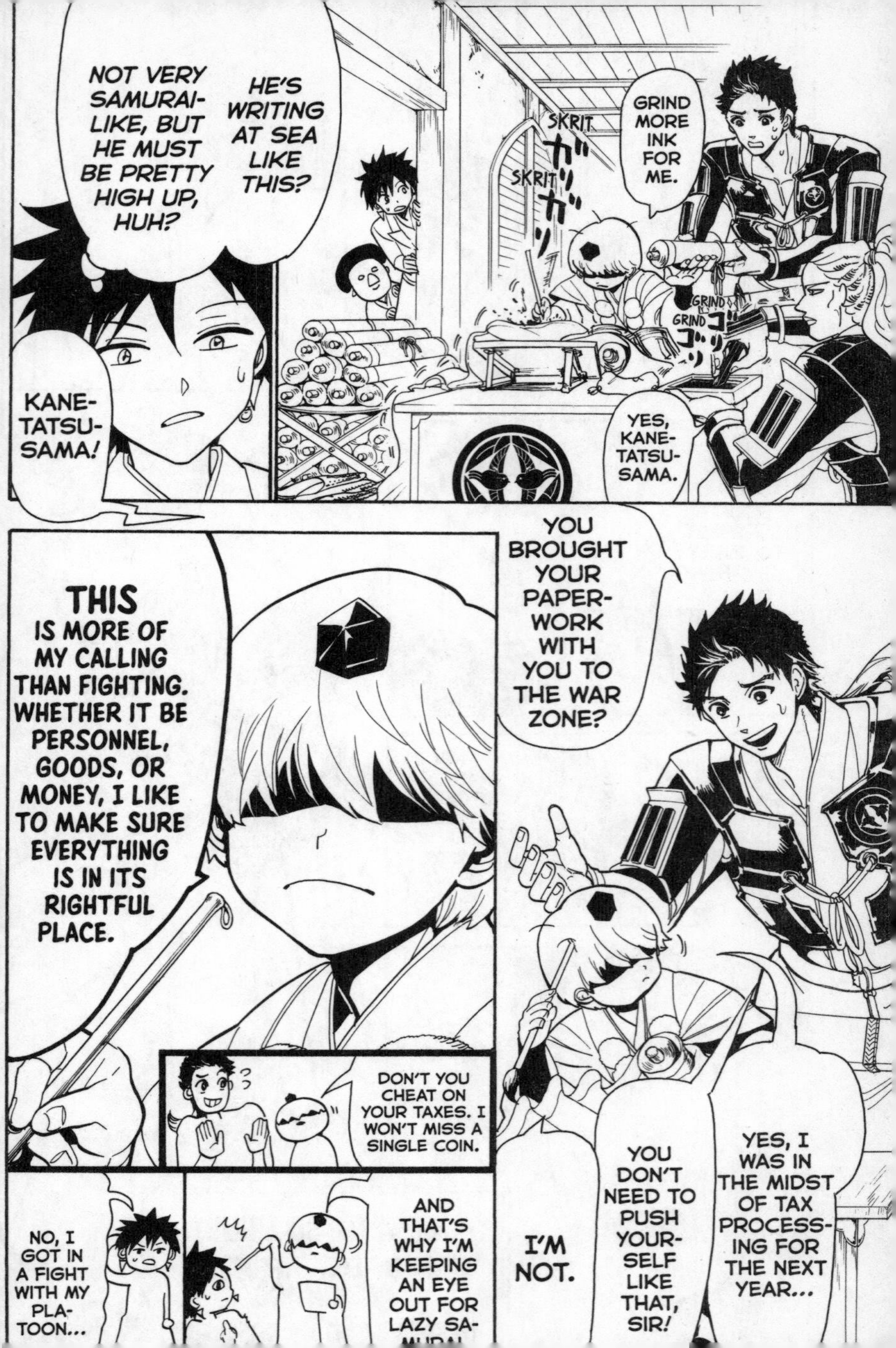
GRIND MORE INK FOR ME.
SKRIT
SKRIT
GRIND
GRIND
YES, KANE-TATSU-SAMA.
HE'S WRITING AT SEA LIKE THIS?
NOT VERY SAMURAI-LIKE, BUT HE MUST BE PRETTY HIGH UP, HUH?
KANE-TATSU-SAMA!
YOU BROUGHT YOUR PAPER-WORK WITH YOU TO THE WAR ZONE?
YES, I WAS IN THE MIDST OF TAX PROCESS-ING FOR THE NEXT YEAR...
YOU DON'T NEED TO PUSH YOUR-SELF LIKE THAT, SIR!
I'M NOT.
THIS IS MORE OF MY CALLING THAN FIGHTING. WHETHER IT BE PERSONNEL, GOODS, OR MONEY, I LIKE TO MAKE SURE EVERYTHING IS IN ITS RIGHTFUL PLACE.
DON'T YOU CHEAT ON YOUR TAXES. I WON'T MISS A SINGLE COIN.
AND THAT'S WHY I'M KEEPING AN EYE OUT FOR LAZY SA-
NO, I GOT IN A FIGHT WITH MY PLA-TOON...

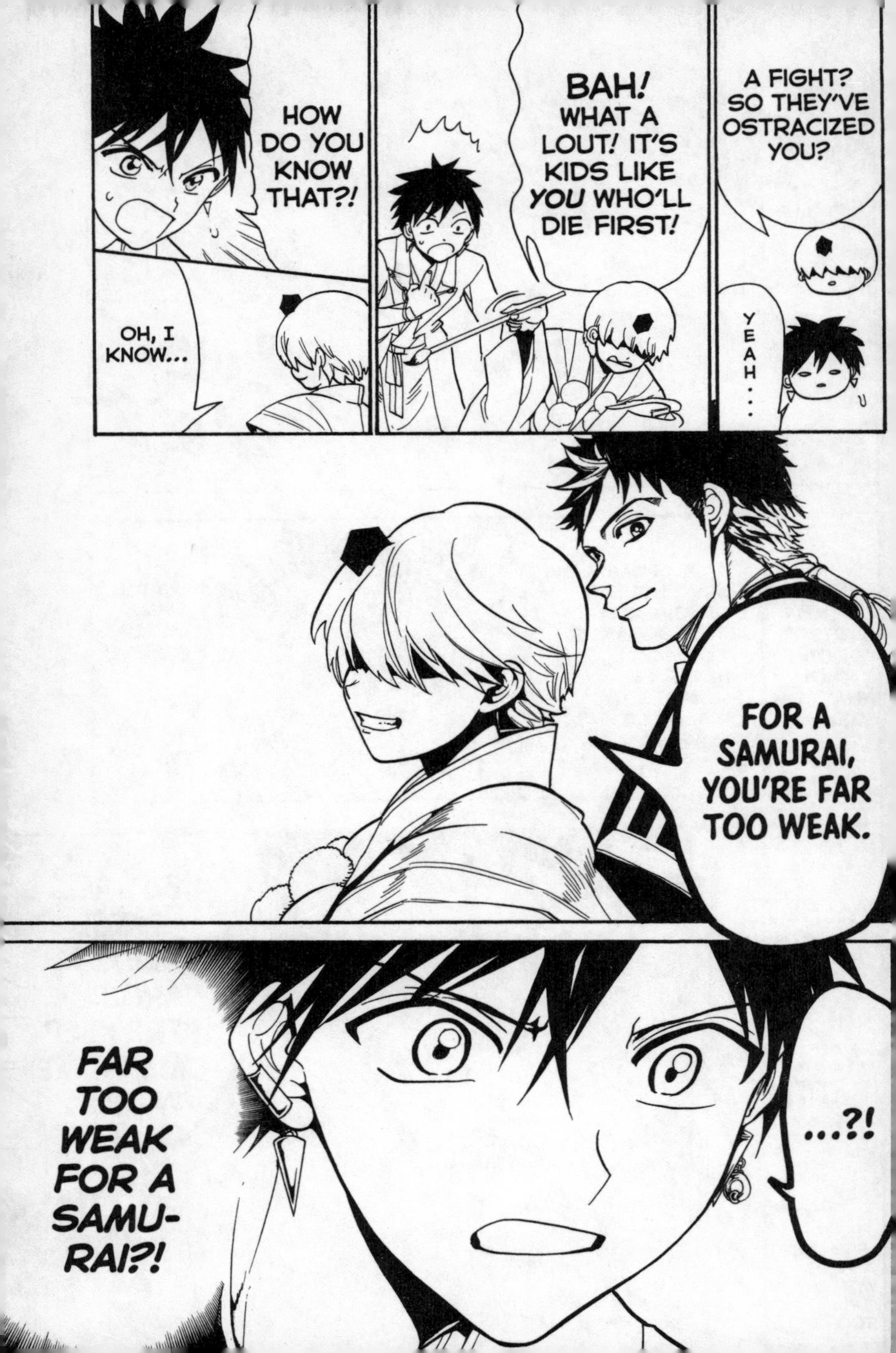
A FIGHT? SO THEY'VE OSTRACIZED YOU?
YEAH...
BAH! WHAT A LOUT! IT'S KIDS LIKE *YOU* WHO'LL DIE FIRST!
HOW DO YOU KNOW THAT?!
OH, I KNOW...
FOR A SAMURAI, YOU'RE FAR TOO WEAK.
...?!
FAR TOO WEAK FOR A SAMU-RAI?!

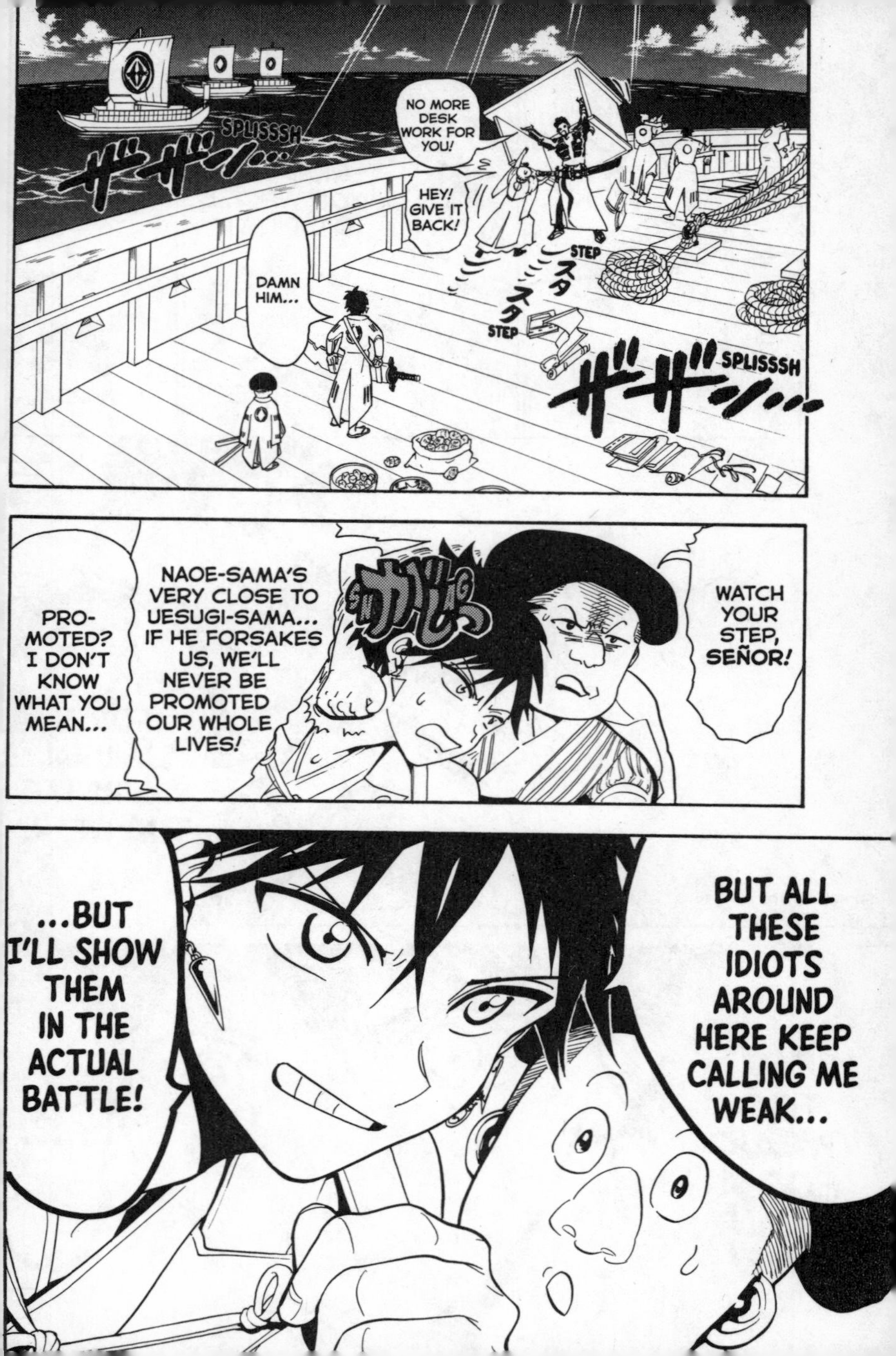
NO MORE DESK WORK FOR YOU!
HEY! GIVE IT BACK!
STEP
STEP
SPLISSSH
SPLISSSH
DAMN HIM...
WATCH YOUR STEP, SEÑOR!
NAOE-SAMA'S VERY CLOSE TO UESUGI-SAMA... IF HE FORSAKES US, WE'LL NEVER BE PROMOTED OUR WHOLE LIVES!
PRO-MOTED? I DON'T KNOW WHAT YOU MEAN...
BUT ALL THESE IDIOTS AROUND HERE KEEP CALLING ME WEAK...
...BUT I'LL SHOW THEM IN THE ACTUAL BATTLE!

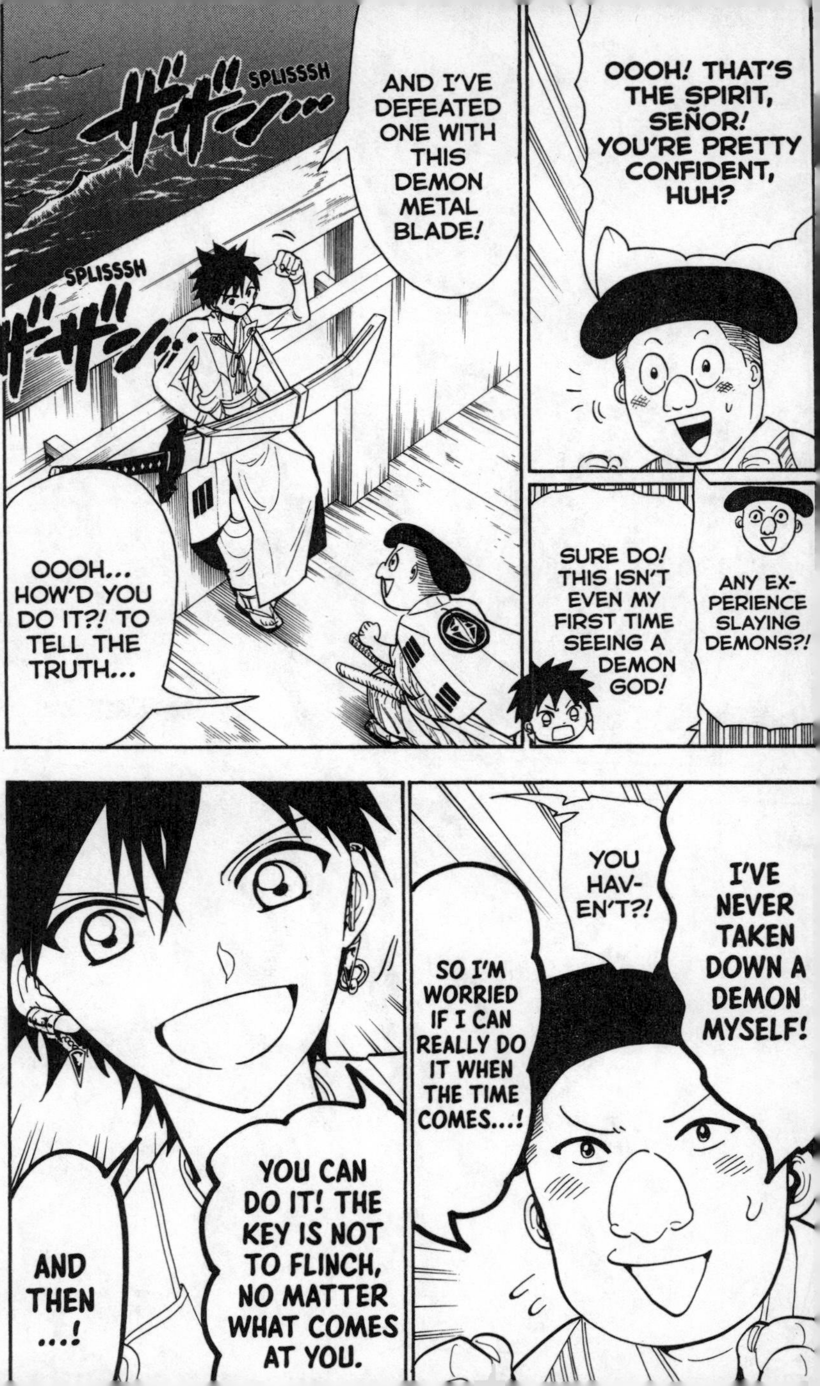
OOOH! THAT'S THE SPIRIT, SEÑOR! YOU'RE PRETTY CONFIDENT, HUH?
ANY EX-PERIENCE SLAYING DEMONS?!
SURE DO! THIS ISN'T EVEN MY FIRST TIME SEEING A DEMON GOD!
SPLISSSH
SPLISSSH
AND I'VE DEFEATED ONE WITH THIS DEMON METAL BLADE!
OOOH... HOW'D YOU DO IT?! TO TELL THE TRUTH...
I'VE NEVER TAKEN DOWN A DEMON MYSELF!
YOU HAV-EN'T?!
SO I'M WORRIED IF I CAN REALLY DO IT WHEN THE TIME COMES...!
YOU CAN DO IT! THE KEY IS NOT TO FLINCH, NO MATTER WHAT COMES AT YOU.
AND THEN ...!

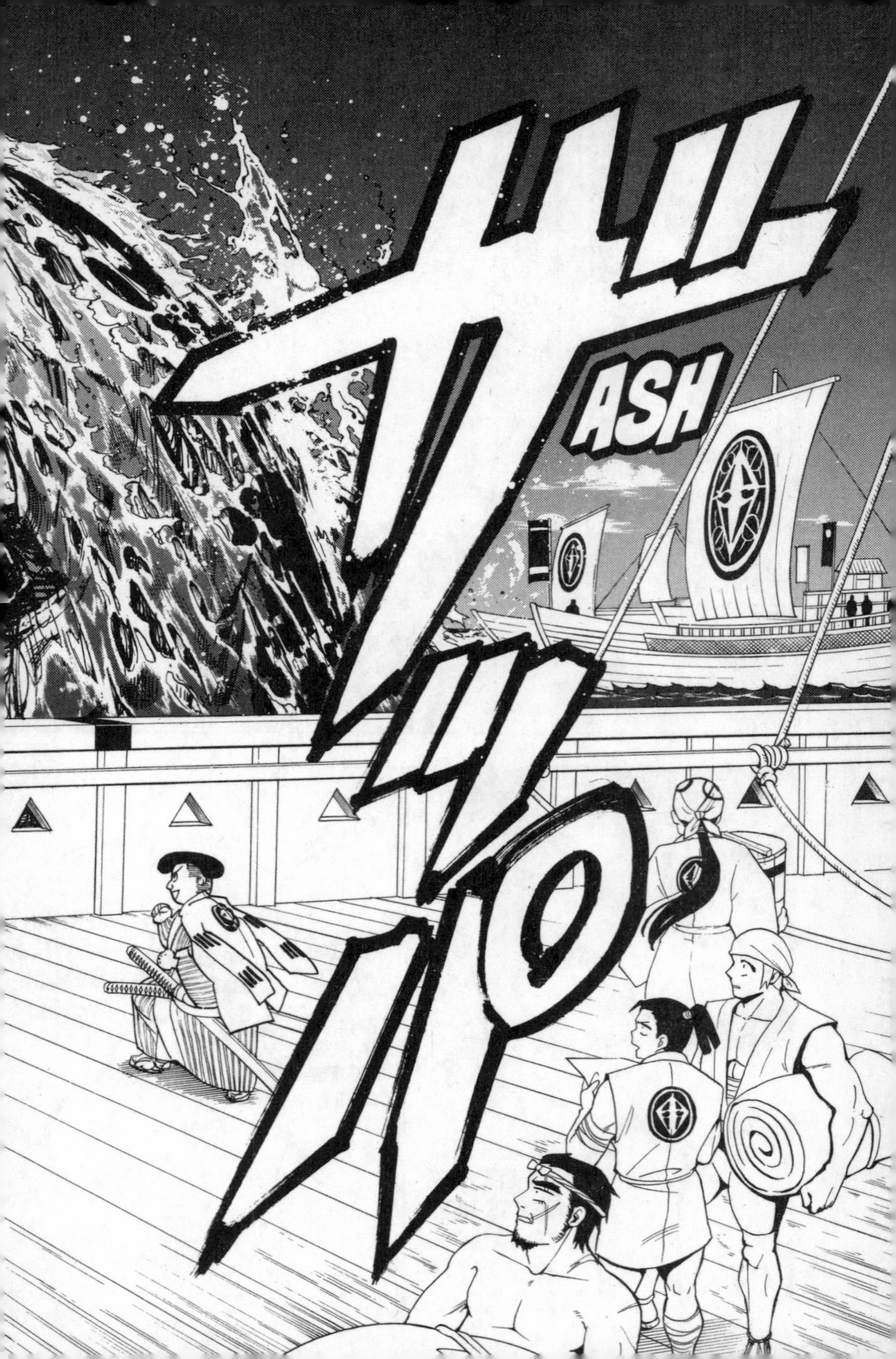
ASH

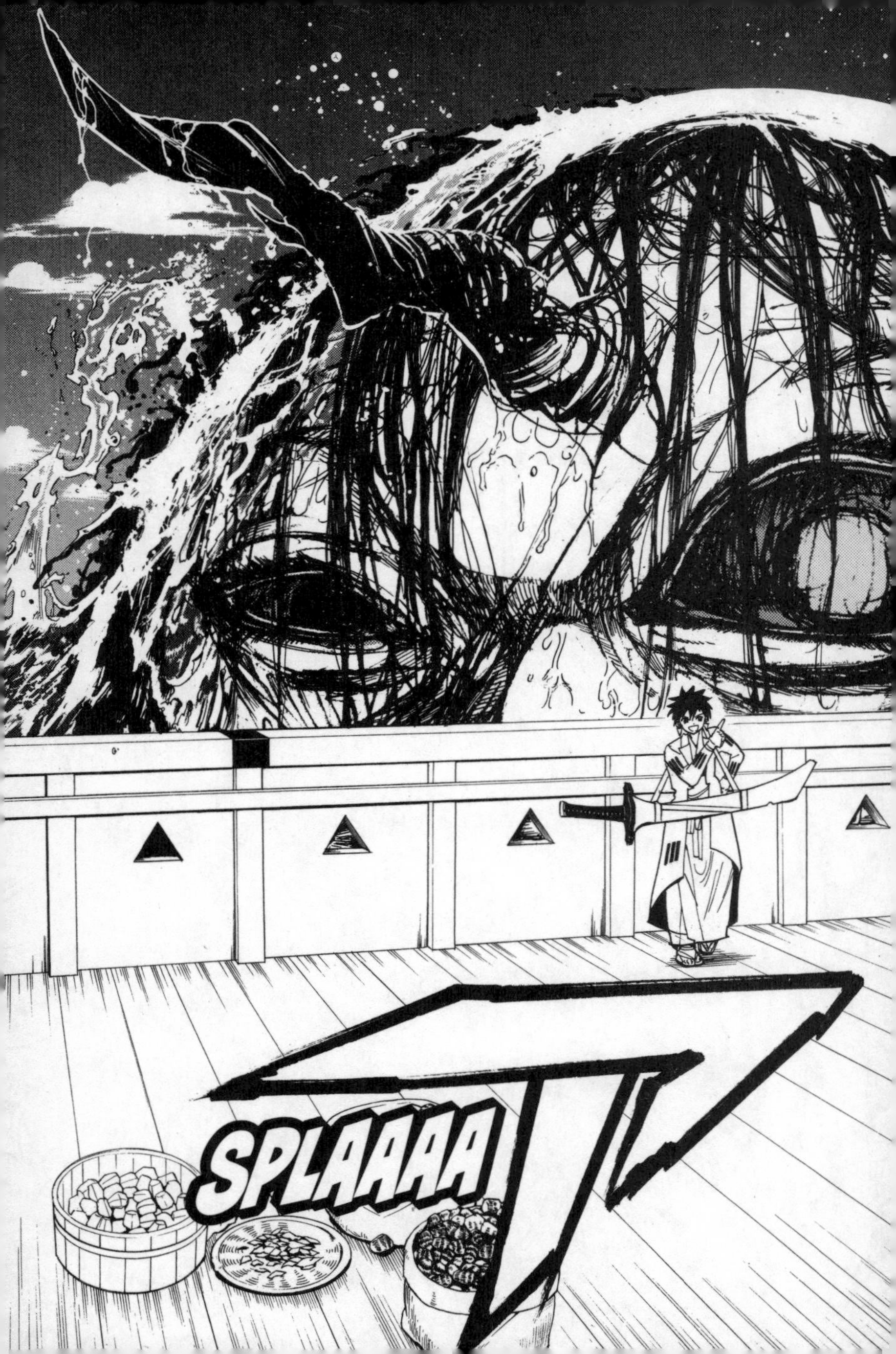
SPLAAAAT

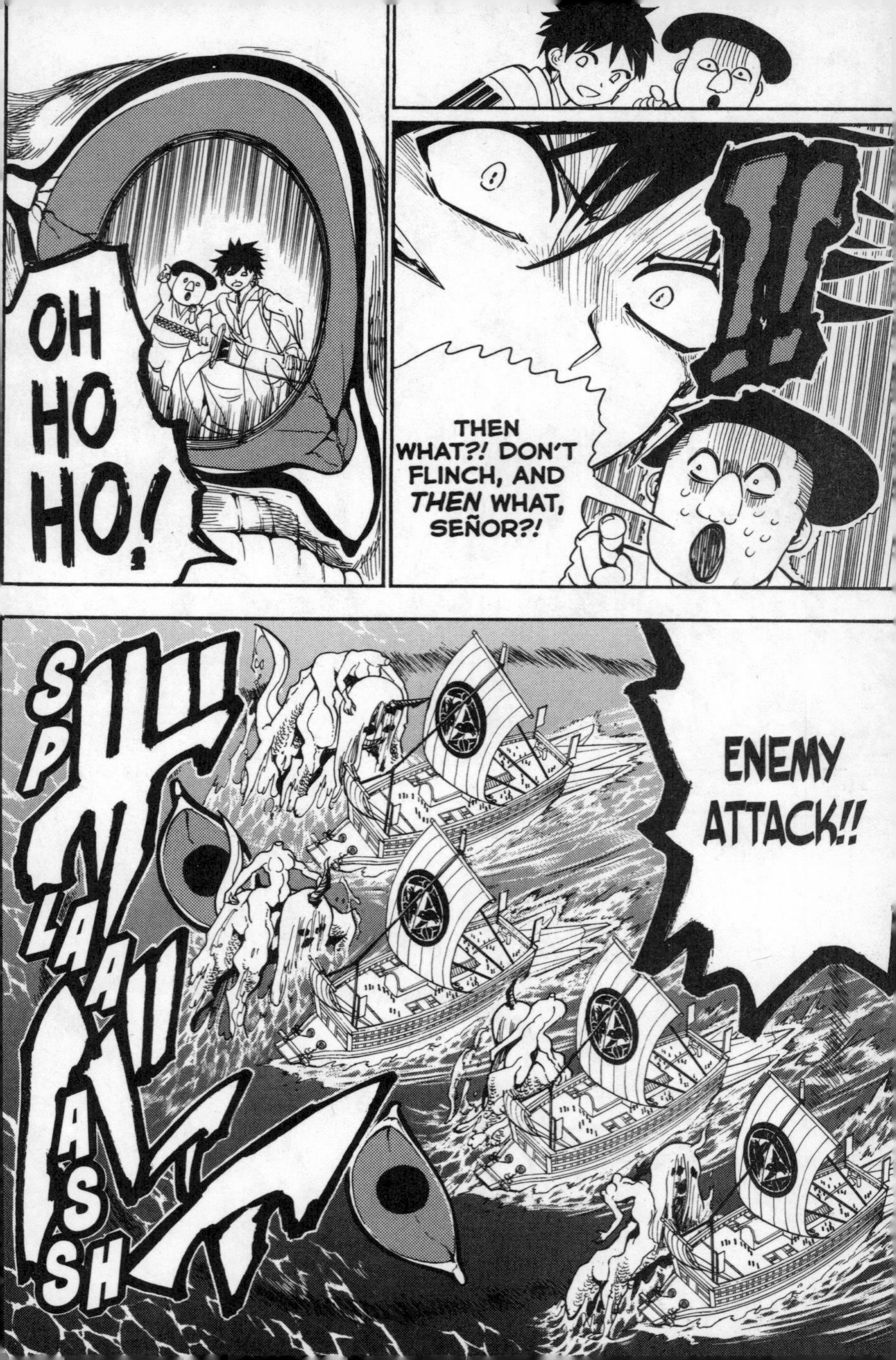
THEN WHAT?! DON'T FLINCH, AND THEN WHAT, SEÑOR?!
OH HO HO!
ENEMY ATTACK!!
SPLAAASH

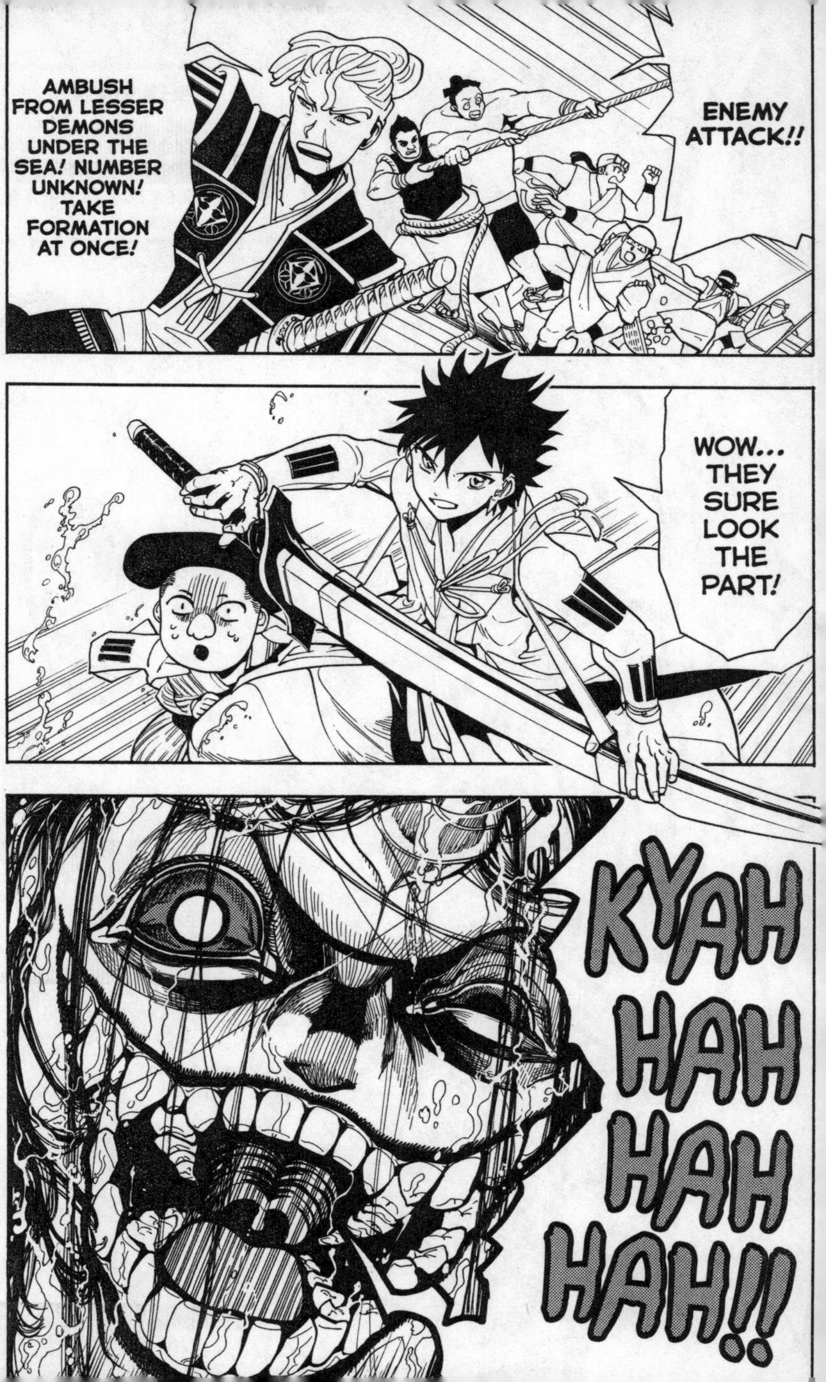
ENEMY ATTACK!!
AMBUSH FROM LESSER DEMONS UNDER THE SEA! NUMBER UNKNOWN! TAKE FORMATION AT ONCE!
WOW... THEY SURE LOOK THE PART!
KYAH HAH HAH HAH!!

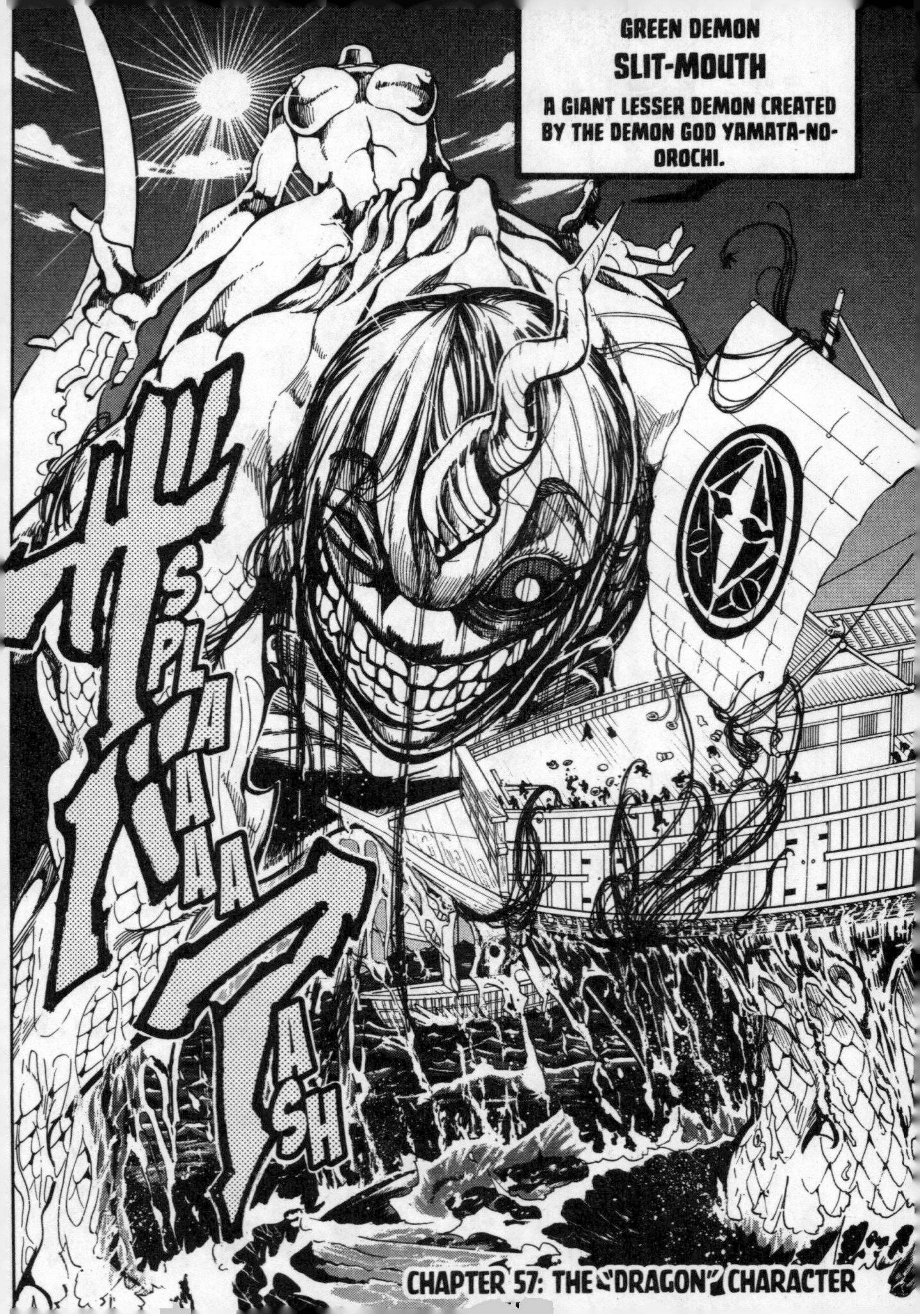
GREEN DEMON
SLIT-MOUTH
A GIANT LESSER DEMON CREATED BY THE DEMON GOD YAMATA-NO-OROCHI.
SPLAAAAASH
CHAPTER 57: THE "DRAGON" CHARACTER

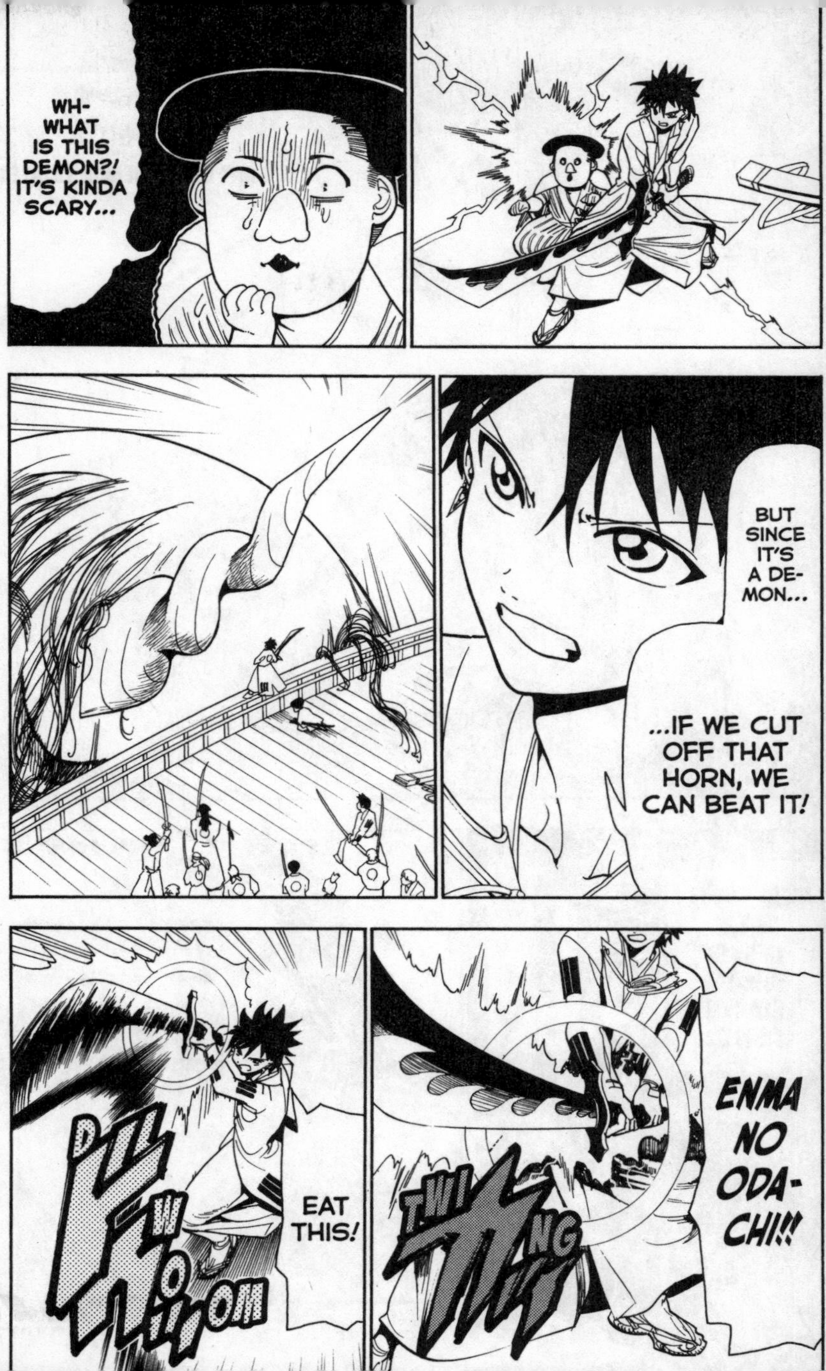
WH- WHAT IS THIS DEMON?! IT'S KINDA SCARY...
BUT SINCE IT'S A DE-MON...
...IF WE CUT OFF THAT HORN, WE CAN BEAT IT!
ENMA NO ODA-CHI!!
TWING
EAT THIS!

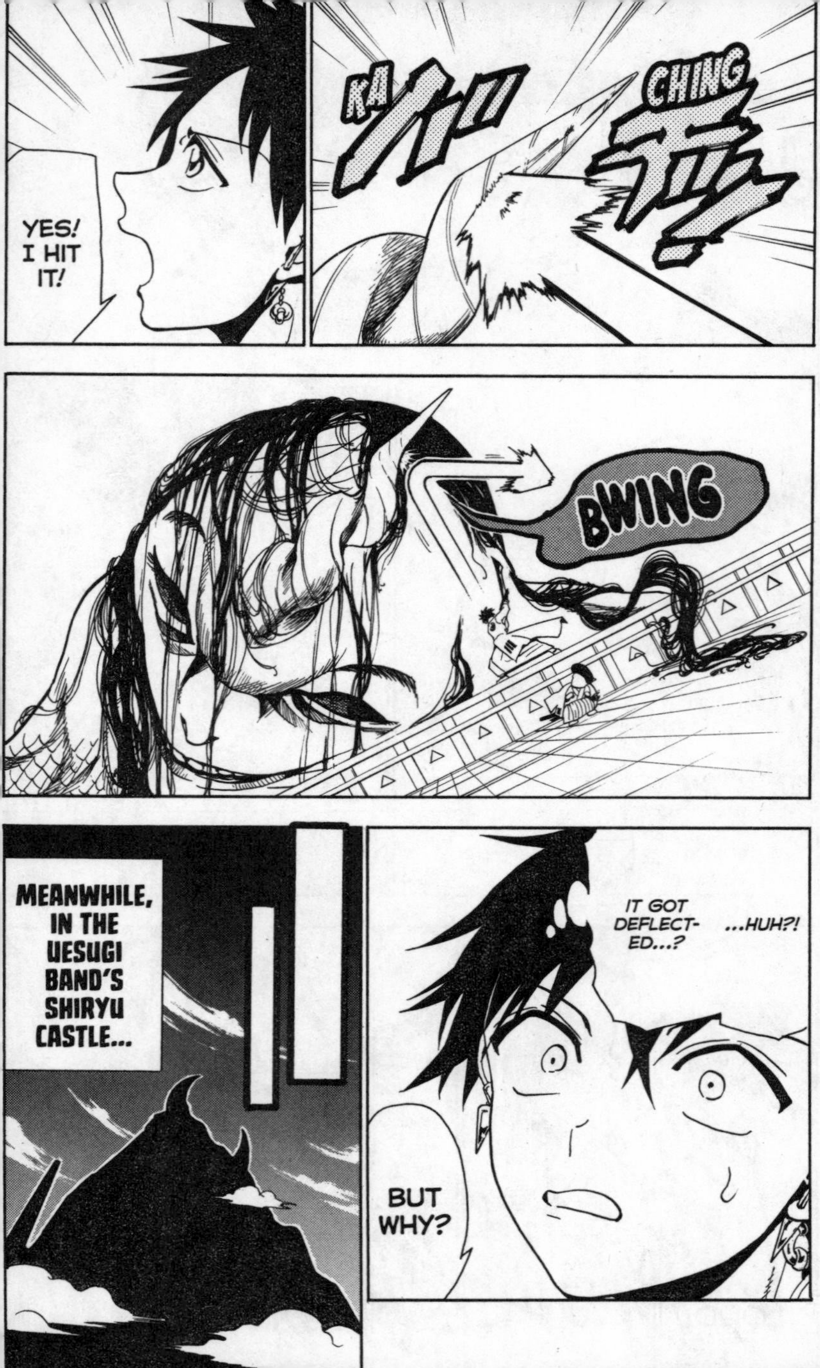
KA
CHING
YES! I HIT IT!
BWING
...HUH?!
IT GOT DEFLECT-ED...?
BUT WHY?
MEANWHILE, IN THE UESUGI BAND'S SHIRYU CASTLE...

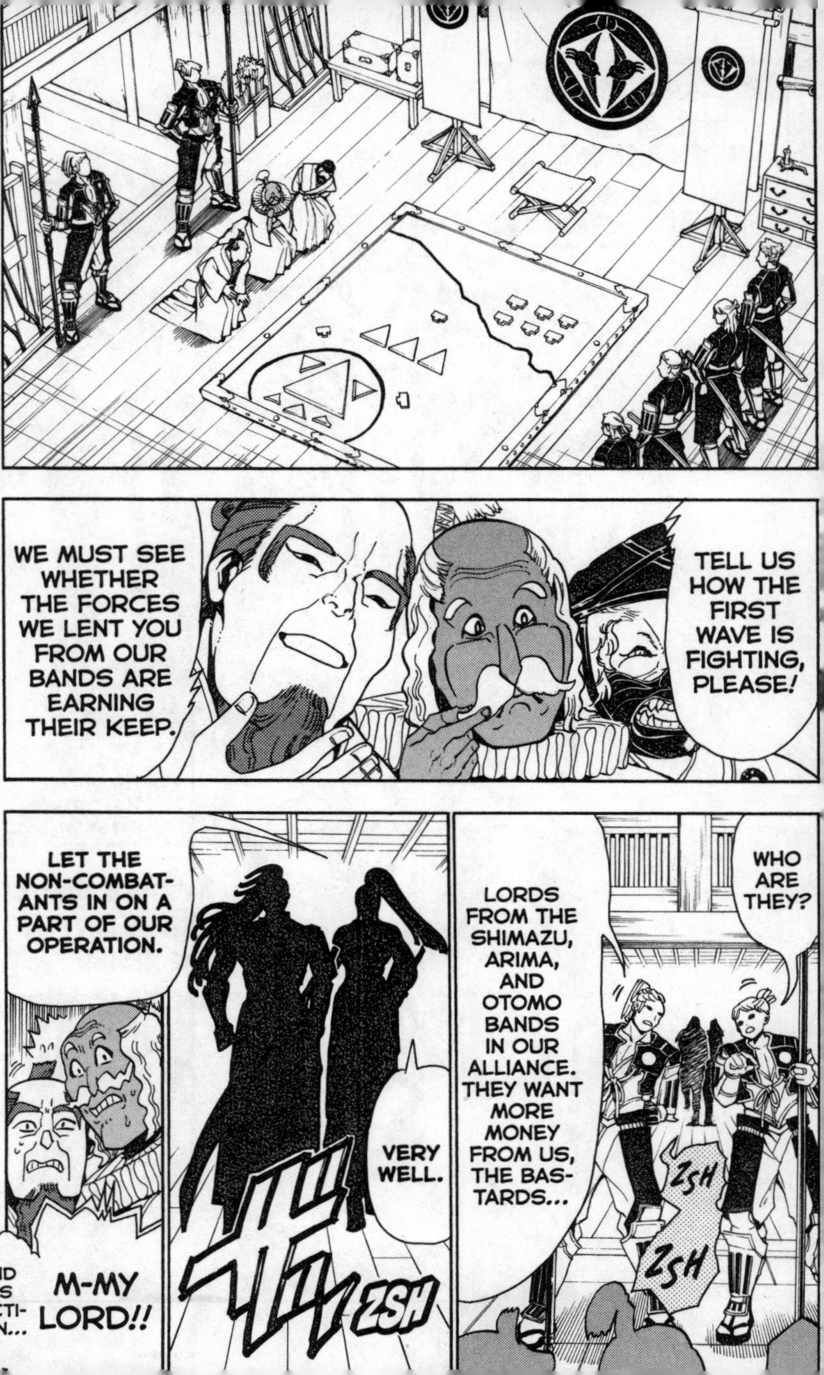
TELL US HOW THE FIRST WAVE IS FIGHTING, PLEASE!
WE MUST SEE WHETHER THE FORCES WE LENT YOU FROM OUR BANDS ARE EARNING THEIR KEEP.
WHO ARE THEY?
LORDS FROM THE SHIMAZU, ARIMA, AND OTOMO BANDS IN OUR ALLIANCE. THEY WANT MORE MONEY FROM US, THE BAS-TARDS...
ZSH
ZSH
VERY WELL.
ZSH
LET THE NON-COMBAT-ANTS IN ON A PART OF OUR OPERATION.
M-MY LORD!!
AND HIS TACTI-CIAN...

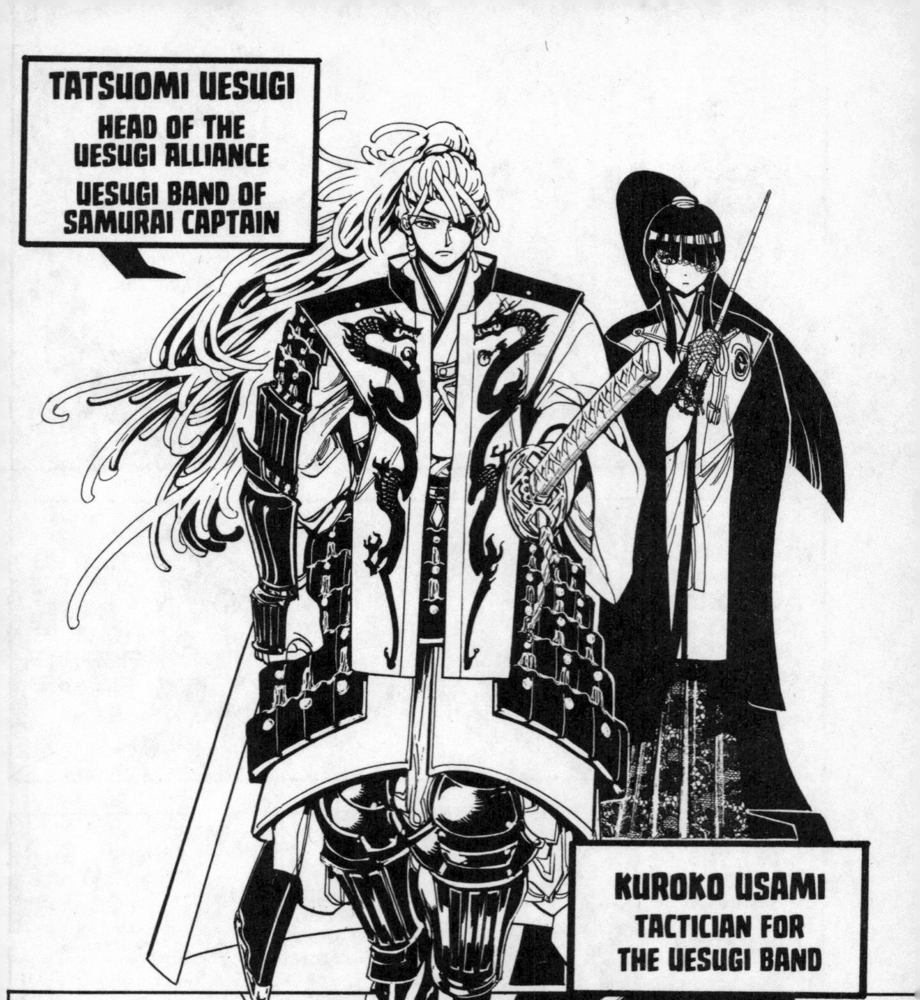
TATSUOMI UESUGI
HEAD OF THE UESUGI ALLIANCE
UESUGI BAND OF SAMURAI CAPTAIN
KUROKO USAMI
TACTICIAN FOR THE UESUGI BAND
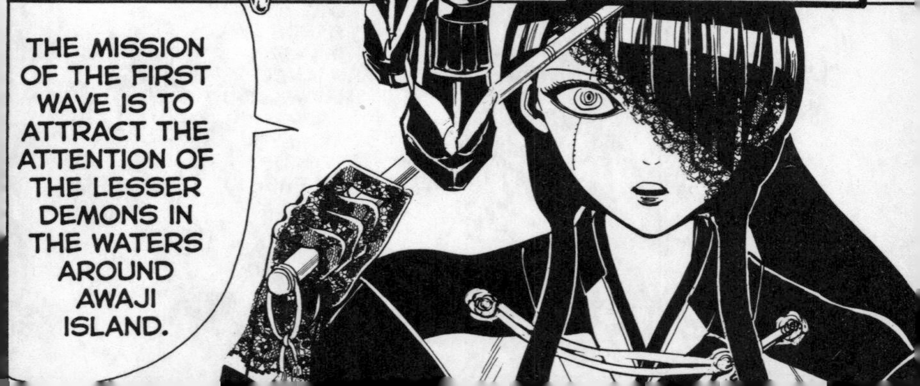
THE MISSION OF THE FIRST WAVE IS TO ATTRACT THE ATTENTION OF THE LESSER DEMONS IN THE WATERS AROUND AWAJI ISLAND.

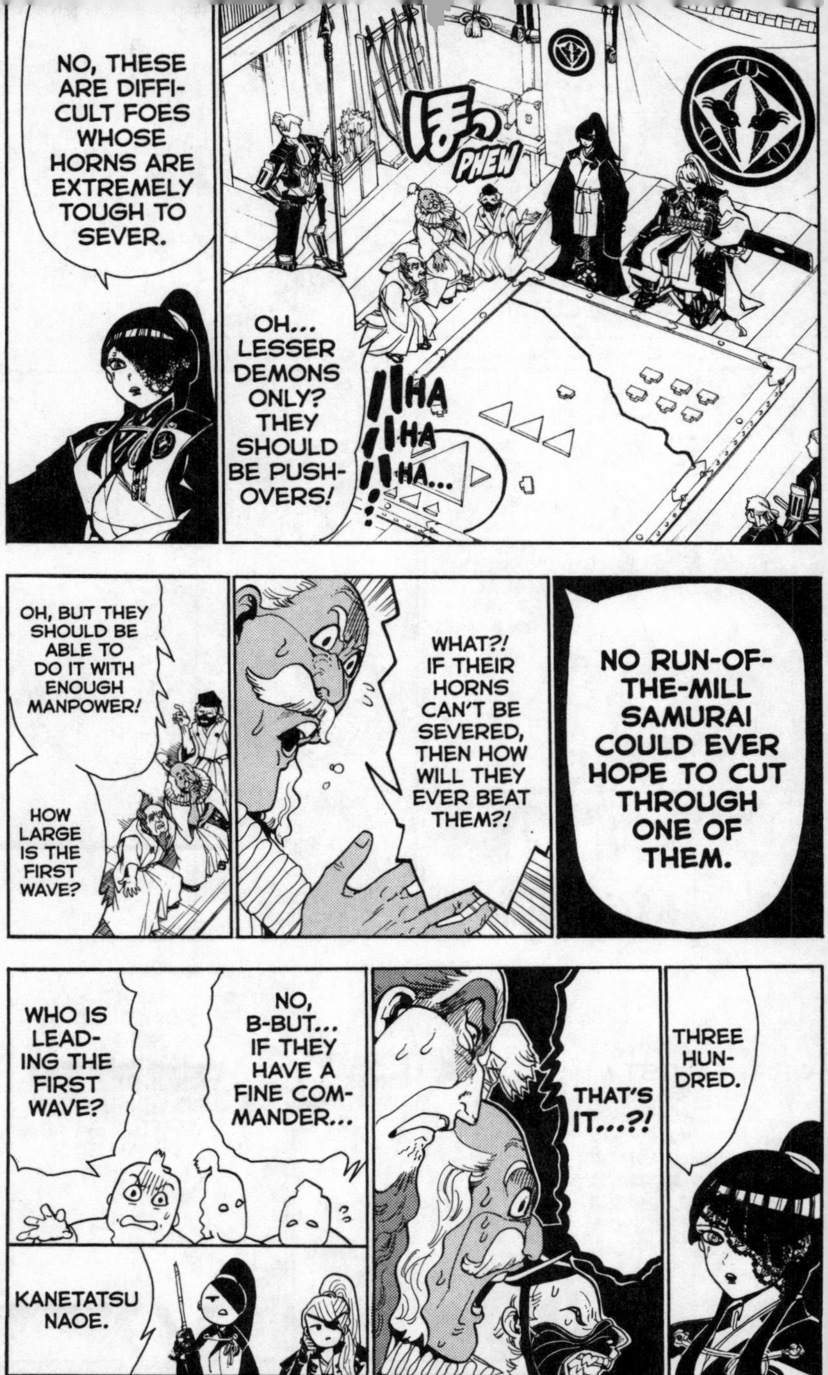

ほっ
PHEW
OH... LESSER DEMONS ONLY? THEY SHOULD BE PUSH-OVERS!
HA HA HA...
NO, THESE ARE DIFFI-CULT FOES WHOSE HORNS ARE EXTREMELY TOUGH TO SEVER.
NO RUN-OF-THE-MILL SAMURAI COULD EVER HOPE TO CUT THROUGH ONE OF THEM.
WHAT?! IF THEIR HORNS CAN'T BE SEVERED, THEN HOW WILL THEY EVER BEAT THEM?!
OH, BUT THEY SHOULD BE ABLE TO DO IT WITH ENOUGH MANPOWER!
HOW LARGE IS THE FIRST WAVE?
THREE HUN-DRED.
THAT'S IT...?!
NO, B-BUT... IF THEY HAVE A FINE COM-MANDER...
WHO IS LEAD-ING THE FIRST WAVE?
KANETATSU NAOE.

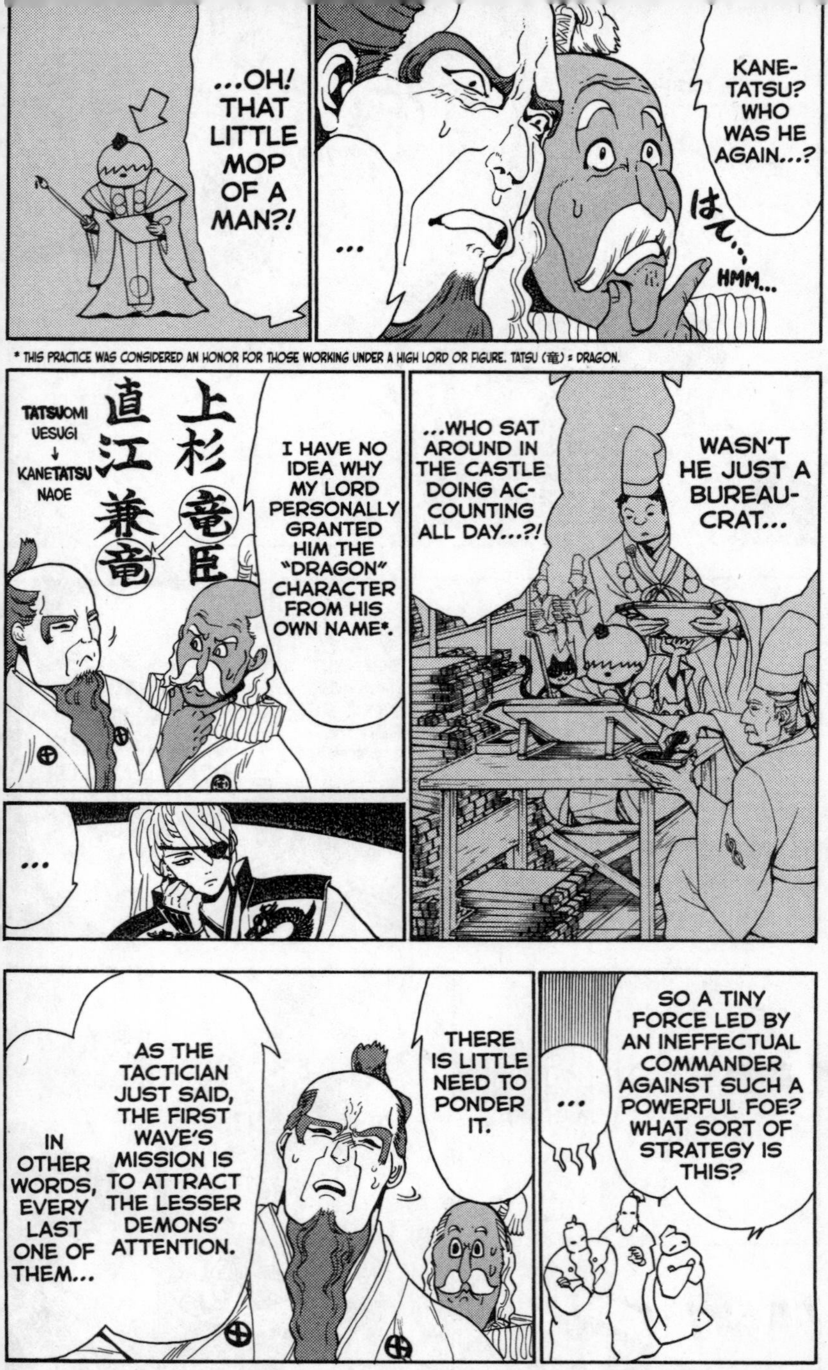
KANE-TATSU? WHO WAS HE AGAIN...?
はて…
HMM...
...
...OH! THAT LITTLE MOP OF A MAN?!
WASN'T HE JUST A BUREAU-CRAT...
...WHO SAT AROUND IN THE CASTLE DOING AC-COUNTING ALL DAY...?!
上杉竜臣
直江兼竜
TATSUOMI UESUGI ↓ KANETATSU NAOE
I HAVE NO IDEA WHY MY LORD PERSONALLY GRANTED HIM THE "DRAGON" CHARACTER FROM HIS OWN NAME*.
...
SO A TINY FORCE LED BY AN INEFFECTUAL COMMANDER AGAINST SUCH A POWERFUL FOE? WHAT SORT OF STRATEGY IS THIS?
...
THERE IS LITTLE NEED TO PONDER IT.
AS THE TACTICIAN JUST SAID, THE FIRST WAVE'S MISSION IS TO ATTRACT THE LESSER DEMONS' ATTENTION.
IN OTHER WORDS, EVERY LAST ONE OF THEM...

* THIS PRACTICE WAS CONSIDERED AN HONOR FOR THOSE WORKING UNDER A HIGH LORD OR FIGURE. TATSU (竜) = DRAGON.

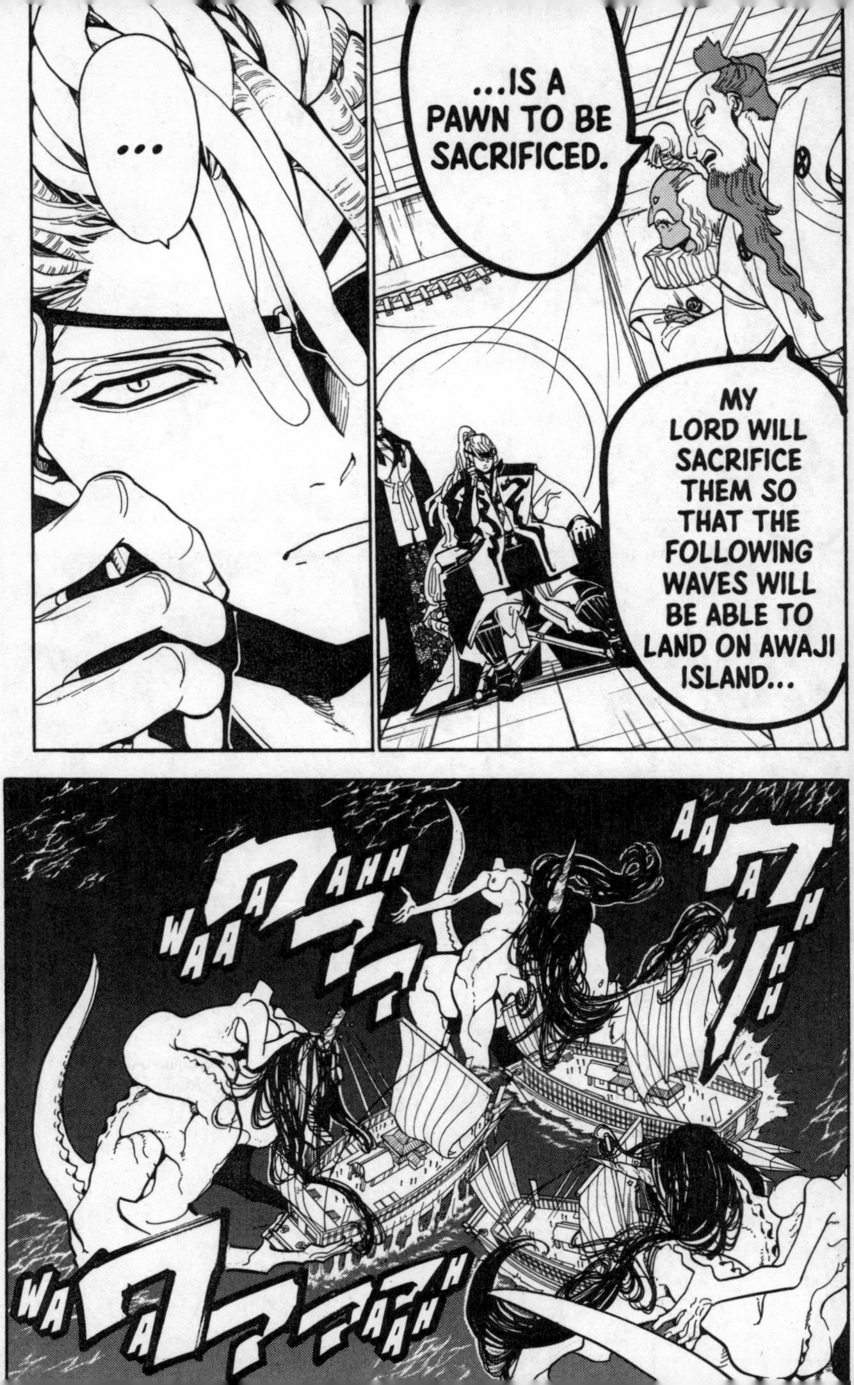
...IS A PAWN TO BE SACRIFICED.
MY LORD WILL SACRIFICE THEM SO THAT THE FOLLOWING WAVES WILL BE ABLE TO LAND ON AWAJI ISLAND...
...
AAAHHHHH
WAAAAHH
WAAAAAAHH

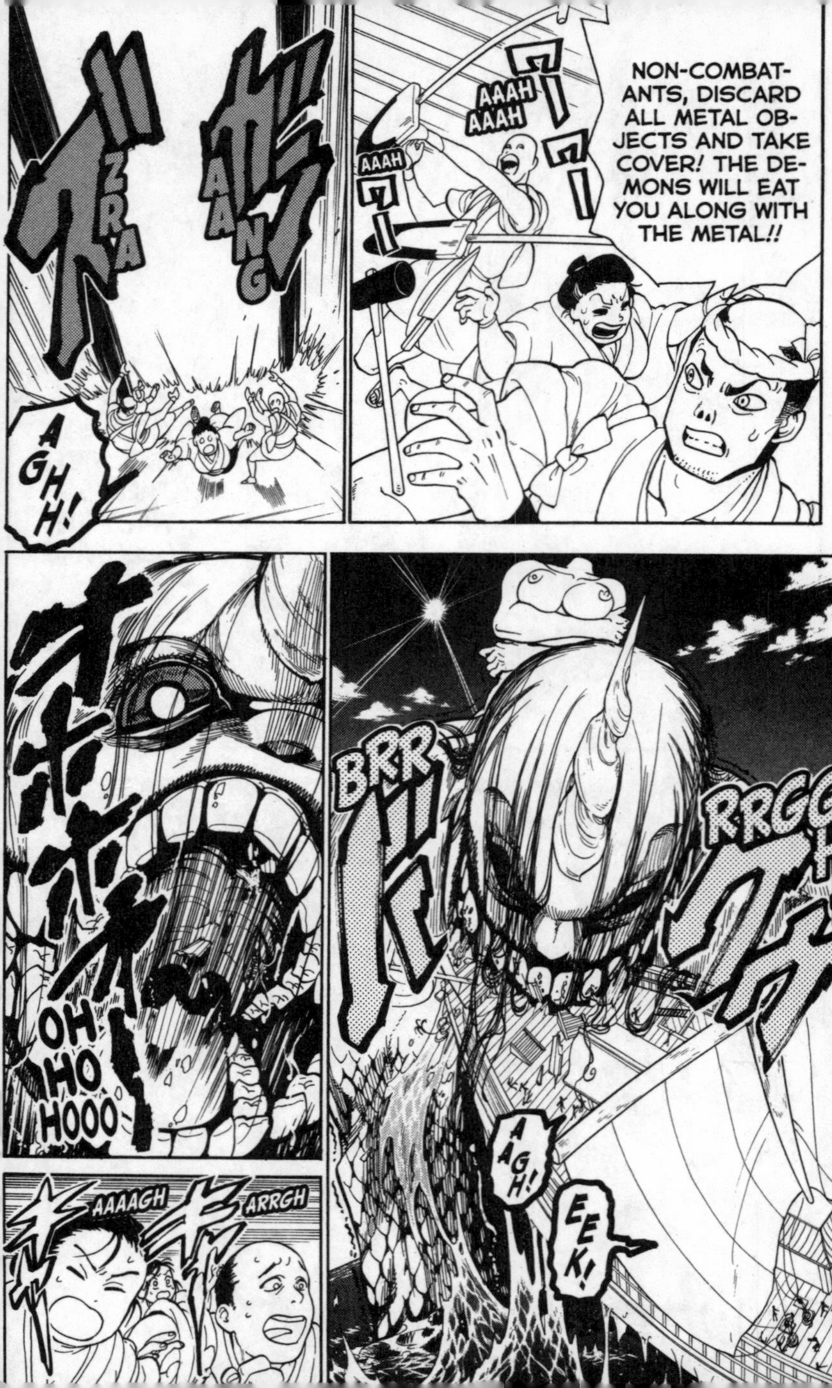
NON-COMBATANTS, DISCARD ALL METAL OBJECTS AND TAKE COVER! THE DEMONS WILL EAT YOU ALONG WITH THE METAL!!
AAAH AAAH
AAAH
ZRA
AANG
AGHH!
BRR
RRGGHHH
AAGH!
EEK!
OH HO HOOO
AAAAGH
ARRGH

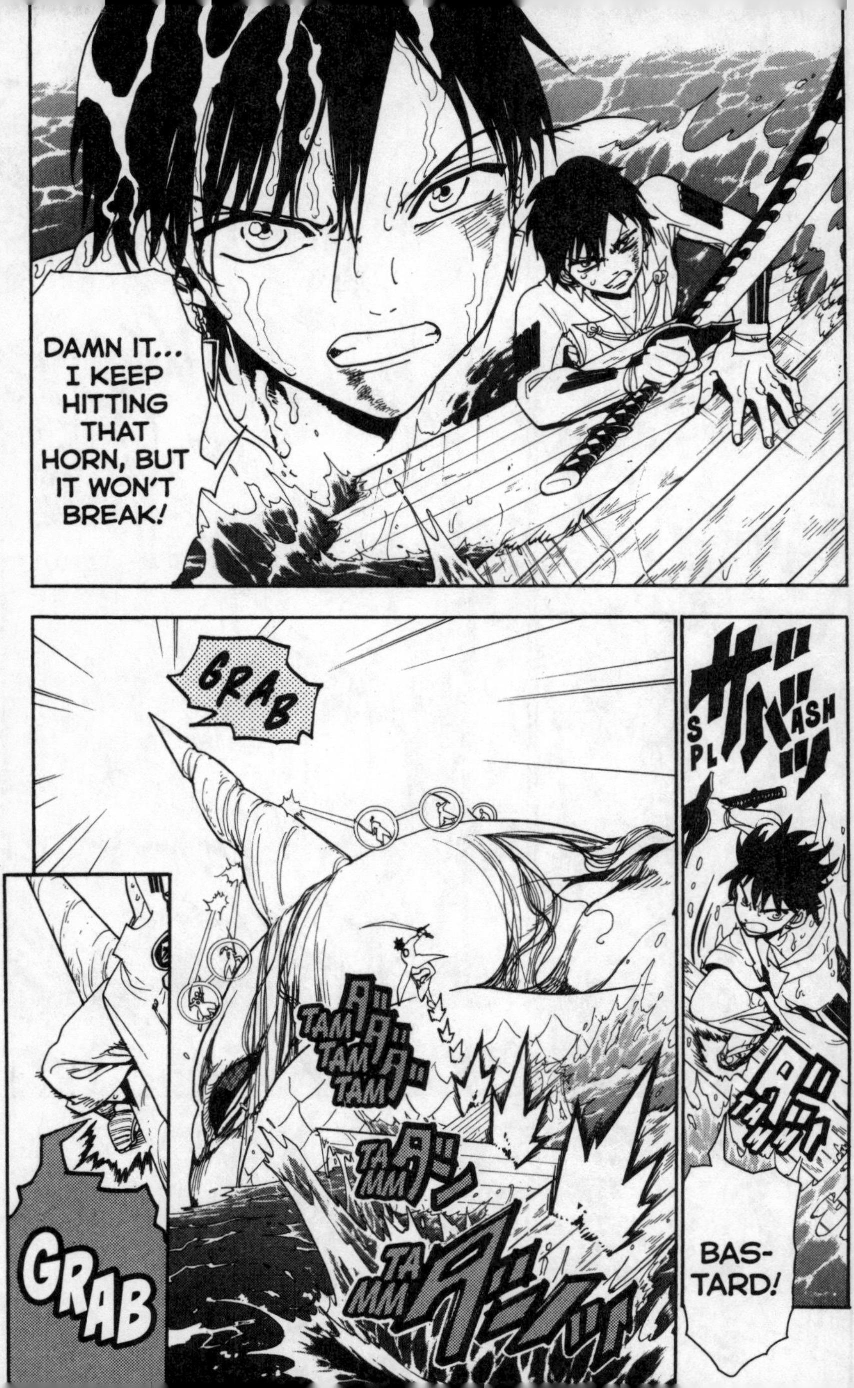
DAMN IT... I KEEP HITTING THAT HORN, BUT IT WON'T BREAK!
SPLASH
TAMMM
BASTARD!
GRAB
TAM TAM TAM
TAMMM
TAMMM
GRAB

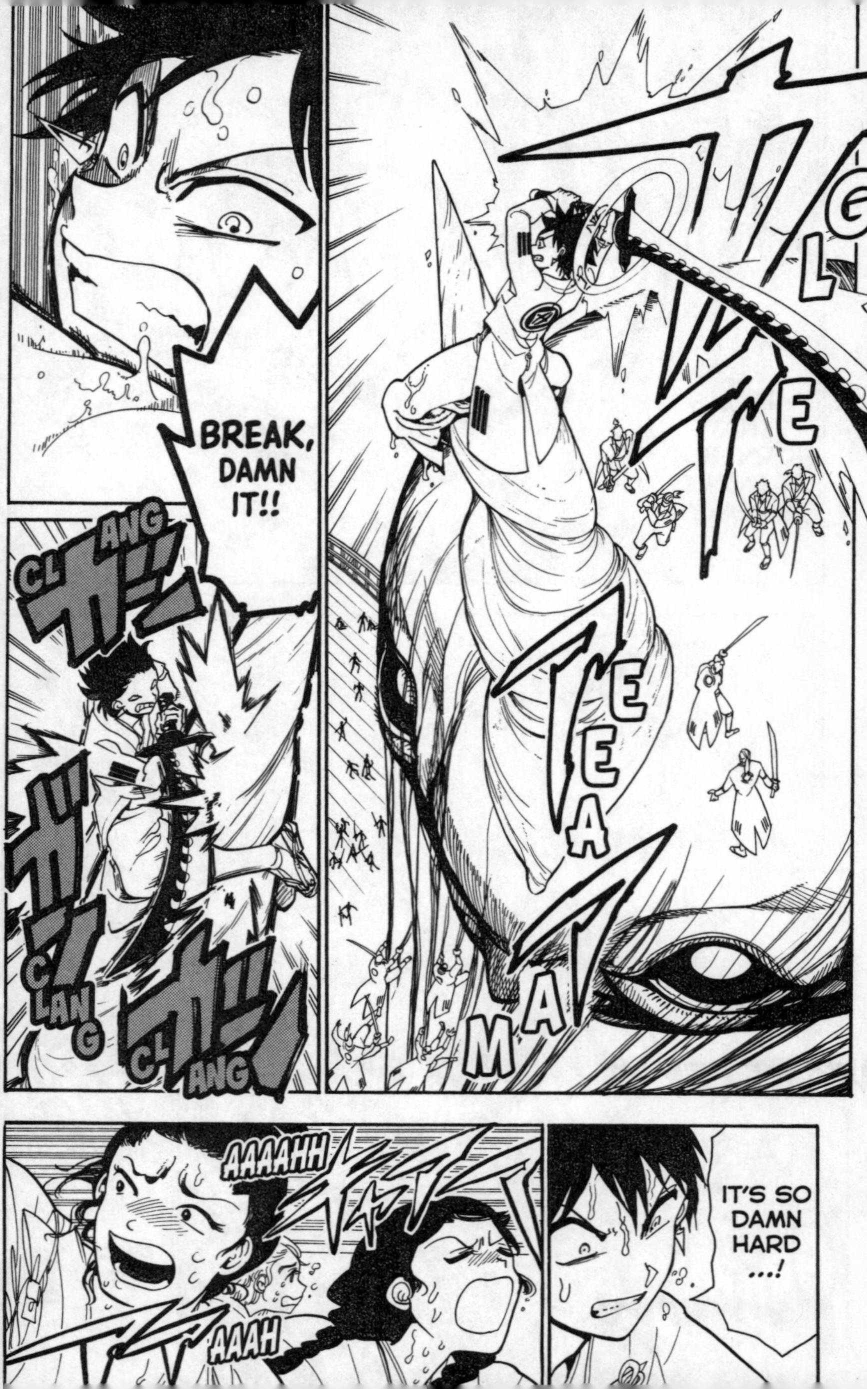
MAAEEELG
BREAK, DAMN IT!!
CLANG
CLANG
CLANG
IT'S SO DAMN HARD ...!
AAAAHH
AAAH

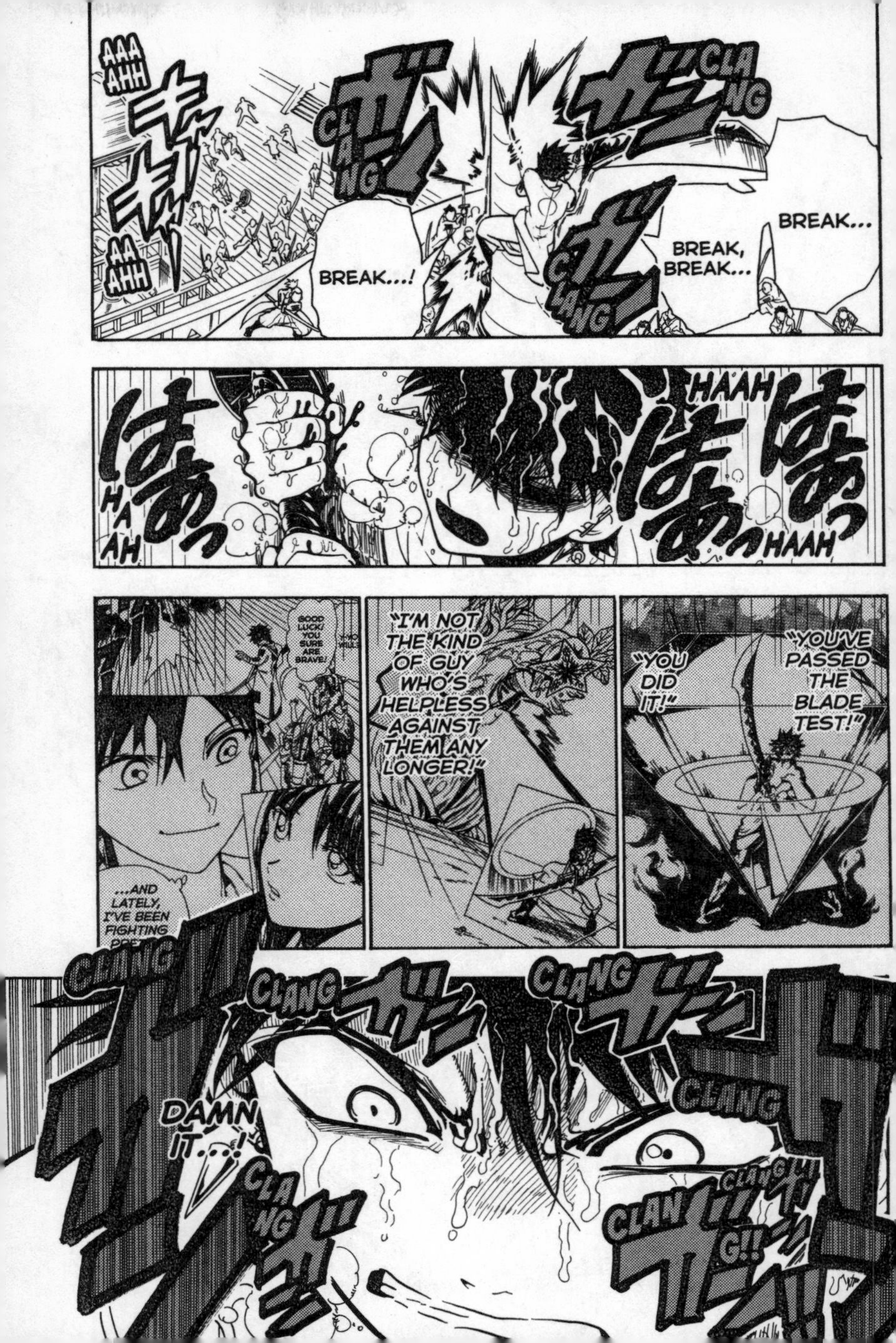
BREAK...
BREAK, BREAK...
CLANG
CLA NG
CLANG
CLANG
BREAK...!
AAAAHH
AAAHH
HAAH
HAAH
HAAH
"YOU'VE PASSED THE BLADE TEST!"
"YOU DID IT!"
"I'M NOT THE KIND OF GUY WHO'S HELPLESS AGAINST THEM ANY LONGER!"
GOOD LUCK! YOU SURE ARE BRAVE!
...AND LATELY, I'VE BEEN FIGHTING
CLANG
CLANG
CLANG
CLANG
CLANG
DAMN IT...!
CLANG
CLANG!!

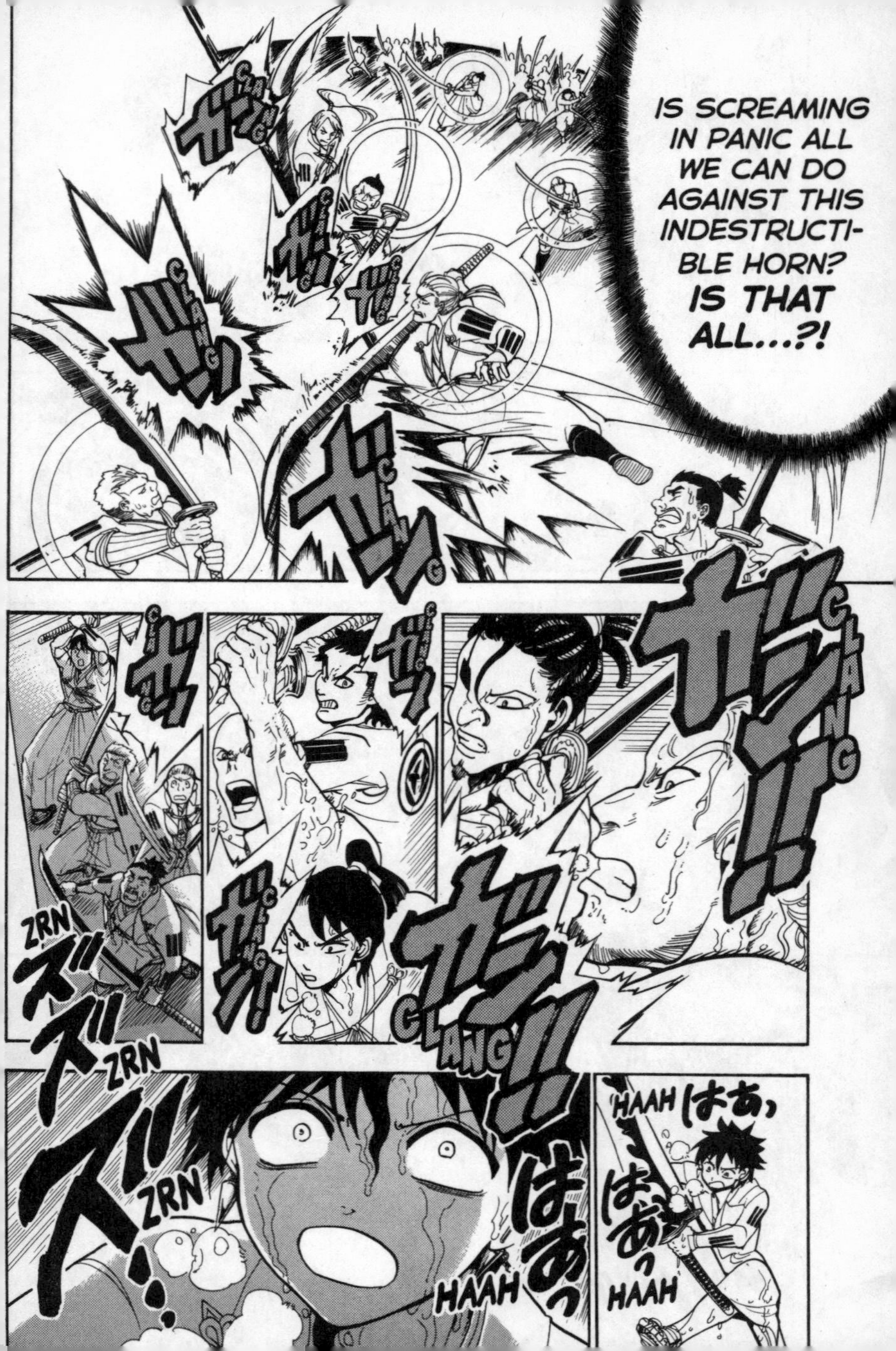
IS SCREAMING IN PANIC ALL WE CAN DO AGAINST THIS INDESTRUCTI-BLE HORN?
IS THAT ALL...?!
ガン CLANG
ガッ CLANG
ガッ CLANG
ガン!! CLANG
ガン CLANG
ガン!! CLANG
ガッ CLANG
ガッ CLANG
ガッ!! CLANG
ガン!! CLANG!!
はあっ HAAH
はあっ HAAH
ZRN ズ
ZRN ズ
ZRN ズ!!...
はあっ HAAH

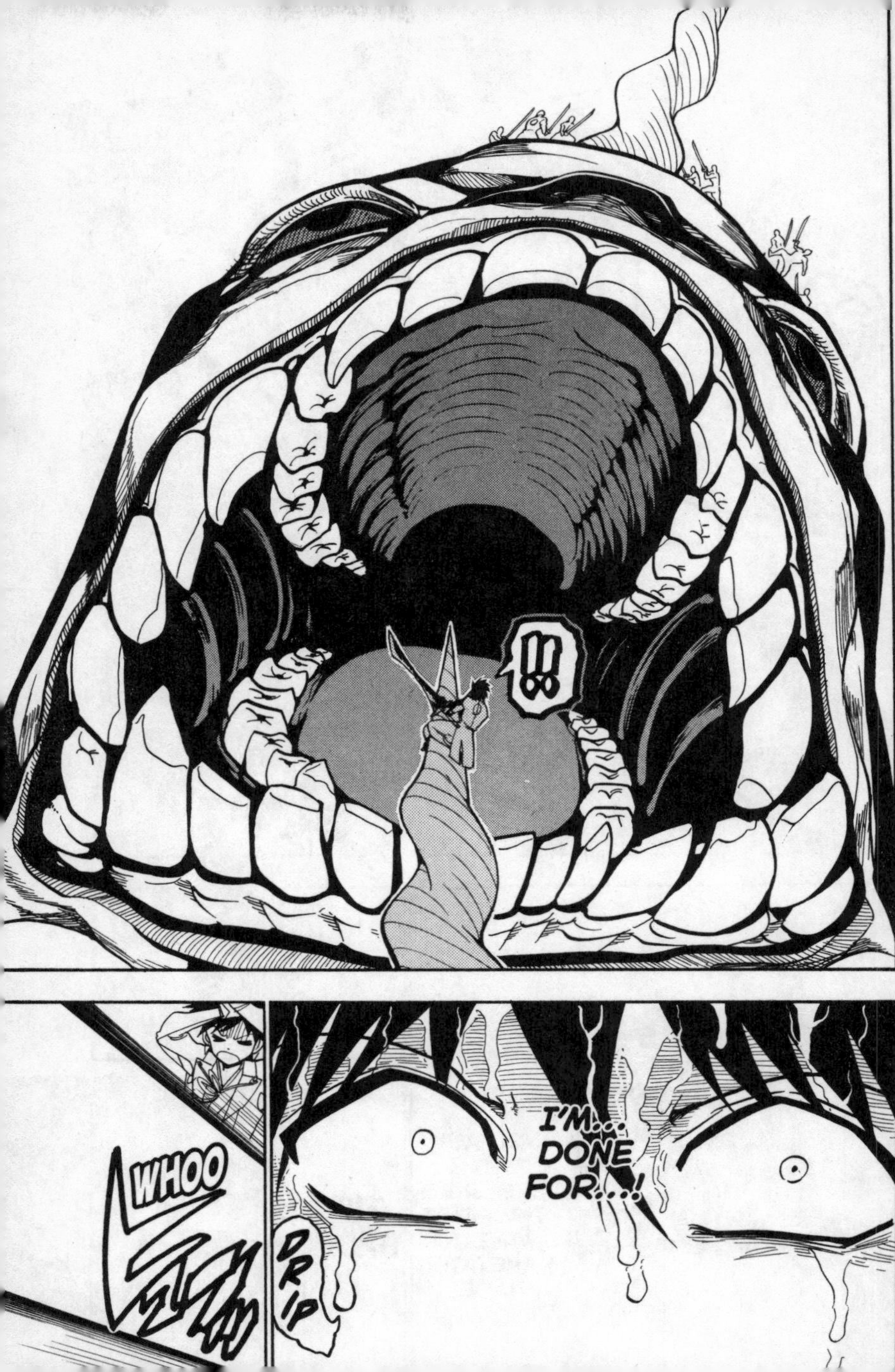

!?
I'M... DONE FOR...!
DRIP
WHOO

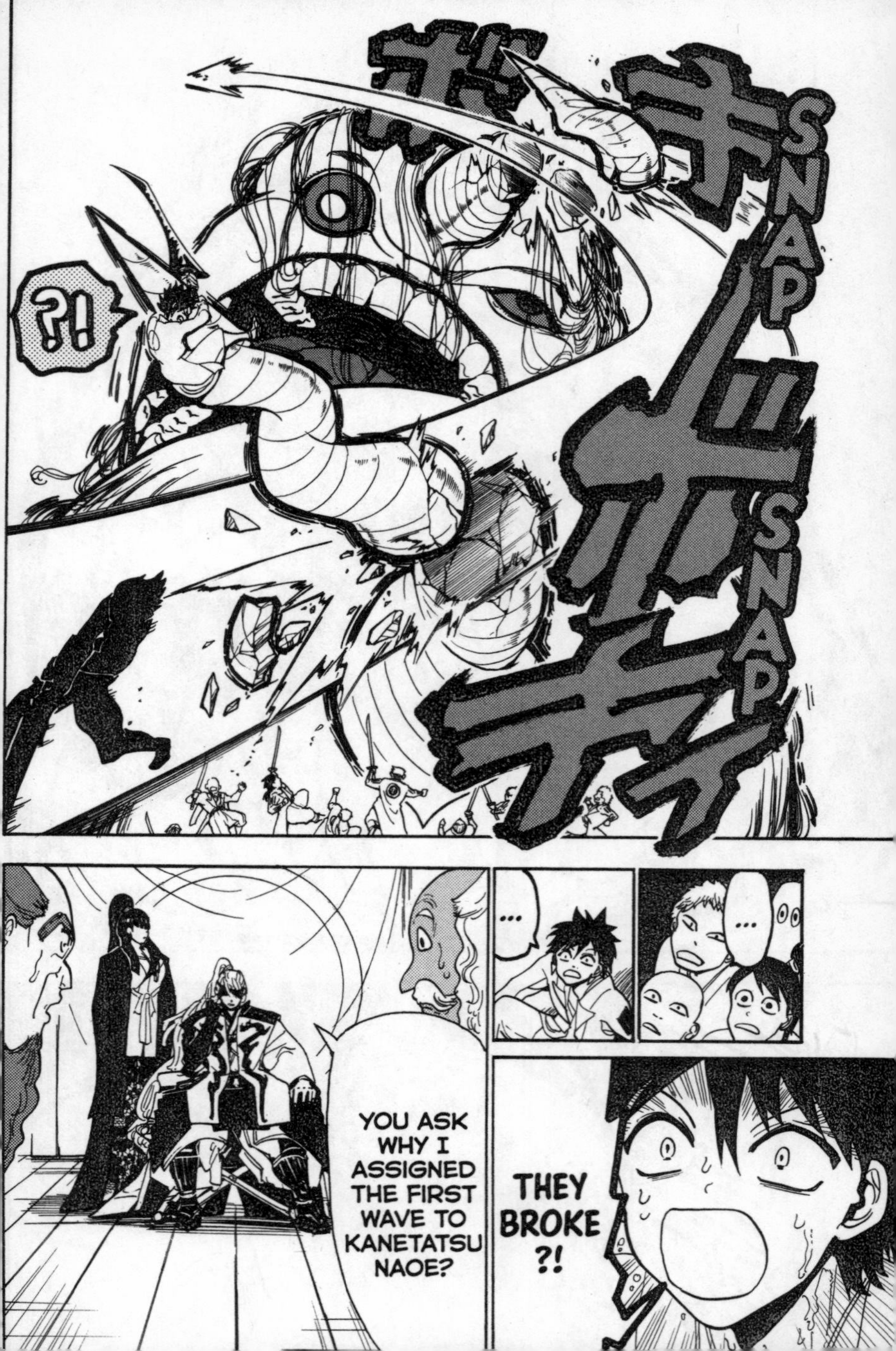
SNAP
SNAP
?!
...
...
THEY BROKE ?!
YOU ASK WHY I ASSIGNED THE FIRST WAVE TO KANETATSU NAOE?

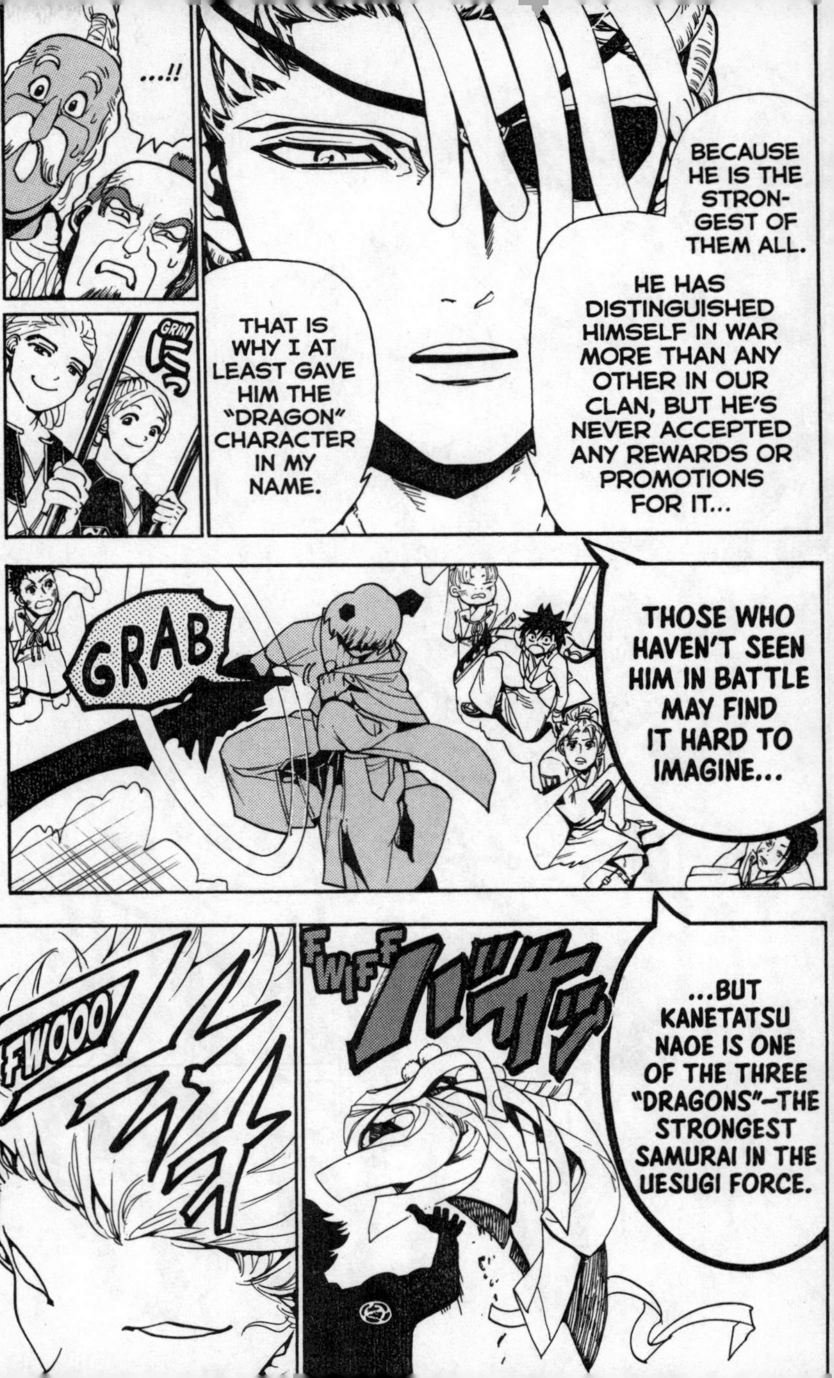
BECAUSE HE IS THE STRON-GEST OF THEM ALL.
HE HAS DISTINGUISHED HIMSELF IN WAR MORE THAN ANY OTHER IN OUR CLAN, BUT HE'S NEVER ACCEPTED ANY REWARDS OR PROMOTIONS FOR IT...
THAT IS WHY I AT LEAST GAVE HIM THE "DRAGON" CHARACTER IN MY NAME.
...!!
GRIN
THOSE WHO HAVEN'T SEEN HIM IN BATTLE MAY FIND IT HARD TO IMAGINE...
GRAB
...BUT KANETATSU NAOE IS ONE OF THE THREE "DRAGONS"—THE STRONGEST SAMURAI IN THE UESUGI FORCE.
FWIFF
FWOOO

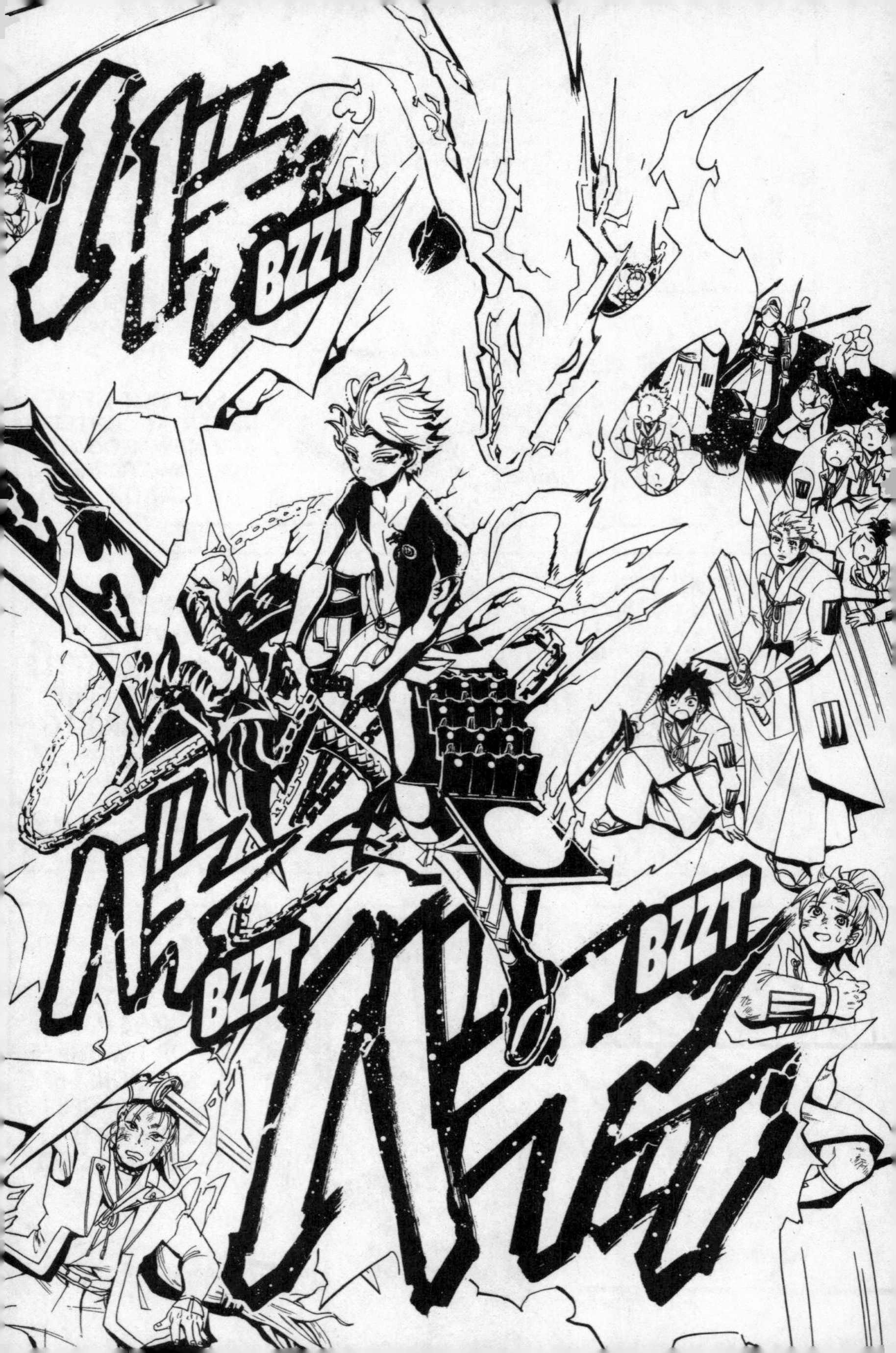
BZZT
BZZT
BZZT

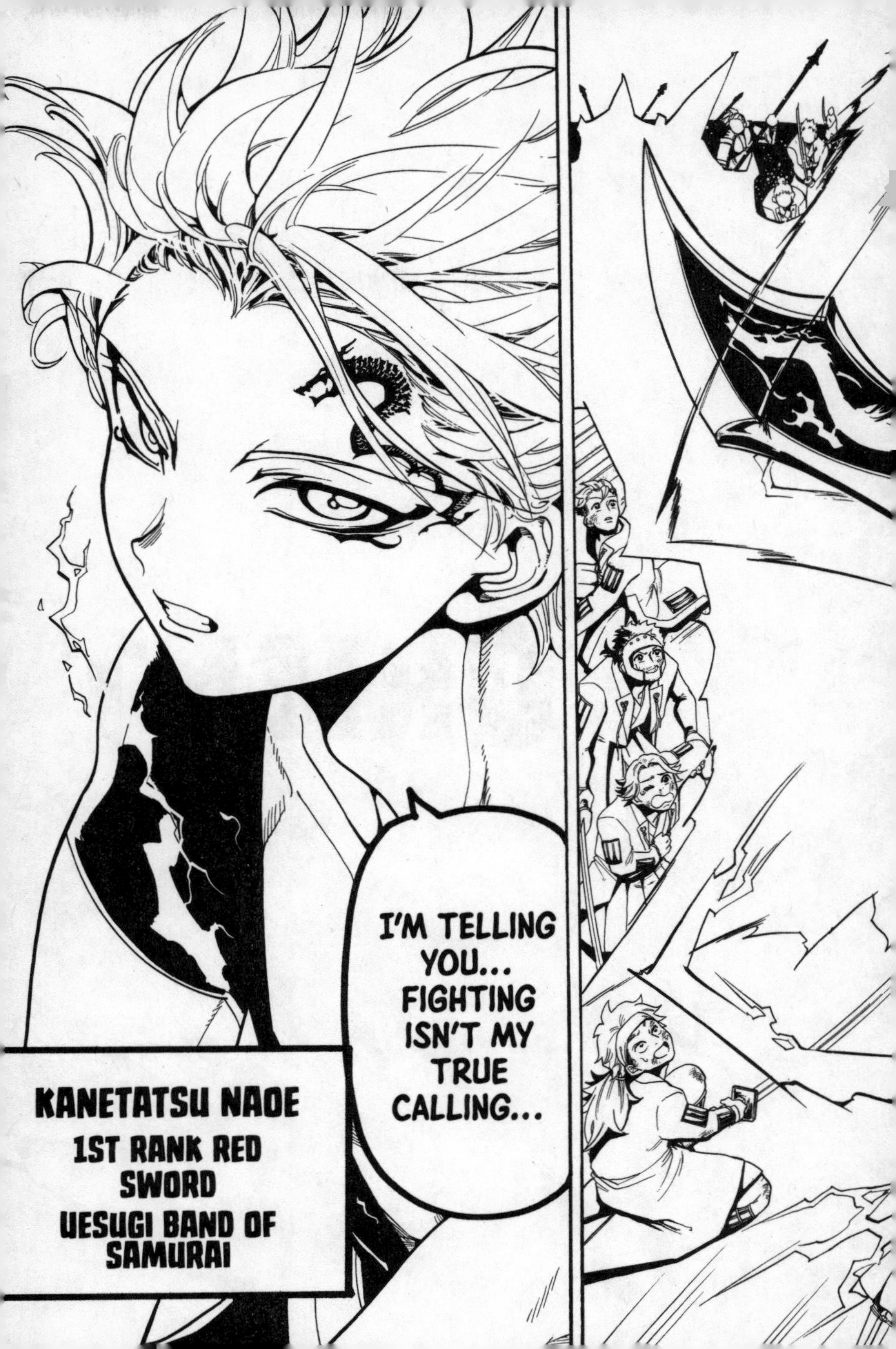
I'M TELLING YOU... FIGHTING ISN'T MY TRUE CALLING...
KANETATSU NAOE
1ST RANK RED SWORD
UESUGI BAND OF SAMURAI

ORIENT

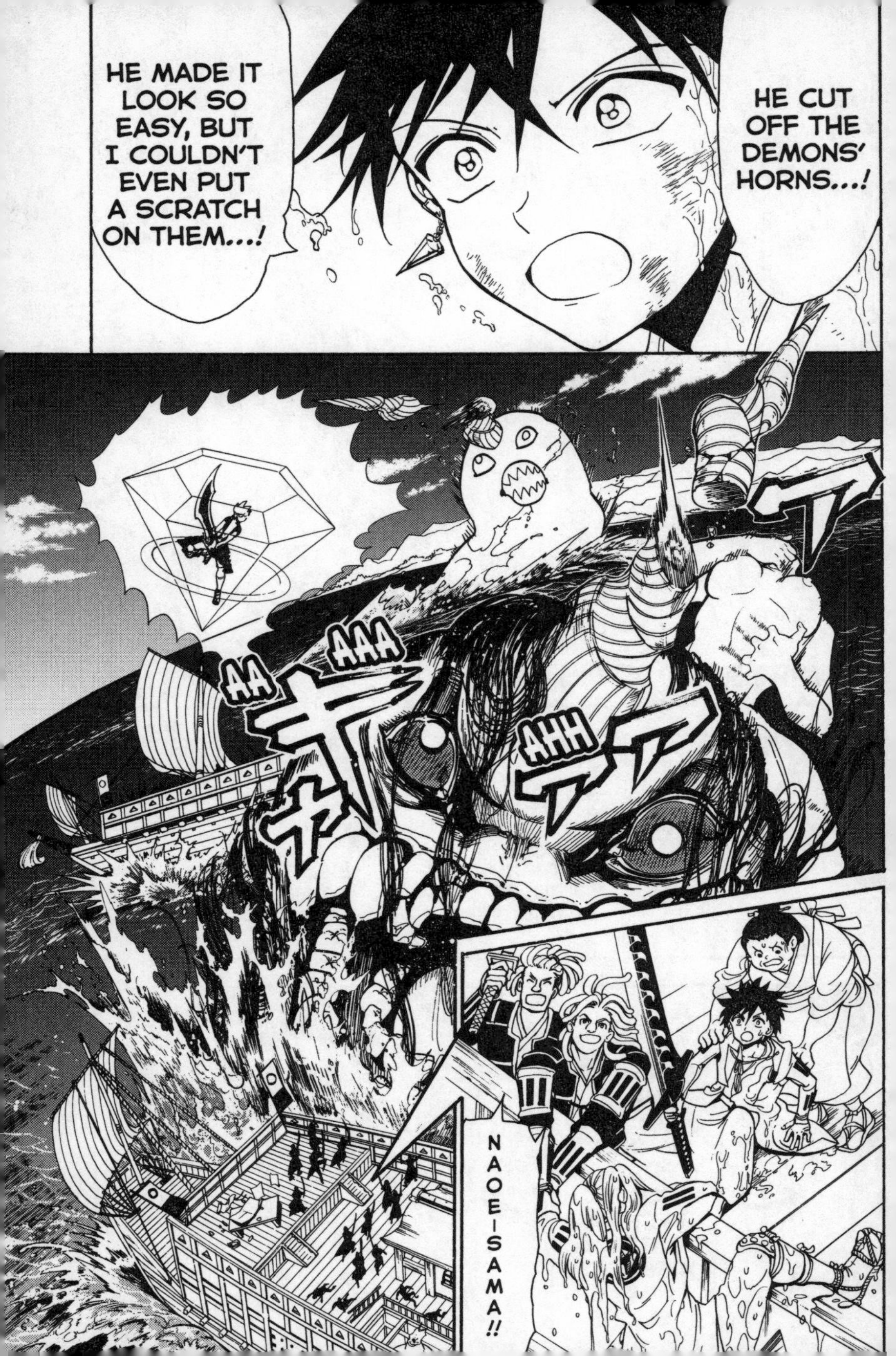
HE CUT OFF THE DEMONS' HORNS...!
HE MADE IT LOOK SO EASY, BUT I COULDN'T EVEN PUT A SCRATCH ON THEM...!
AA
AAA
AHH
NAOE-SAMA!!

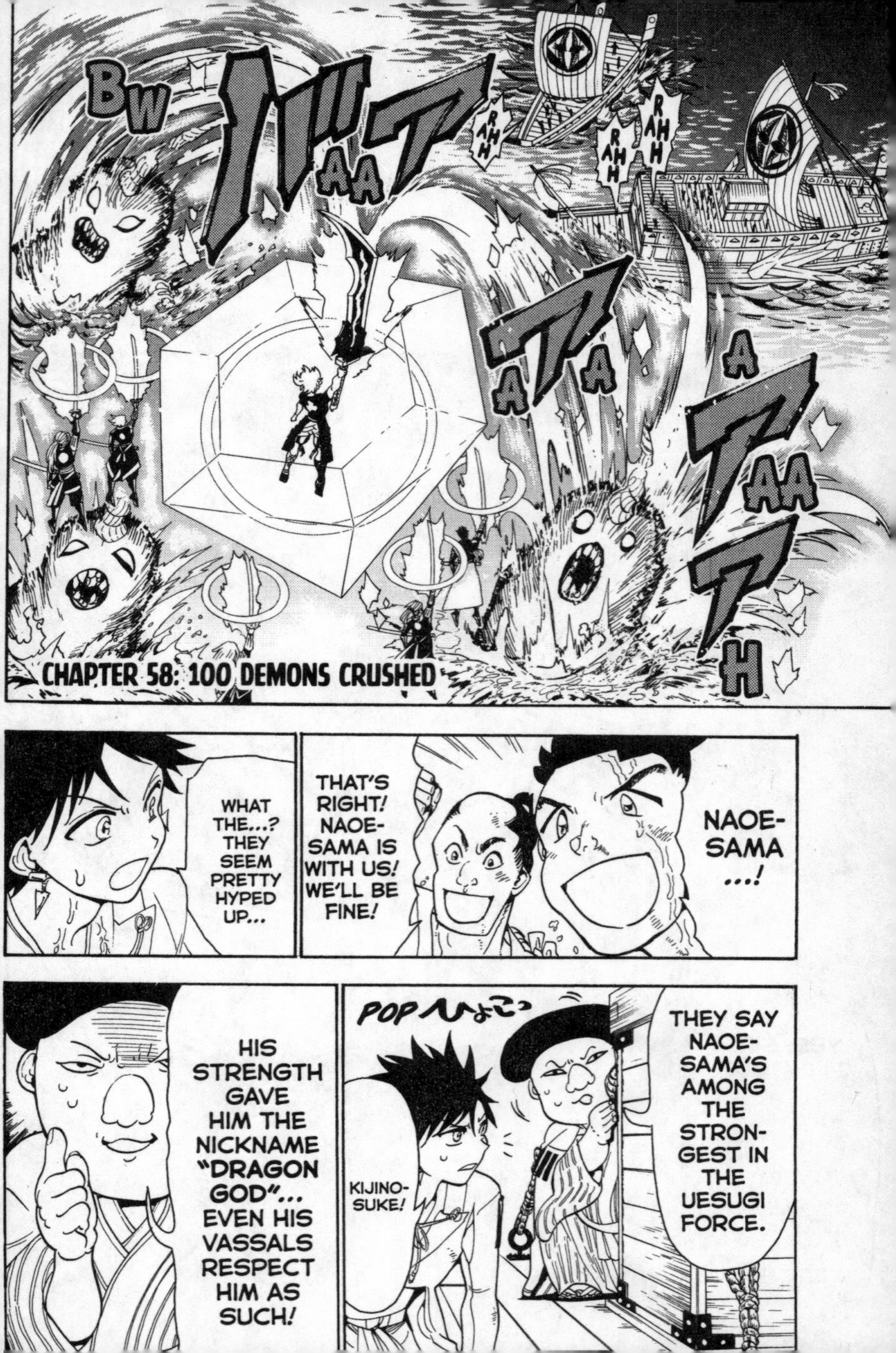

BW
AA
RAH RAH
RAHH
RAHH
A A A
A AA H
CHAPTER 58: 100 DEMONS CRUSHED
NAOE-SAMA ...!
THAT'S RIGHT! NAOE-SAMA IS WITH US! WE'LL BE FINE!
WHAT THE...? THEY SEEM PRETTY HYPED UP...
THEY SAY NAOE-SAMA'S AMONG THE STRONGEST IN THE UESUGI FORCE.
POP
KIJINO-SUKE!
HIS STRENGTH GAVE HIM THE NICKNAME "DRAGON GOD"... EVEN HIS VASSALS RESPECT HIM AS SUCH!

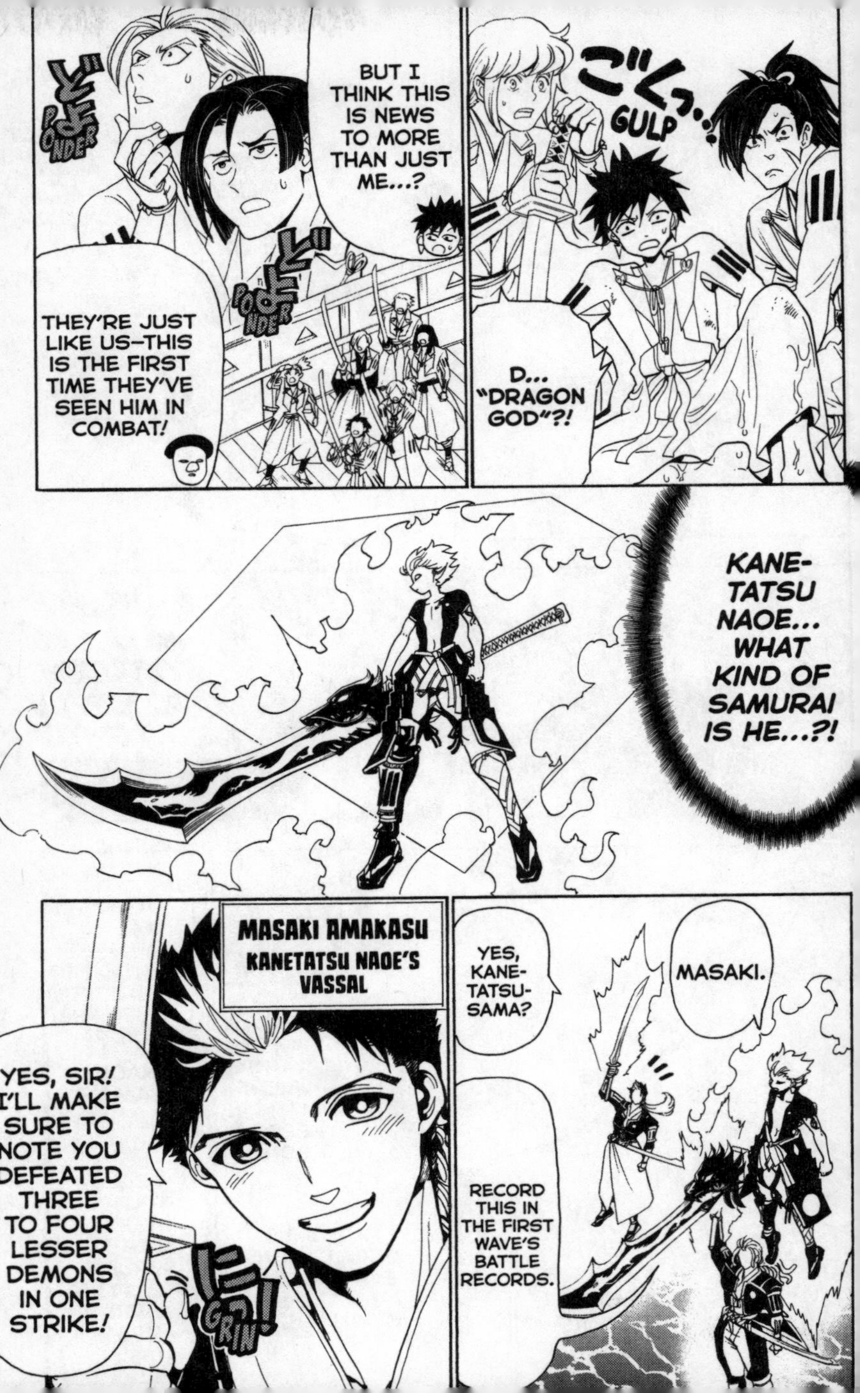
ごくっ
GULP
D... "DRAGON GOD"?!
BUT I THINK THIS IS NEWS TO MORE THAN JUST ME...?
PONDER
THEY'RE JUST LIKE US—THIS IS THE FIRST TIME THEY'VE SEEN HIM IN COMBAT!
PONDER
KANE-TATSU NAOE... WHAT KIND OF SAMURAI IS HE...?!
MASAKI.
YES, KANE-TATSU-SAMA?
RECORD THIS IN THE FIRST WAVE'S BATTLE RECORDS.
MASAKI AMAKASU KANETATSU NAOE'S VASSAL
YES, SIR! I'LL MAKE SURE TO NOTE YOU DEFEATED THREE TO FOUR LESSER DEMONS IN ONE STRIKE!
GRIN

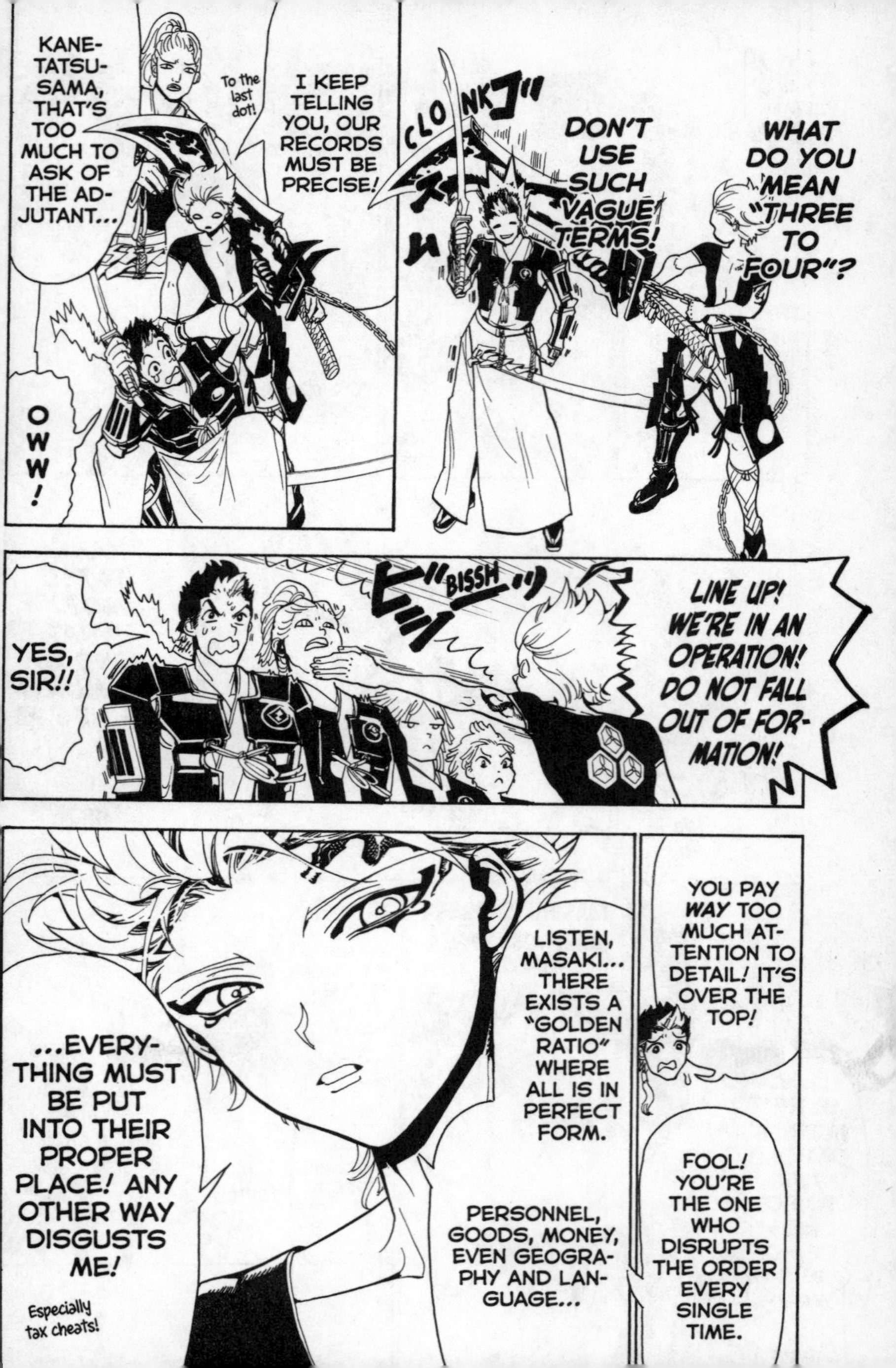

WHAT DO YOU MEAN "THREE TO FOUR"?
DON'T USE SUCH VAGUE TERMS!
CLONK
I KEEP TELLING YOU, OUR RECORDS MUST BE PRECISE!
To the last dot!
KANE-TATSU-SAMA, THAT'S TOO MUCH TO ASK OF THE AD-JUTANT...
OWW!
LINE UP! WE'RE IN AN OPERATION! DO NOT FALL OUT OF FOR-MATION!
BISSH
YES, SIR!!
YOU PAY WAY TOO MUCH AT-TENTION TO DETAIL! IT'S OVER THE TOP!
FOOL! YOU'RE THE ONE WHO DISRUPTS THE ORDER EVERY SINGLE TIME.
LISTEN, MASAKI... THERE EXISTS A "GOLDEN RATIO" WHERE ALL IS IN PERFECT FORM.
PERSONNEL, GOODS, MONEY, EVEN GEOGRA-PHY AND LAN-GUAGE...
...EVERY-THING MUST BE PUT INTO THEIR PROPER PLACE! ANY OTHER WAY DISGUSTS ME!
Especially tax cheats!

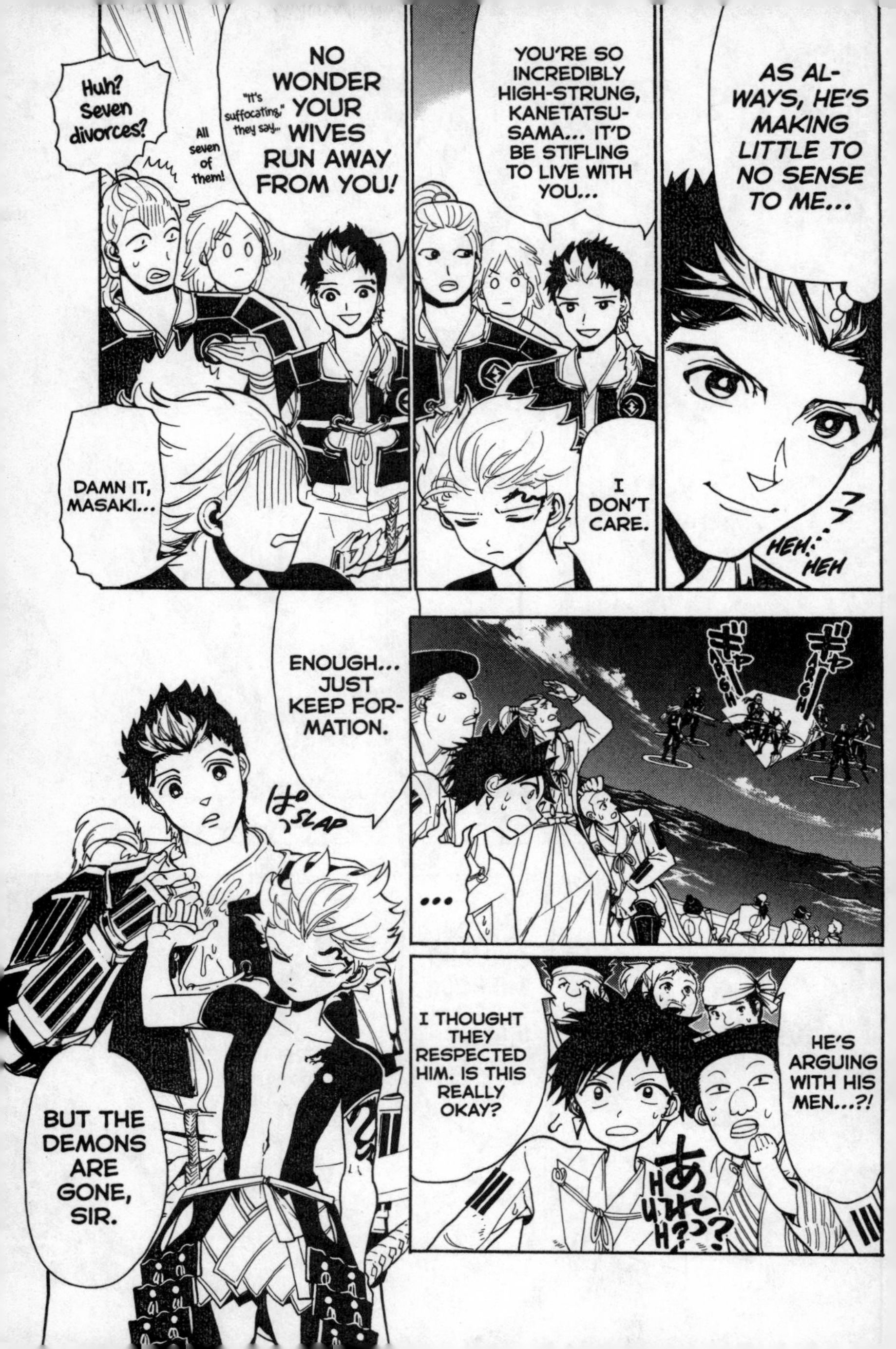
AS AL-WAYS, HE'S MAKING LITTLE TO NO SENSE TO ME...
HEH HEH
YOU'RE SO INCREDIBLY HIGH-STRUNG, KANETATSU-SAMA... IT'D BE STIFLING TO LIVE WITH YOU...
I DON'T CARE.
NO WONDER YOUR WIVES RUN AWAY FROM YOU!
"It's suffocating," they say...
All seven of them!
Huh? Seven divorces?
DAMN IT, MASAKI...
ギャ ARGH
ギャ ARGH
...
HE'S ARGUING WITH HIS MEN...?!
I THOUGHT THEY RESPECTED HIM. IS THIS REALLY OKAY?
ENOUGH... JUST KEEP FOR-MATION.
ぱっ SLAP
BUT THE DEMONS ARE GONE, SIR.

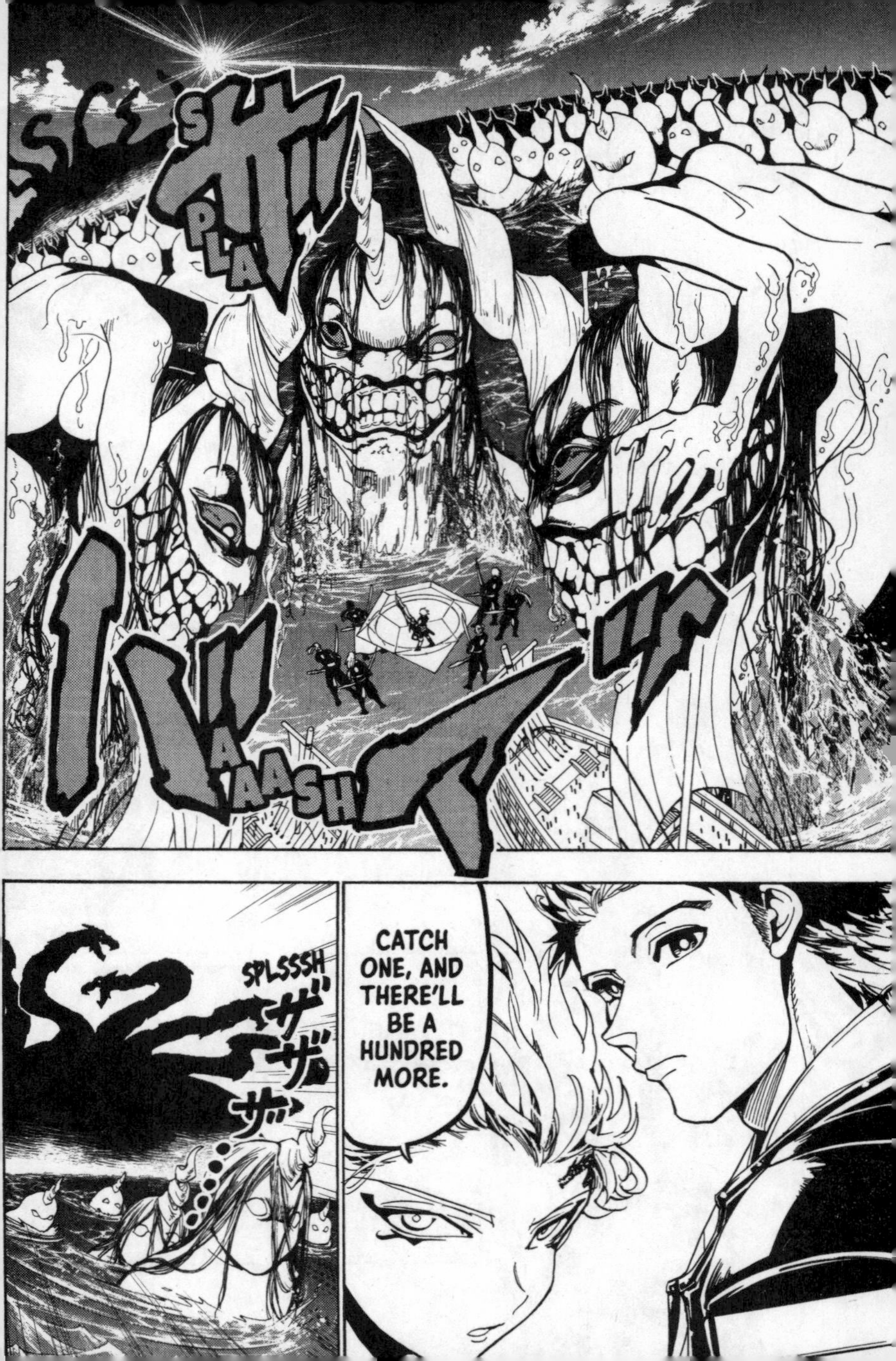
SPLAAAASH
CATCH ONE, AND THERE'LL BE A HUNDRED MORE.
SPLSSSH

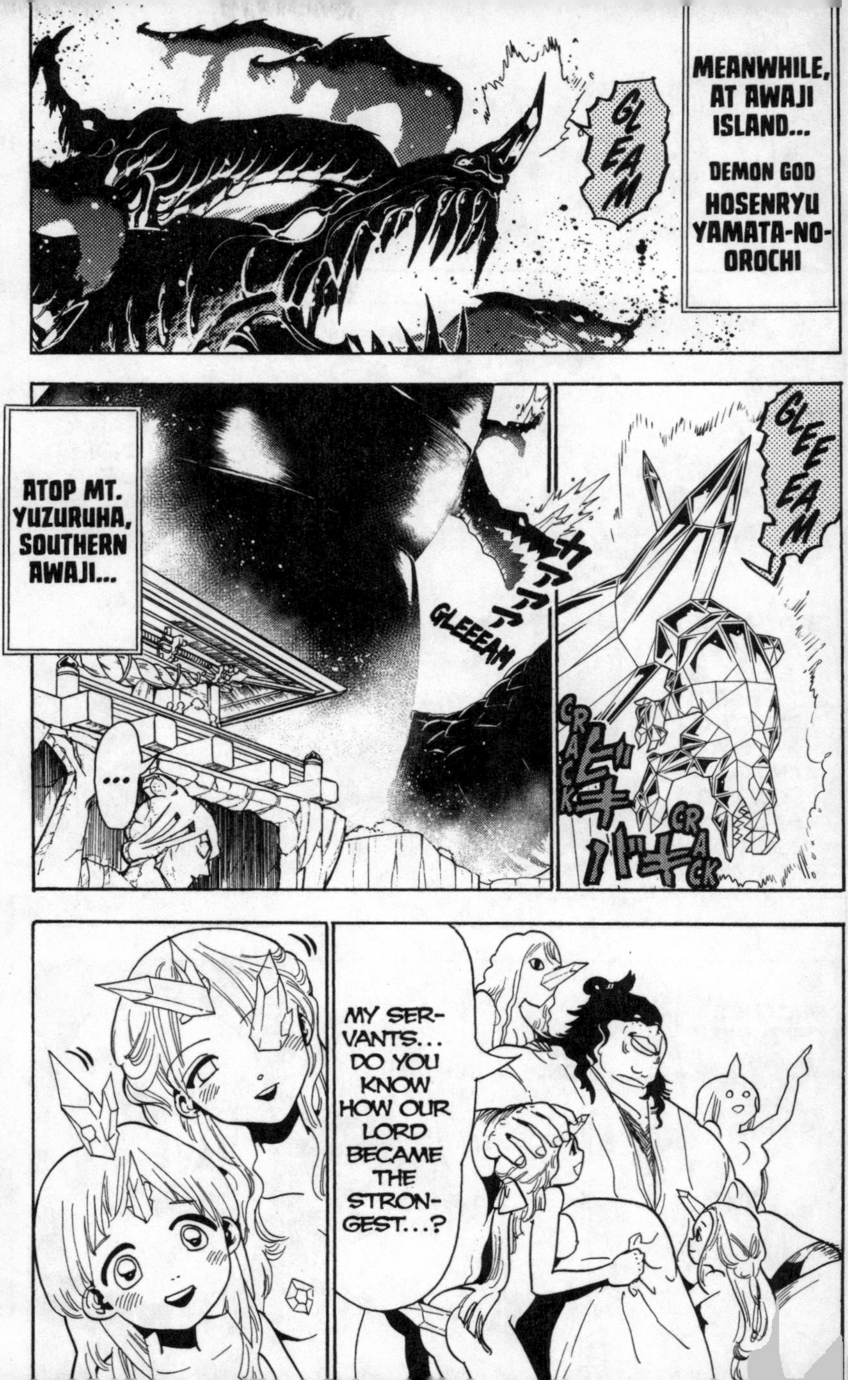
MEANWHILE, AT AWAJI ISLAND...
DEMON GOD
HOSENRYU YAMATA-NO-OROCHI
GLEAM
GLEEEAM
CRACK
CRACK
ATOP MT. YUZURUHA, SOUTHERN AWAJI...
GLEEEAM
...
MY SER-VANTS... DO YOU KNOW HOW OUR LORD BECAME THE STRON-GEST...?

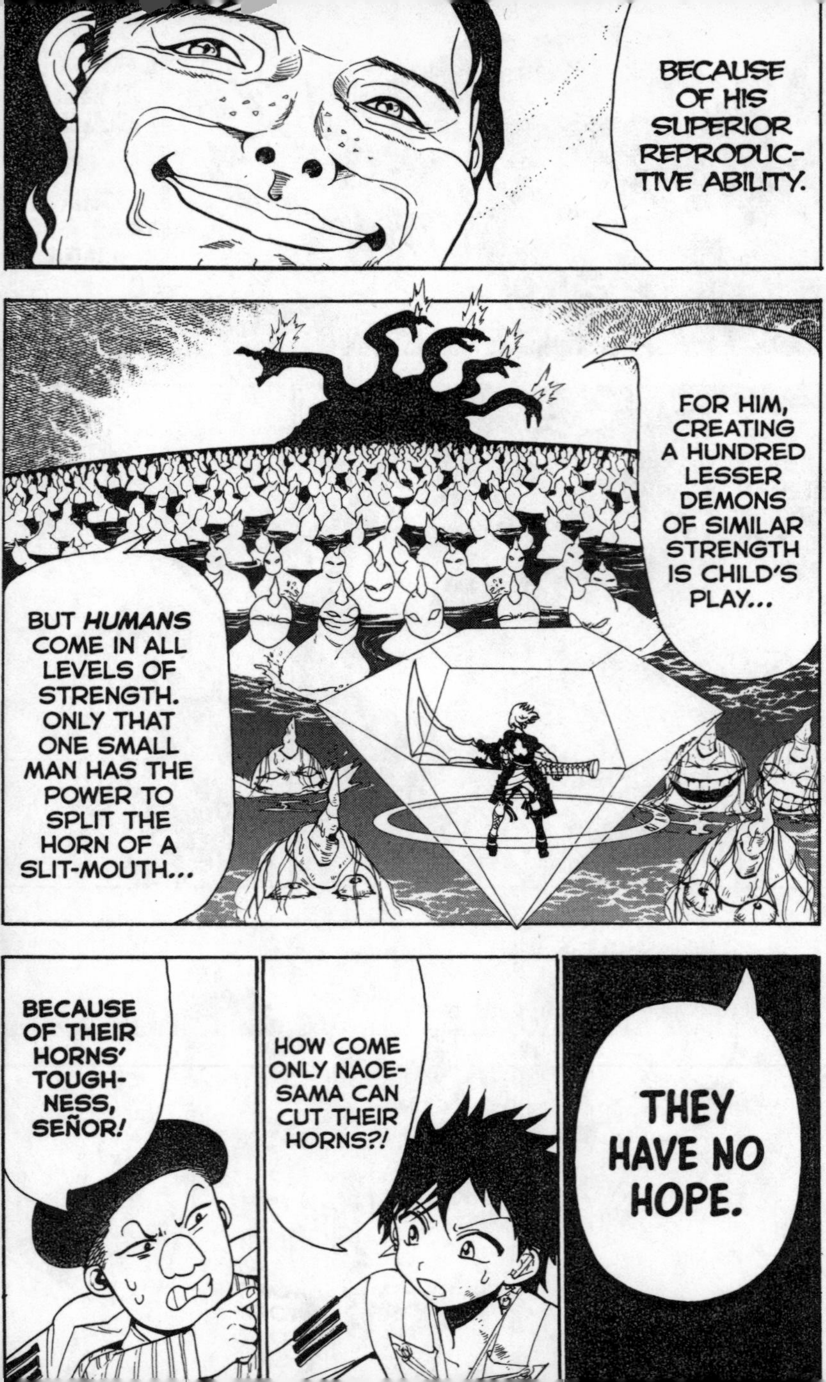
BECAUSE OF HIS SUPERIOR REPRODUC-TIVE ABILITY.
FOR HIM, CREATING A HUNDRED LESSER DEMONS OF SIMILAR STRENGTH IS CHILD'S PLAY...
BUT *HUMANS* COME IN ALL LEVELS OF STRENGTH. ONLY THAT ONE SMALL MAN HAS THE POWER TO SPLIT THE HORN OF A SLIT-MOUTH...
THEY HAVE NO HOPE.
HOW COME ONLY NAOE-SAMA CAN CUT THEIR HORNS?!
BECAUSE OF THEIR HORNS' TOUGH-NESS, SEÑOR!

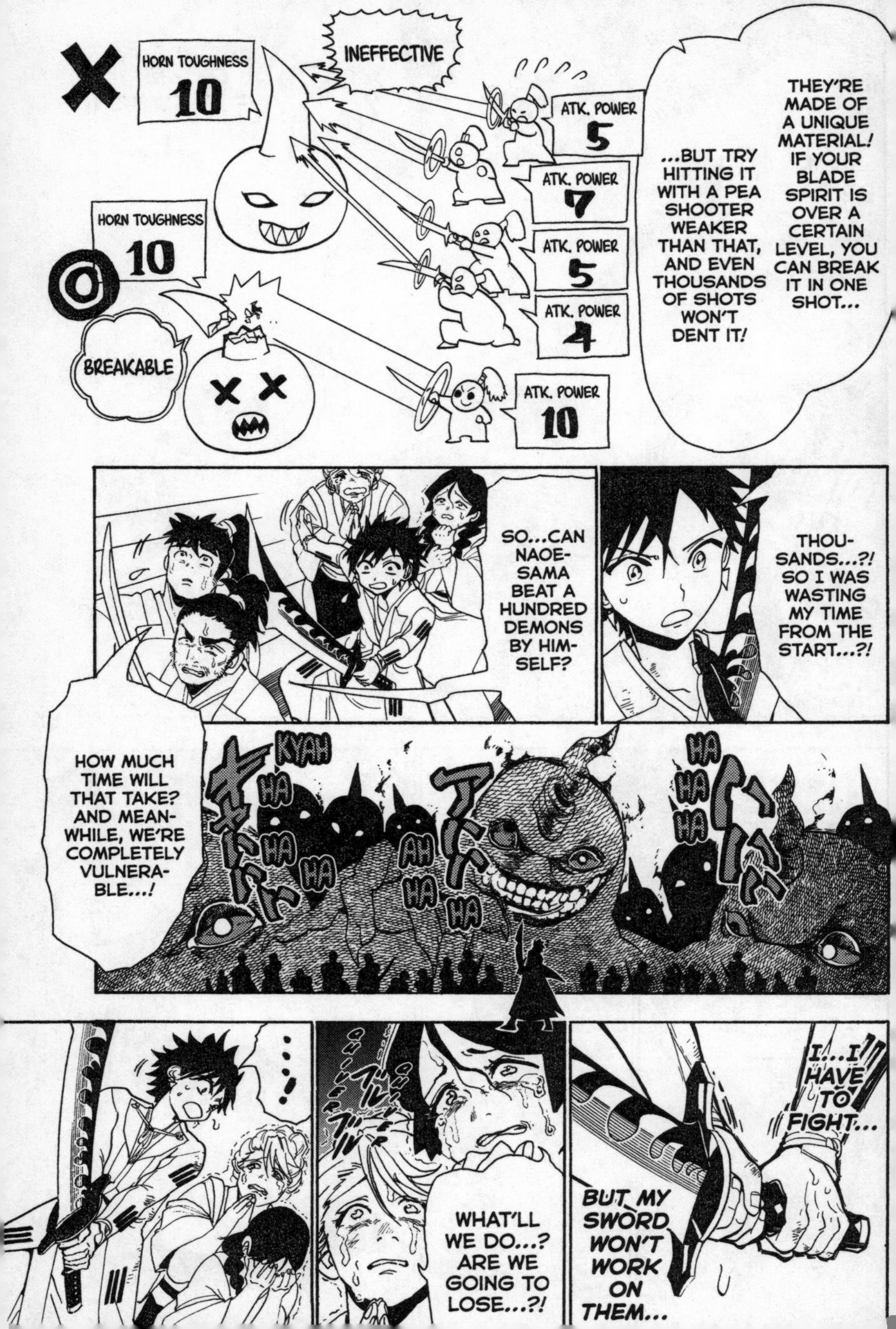
THEY'RE MADE OF A UNIQUE MATERIAL! IF YOUR BLADE SPIRIT IS OVER A CERTAIN LEVEL, YOU CAN BREAK IT IN ONE SHOT...
...BUT TRY HITTING IT WITH A PEA SHOOTER WEAKER THAN THAT, AND EVEN THOUSANDS OF SHOTS WON'T DENT IT!
INEFFECTIVE
HORN TOUGHNESS 10
ATK. POWER 5
ATK. POWER 7
ATK. POWER 5
ATK. POWER 4
HORN TOUGHNESS 10
BREAKABLE
ATK. POWER 10
THOU-SANDS...?! SO I WAS WASTING MY TIME FROM THE START...?!
SO...CAN NAOE-SAMA BEAT A HUNDRED DEMONS BY HIM-SELF?
HA HA HA HA
KYAH HA HA HA
AH HA HA HA
HOW MUCH TIME WILL THAT TAKE? AND MEAN-WHILE, WE'RE COMPLETELY VULNERA-BLE...!
I...I HAVE TO FIGHT...
BUT MY SWORD WON'T WORK ON THEM...
WHAT'LL WE DO...? ARE WE GOING TO LOSE...?!
...!

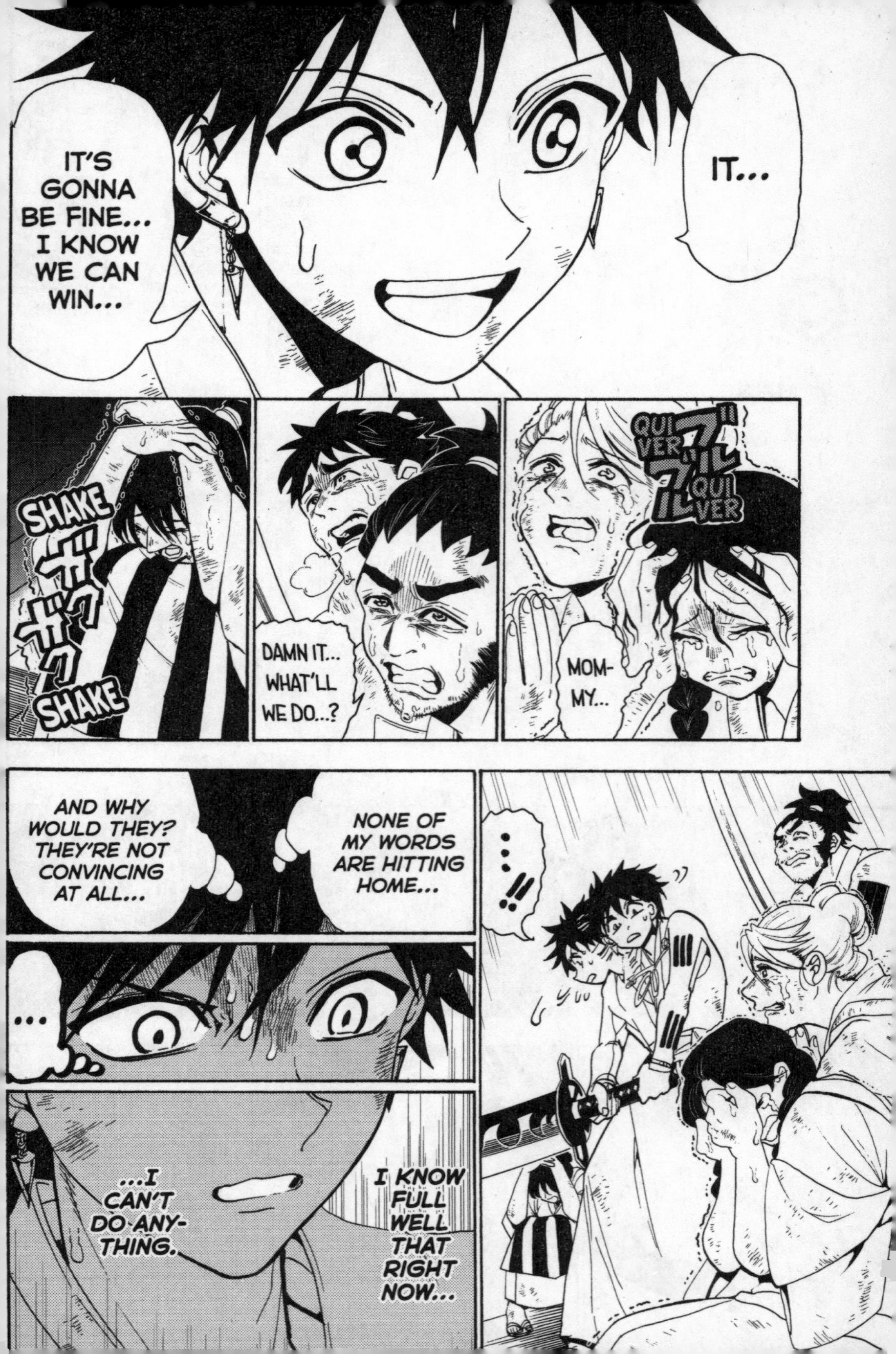

IT...
IT'S GONNA BE FINE... I KNOW WE CAN WIN...
QUIVER QUIVER
MOM-MY...
DAMN IT... WHAT'LL WE DO...?
SHAKE SHAKE
...!!
NONE OF MY WORDS ARE HITTING HOME...
AND WHY WOULD THEY? THEY'RE NOT CONVINCING AT ALL...
...
I KNOW FULL WELL THAT RIGHT NOW...
...I CAN'T DO ANYTHING.

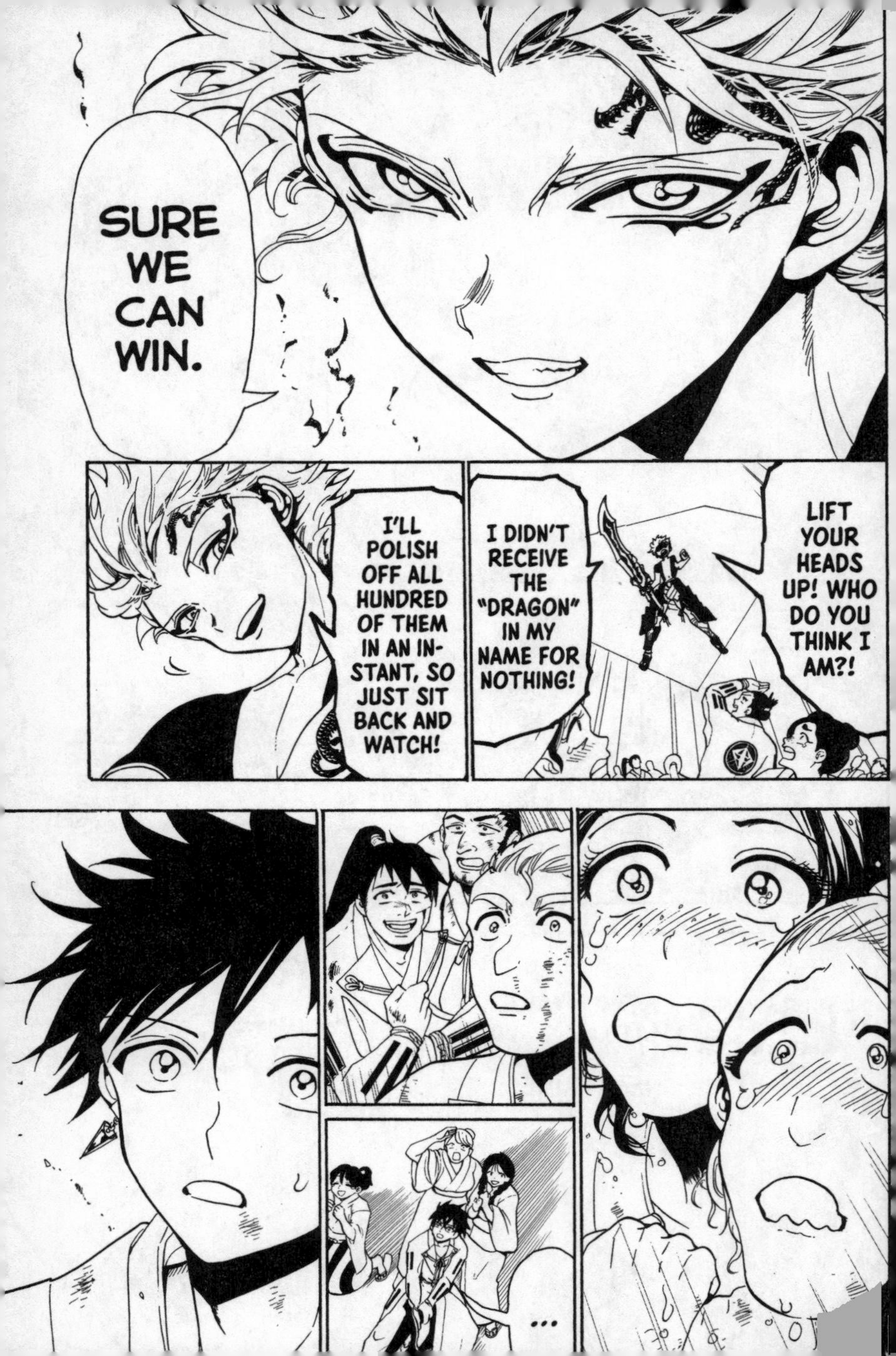
SURE WE CAN WIN.
LIFT YOUR HEADS UP! WHO DO YOU THINK I AM?!
I DIDN'T RECEIVE THE "DRAGON" IN MY NAME FOR NOTHING!
I'LL POLISH OFF ALL HUNDRED OF THEM IN AN IN-STANT, SO JUST SIT BACK AND WATCH!
...

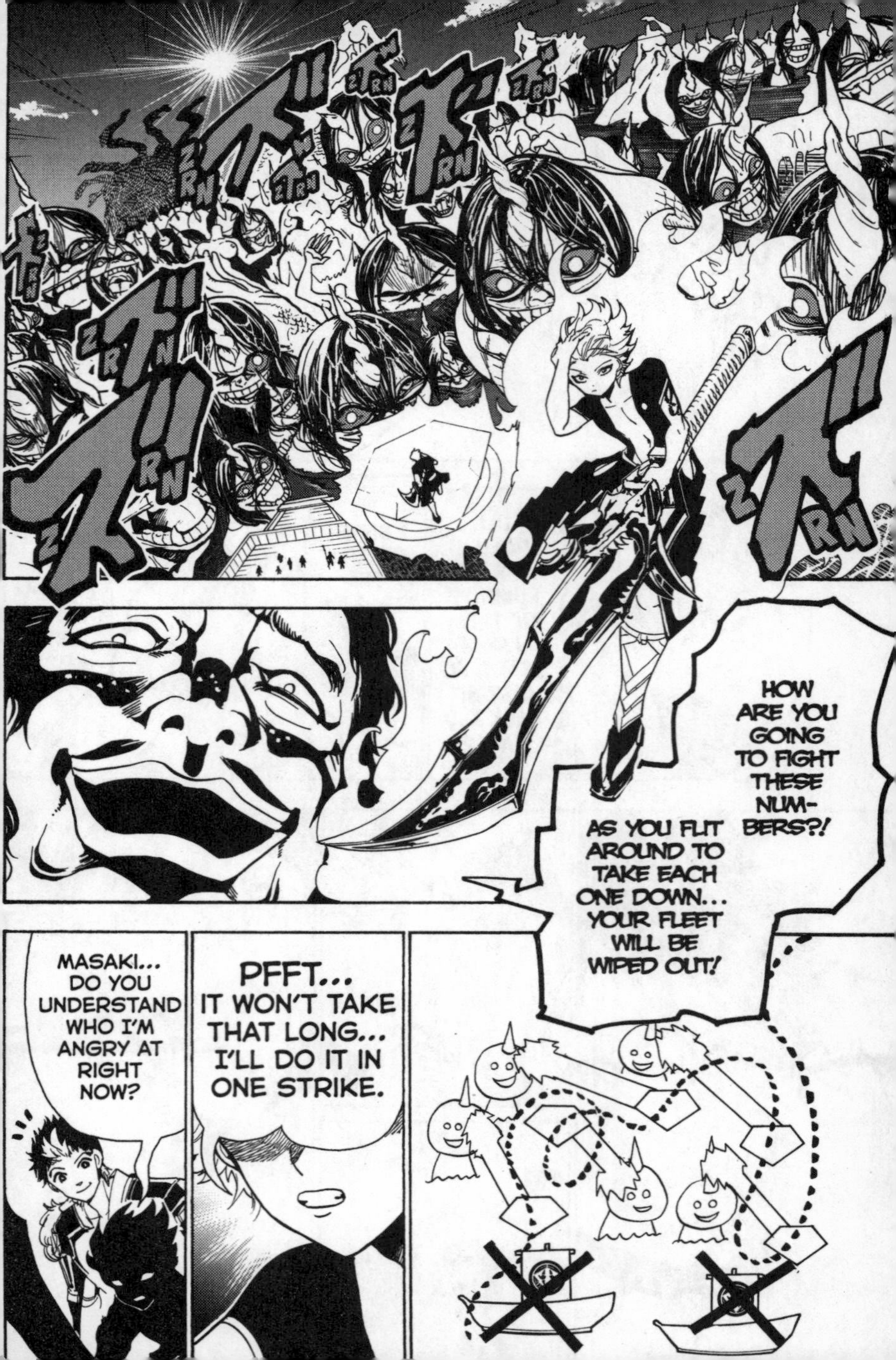
ZRN
ZRN
ZRN
ZRN
ZRN
HOW ARE YOU GOING TO FIGHT THESE NUM-BERS?!
AS YOU FLIT AROUND TO TAKE EACH ONE DOWN... YOUR FLEET WILL BE WIPED OUT!
PFFT... IT WON'T TAKE THAT LONG... I'LL DO IT IN ONE STRIKE.
MASAKI... DO YOU UNDERSTAND WHO I'M ANGRY AT RIGHT NOW?

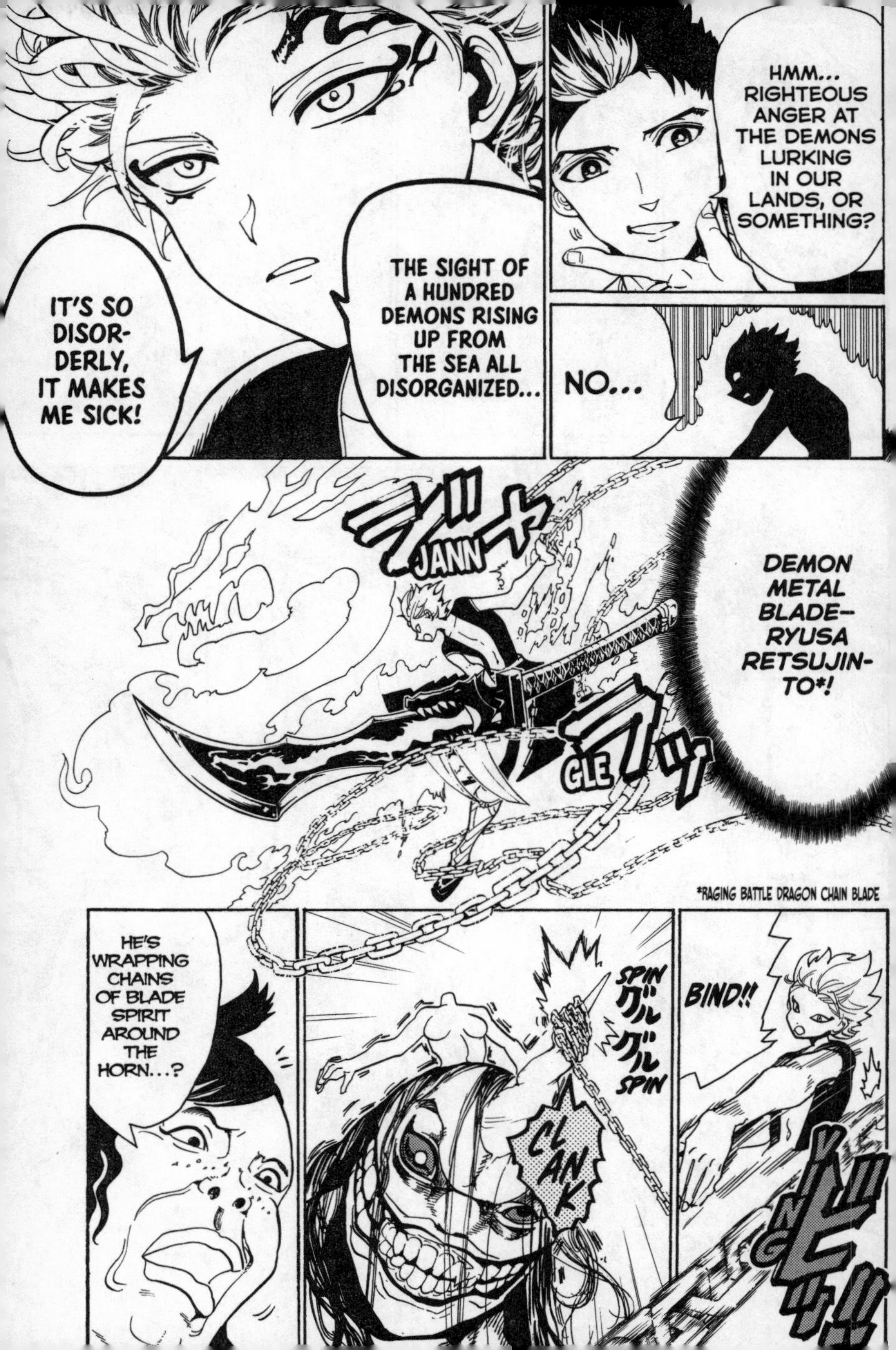

HMM... RIGHTEOUS ANGER AT THE DEMONS LURKING IN OUR LANDS, OR SOMETHING?
NO...
THE SIGHT OF A HUNDRED DEMONS RISING UP FROM THE SEA ALL DISORGANIZED...
IT'S SO DISORDERLY, IT MAKES ME SICK!
DEMON METAL BLADE-- RYUSA RETSUJIN-TO*!
JANN
GLE
*RAGING BATTLE DRAGON CHAIN BLADE
BIND!!
ZING
SPIN
SPIN
CLANK
HE'S WRAPPING CHAINS OF BLADE SPIRIT AROUND THE HORN...?

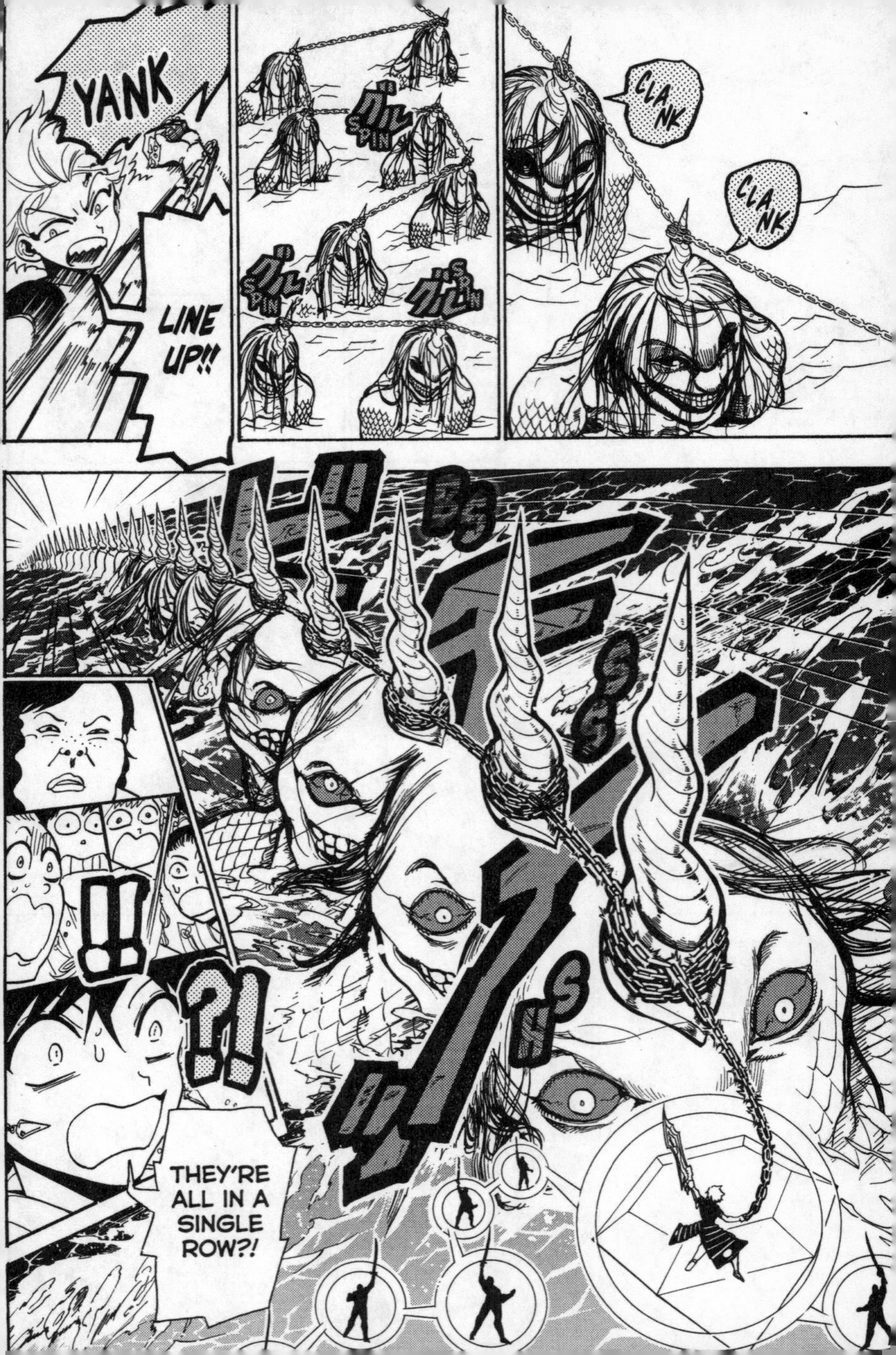

CLANK
CLANK
SPIN
SPIN
SPIN
YANK
LINE UP!!
!!
?!
THEY'RE ALL IN A SINGLE ROW?!

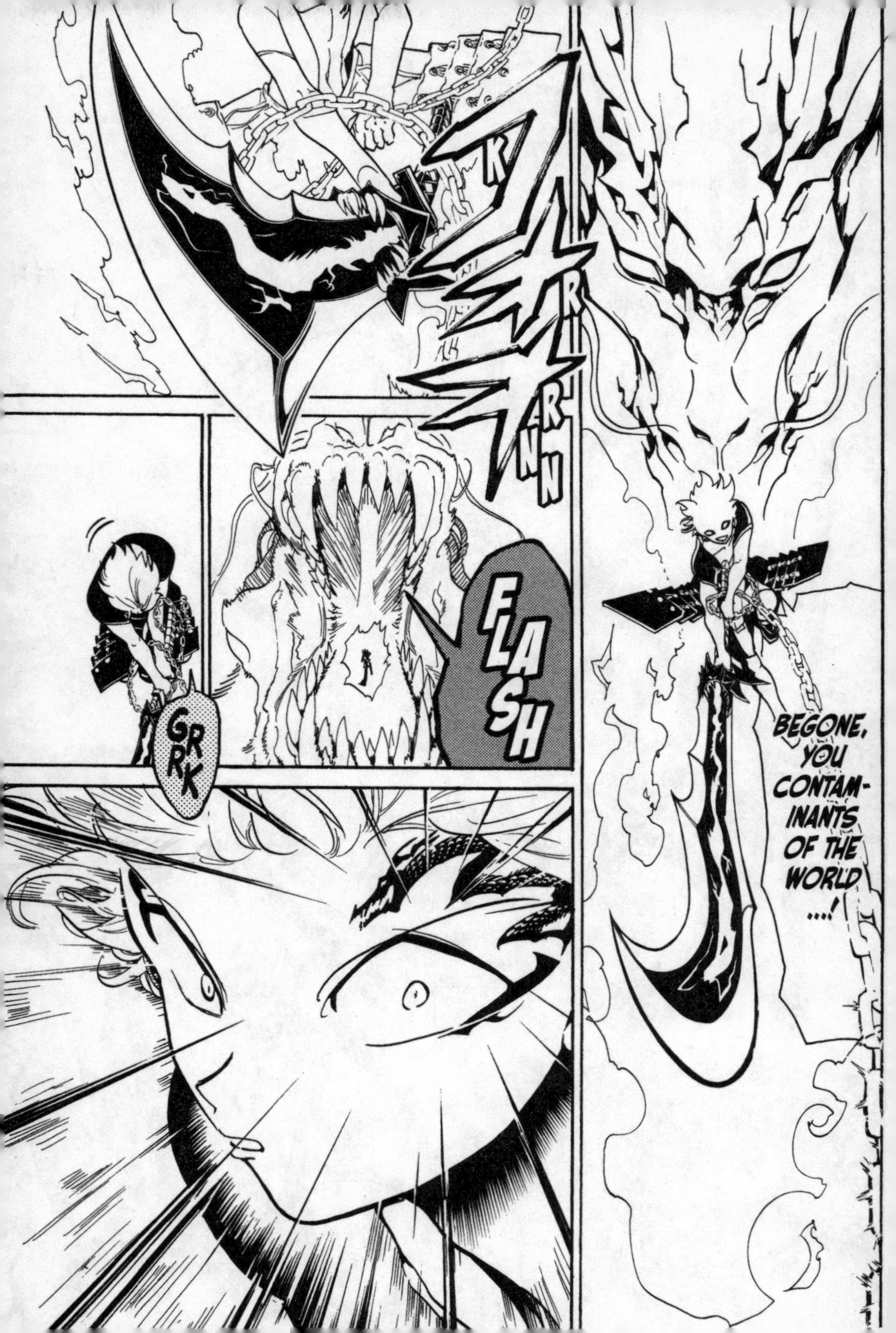
BEGONE, YOU CONTAM-INANTS OF THE WORLD...!
KRRNN
FLASH
GRRK

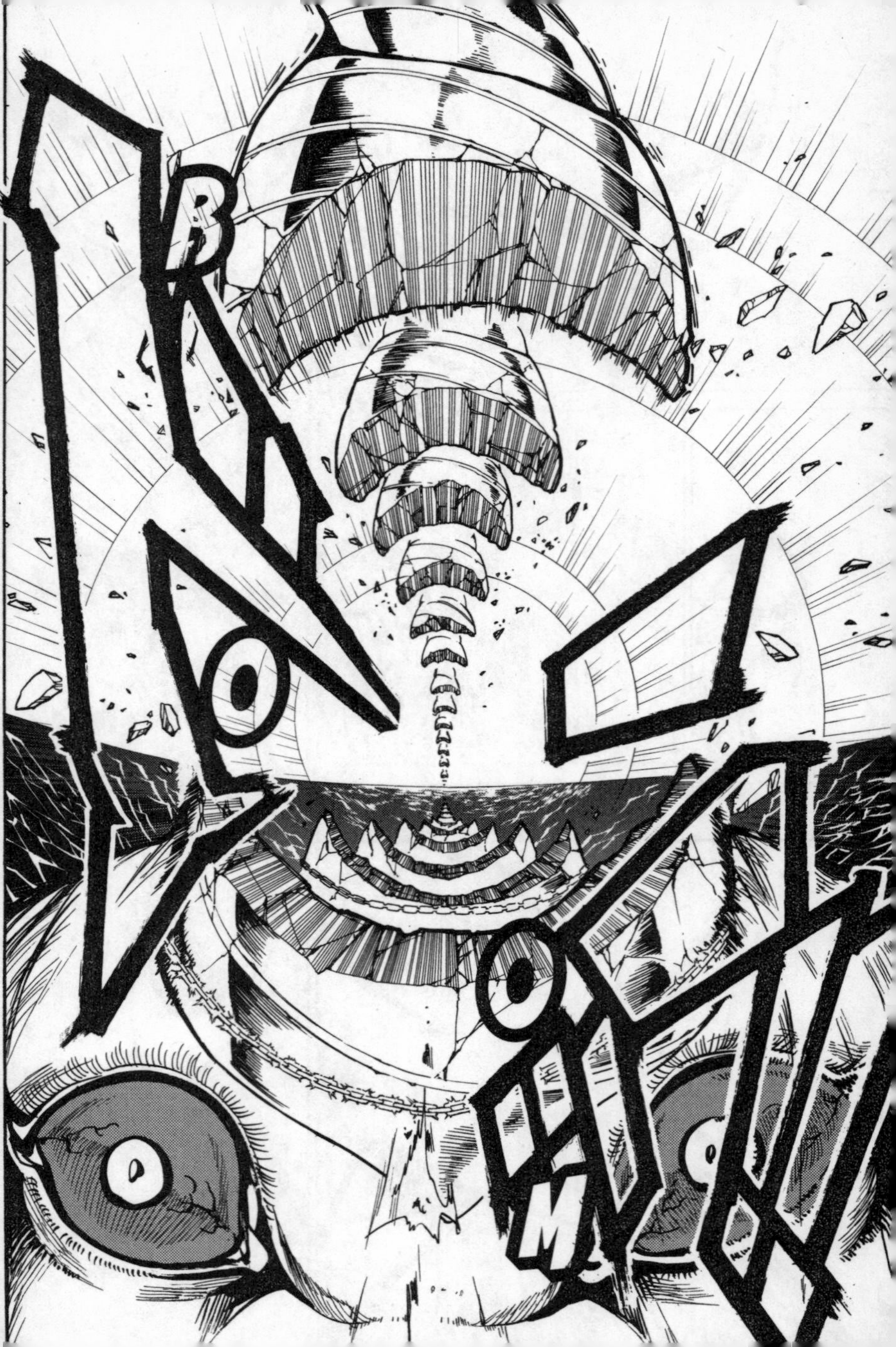

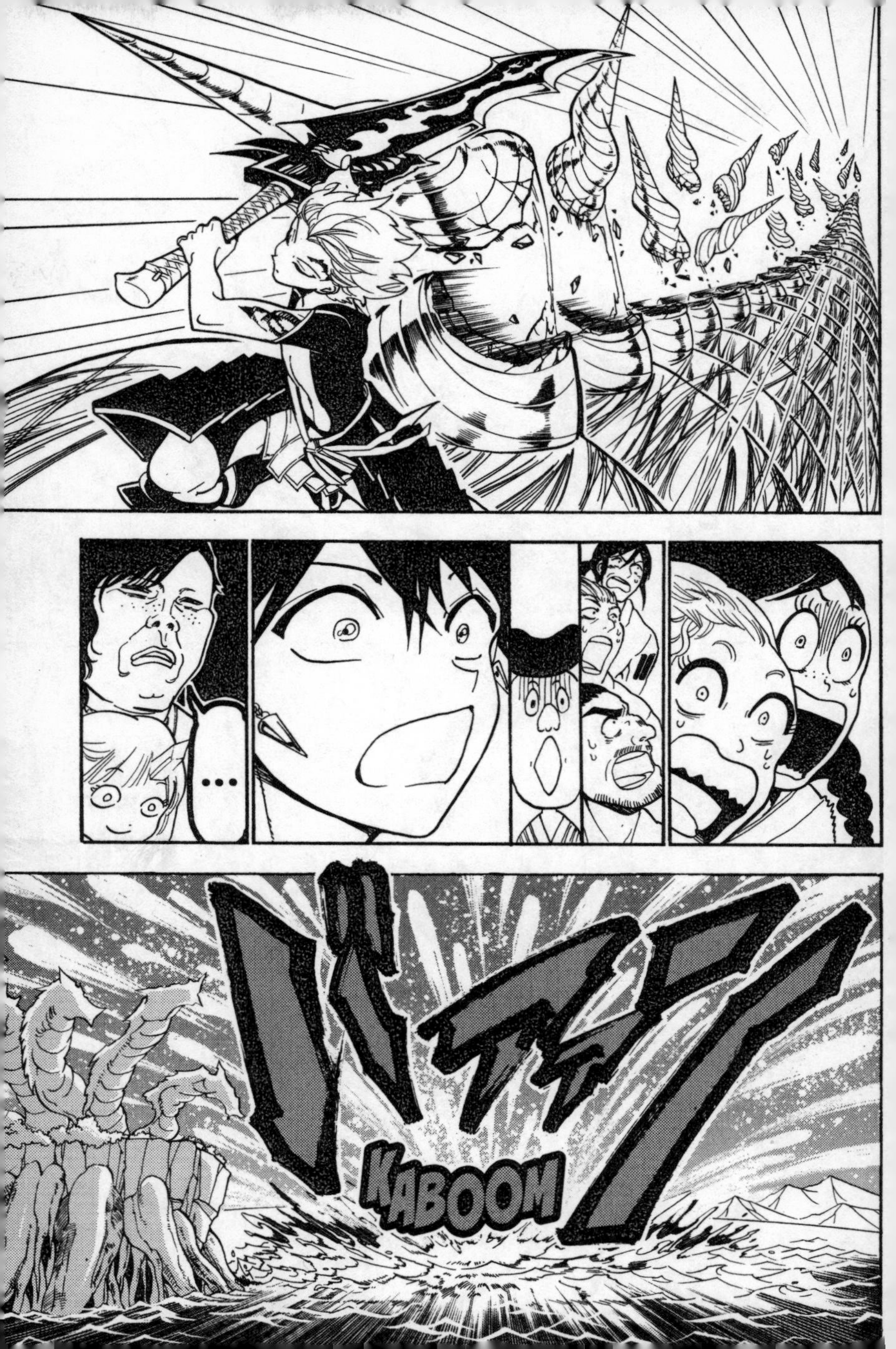
...
KABOOM

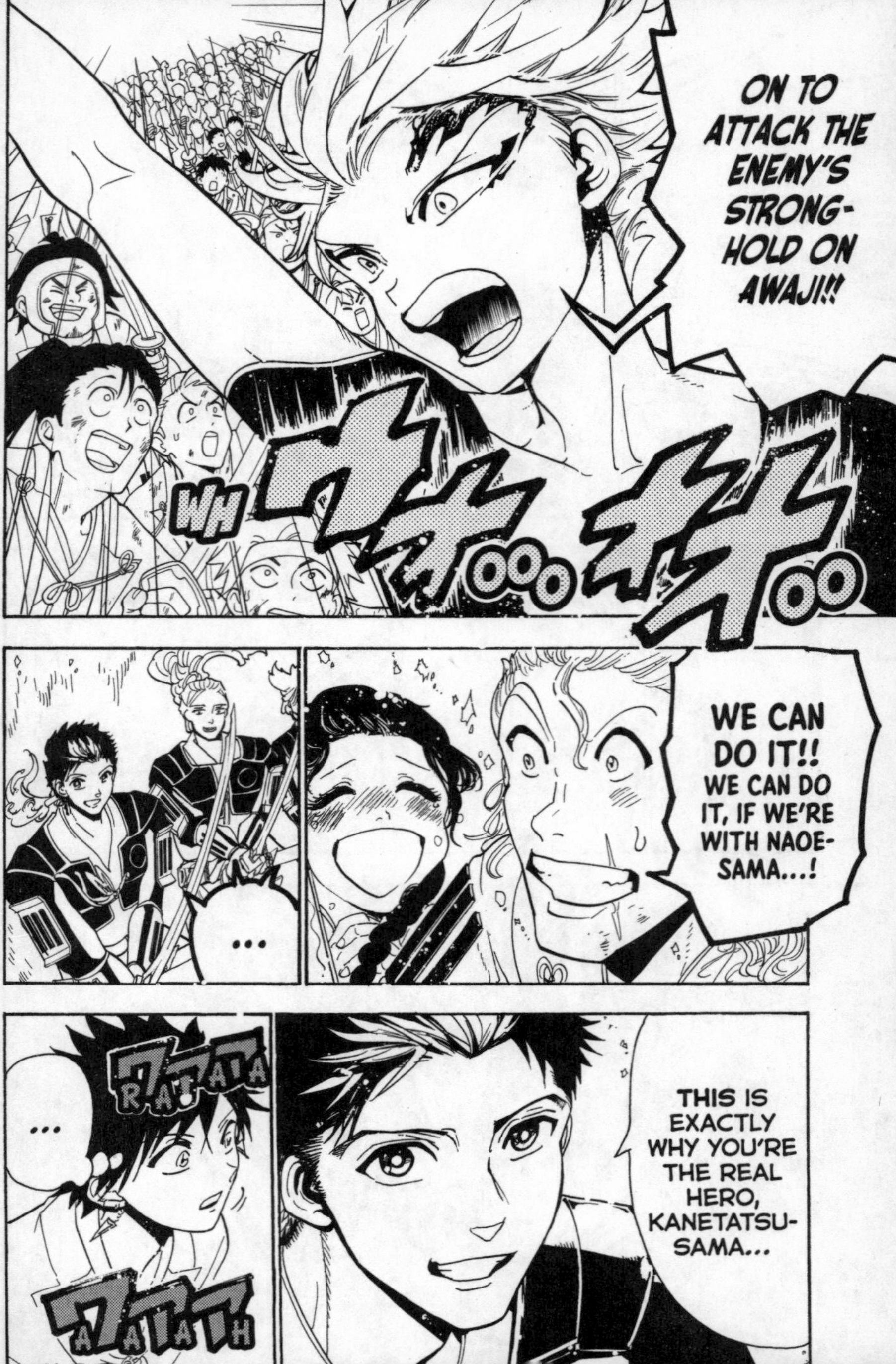
ON TO ATTACK THE ENEMY'S STRONGHOLD ON AWAJI!!
WH OOO OO
WE CAN DO IT!! WE CAN DO IT, IF WE'RE WITH NAOE-SAMA...!
...
THIS IS EXACTLY WHY YOU'RE THE REAL HERO, KANETATSU-SAMA...
RATATA
...
AAATATH

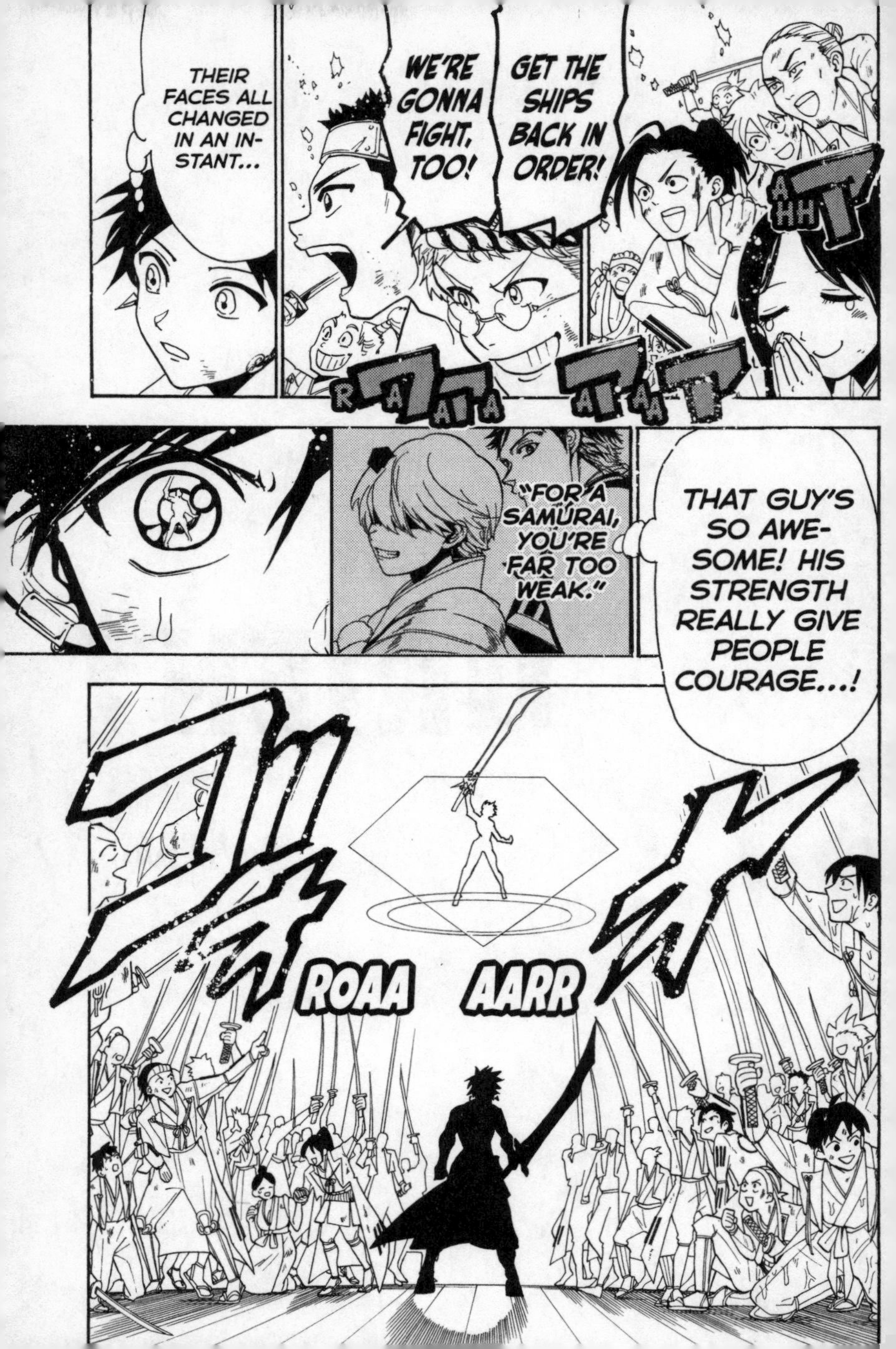
GET THE SHIPS BACK IN ORDER!
WE'RE GONNA FIGHT, TOO!
AHHH
THEIR FACES ALL CHANGED IN AN INSTANT...
RAAAA AAAT
THAT GUY'S SO AWESOME! HIS STRENGTH REALLY GIVE PEOPLE COURAGE...!
"FOR A SAMURAI, YOU'RE FAR TOO WEAK."
ROAA AARR

ORIENT

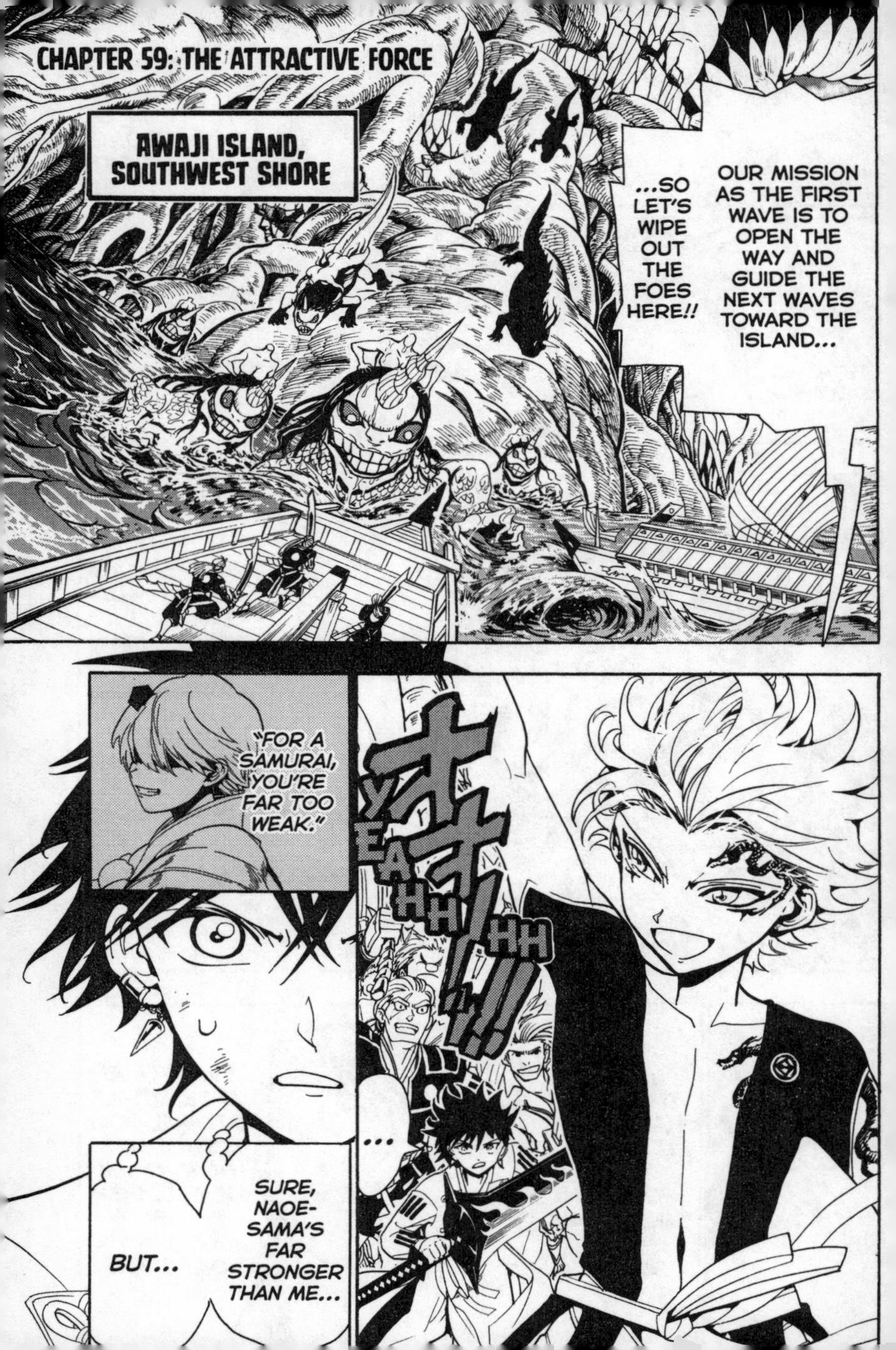
CHAPTER 59: THE ATTRACTIVE FORCE
AWAJI ISLAND, SOUTHWEST SHORE
OUR MISSION AS THE FIRST WAVE IS TO OPEN THE WAY AND GUIDE THE NEXT WAVES TOWARD THE ISLAND...
...SO LET'S WIPE OUT THE FOES HERE!!
YEAHHHH!!
"FOR A SAMURAI, YOU'RE FAR TOO WEAK."
...
SURE, NAOE-SAMA'S FAR STRONGER THAN ME...
BUT...

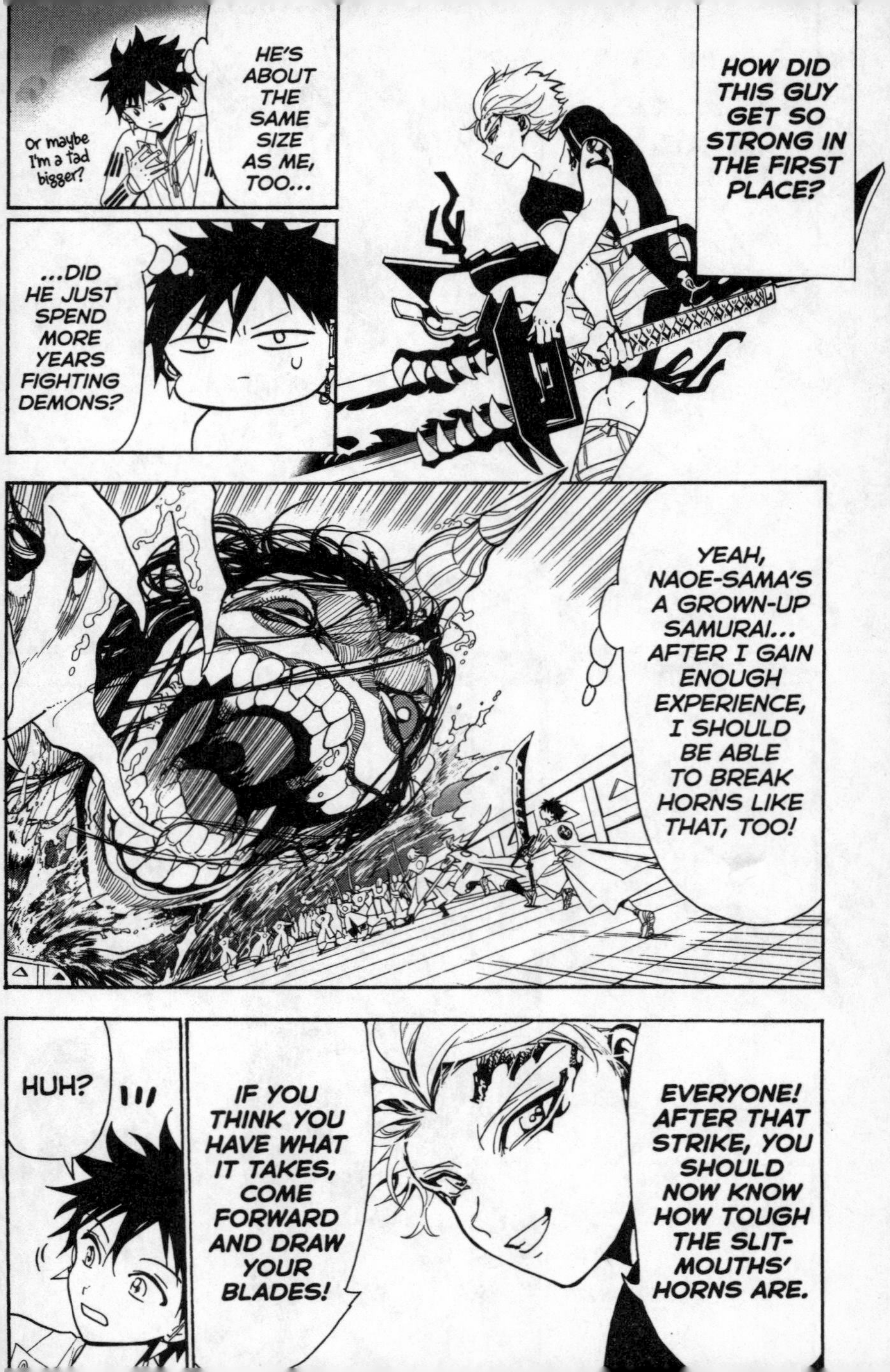
HOW DID THIS GUY GET SO STRONG IN THE FIRST PLACE?
HE'S ABOUT THE SAME SIZE AS ME, TOO...
Or maybe I'm a tad bigger?
...DID HE JUST SPEND MORE YEARS FIGHTING DEMONS?
YEAH, NAOE-SAMA'S A GROWN-UP SAMURAI... AFTER I GAIN ENOUGH EXPERIENCE, I SHOULD BE ABLE TO BREAK HORNS LIKE THAT, TOO!
EVERYONE! AFTER THAT STRIKE, YOU SHOULD NOW KNOW HOW TOUGH THE SLIT-MOUTHS' HORNS ARE.
IF YOU THINK YOU HAVE WHAT IT TAKES, COME FORWARD AND DRAW YOUR BLADES!
HUH?

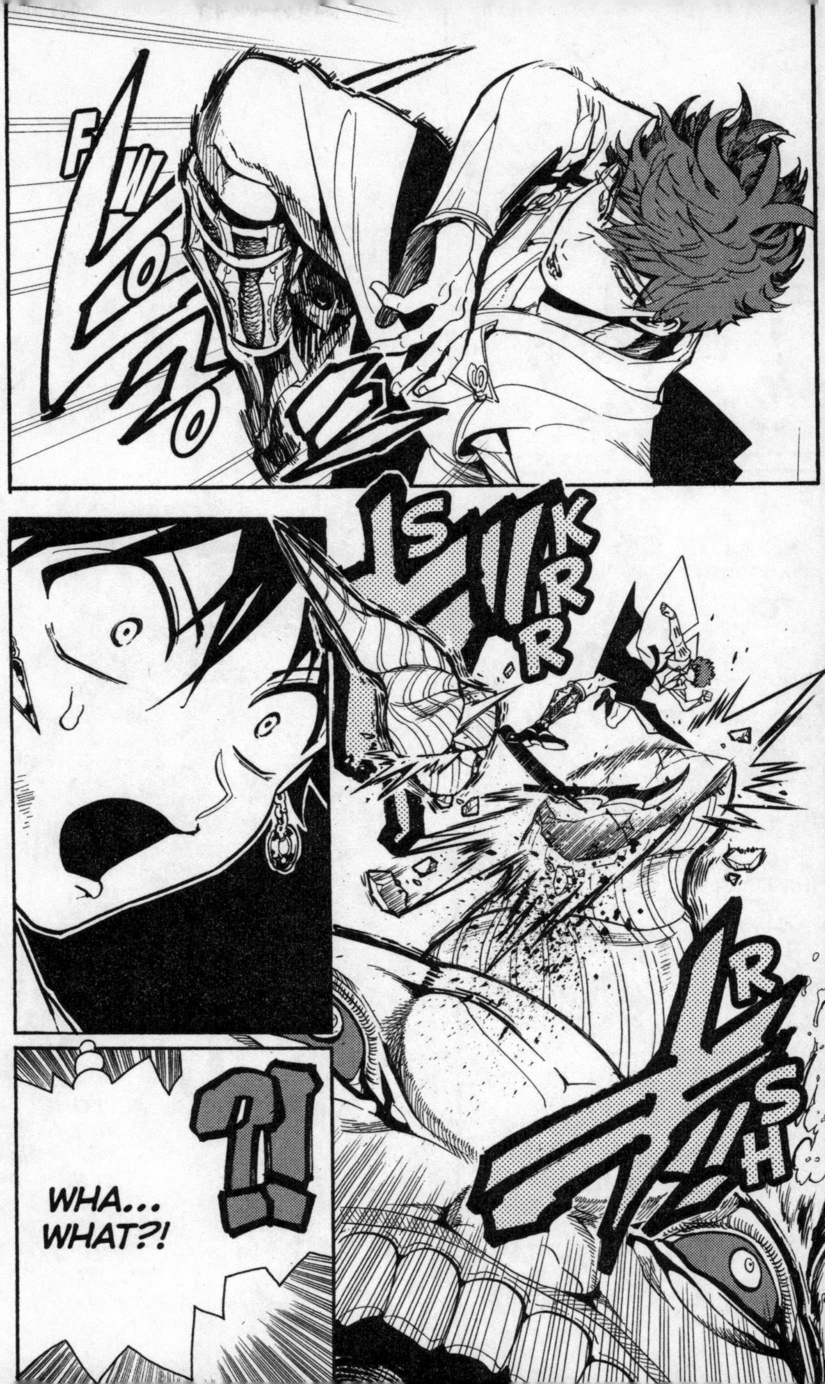
FWOOSH
SKRR
RSH
?!
WHA...
WHAT?!

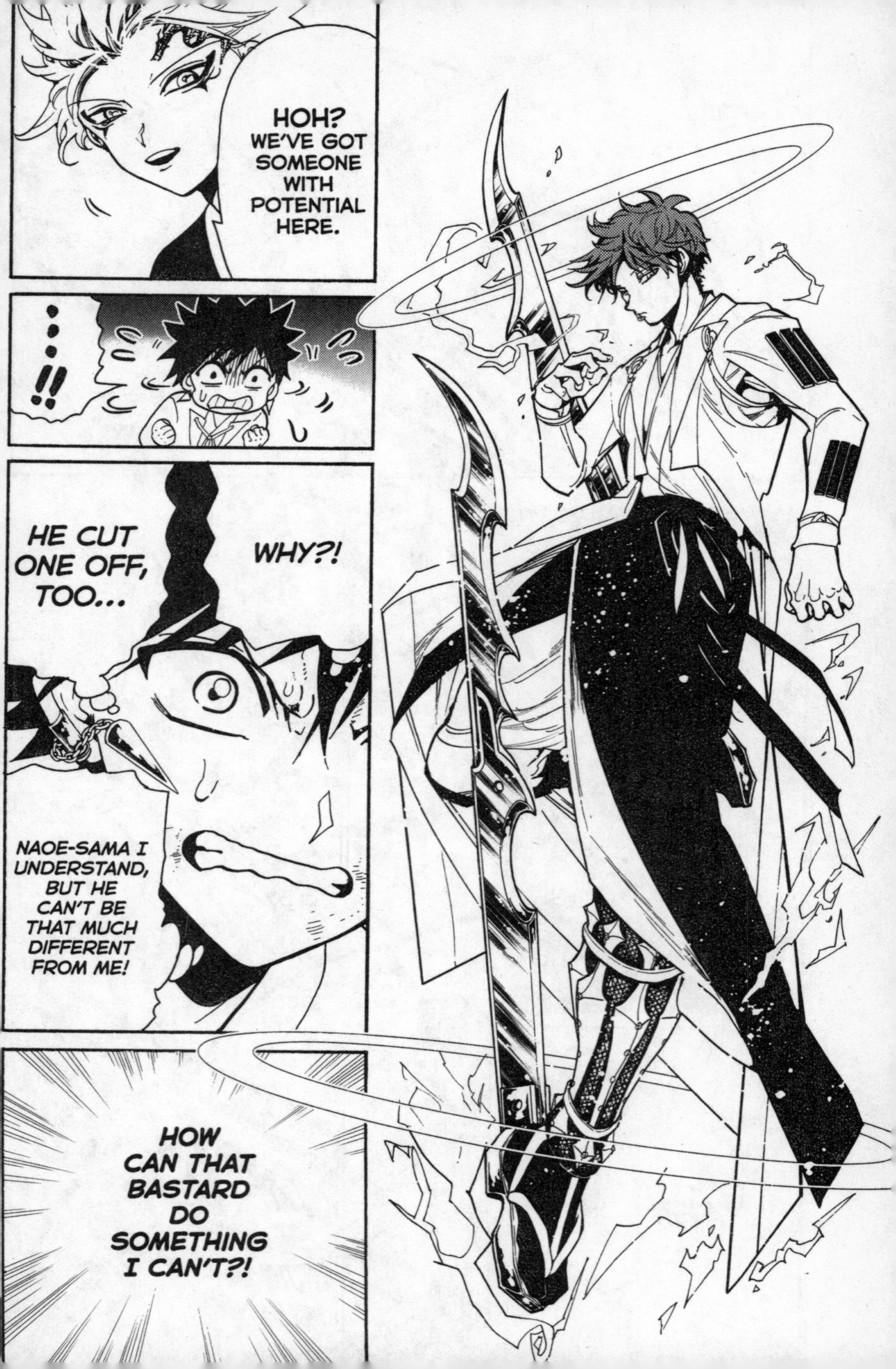
HOH? WE'VE GOT SOMEONE WITH POTENTIAL HERE.
...!!
WHY?!
HE CUT ONE OFF, TOO...
NAOE-SAMA I UNDERSTAND, BUT HE CAN'T BE THAT MUCH DIFFERENT FROM ME!
HOW CAN THAT BASTARD DO SOMETHING I CAN'T?!

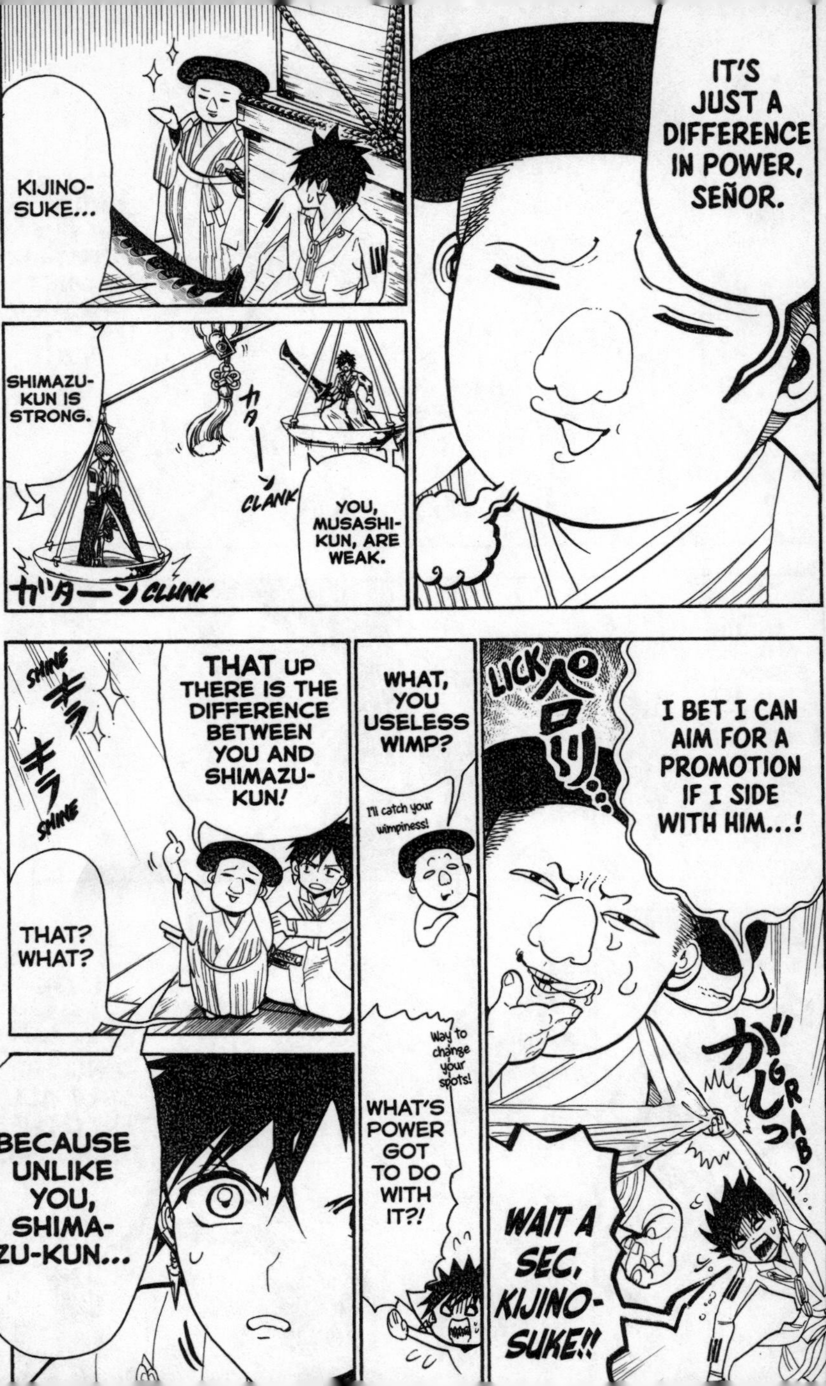
IT'S JUST A DIFFERENCE IN POWER, SEÑOR.
KIJINO-SUKE...
SHIMAZU-KUN IS STRONG.
カタ— CLANK
YOU, MUSASHI-KUN, ARE WEAK.
ガターン CLUNK
I BET I CAN AIM FOR A PROMOTION IF I SIDE WITH HIM...!
ペロリ LICK
がしっ GRAB
WAIT A SEC, KIJINO-SUKE!!
WHAT, YOU USELESS WIMP?
I'll catch your wimpiness!
Way to change your spots!
WHAT'S POWER GOT TO DO WITH IT?!
THAT UP THERE IS THE DIFFERENCE BETWEEN YOU AND SHIMAZU-KUN!
キラ SHINE
キラ SHINE
THAT? WHAT?
BECAUSE UNLIKE YOU, SHIMA-ZU-KUN...

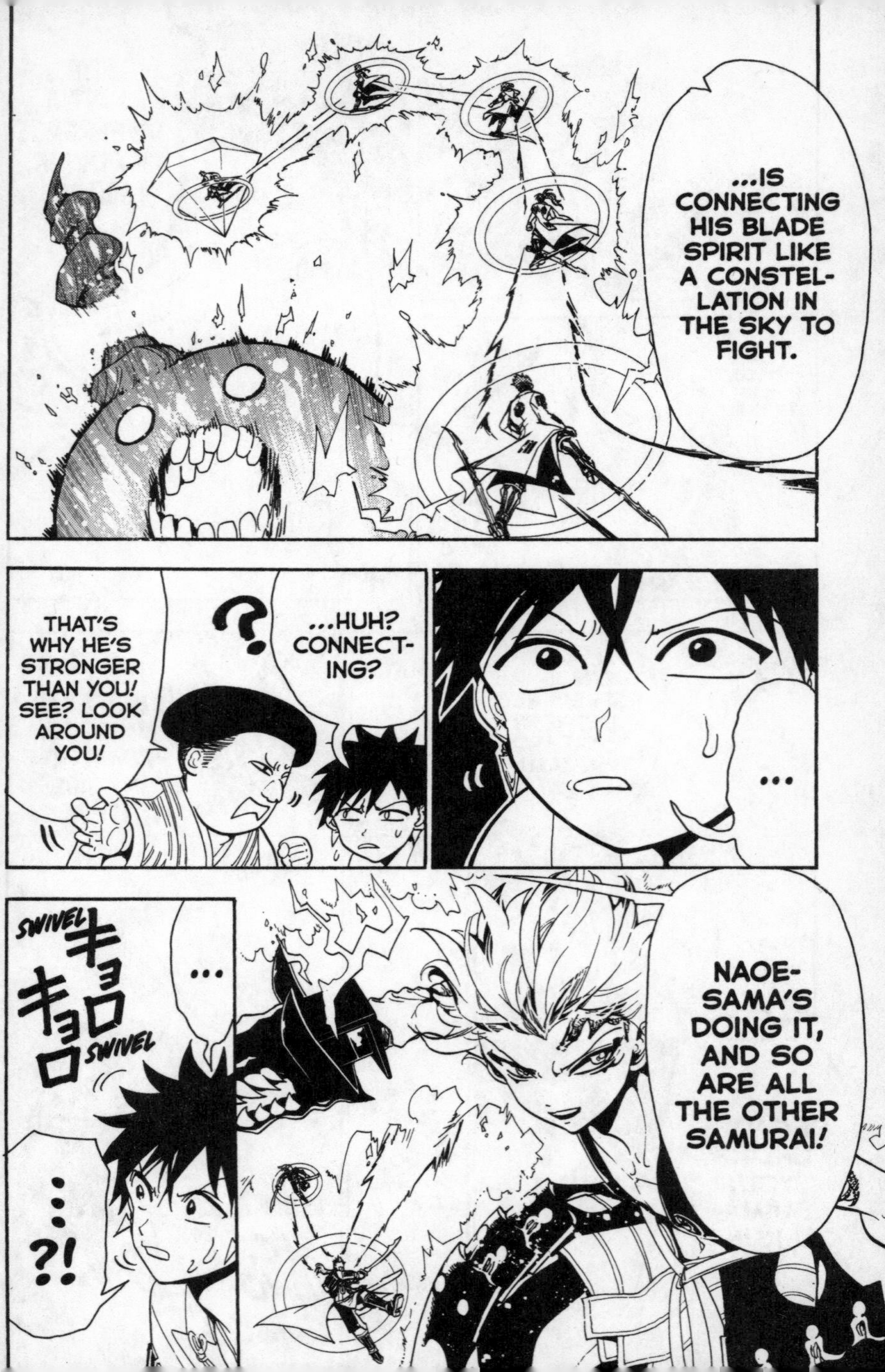
...IS CONNECTING HIS BLADE SPIRIT LIKE A CONSTEL-LATION IN THE SKY TO FIGHT.
...
...HUH? CONNECT-ING?
?
THAT'S WHY HE'S STRONGER THAN YOU! SEE? LOOK AROUND YOU!
NAOE-SAMA'S DOING IT, AND SO ARE ALL THE OTHER SAMURAI!
SWIVEL キョロ
キョロ SWIVEL
...
...?!

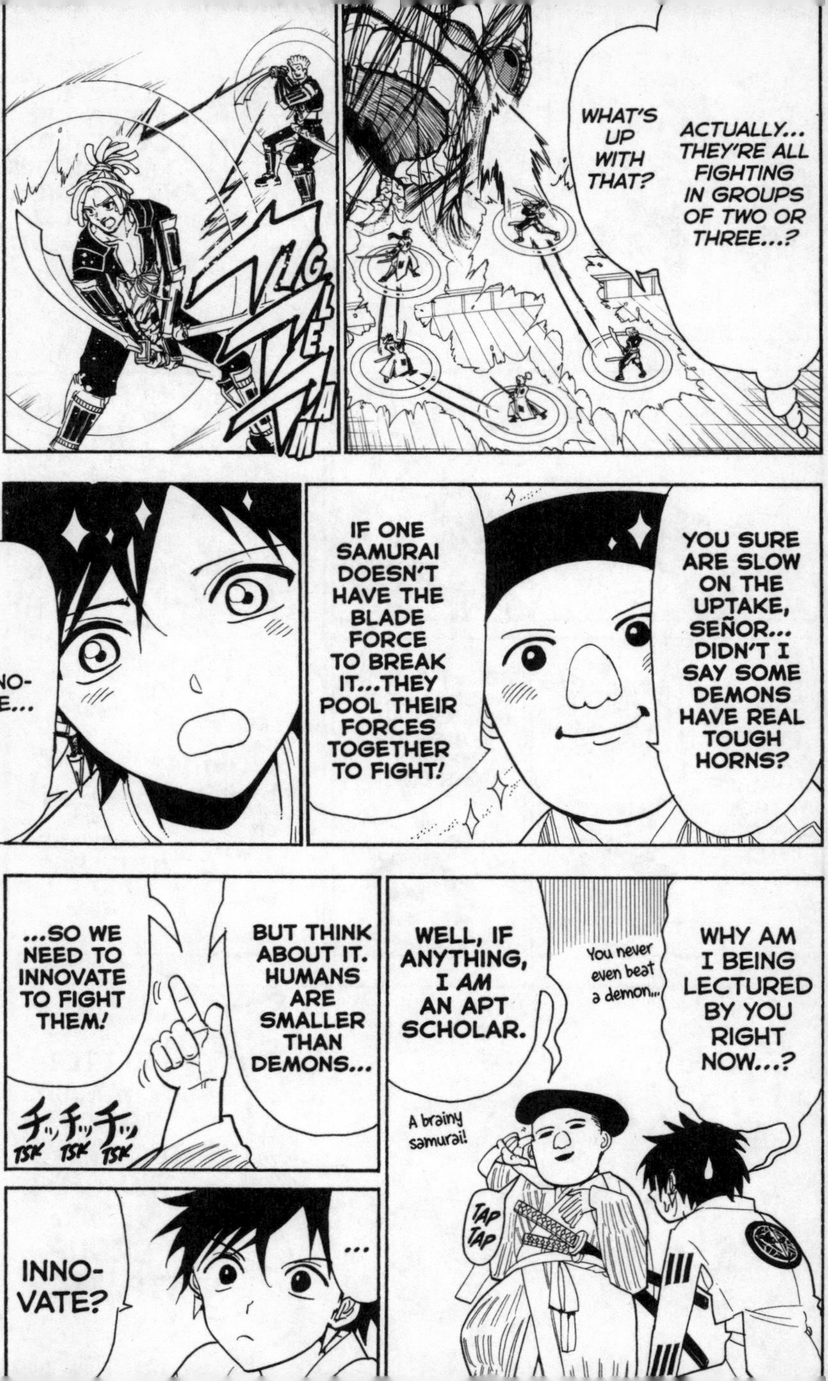
ACTUALLY... THEY'RE ALL FIGHTING IN GROUPS OF TWO OR THREE...?
WHAT'S UP WITH THAT?
YOU SURE ARE SLOW ON THE UPTAKE, SEÑOR... DIDN'T I SAY SOME DEMONS HAVE REAL TOUGH HORNS?
IF ONE SAMURAI DOESN'T HAVE THE BLADE FORCE TO BREAK IT...THEY POOL THEIR FORCES TOGETHER TO FIGHT!
KIJINO-SUKE...
WHY AM I BEING LECTURED BY YOU RIGHT NOW...?
You never even beat a demon...
WELL, IF ANYTHING, I *AM* AN APT SCHOLAR.
A brainy samurai!
TAP TAP
BUT THINK ABOUT IT. HUMANS ARE SMALLER THAN DEMONS...
...SO WE NEED TO INNOVATE TO FIGHT THEM!
チッチッチッ
TSK TSK TSK
...
INNO-VATE?

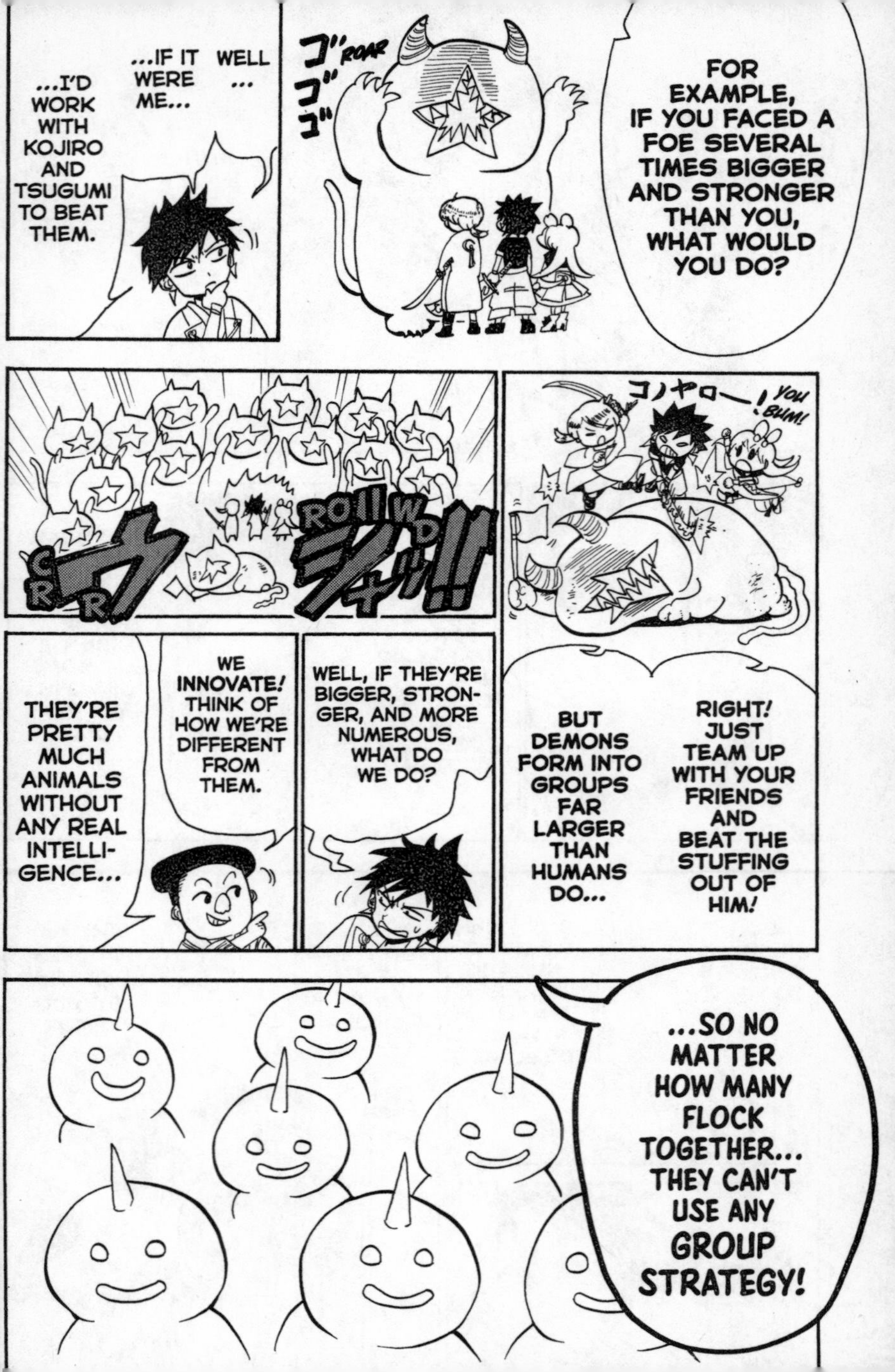
ゴゴゴ ROAR
FOR EXAMPLE, IF YOU FACED A FOE SEVERAL TIMES BIGGER AND STRONGER THAN YOU, WHAT WOULD YOU DO?
WELL ...
...IF IT WERE ME...
...I'D WORK WITH KOJIRO AND TSUGUMI TO BEAT THEM.
コノヤロー! YOU BUM!
RIGHT! JUST TEAM UP WITH YOUR FRIENDS AND BEAT THE STUFFING OUT OF HIM!
BUT DEMONS FORM INTO GROUPS FAR LARGER THAN HUMANS DO...
シャッ!! ROWD
CRR
WELL, IF THEY'RE BIGGER, STRONGER, AND MORE NUMEROUS, WHAT DO WE DO?
WE INNOVATE! THINK OF HOW WE'RE DIFFERENT FROM THEM.
THEY'RE PRETTY MUCH ANIMALS WITHOUT ANY REAL INTELLIGENCE...
...SO NO MATTER HOW MANY FLOCK TOGETHER... THEY CAN'T USE ANY GROUP STRATEGY!

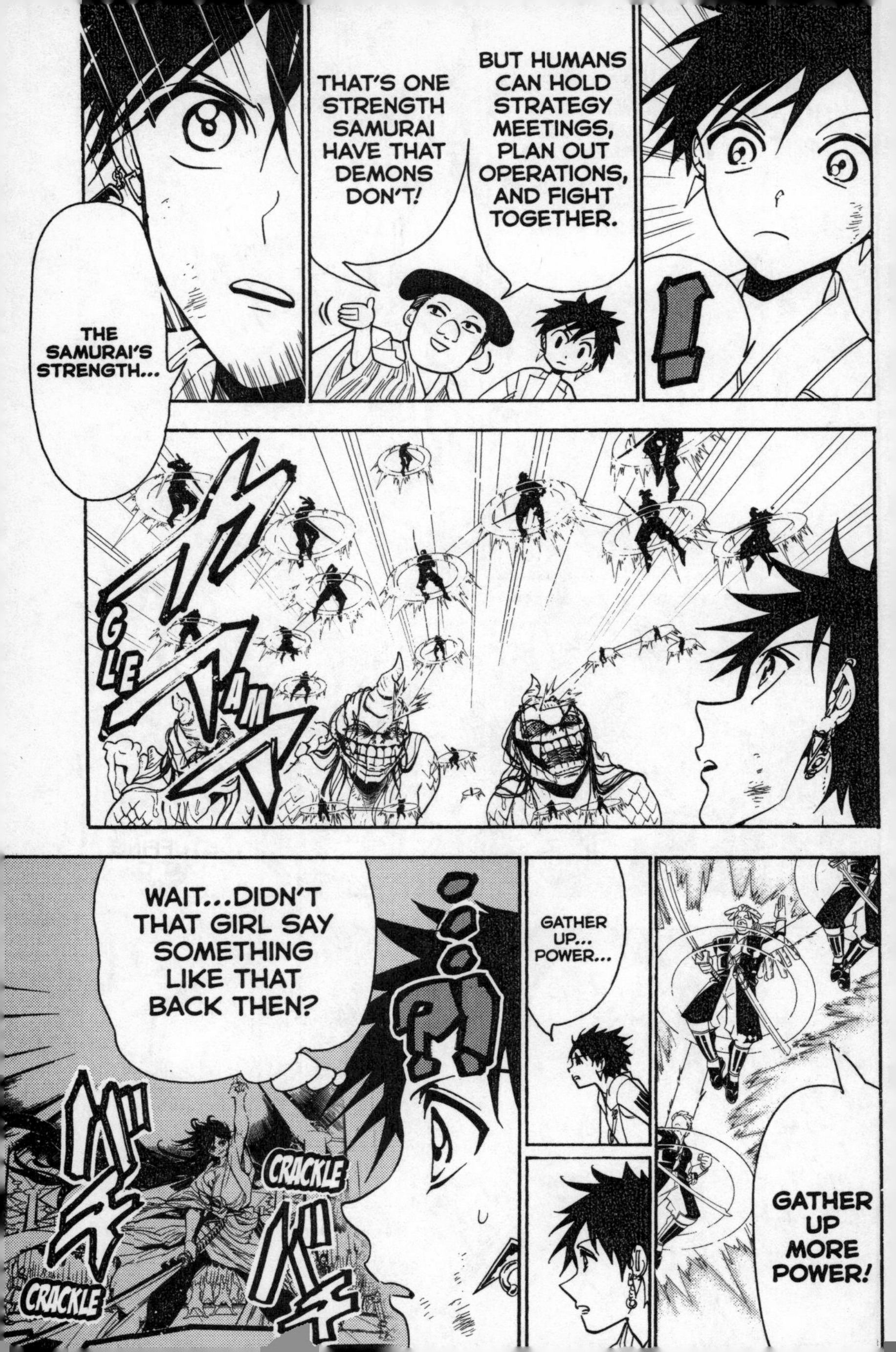
BUT HUMANS CAN HOLD STRATEGY MEETINGS, PLAN OUT OPERATIONS, AND FIGHT TOGETHER.
THAT'S ONE STRENGTH SAMURAI HAVE THAT DEMONS DON'T!
THE SAMURAI'S STRENGTH...
GLEAM
GATHER UP MORE POWER!
GATHER UP... POWER...
WAIT...DIDN'T THAT GIRL SAY SOMETHING LIKE THAT BACK THEN?
CRACKLE
CRACKLE

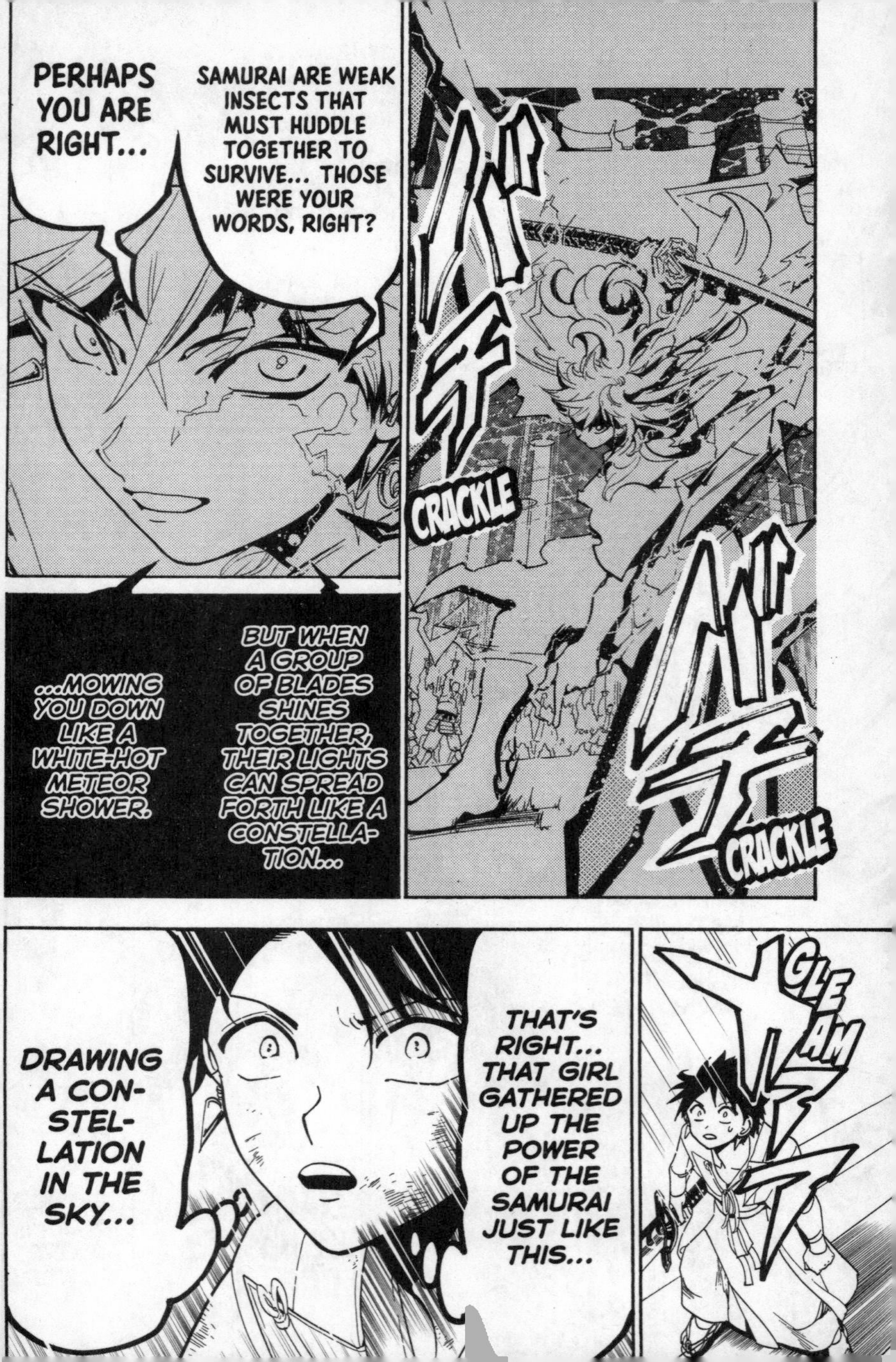
CRACKLE
CRACKLE
SAMURAI ARE WEAK INSECTS THAT MUST HUDDLE TOGETHER TO SURVIVE... THOSE WERE YOUR WORDS, RIGHT?
PERHAPS YOU ARE RIGHT...
BUT WHEN A GROUP OF BLADES SHINES TOGETHER, THEIR LIGHTS CAN SPREAD FORTH LIKE A CONSTELLATION...
...MOWING YOU DOWN LIKE A WHITE-HOT METEOR SHOWER.
GLEAM
THAT'S RIGHT... THAT GIRL GATHERED UP THE POWER OF THE SAMURAI JUST LIKE THIS...
DRAWING A CONSTELLATION IN THE SKY...

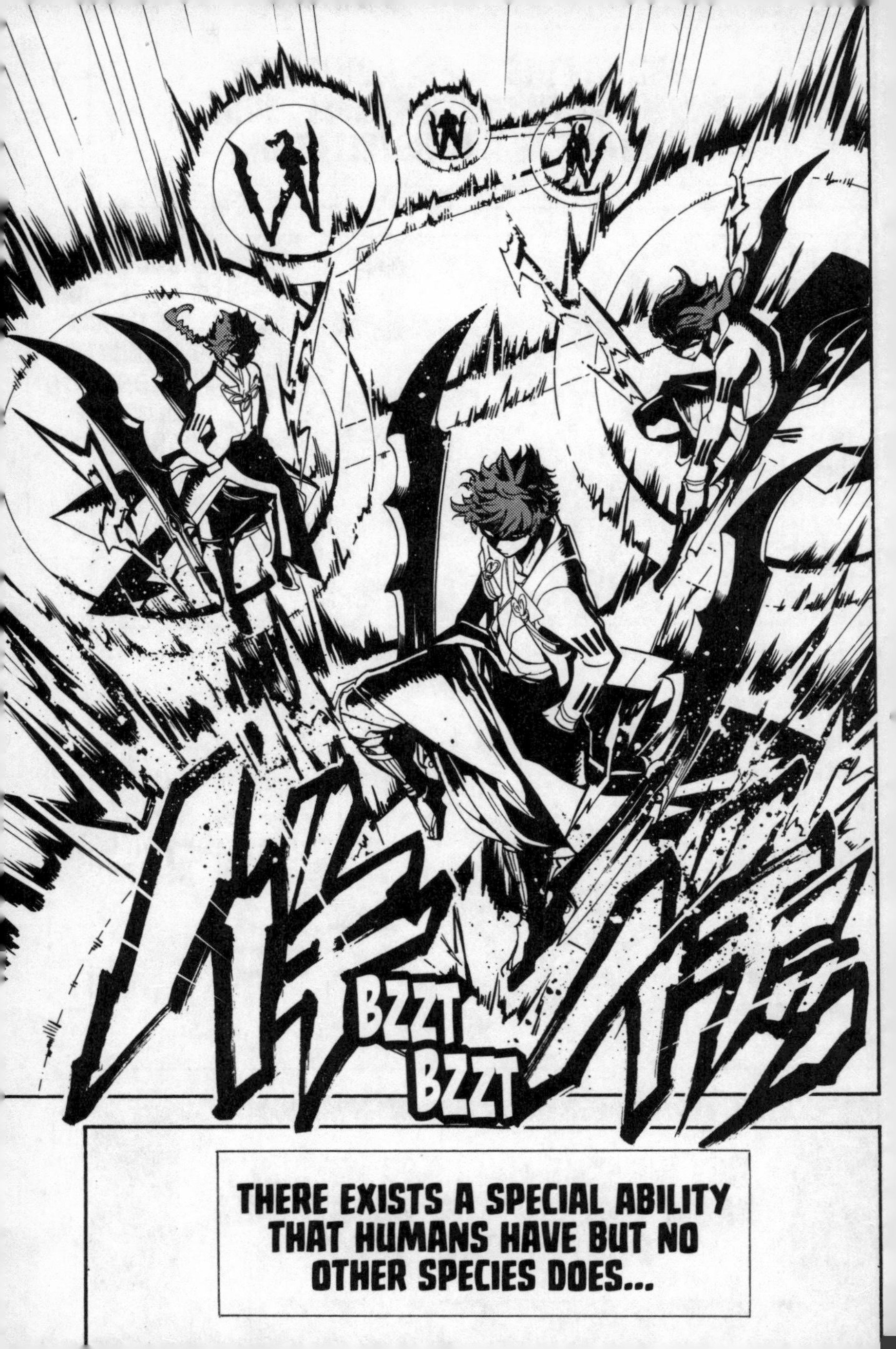
BZZT
BZZT
THERE EXISTS A SPECIAL ABILITY THAT HUMANS HAVE BUT NO OTHER SPECIES DOES...

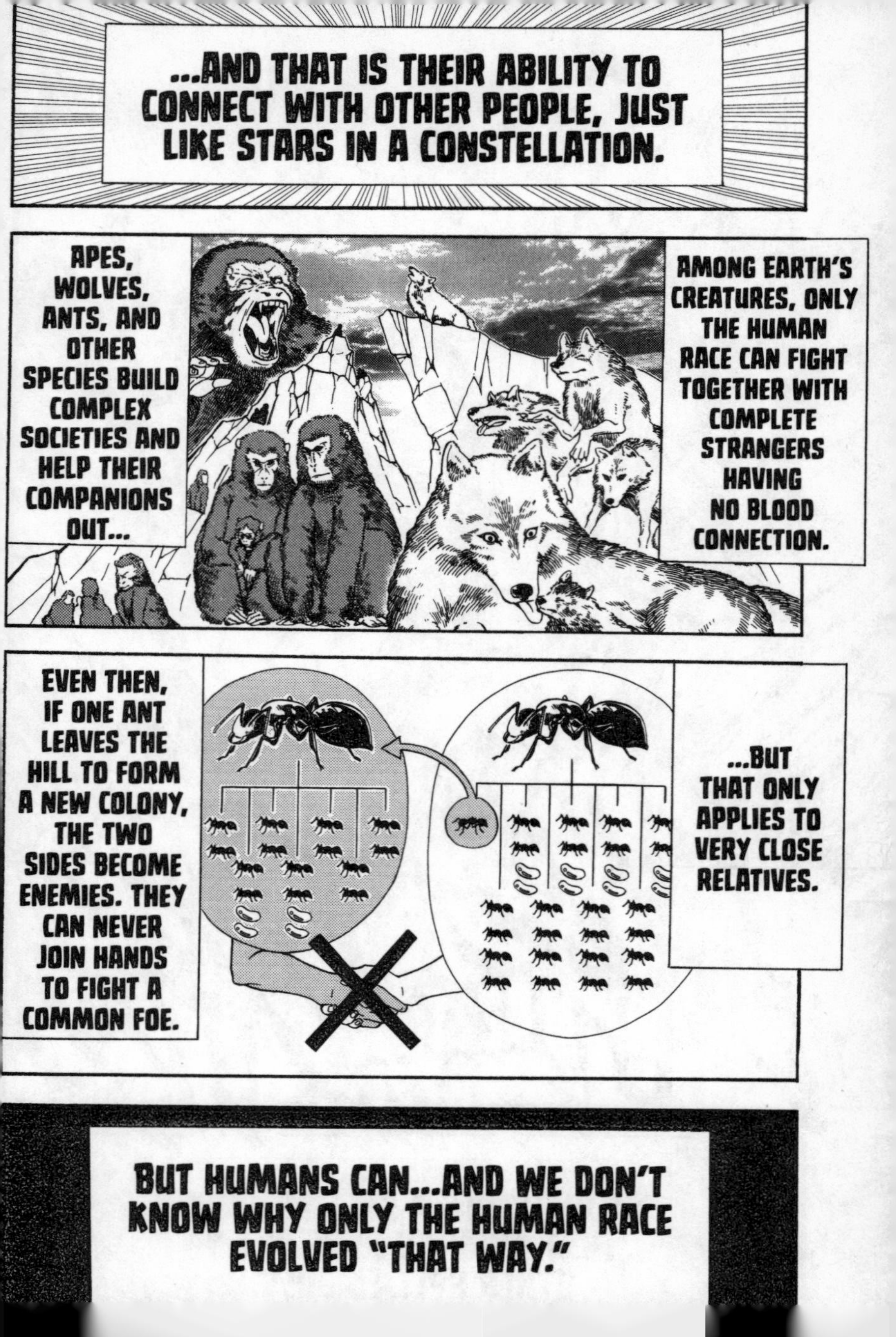
...AND THAT IS THEIR ABILITY TO CONNECT WITH OTHER PEOPLE, JUST LIKE STARS IN A CONSTELLATION.
AMONG EARTH'S CREATURES, ONLY THE HUMAN RACE CAN FIGHT TOGETHER WITH COMPLETE STRANGERS HAVING NO BLOOD CONNECTION.
APES, WOLVES, ANTS, AND OTHER SPECIES BUILD COMPLEX SOCIETIES AND HELP THEIR COMPANIONS OUT...
...BUT THAT ONLY APPLIES TO VERY CLOSE RELATIVES.
EVEN THEN, IF ONE ANT LEAVES THE HILL TO FORM A NEW COLONY, THE TWO SIDES BECOME ENEMIES. THEY CAN NEVER JOIN HANDS TO FIGHT A COMMON FOE.
BUT HUMANS CAN...AND WE DON'T KNOW WHY ONLY THE HUMAN RACE EVOLVED "THAT WAY."

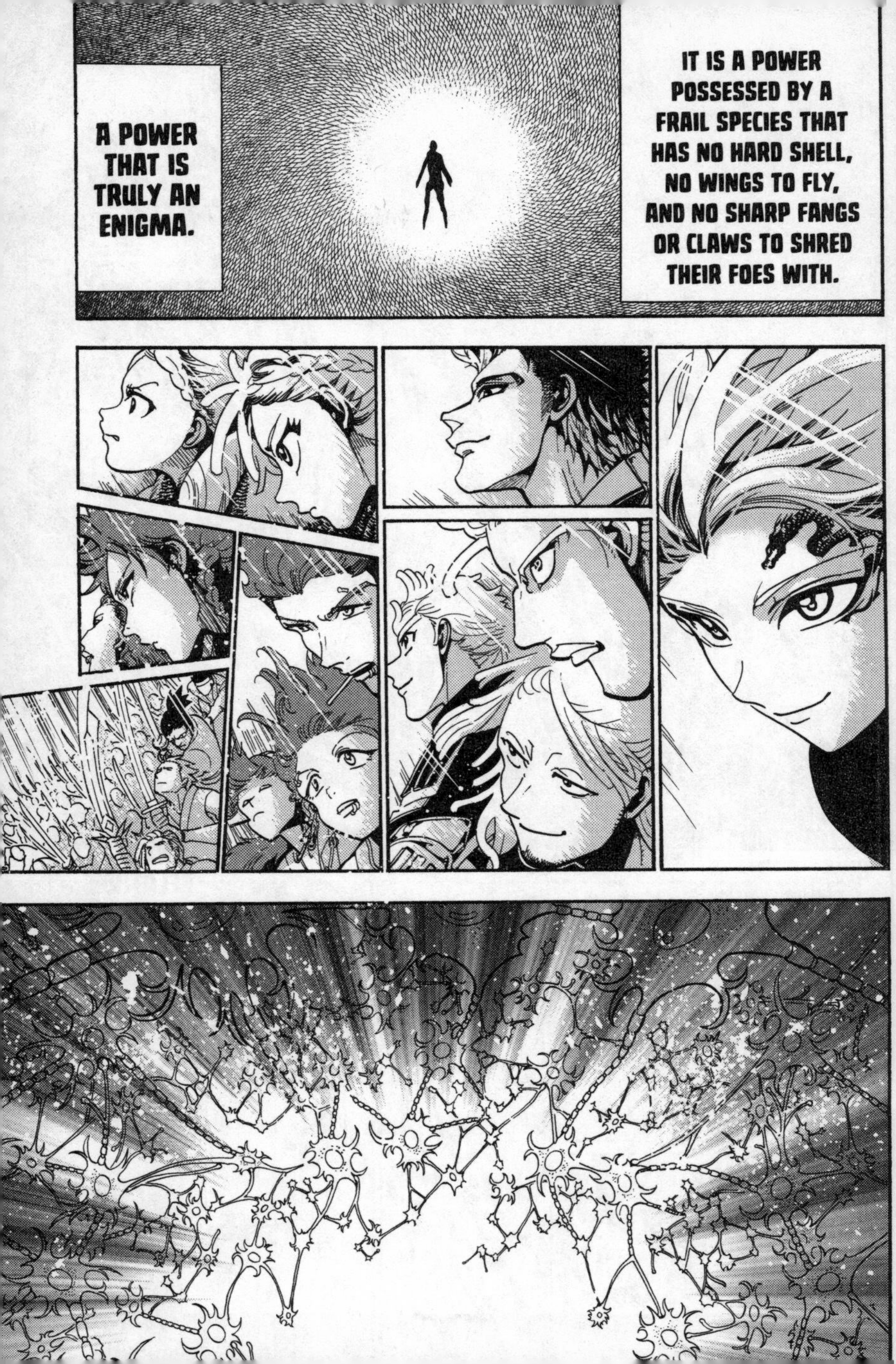
IT IS A POWER POSSESSED BY A FRAIL SPECIES THAT HAS NO HARD SHELL, NO WINGS TO FLY, AND NO SHARP FANGS OR CLAWS TO SHRED THEIR FOES WITH.
A POWER THAT IS TRULY AN ENIGMA.

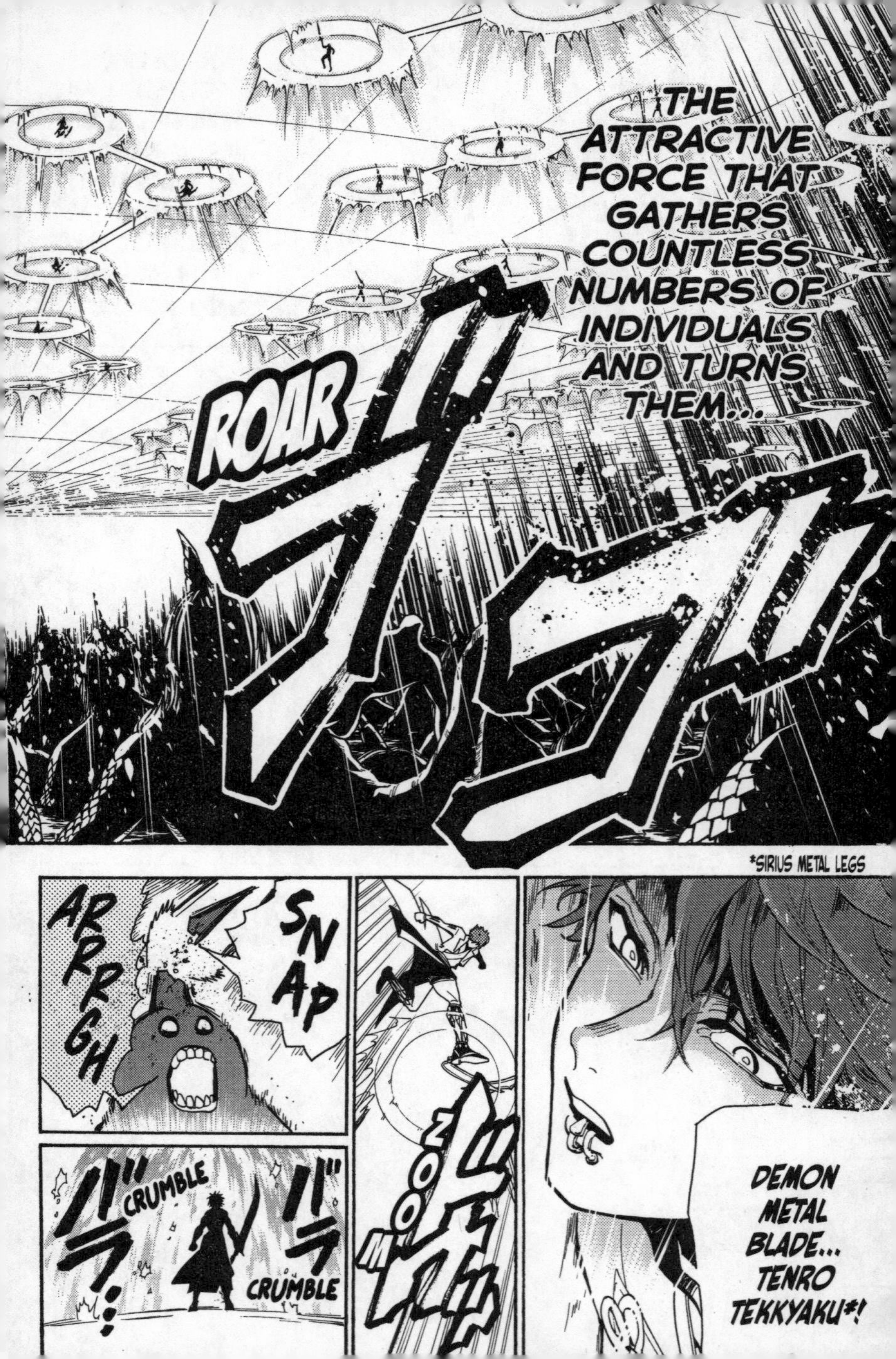
THE ATTRACTIVE FORCE THAT GATHERS COUNTLESS NUMBERS OF INDIVIDUALS AND TURNS THEM...
ROAR
*SIRIUS METAL LEGS
DEMON METAL BLADE... TENRO TEKKYAKU*!
ZOOOM
SNAP
ARRRGH
CRUMBLE
CRUMBLE

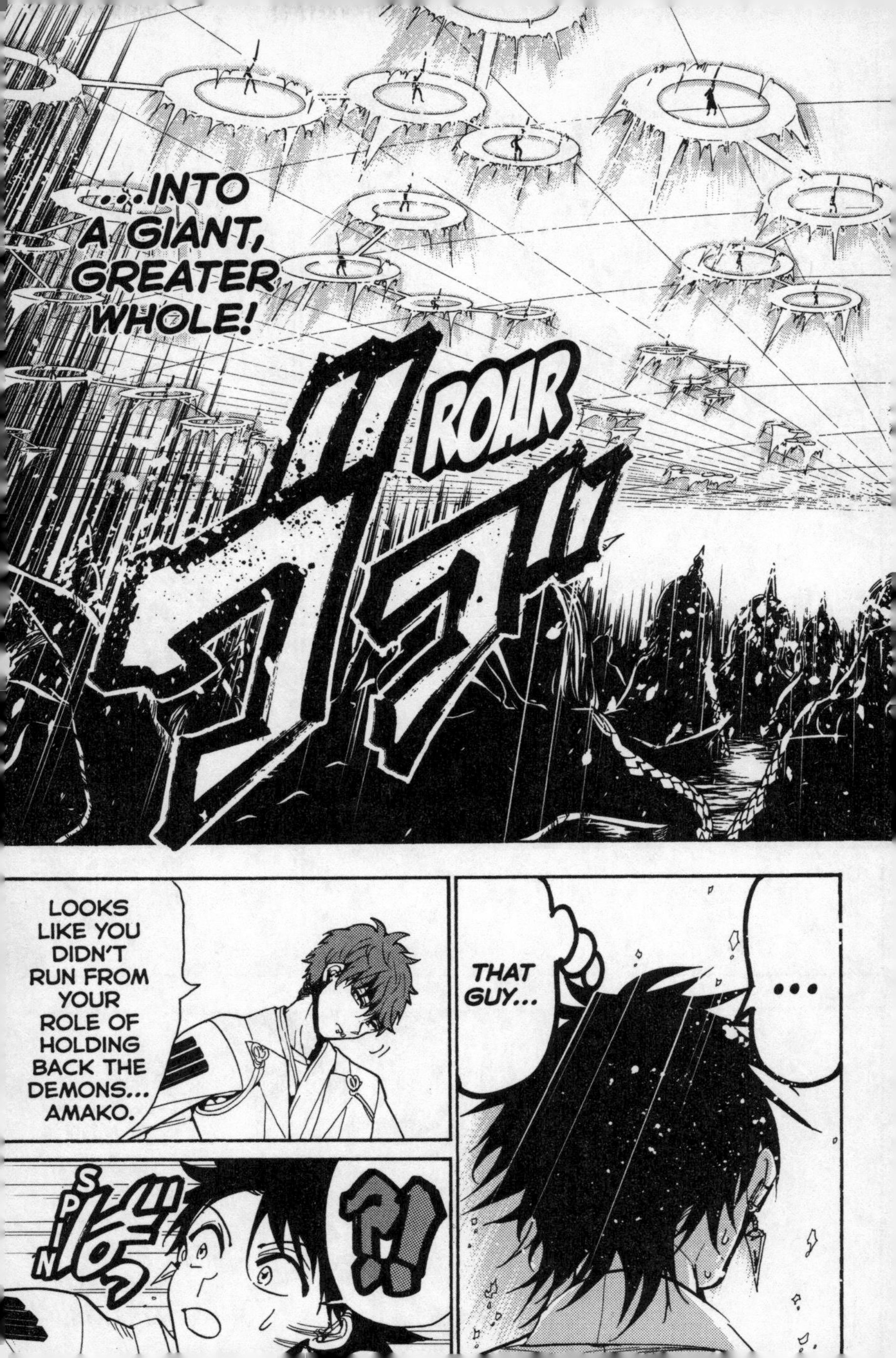
...INTO A GIANT, GREATER WHOLE!
ROAR
...
THAT GUY...
LOOKS LIKE YOU DIDN'T RUN FROM YOUR ROLE OF HOLDING BACK THE DEMONS... AMAKO.
SPIN
?!

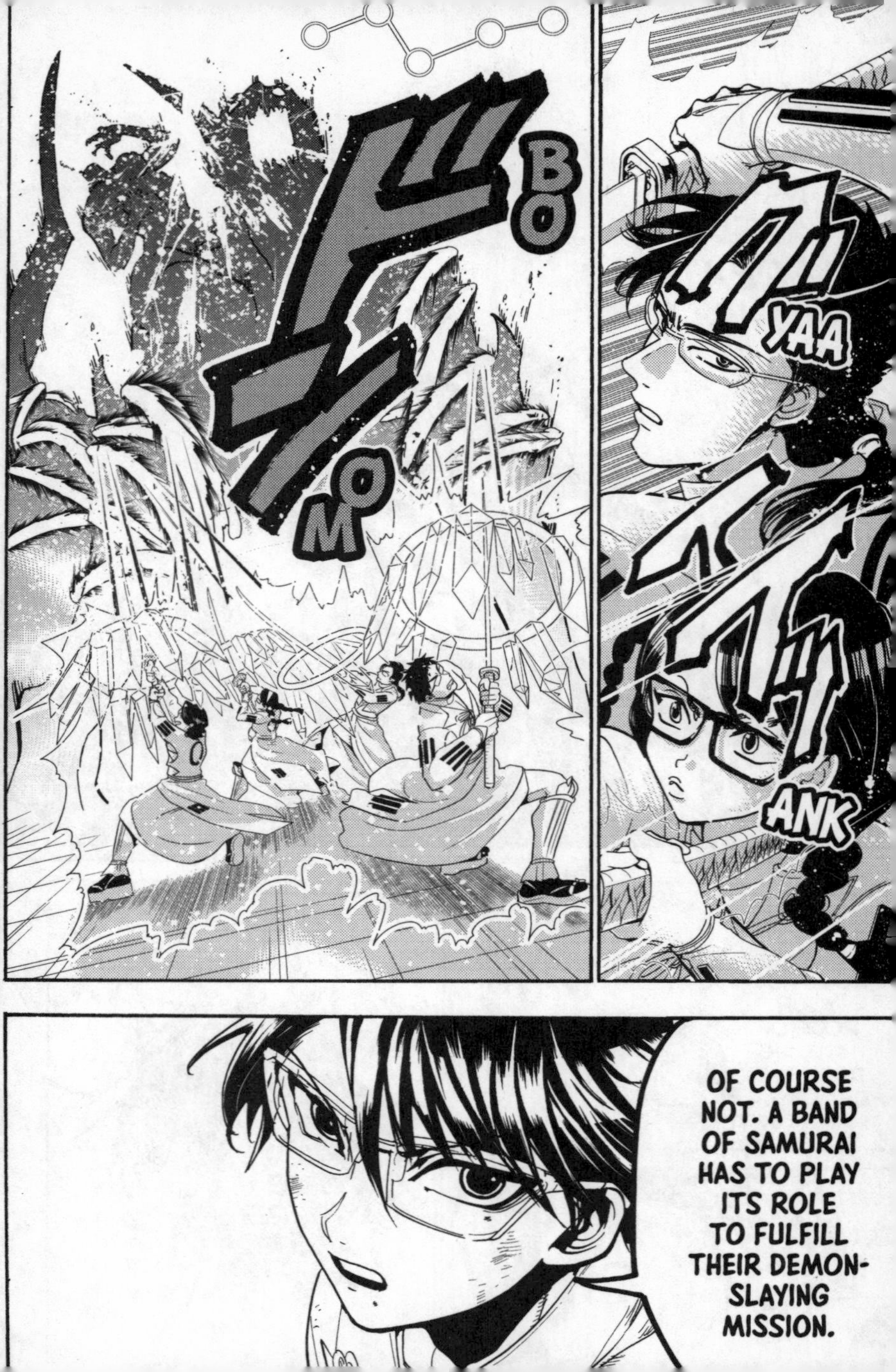
YAA
ANK
BOOM
OF COURSE NOT. A BAND OF SAMURAI HAS TO PLAY ITS ROLE TO FULFILL THEIR DEMON-SLAYING MISSION.

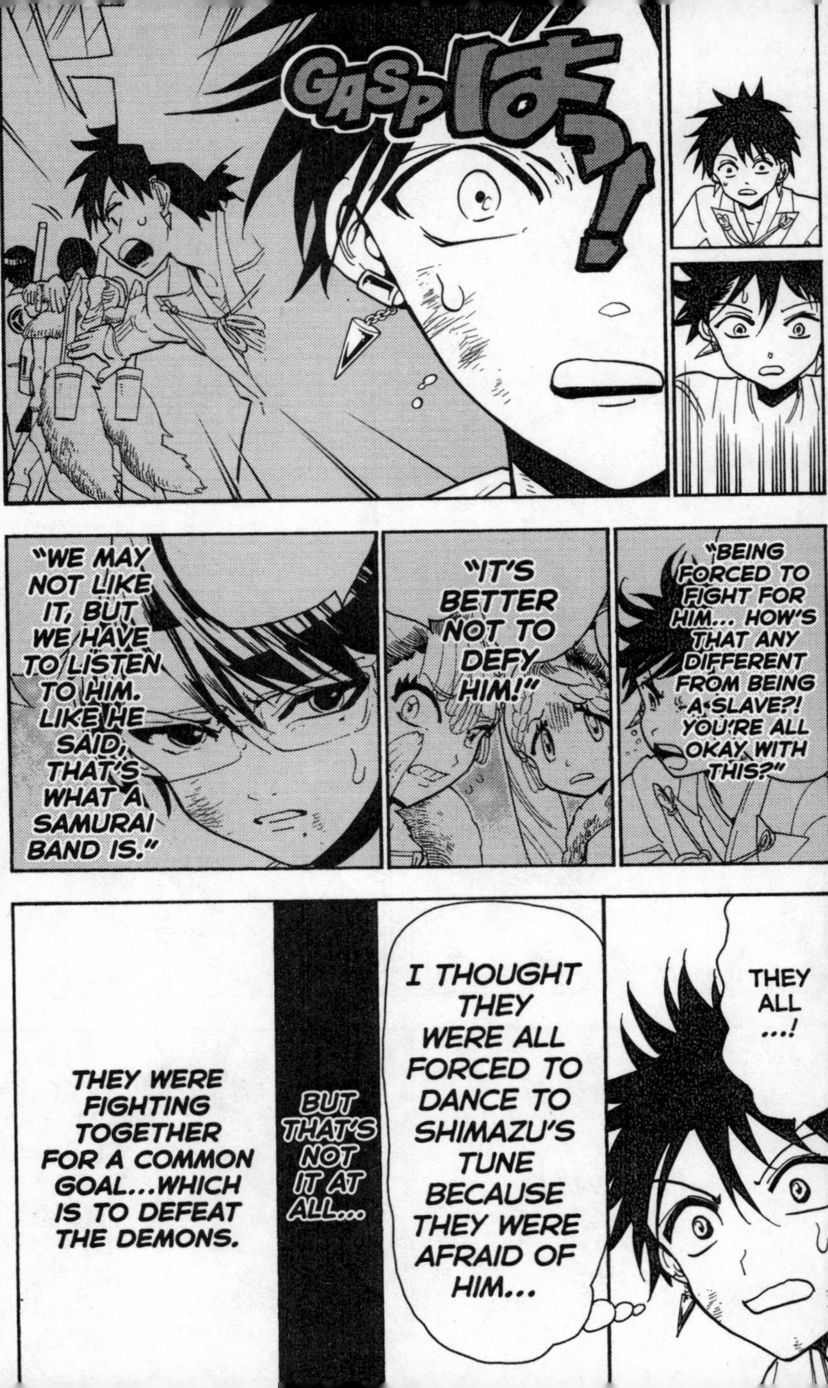
GASP はっ!
"BEING FORCED TO FIGHT FOR HIM... HOW'S THAT ANY DIFFERENT FROM BEING A SLAVE?! YOU'RE ALL OKAY WITH THIS?"
"IT'S BETTER NOT TO DEFY HIM!"
"WE MAY NOT LIKE IT, BUT WE HAVE TO LISTEN TO HIM. LIKE HE SAID, THAT'S WHAT A SAMURAI BAND IS."
THEY ALL ...!
I THOUGHT THEY WERE ALL FORCED TO DANCE TO SHIMAZU'S TUNE BECAUSE THEY WERE AFRAID OF HIM...
BUT THAT'S NOT IT AT ALL...
THEY WERE FIGHTING TOGETHER FOR A COMMON GOAL...WHICH IS TO DEFEAT THE DEMONS.

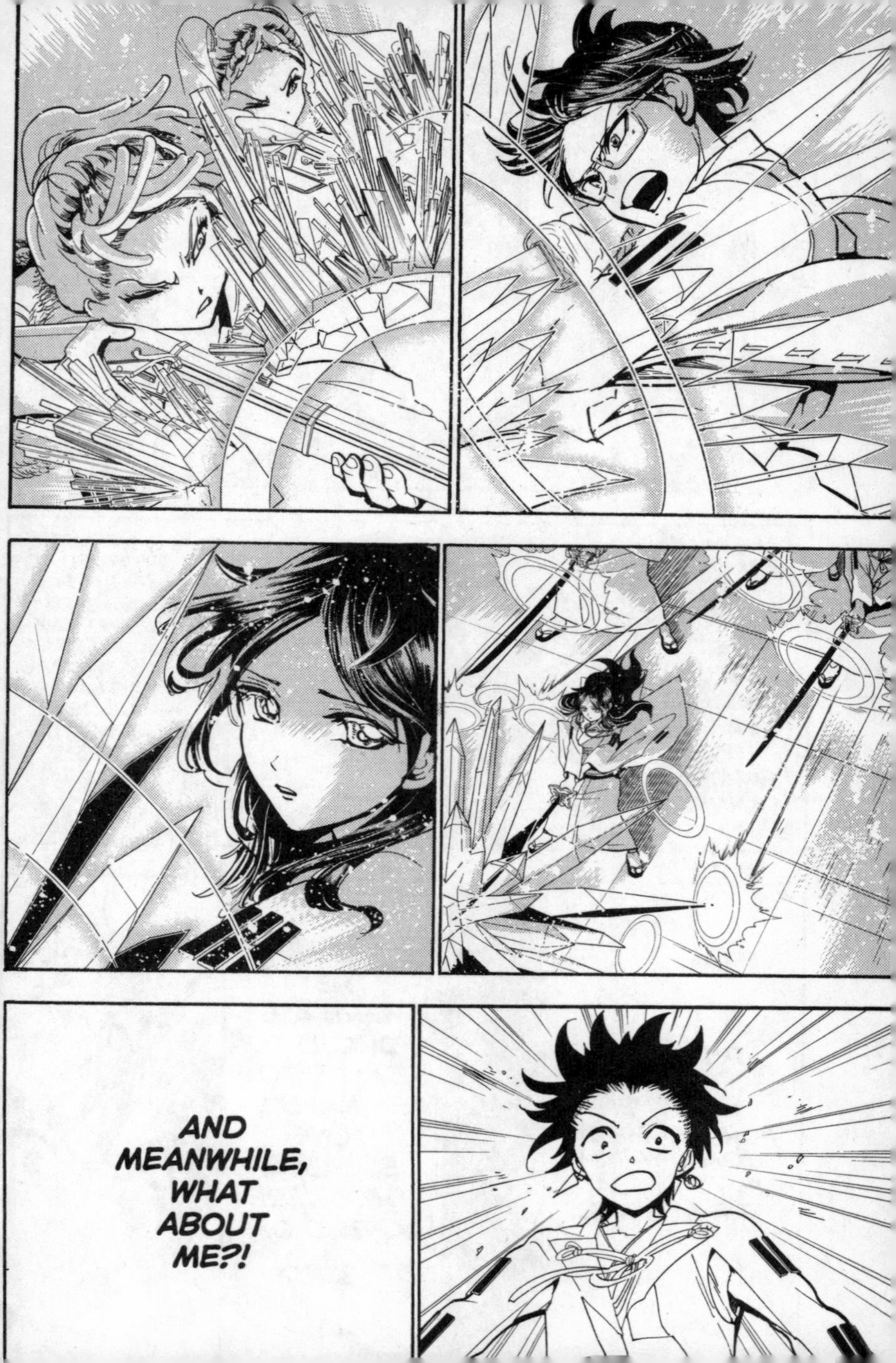
AND MEANWHILE, WHAT ABOUT ME?!

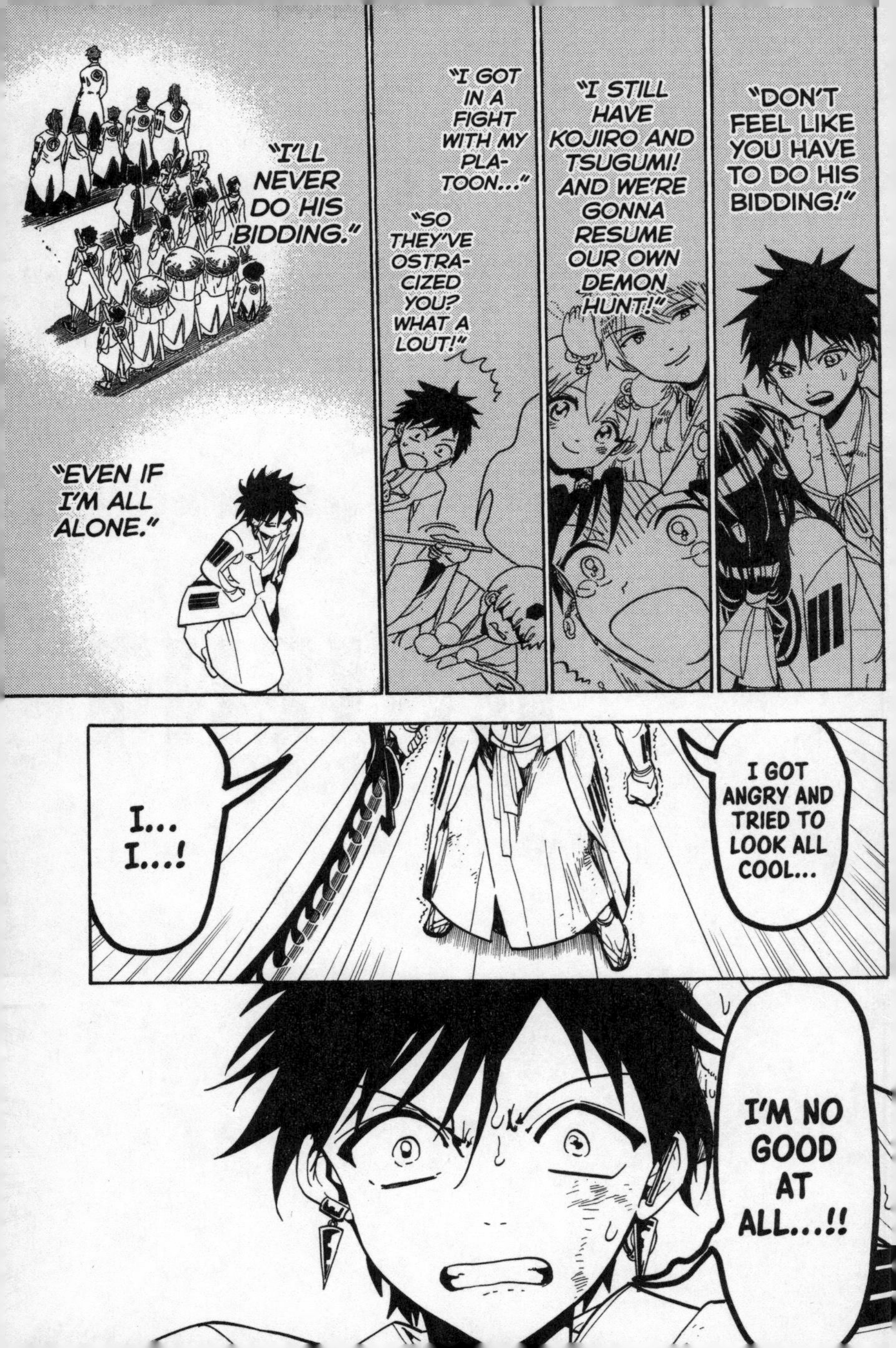
"DON'T FEEL LIKE YOU HAVE TO DO HIS BIDDING!"
"I STILL HAVE KOJIRO AND TSUGUMI! AND WE'RE GONNA RESUME OUR OWN DEMON HUNT!"
"I GOT IN A FIGHT WITH MY PLA-TOON..."
"SO THEY'VE OSTRA-CIZED YOU? WHAT A LOUT!"
"I'LL NEVER DO HIS BIDDING."
"EVEN IF I'M ALL ALONE."
I GOT ANGRY AND TRIED TO LOOK ALL COOL...
I... I...!
I'M NO GOOD AT ALL...!!

ORIENT

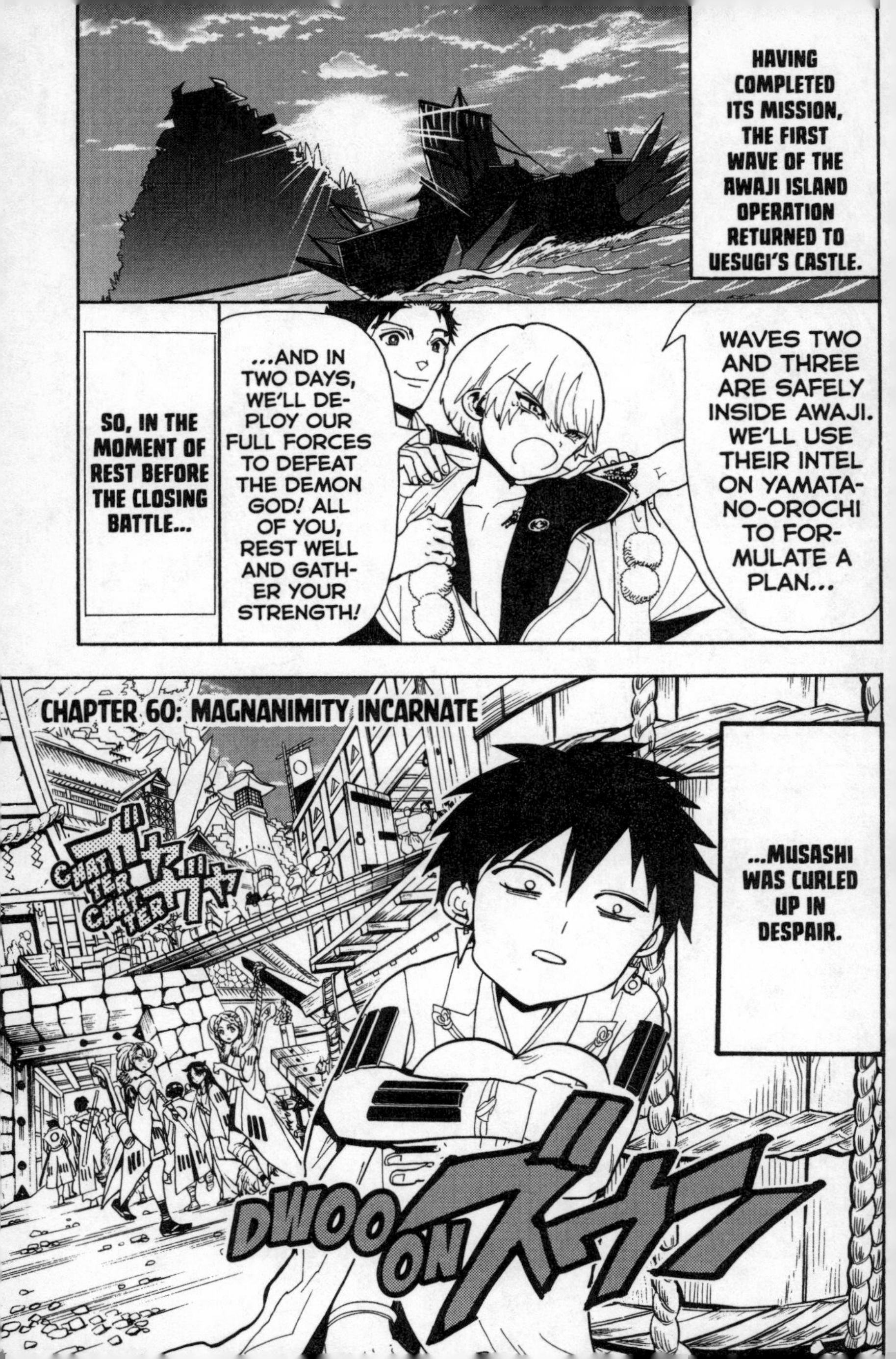
HAVING COMPLETED ITS MISSION, THE FIRST WAVE OF THE AWAJI ISLAND OPERATION RETURNED TO UESUGI'S CASTLE.
WAVES TWO AND THREE ARE SAFELY INSIDE AWAJI. WE'LL USE THEIR INTEL ON YAMATA-NO-OROCHI TO FORMULATE A PLAN...
...AND IN TWO DAYS, WE'LL DEPLOY OUR FULL FORCES TO DEFEAT THE DEMON GOD! ALL OF YOU, REST WELL AND GATHER YOUR STRENGTH!
SO, IN THE MOMENT OF REST BEFORE THE CLOSING BATTLE...
CHAPTER 60: MAGNANIMITY INCARNATE
...MUSASHI WAS CURLED UP IN DESPAIR.
CHATTER CHATTER
DWOOON

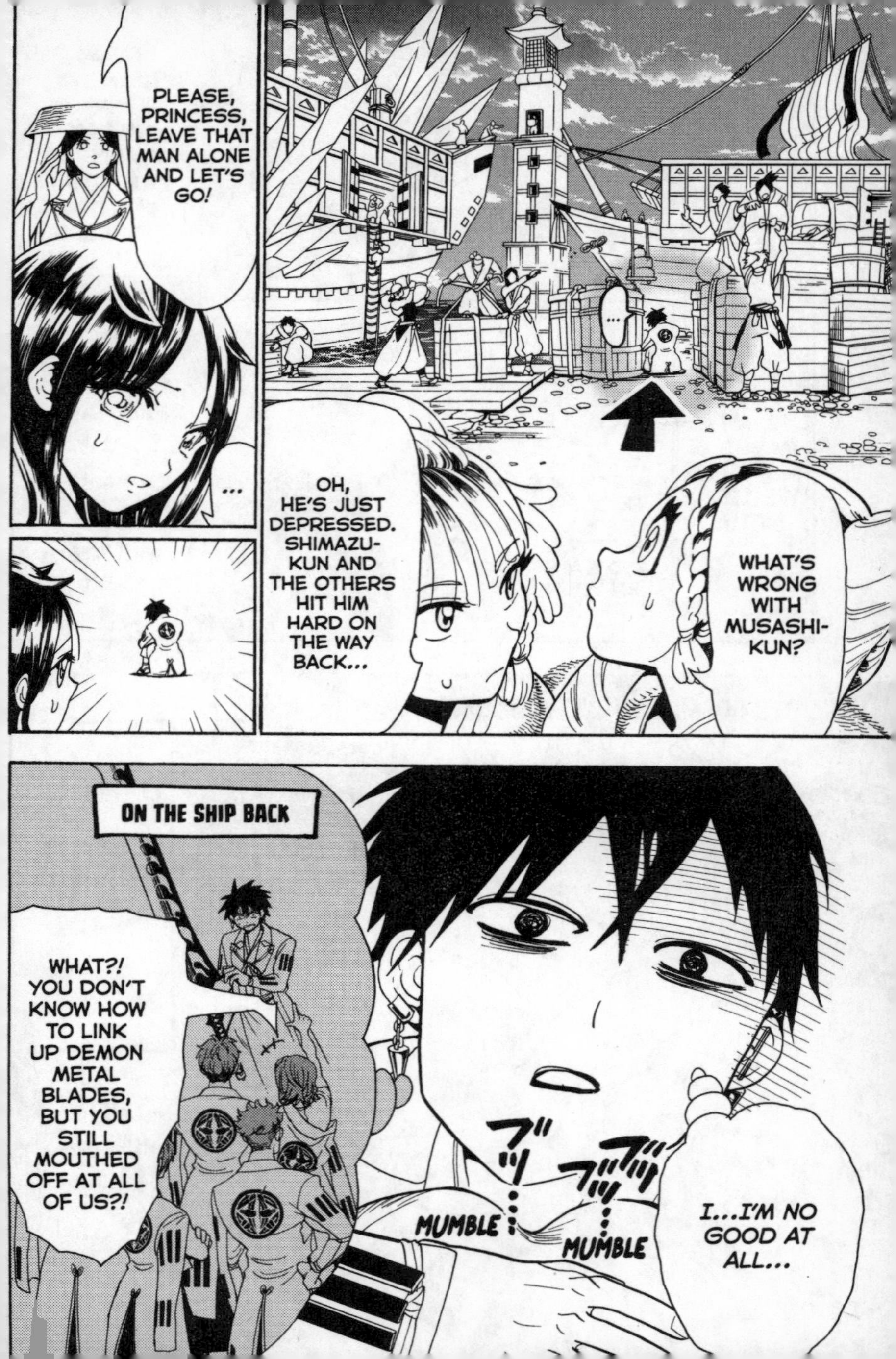
...
WHAT'S WRONG WITH MUSASHI-KUN?
OH, HE'S JUST DEPRESSED. SHIMAZU-KUN AND THE OTHERS HIT HIM HARD ON THE WAY BACK...
PLEASE, PRINCESS, LEAVE THAT MAN ALONE AND LET'S GO!
...
ON THE SHIP BACK
WHAT?! YOU DON'T KNOW HOW TO LINK UP DEMON METAL BLADES, BUT YOU STILL MOUTHED OFF AT ALL OF US?!
ブツ…
MUMBLE
ブツブツ…
MUMBLE
I...I'M NO GOOD AT ALL...

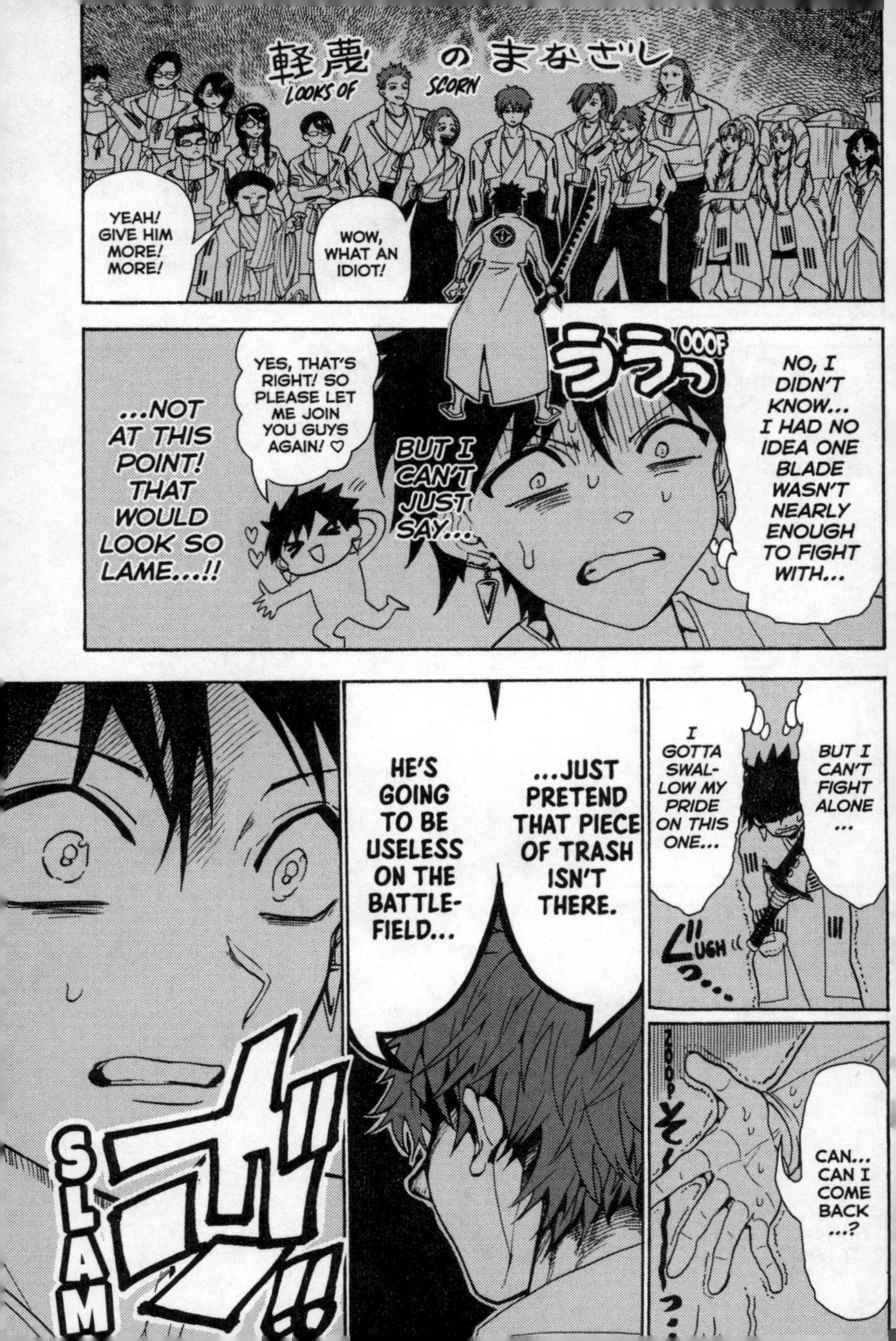

軽蔑のまなざし
LOOKS OF SCORN
WOW, WHAT AN IDIOT!
YEAH! GIVE HIM MORE! MORE!
NO, I DIDN'T KNOW... I HAD NO IDEA ONE BLADE WASN'T NEARLY ENOUGH TO FIGHT WITH...
ううっ
OOOF
BUT I CAN'T JUST SAY...
YES, THAT'S RIGHT! SO PLEASE LET ME JOIN YOU GUYS AGAIN! ♡
...NOT AT THIS POINT! THAT WOULD LOOK SO LAME...!!
BUT I CAN'T FIGHT ALONE...
I GOTTA SWAL-LOW MY PRIDE ON THIS ONE...
ぐっ...
UGH
そ〜
ZOOP
CAN... CAN I COME BACK...?
...JUST PRETEND THAT PIECE OF TRASH ISN'T THERE.
HE'S GOING TO BE USELESS ON THE BATTLE-FIELD...
ゴッ!!
SLAM

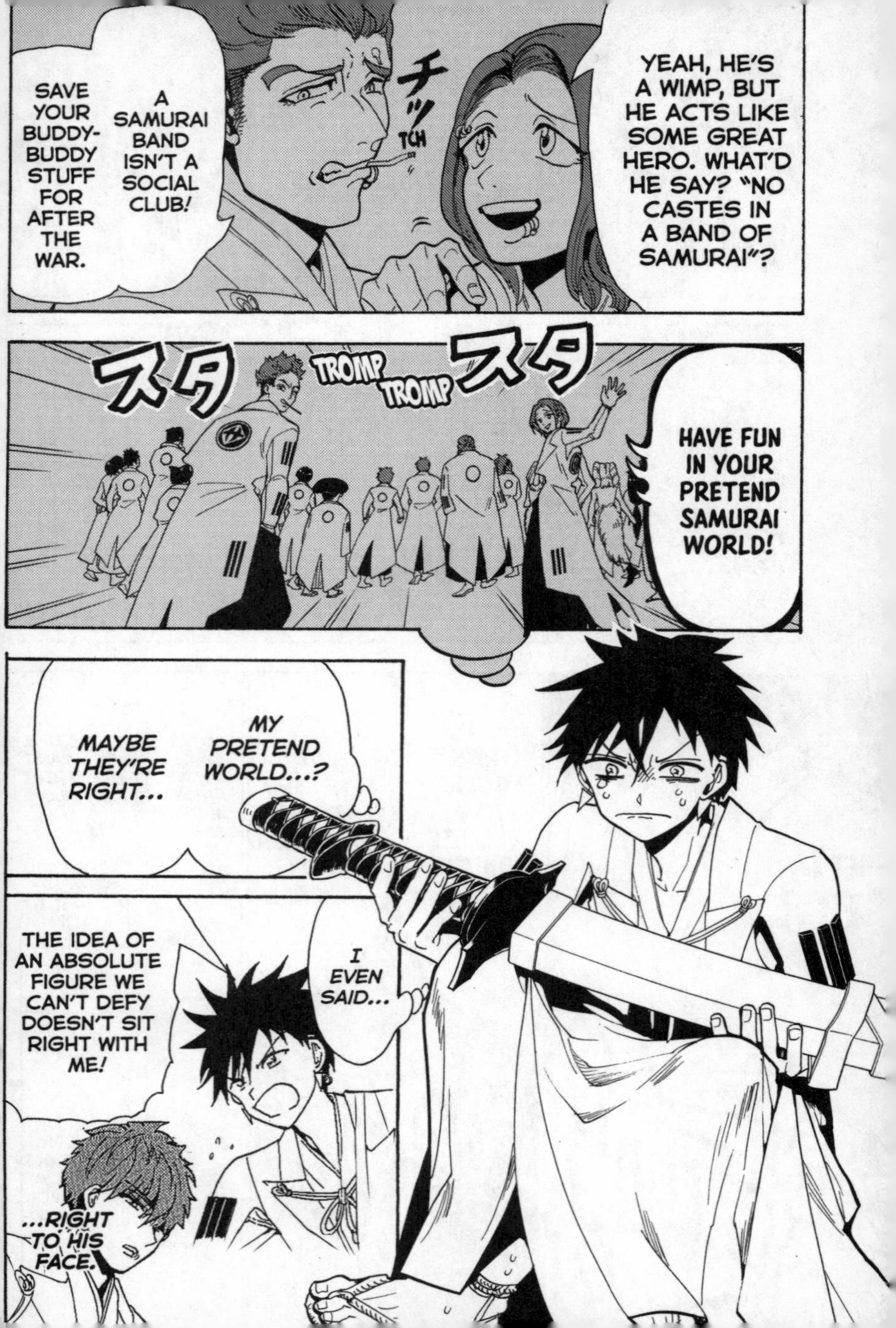
YEAH, HE'S A WIMP, BUT HE ACTS LIKE SOME GREAT HERO. WHAT'D HE SAY? "NO CASTES IN A BAND OF SAMURAI"?
チッ
TCH
A SAMURAI BAND ISN'T A SOCIAL CLUB!
SAVE YOUR BUDDY-BUDDY STUFF FOR AFTER THE WAR.
HAVE FUN IN YOUR PRETEND SAMURAI WORLD!
スタ
TROMP TROMP
スタ
MY PRETEND WORLD...?
MAYBE THEY'RE RIGHT...
I EVEN SAID...
THE IDEA OF AN ABSOLUTE FIGURE WE CAN'T DEFY DOESN'T SIT RIGHT WITH ME!
...RIGHT TO HIS FACE.

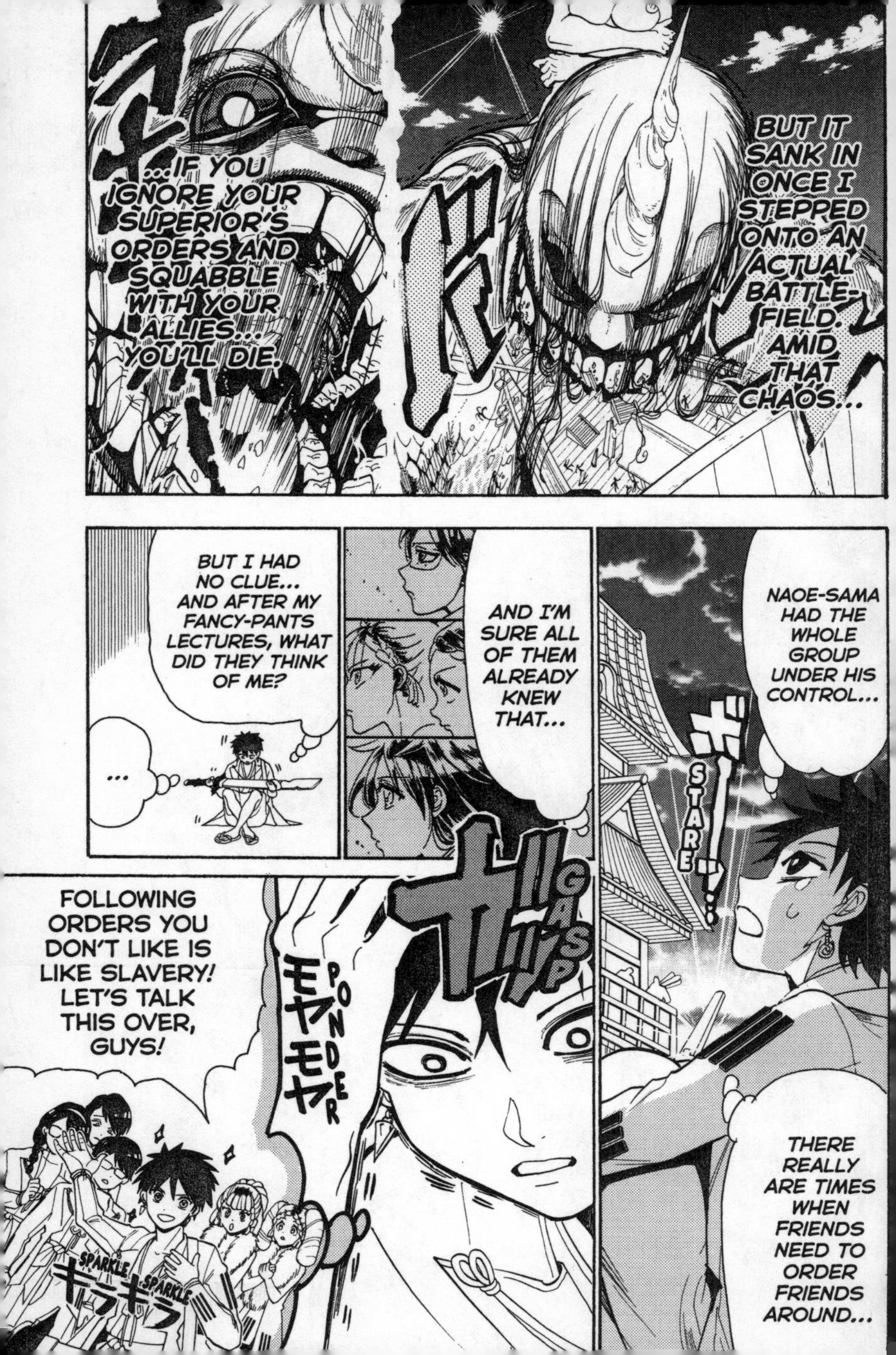
BUT IT SANK IN ONCE I STEPPED ONTO AN ACTUAL BATTLE-FIELD. AMID THAT CHAOS...
...IF YOU IGNORE YOUR SUPERIOR'S ORDERS AND SQUABBLE WITH YOUR ALLIES... YOU'LL DIE.
NAOE-SAMA HAD THE WHOLE GROUP UNDER HIS CONTROL...
STARE
AND I'M SURE ALL OF THEM ALREADY KNEW THAT...
BUT I HAD NO CLUE... AND AFTER MY FANCY-PANTS LECTURES, WHAT DID THEY THINK OF ME?
...
THERE REALLY ARE TIMES WHEN FRIENDS NEED TO ORDER FRIENDS AROUND...
GASP
モヤモヤ
PONDER
FOLLOWING ORDERS YOU DON'T LIKE IS LIKE SLAVERY! LET'S TALK THIS OVER, GUYS!
キラキラ
SPARKLE SPARKLE

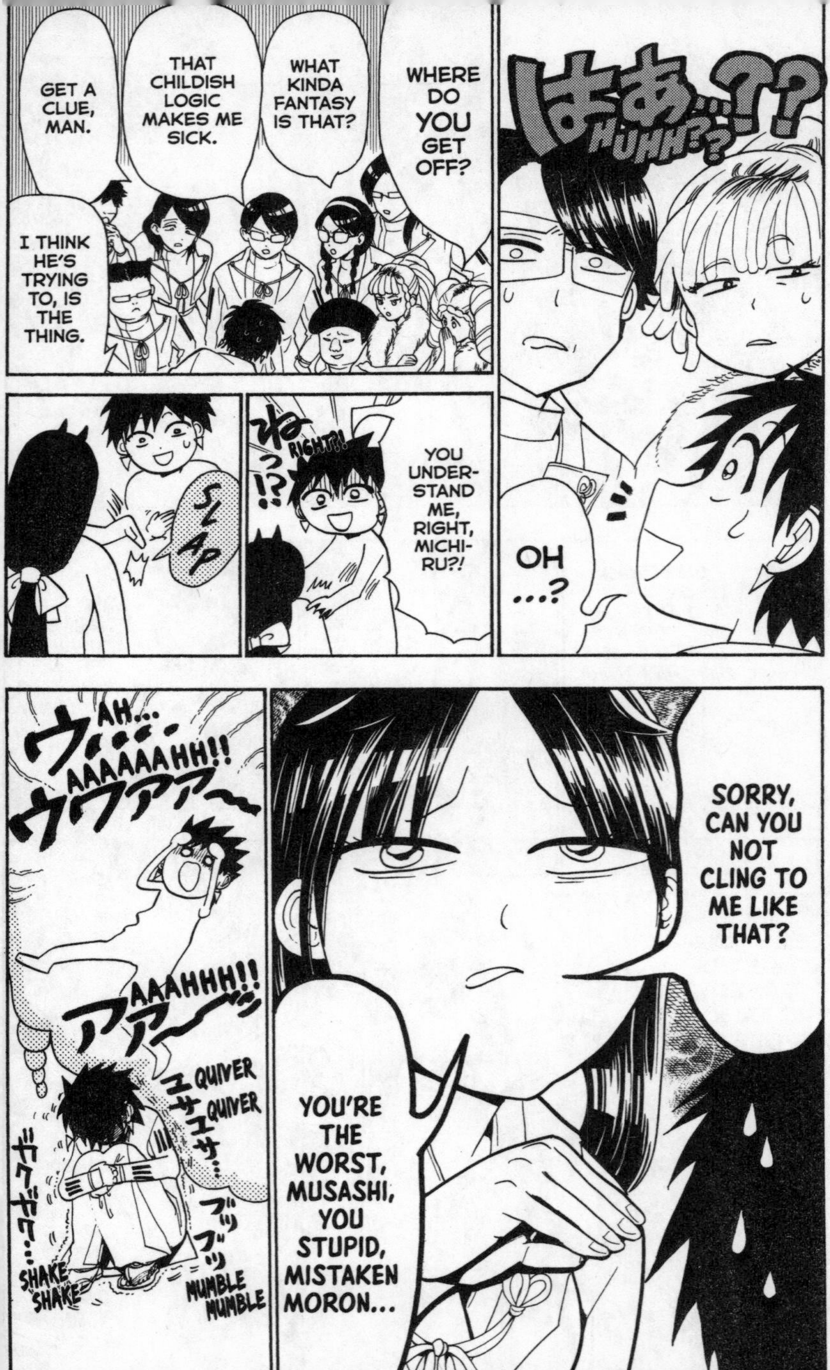
はあ…??
HUHH??
OH ...?
WHERE DO YOU GET OFF?
WHAT KINDA FANTASY IS THAT?
THAT CHILDISH LOGIC MAKES ME SICK.
GET A CLUE, MAN.
I THINK HE'S TRYING TO, IS THE THING.
YOU UNDERSTAND ME, RIGHT, MICHIRU?!
ねっ!?
RIGHT?!
SLAP
SORRY, CAN YOU NOT CLING TO ME LIKE THAT?
YOU'RE THE WORST, MUSASHI, YOU STUPID, MISTAKEN MORON...
ウァ…
AH...
ウワアア〜
AAAAAAHH!!
アアー〜ッ
AAAAHHH!!
ユサユサ…
QUIVER QUIVER
ブツブツ
MUMBLE MUMBLE
ガクガク…
SHAKE SHAKE

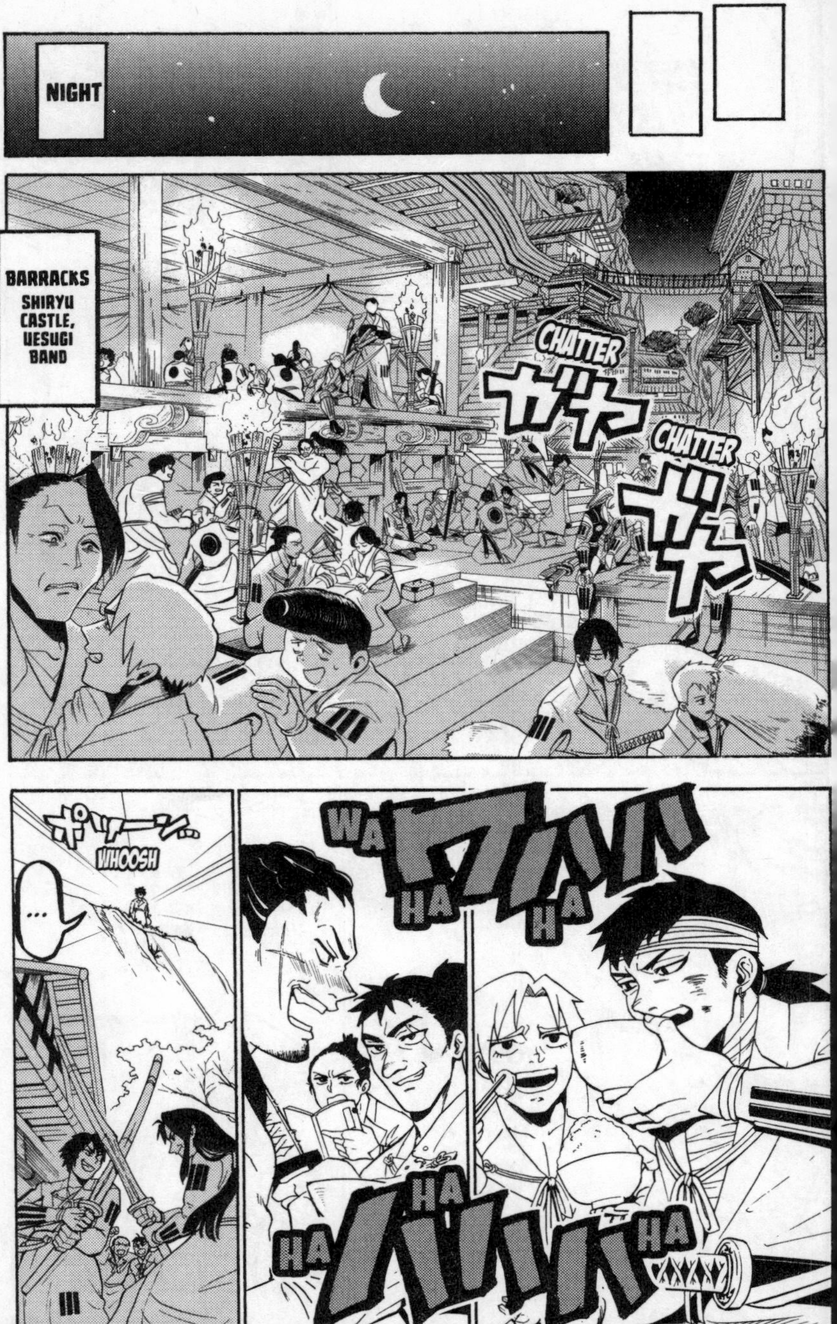
NIGHT
BARRACKS
SHIRYU CASTLE, UESUGI BAND
CHATTER
ガヤ
CHATTER
ガヤ
WA
ワハハハ
HA
HA
HA
HA
ハハハハ
HA
HA
WHOOSH
...

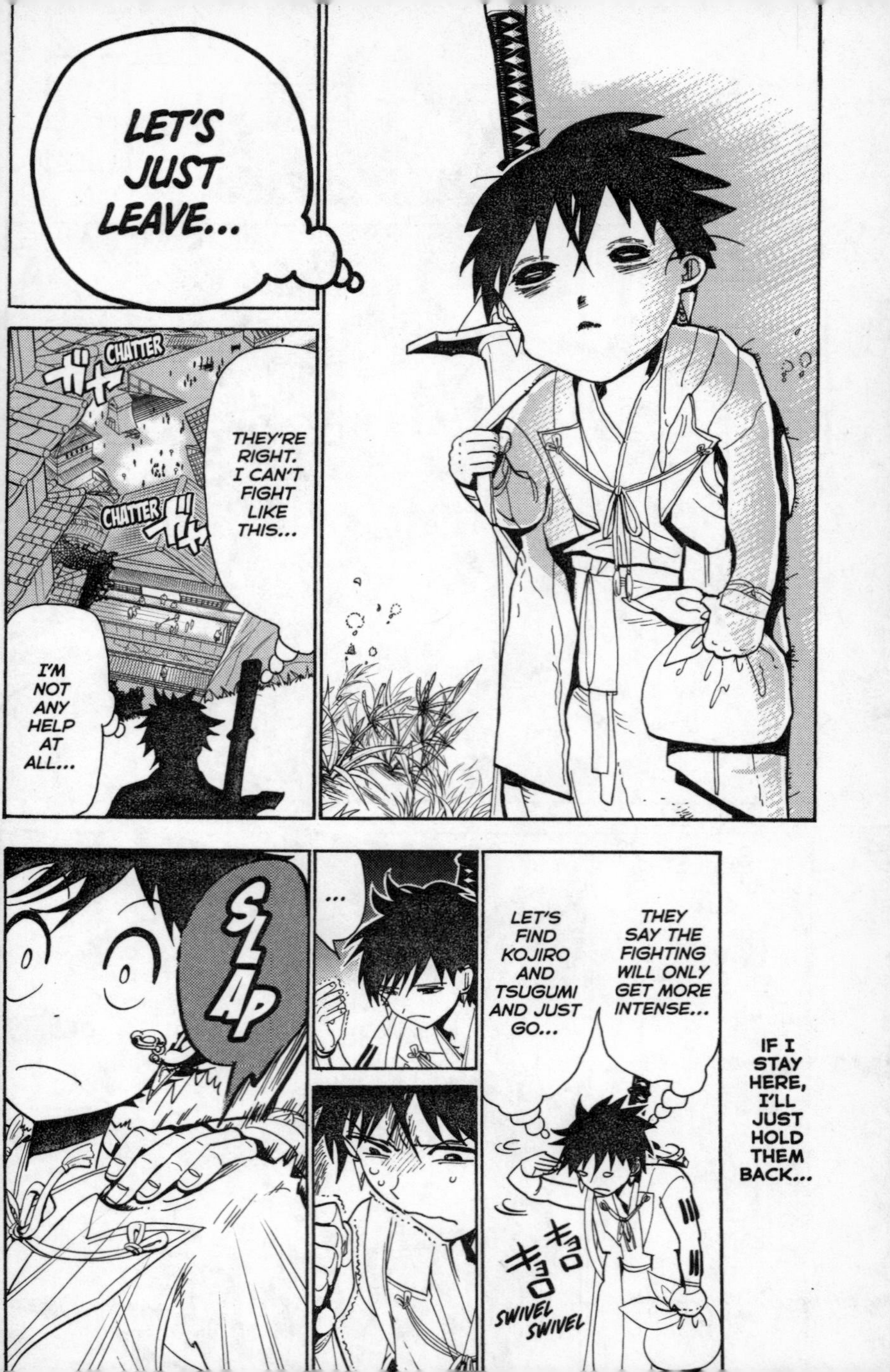

LET'S JUST LEAVE...
ガヤ CHATTER
THEY'RE RIGHT. I CAN'T FIGHT LIKE THIS...
ガヤ CHATTER
I'M NOT ANY HELP AT ALL...
IF I STAY HERE, I'LL JUST HOLD THEM BACK...
THEY SAY THE FIGHTING WILL ONLY GET MORE INTENSE...
LET'S FIND KOJIRO AND TSUGUMI AND JUST GO...
キョロ キョロ SWIVEL SWIVEL
...
SLAP

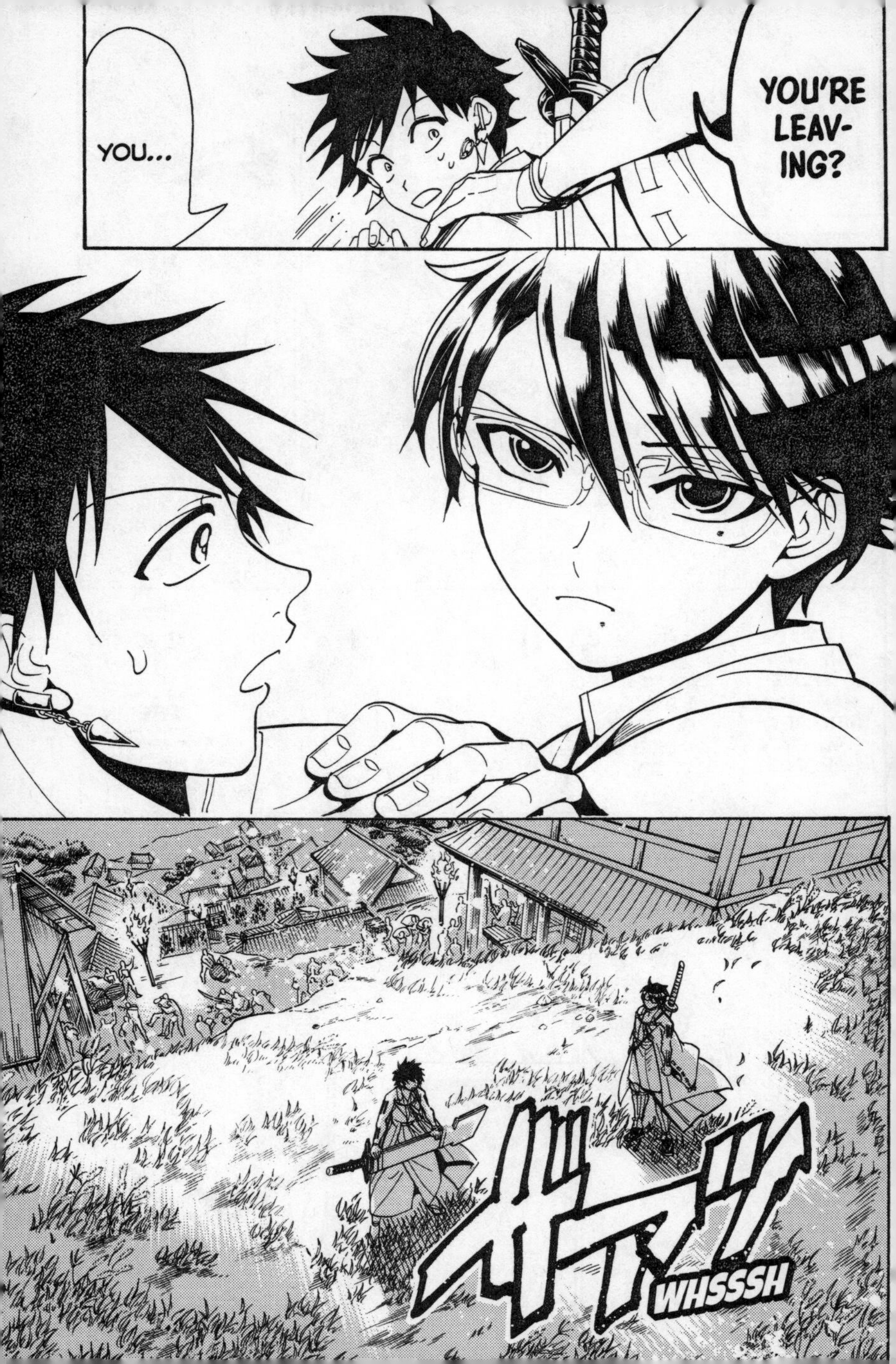
YOU'RE LEAVING?
YOU...
WHSSSH

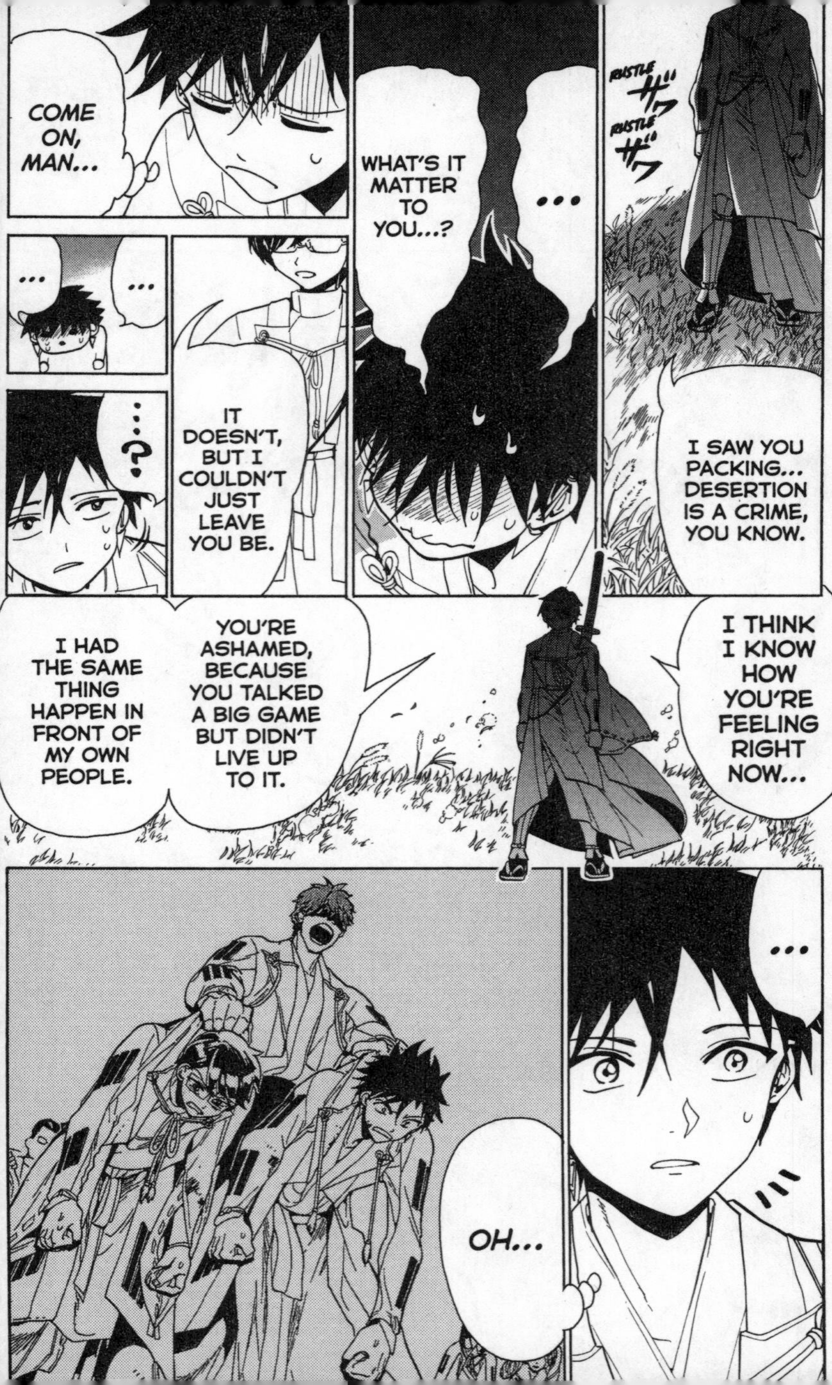

RUSTLE ザッ
RUSTLE ザッ
I SAW YOU PACKING... DESERTION IS A CRIME, YOU KNOW.
...
WHAT'S IT MATTER TO YOU...?
COME ON, MAN...
IT DOESN'T, BUT I COULDN'T JUST LEAVE YOU BE.
...
...
...?
I THINK I KNOW HOW YOU'RE FEELING RIGHT NOW...
YOU'RE ASHAMED, BECAUSE YOU TALKED A BIG GAME BUT DIDN'T LIVE UP TO IT.
I HAD THE SAME THING HAPPEN IN FRONT OF MY OWN PEOPLE.
...
OH...

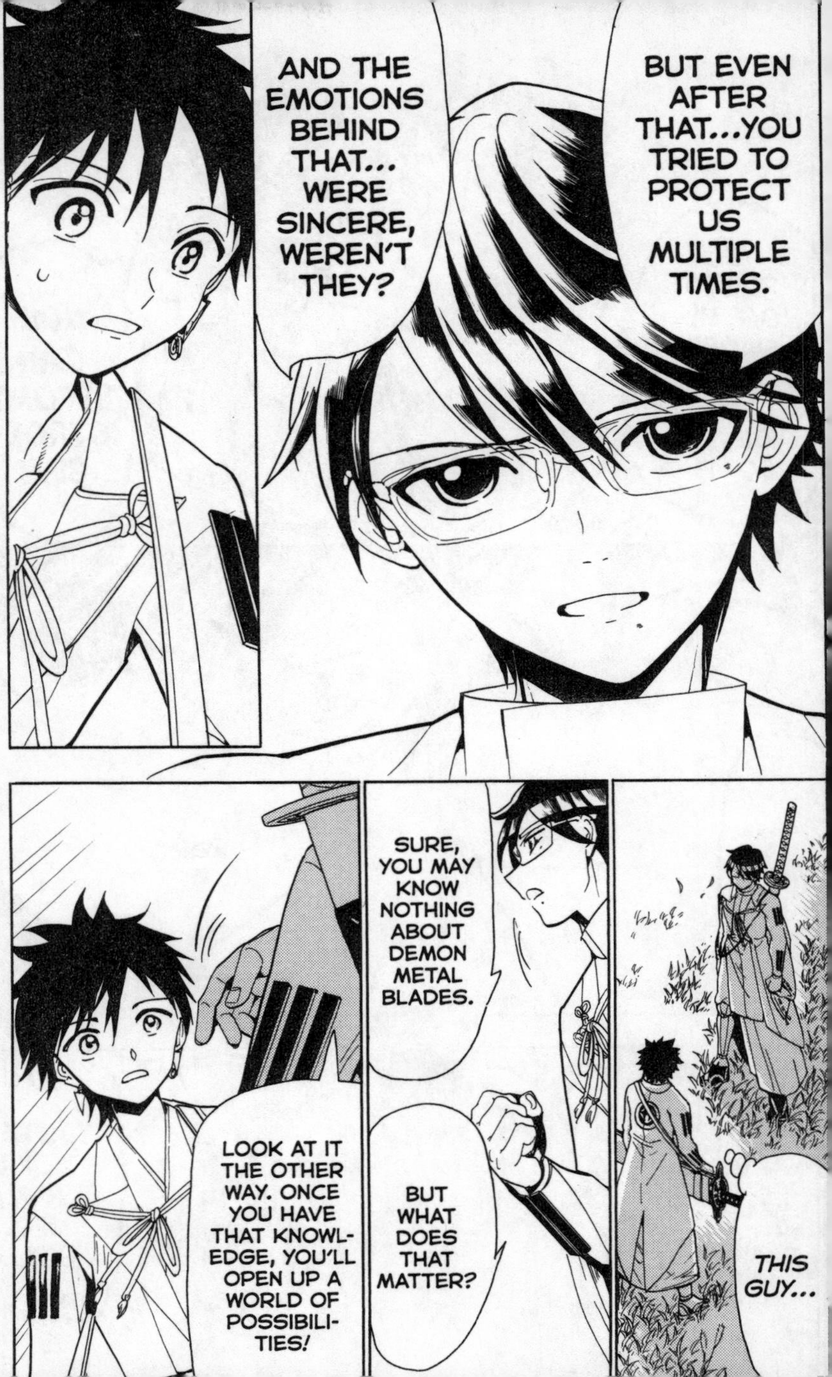
BUT EVEN AFTER THAT...YOU TRIED TO PROTECT US MULTIPLE TIMES.
AND THE EMOTIONS BEHIND THAT... WERE SINCERE, WEREN'T THEY?
THIS GUY...
SURE, YOU MAY KNOW NOTHING ABOUT DEMON METAL BLADES.
BUT WHAT DOES THAT MATTER?
LOOK AT IT THE OTHER WAY. ONCE YOU HAVE THAT KNOWL-EDGE, YOU'LL OPEN UP A WORLD OF POSSIBILI-TIES!

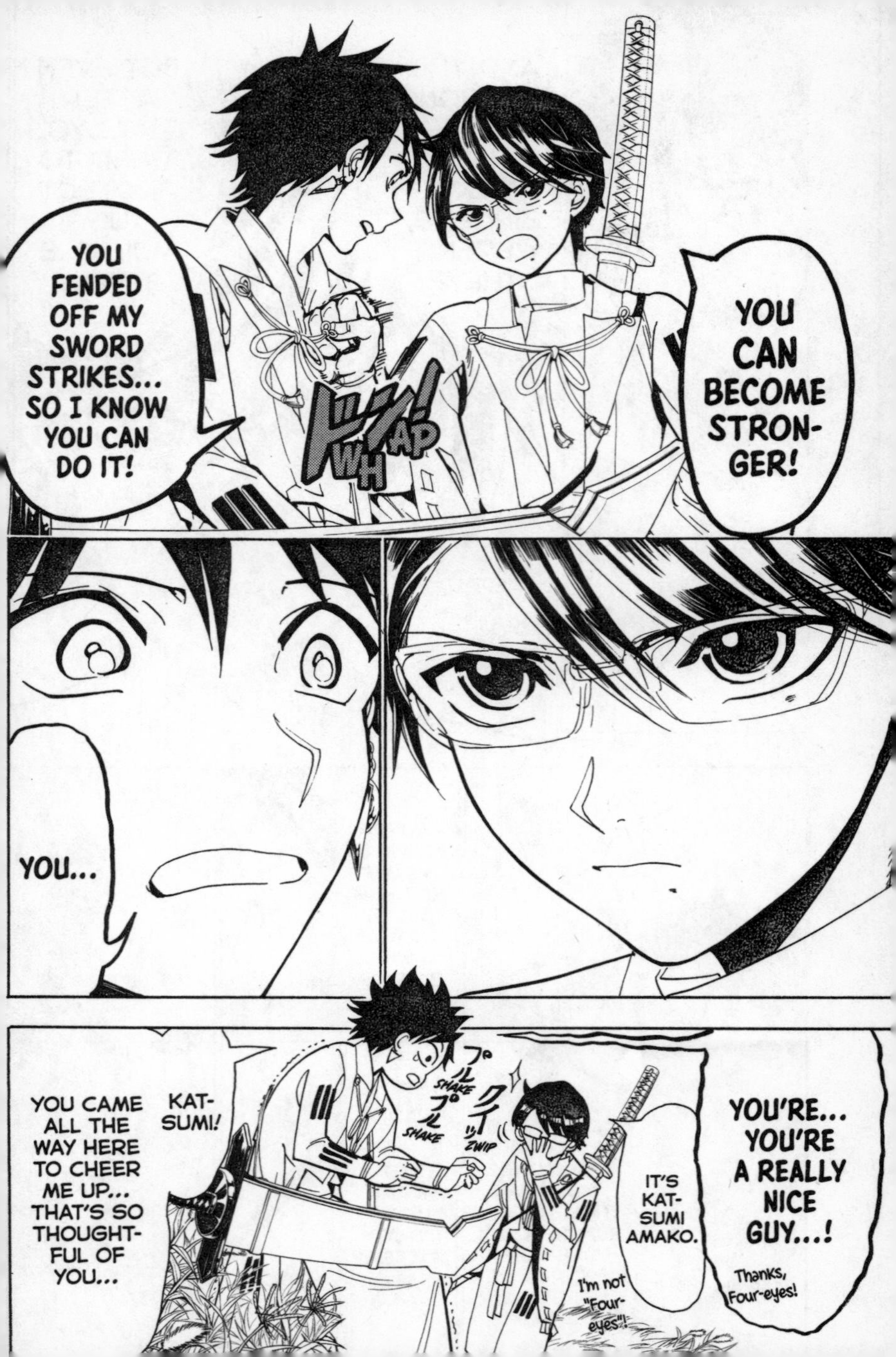
YOU CAN BECOME STRONGER!
WHAP
YOU FENDED OFF MY SWORD STRIKES... SO I KNOW YOU CAN DO IT!
YOU...
YOU'RE... YOU'RE A REALLY NICE GUY...!
Thanks, Four-eyes!
IT'S KATSUMI AMAKO.
I'm not "Four-eyes"!
クイッ ZWIP
プルプル SHAKE SHAKE
KATSUMI!
YOU CAME ALL THE WAY HERE TO CHEER ME UP... THAT'S SO THOUGHTFUL OF YOU...

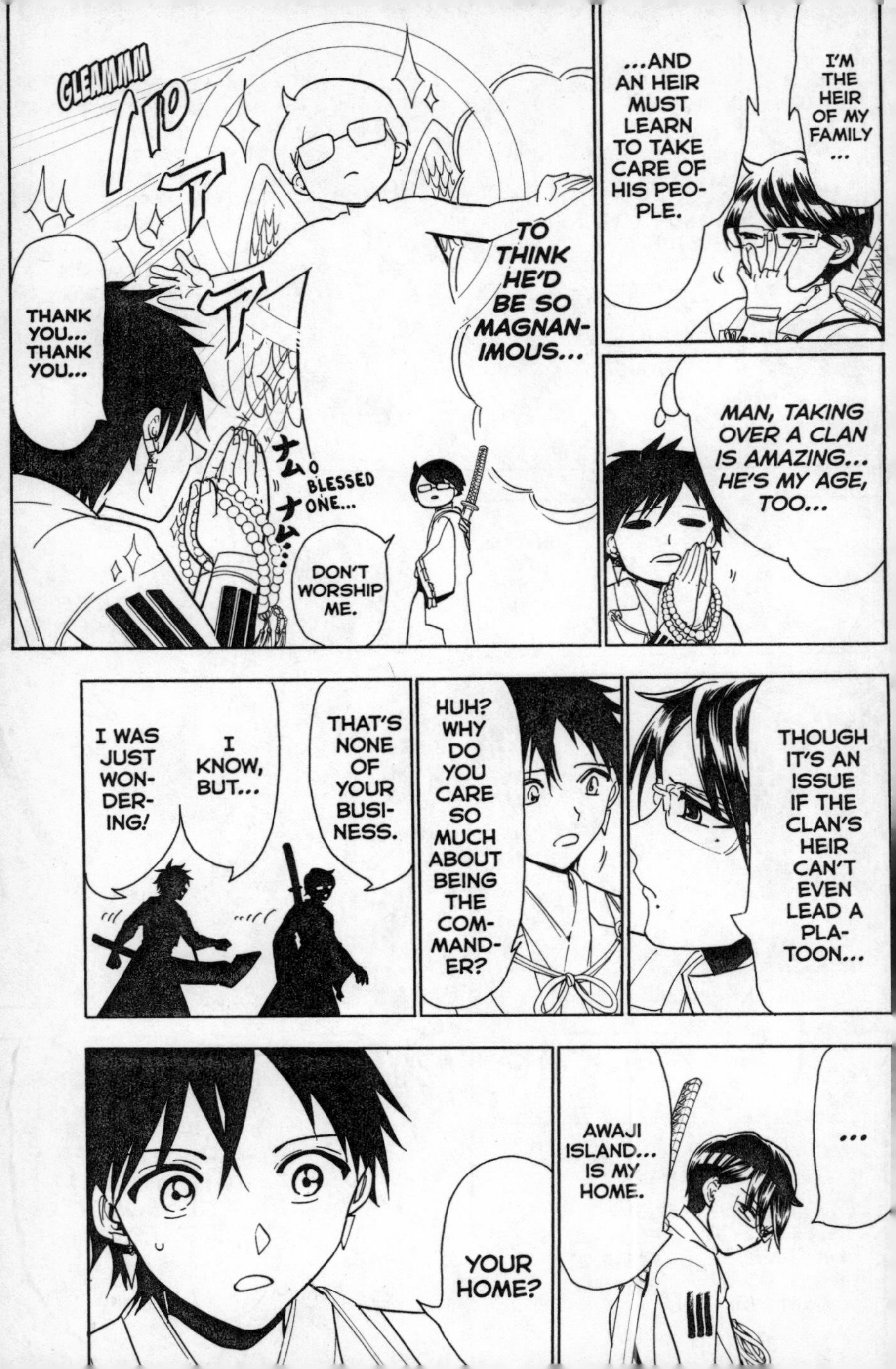
I'M THE HEIR OF MY FAMILY...
...AND AN HEIR MUST LEARN TO TAKE CARE OF HIS PEOPLE.
MAN, TAKING OVER A CLAN IS AMAZING... HE'S MY AGE, TOO...
TO THINK HE'D BE SO MAGNANIMOUS...
GLEAMMM
パア
THANK YOU... THANK YOU...
ナムナム…
O BLESSED ONE...
DON'T WORSHIP ME.
THOUGH IT'S AN ISSUE IF THE CLAN'S HEIR CAN'T EVEN LEAD A PLATOON...
HUH? WHY DO YOU CARE SO MUCH ABOUT BEING THE COMMANDER?
THAT'S NONE OF YOUR BUSINESS.
I KNOW, BUT...
I WAS JUST WONDERING!
...
AWAJI ISLAND... IS MY HOME.
YOUR HOME?

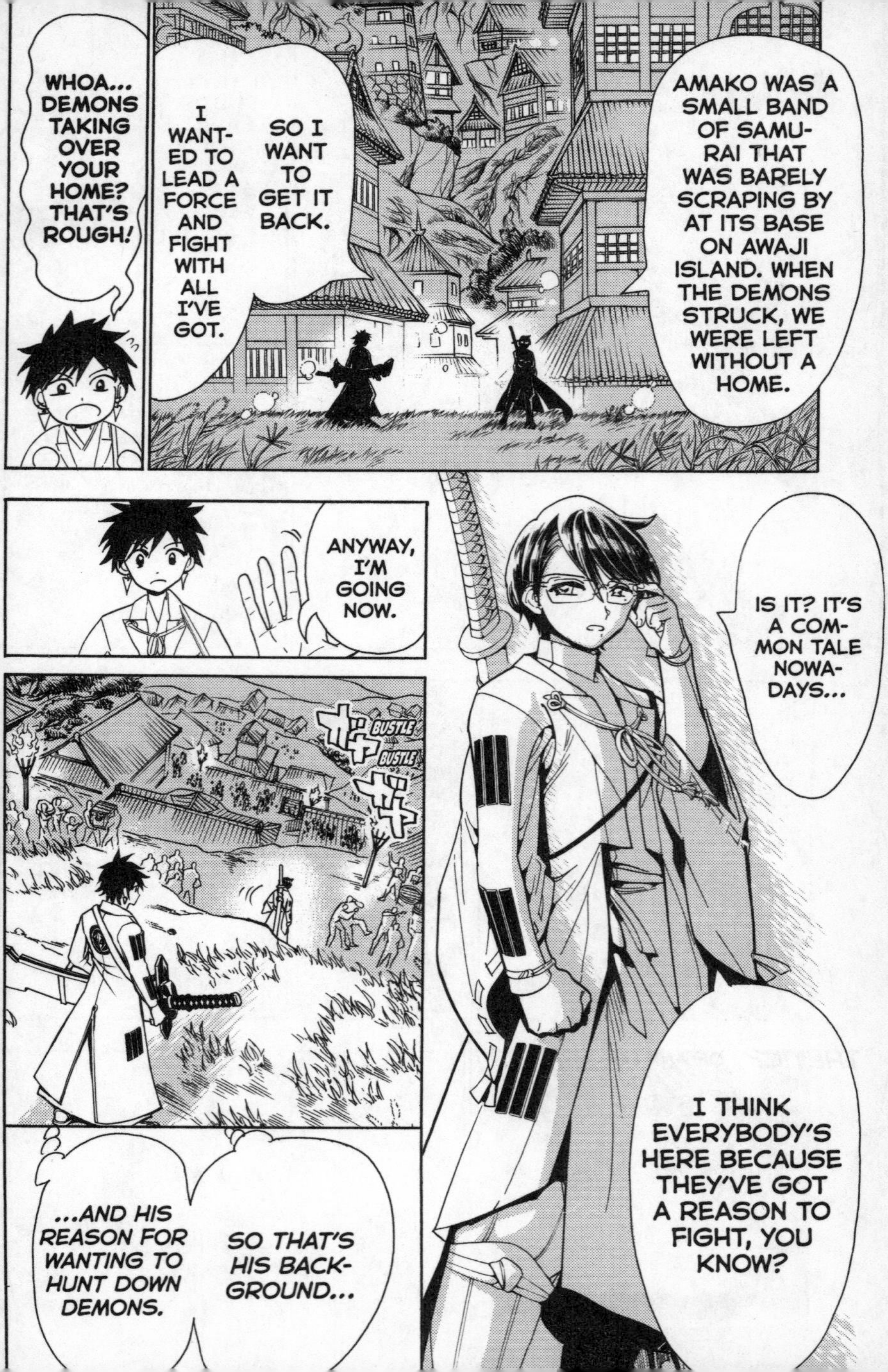
AMAKO WAS A SMALL BAND OF SAMURAI THAT WAS BARELY SCRAPING BY AT ITS BASE ON AWAJI ISLAND. WHEN THE DEMONS STRUCK, WE WERE LEFT WITHOUT A HOME.
I WANTED TO LEAD A FORCE AND FIGHT WITH ALL I'VE GOT.
SO I WANT TO GET IT BACK.
WHOA... DEMONS TAKING OVER YOUR HOME? THAT'S ROUGH!
IS IT? IT'S A COMMON TALE NOWADAYS...
I THINK EVERYBODY'S HERE BECAUSE THEY'VE GOT A REASON TO FIGHT, YOU KNOW?
ANYWAY, I'M GOING NOW.
ガヤ BUSTLE
BUSTLE ガヤ
SO THAT'S HIS BACKGROUND...
...AND HIS REASON FOR WANTING TO HUNT DOWN DEMONS.

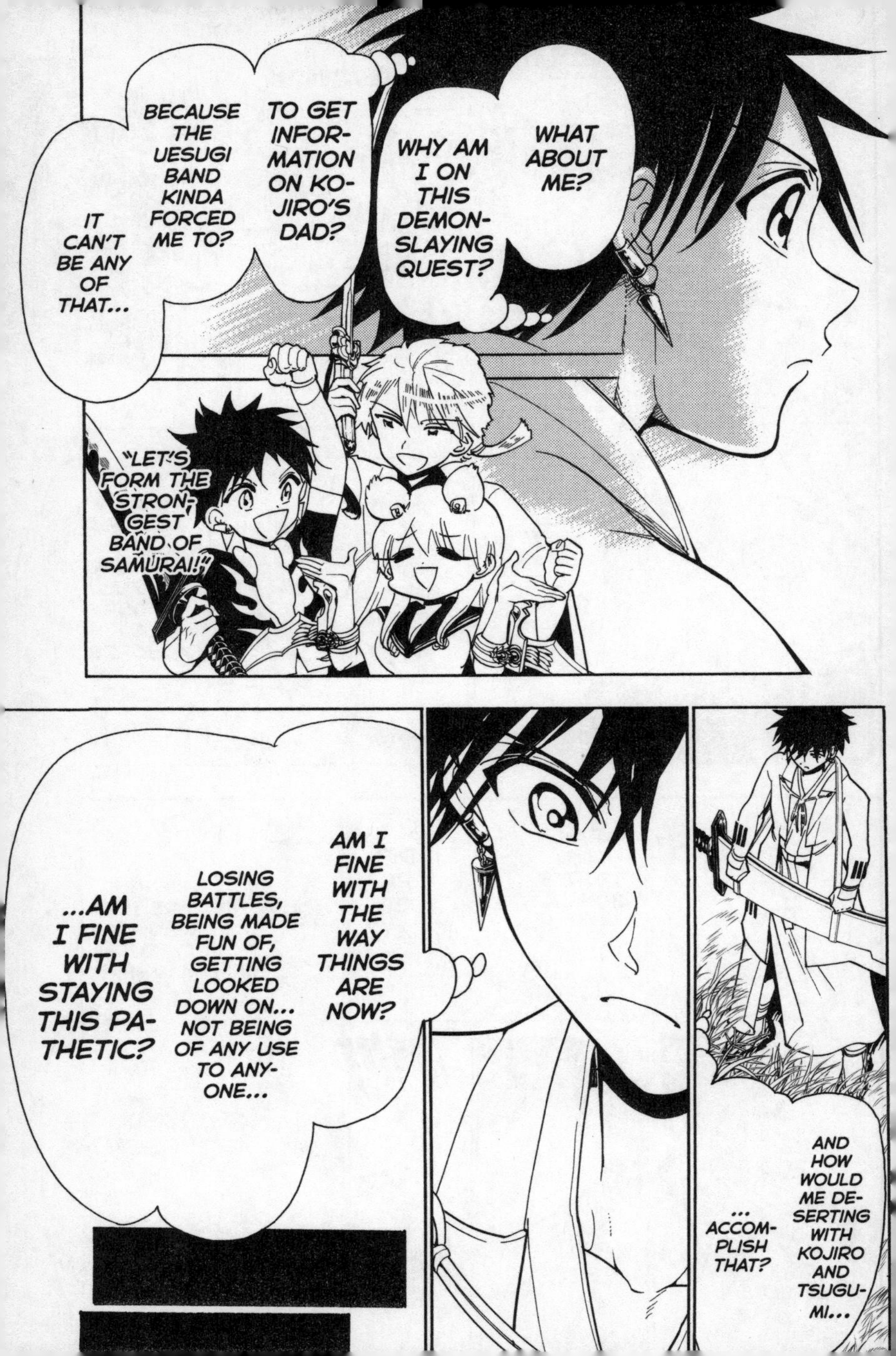

WHAT ABOUT ME?
WHY AM I ON THIS DEMON-SLAYING QUEST?
TO GET INFORMATION ON KOJIRO'S DAD?
BECAUSE THE UESUGI BAND KINDA FORCED ME TO?
IT CAN'T BE ANY OF THAT...
"LET'S FORM THE STRONGEST BAND OF SAMURAI!"
AND HOW WOULD ME DESERTING WITH KOJIRO AND TSUGUMI...
...ACCOMPLISH THAT?
AM I FINE WITH THE WAY THINGS ARE NOW?
LOSING BATTLES, BEING MADE FUN OF, GETTING LOOKED DOWN ON... NOT BEING OF ANY USE TO ANYONE...
...AM I FINE WITH STAYING THIS PATHETIC?
[redacted]

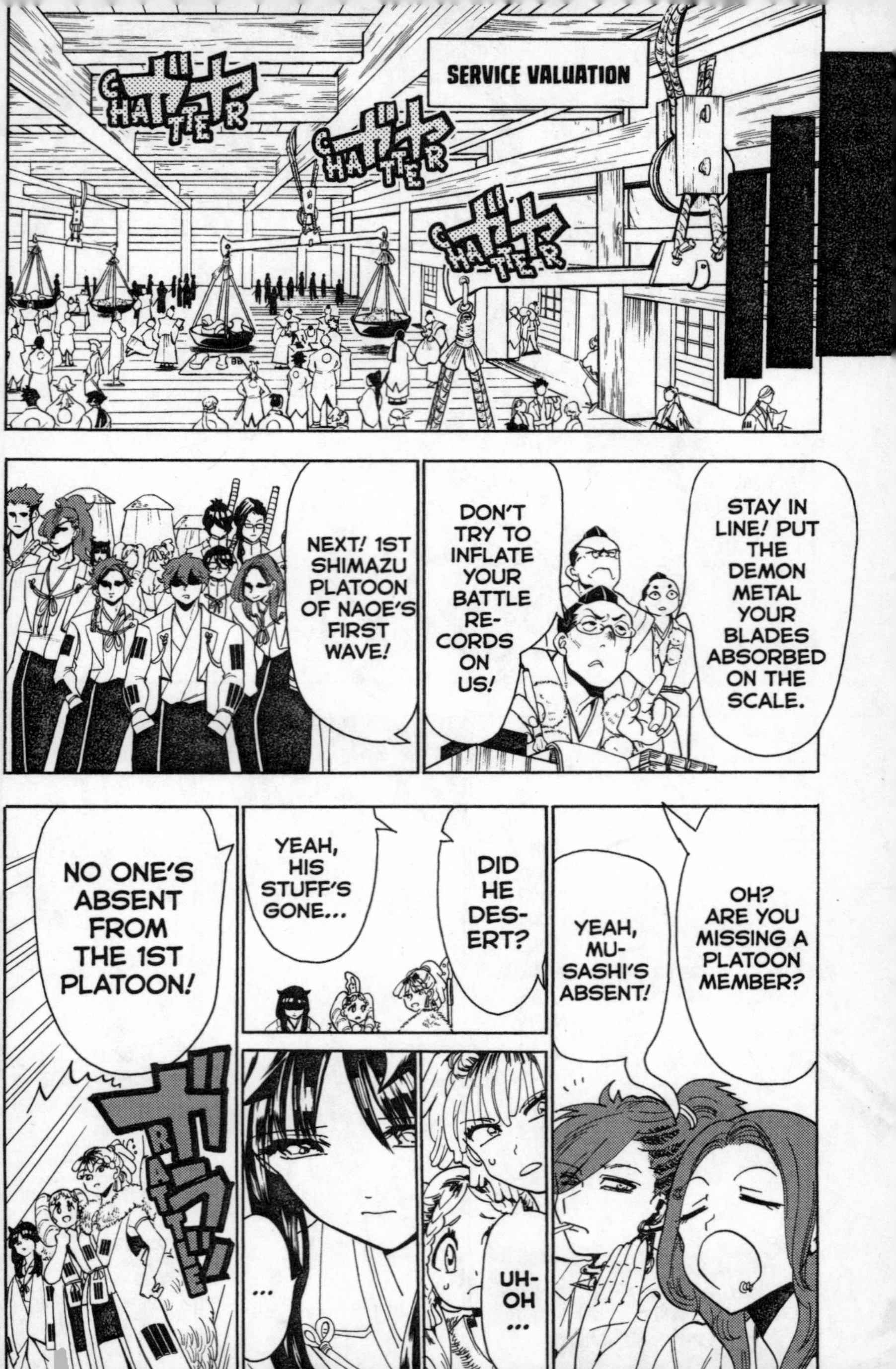
SERVICE VALUATION
CHATTER
CHATTER
CHATTER
[redacted]
STAY IN LINE! PUT THE DEMON METAL YOUR BLADES ABSORBED ON THE SCALE.
DON'T TRY TO INFLATE YOUR BATTLE RE-CORDS ON US!
NEXT! 1ST SHIMAZU PLATOON OF NAOE'S FIRST WAVE!
OH? ARE YOU MISSING A PLATOON MEMBER?
YEAH, MU-SASHI'S ABSENT!
DID HE DES-ERT?
YEAH, HIS STUFF'S GONE...
UH-OH ...
...
NO ONE'S ABSENT FROM THE 1ST PLATOON!
RATTLE

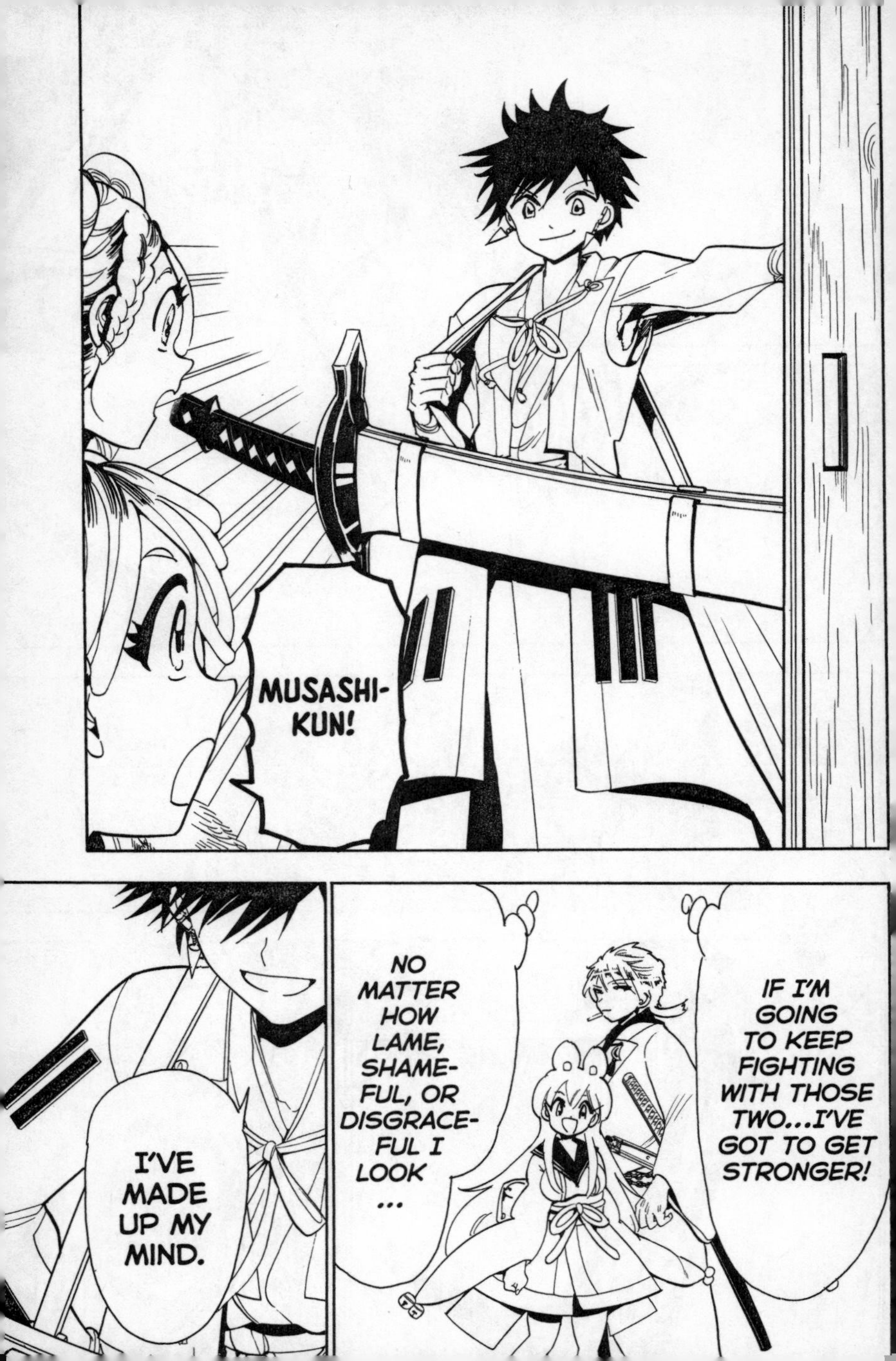
MUSASHI-KUN!
IF I'M GOING TO KEEP FIGHTING WITH THOSE TWO...I'VE GOT TO GET STRONGER!
NO MATTER HOW LAME, SHAME-FUL, OR DISGRACE-FUL I LOOK ...
I'VE MADE UP MY MIND.

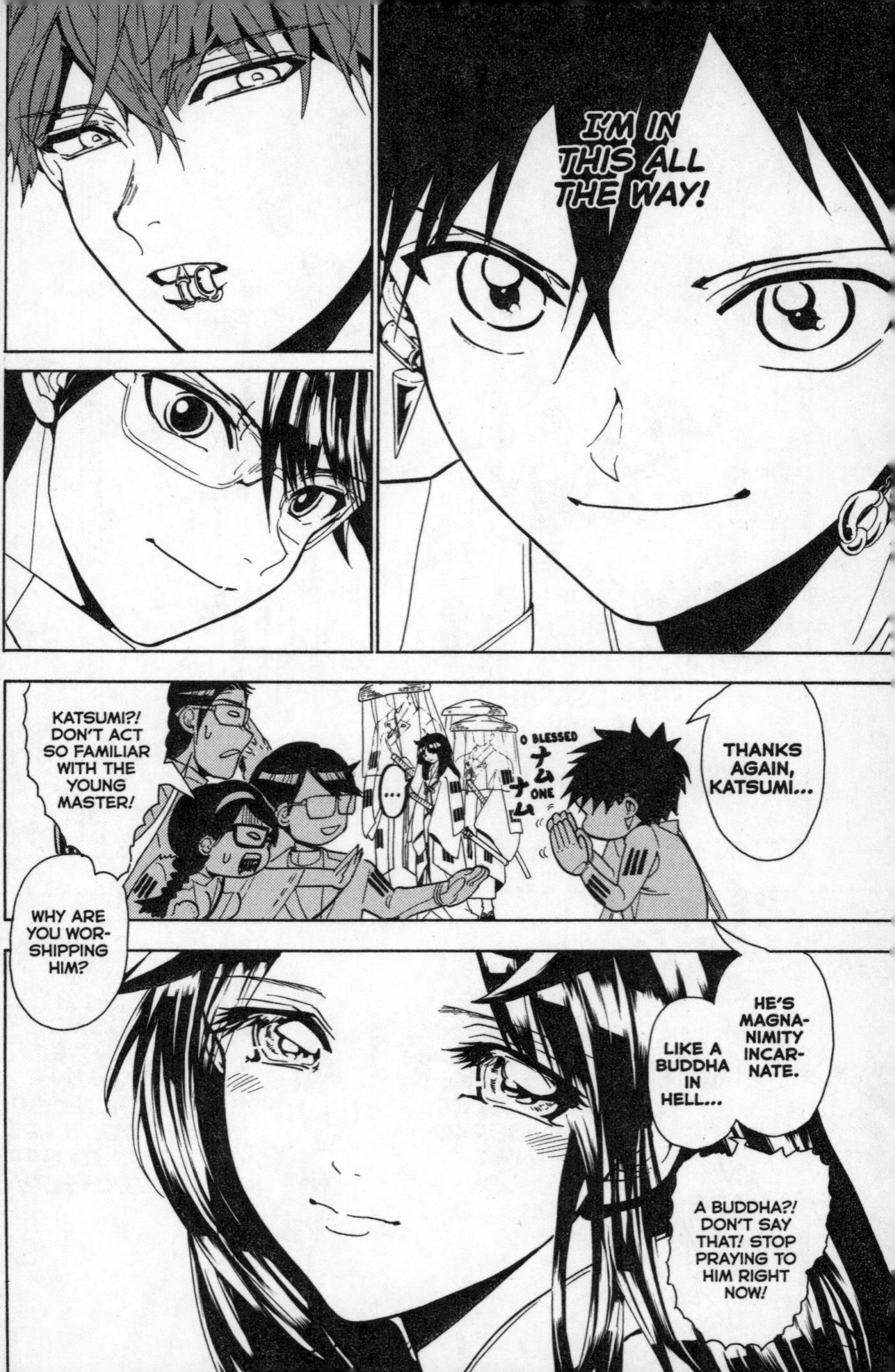
I'M IN THIS ALL THE WAY!
THANKS AGAIN, KATSUMI...
O BLESSED ナム ONE ナム
...
KATSUMI?! DON'T ACT SO FAMILIAR WITH THE YOUNG MASTER!
WHY ARE YOU WOR-SHIPPING HIM?
HE'S MAGNA-NIMITY INCAR-NATE.
LIKE A BUDDHA IN HELL...
A BUDDHA?! DON'T SAY THAT! STOP PRAYING TO HIM RIGHT NOW!

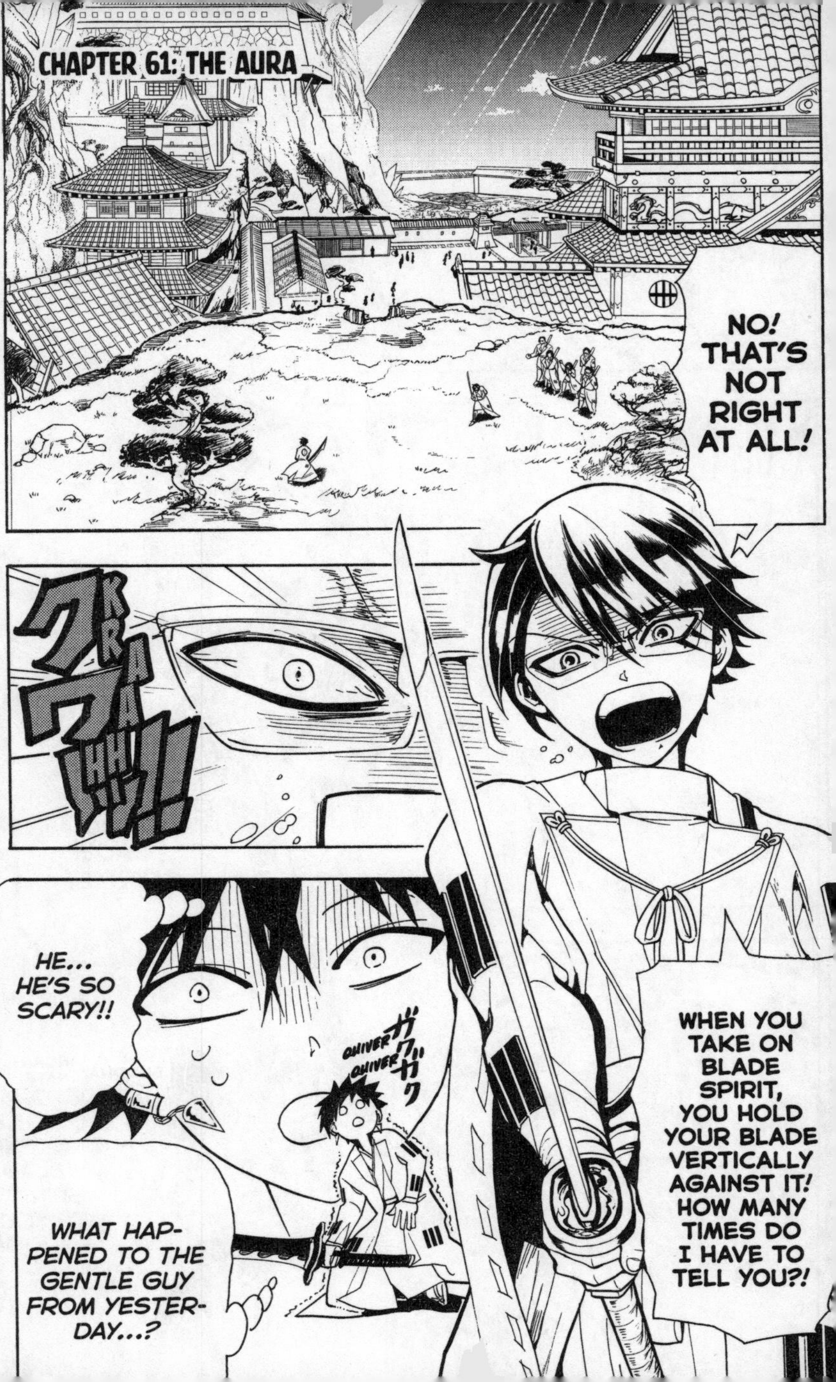
CHAPTER 61: THE AURA
NO! THAT'S NOT RIGHT AT ALL!
KRAAAHH!!
WHEN YOU TAKE ON BLADE SPIRIT, YOU HOLD YOUR BLADE VERTICALLY AGAINST IT! HOW MANY TIMES DO I HAVE TO TELL YOU?!
HE... HE'S SO SCARY!!
QUIVER QUIVER
WHAT HAPPENED TO THE GENTLE GUY FROM YESTERDAY...?

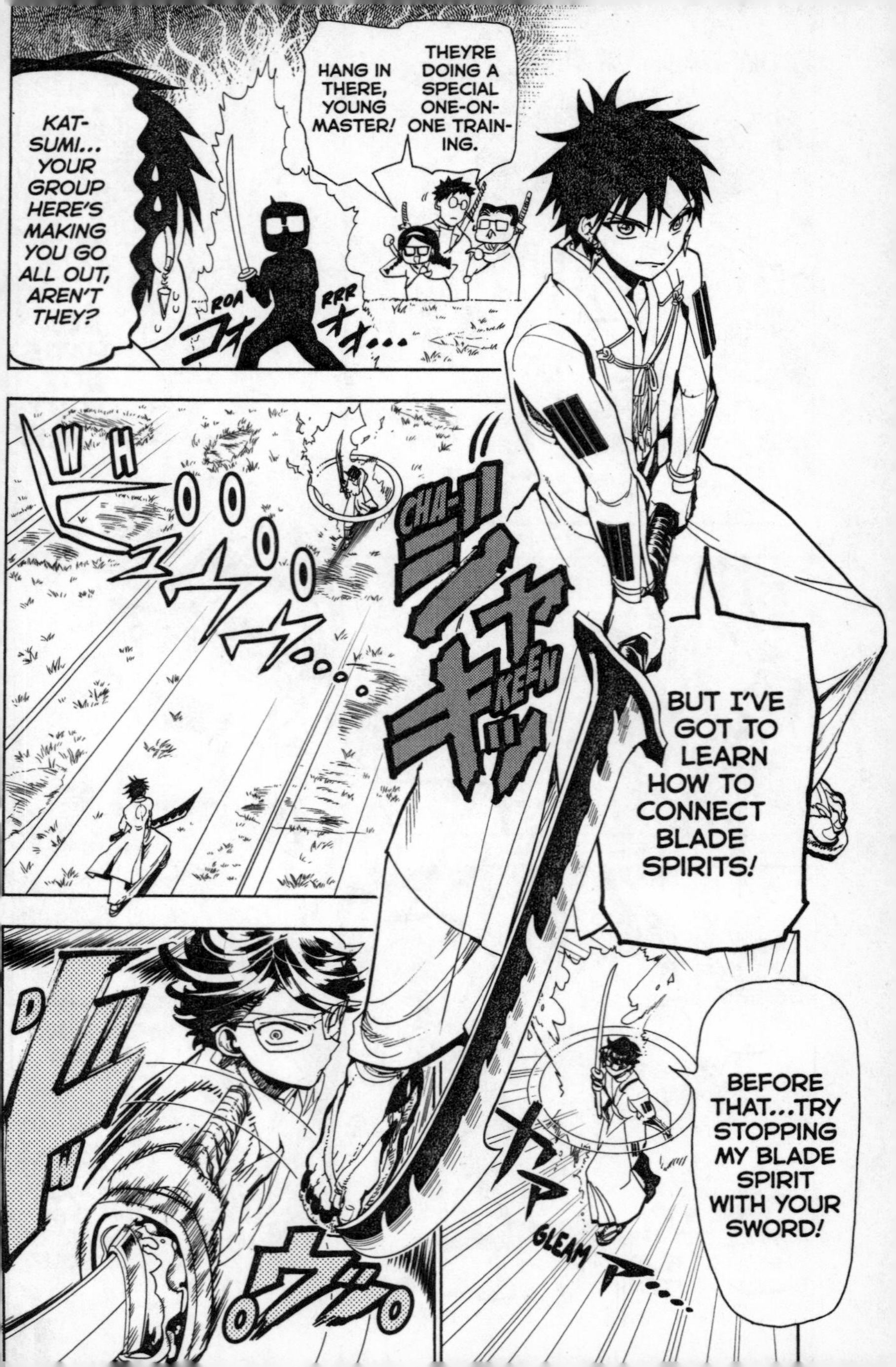
THEYRE DOING A SPECIAL ONE-ON-ONE TRAINING.
HANG IN THERE, YOUNG MASTER!
KAT-SUMI... YOUR GROUP HERE'S MAKING YOU GO ALL OUT, AREN'T THEY?
ROA
RRR
CHA-
KE-EN
WH
BUT I'VE GOT TO LEARN HOW TO CONNECT BLADE SPIRITS!
BEFORE THAT...TRY STOPPING MY BLADE SPIRIT WITH YOUR SWORD!
GLEAM

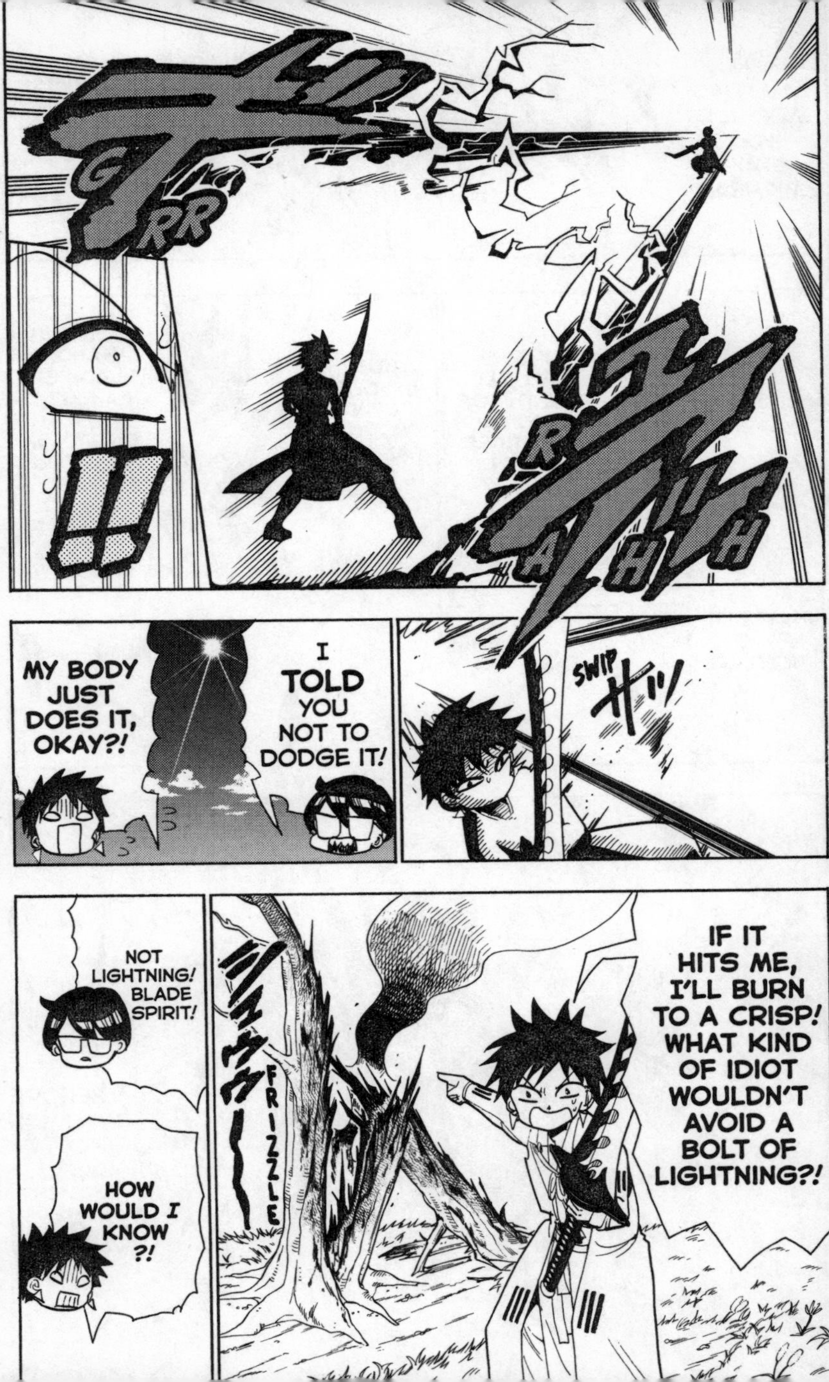
GRR
!!
RAHHH
SWIP
I TOLD YOU NOT TO DODGE IT!
MY BODY JUST DOES IT, OKAY?!
IF IT HITS ME, I'LL BURN TO A CRISP! WHAT KIND OF IDIOT WOULDN'T AVOID A BOLT OF LIGHTNING?!
FRIZZLE
NOT LIGHTNING! BLADE SPIRIT!
HOW WOULD I KNOW ?!

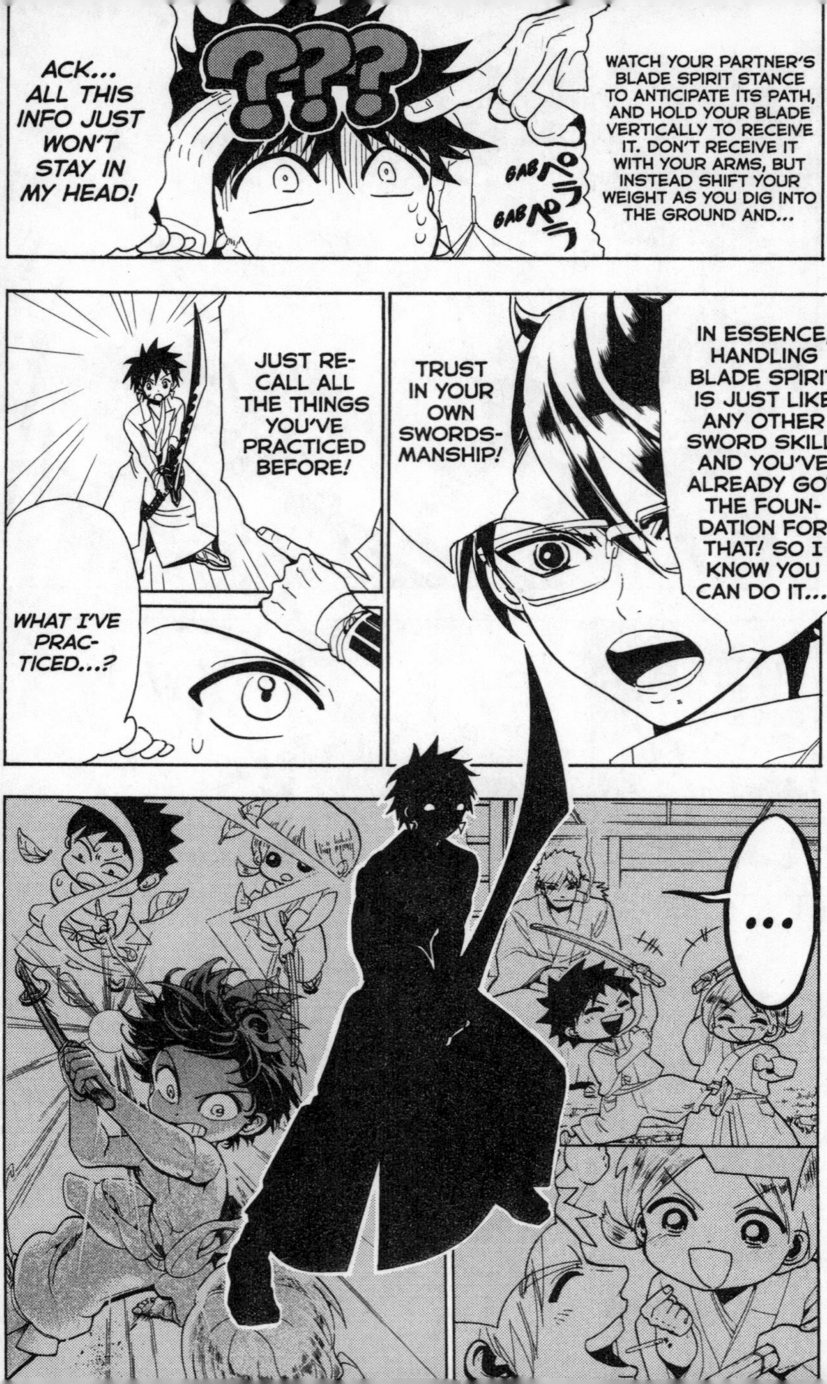
WATCH YOUR PARTNER'S BLADE SPIRIT STANCE TO ANTICIPATE ITS PATH, AND HOLD YOUR BLADE VERTICALLY TO RECEIVE IT. DON'T RECEIVE IT WITH YOUR ARMS, BUT INSTEAD SHIFT YOUR WEIGHT AS YOU DIG INTO THE GROUND AND...
GAB
GAB
ACK... ALL THIS INFO JUST WON'T STAY IN MY HEAD!
IN ESSENCE, HANDLING BLADE SPIRIT IS JUST LIKE ANY OTHER SWORD SKILL, AND YOU'VE ALREADY GOT THE FOUNDATION FOR THAT! SO I KNOW YOU CAN DO IT...
TRUST IN YOUR OWN SWORDSMANSHIP!
JUST RECALL ALL THE THINGS YOU'VE PRACTICED BEFORE!
WHAT I'VE PRACTICED...?
...

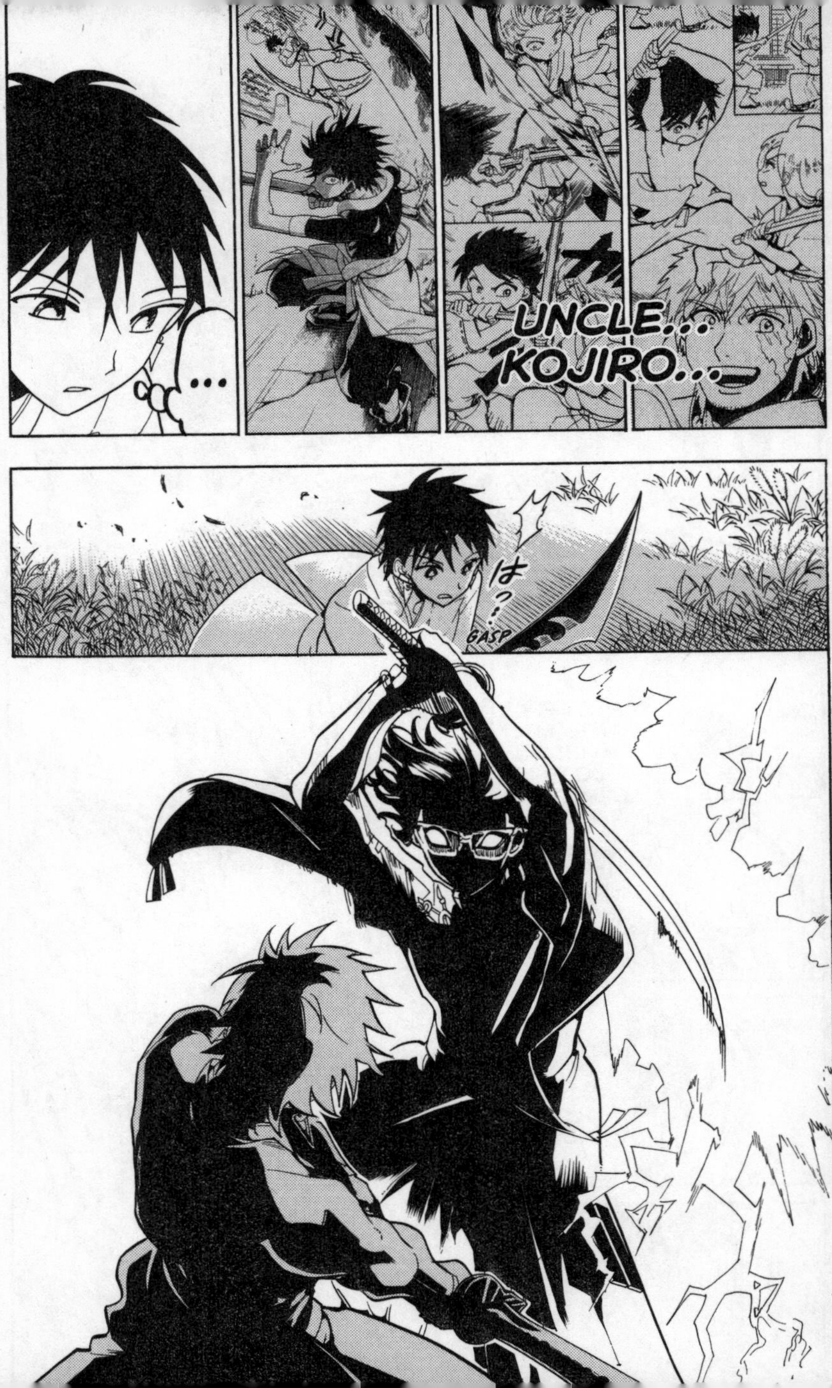
UNCLE... KOJIRO...
...
はっ…
GASP

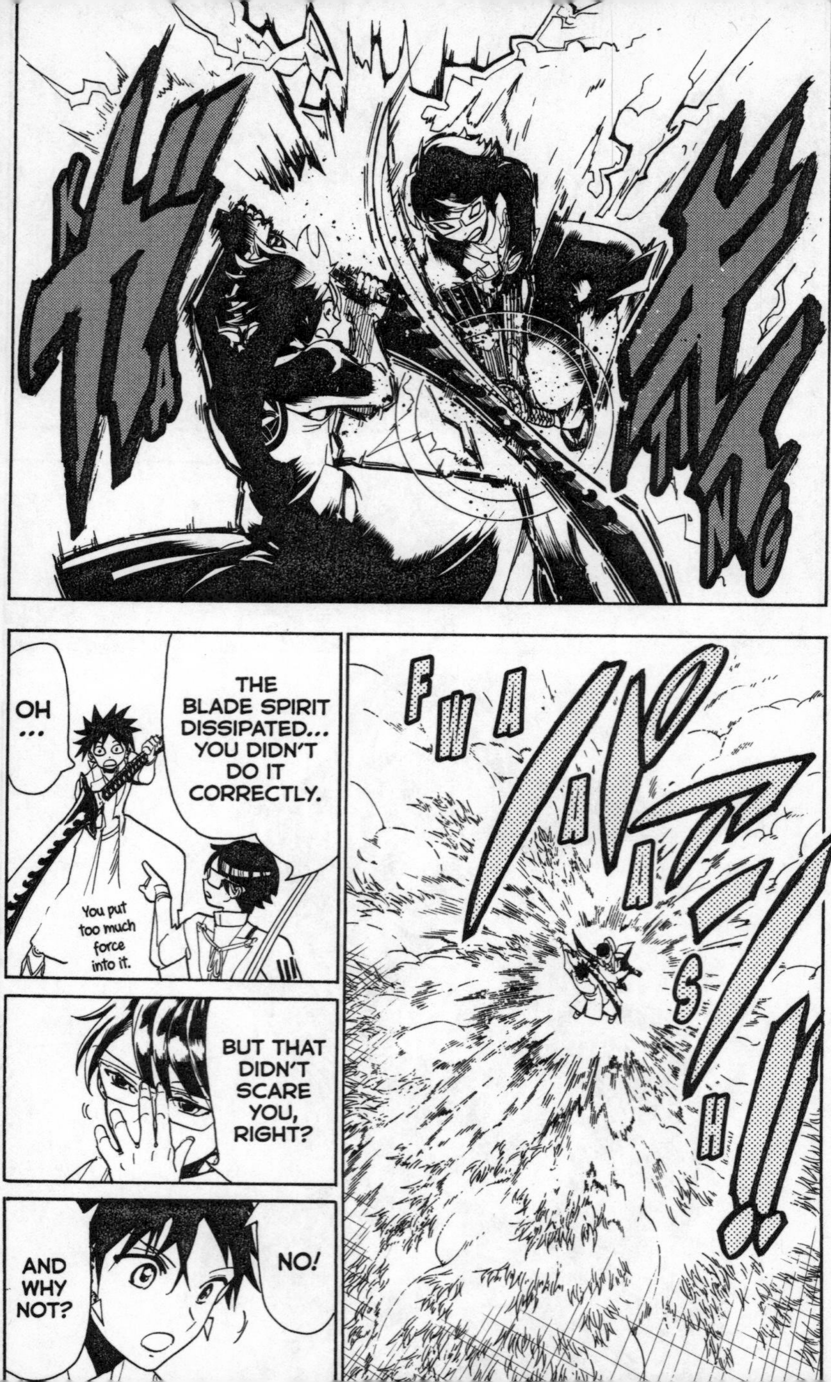

FWAAASH
THE BLADE SPIRIT DISSIPATED... YOU DIDN'T DO IT CORRECTLY.
OH ...
You put too much force into it.
BUT THAT DIDN'T SCARE YOU, RIGHT?
NO!
AND WHY NOT?

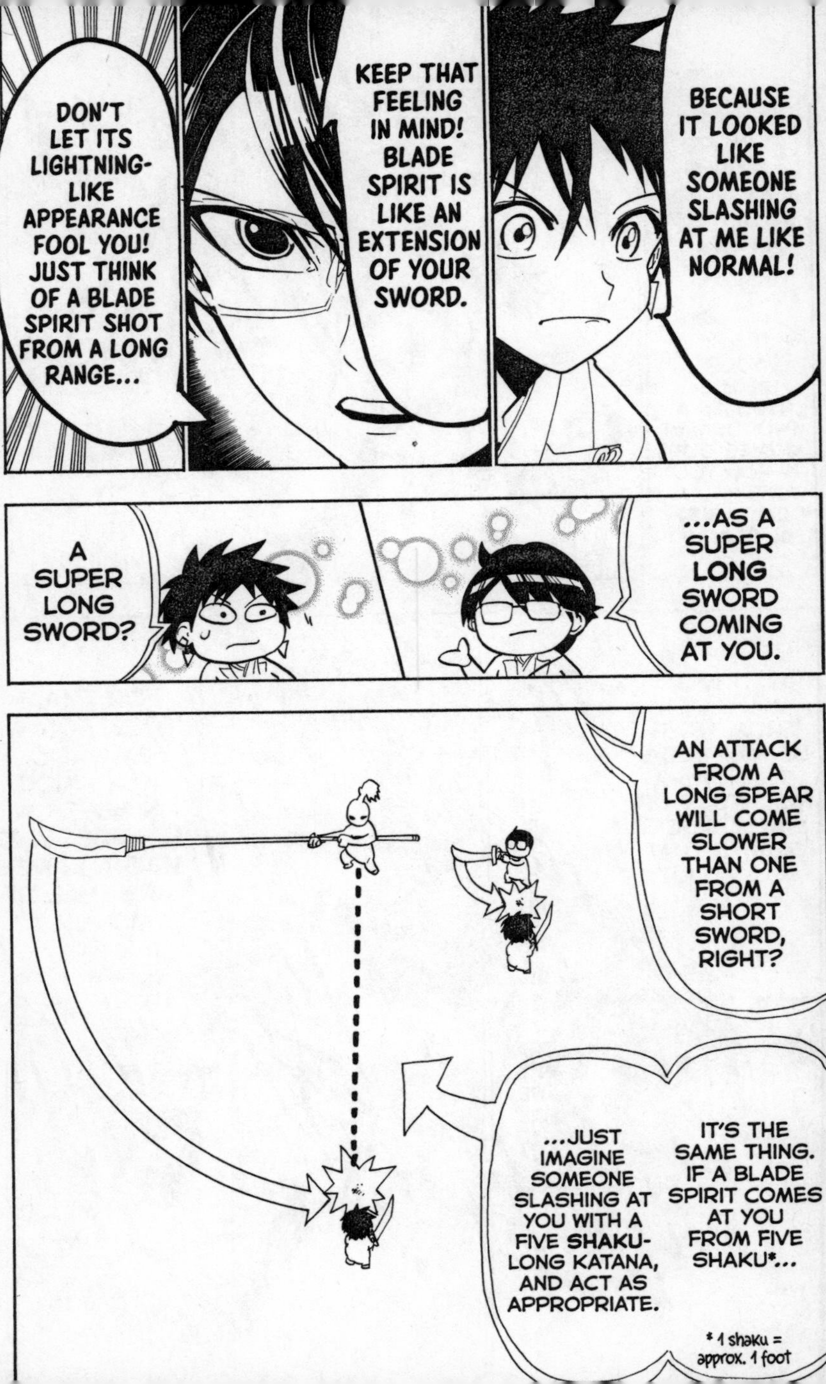
BECAUSE IT LOOKED LIKE SOMEONE SLASHING AT ME LIKE NORMAL!
KEEP THAT FEELING IN MIND! BLADE SPIRIT IS LIKE AN EXTENSION OF YOUR SWORD.
DON'T LET ITS LIGHTNING-LIKE APPEARANCE FOOL YOU! JUST THINK OF A BLADE SPIRIT SHOT FROM A LONG RANGE...
...AS A SUPER LONG SWORD COMING AT YOU.
A SUPER LONG SWORD?
AN ATTACK FROM A LONG SPEAR WILL COME SLOWER THAN ONE FROM A SHORT SWORD, RIGHT?
IT'S THE SAME THING. IF A BLADE SPIRIT COMES AT YOU FROM FIVE SHAKU*...
...JUST IMAGINE SOMEONE SLASHING AT YOU WITH A FIVE SHAKU-LONG KATANA, AND ACT AS APPROPRIATE.
* 1 shaku = approx. 1 foot

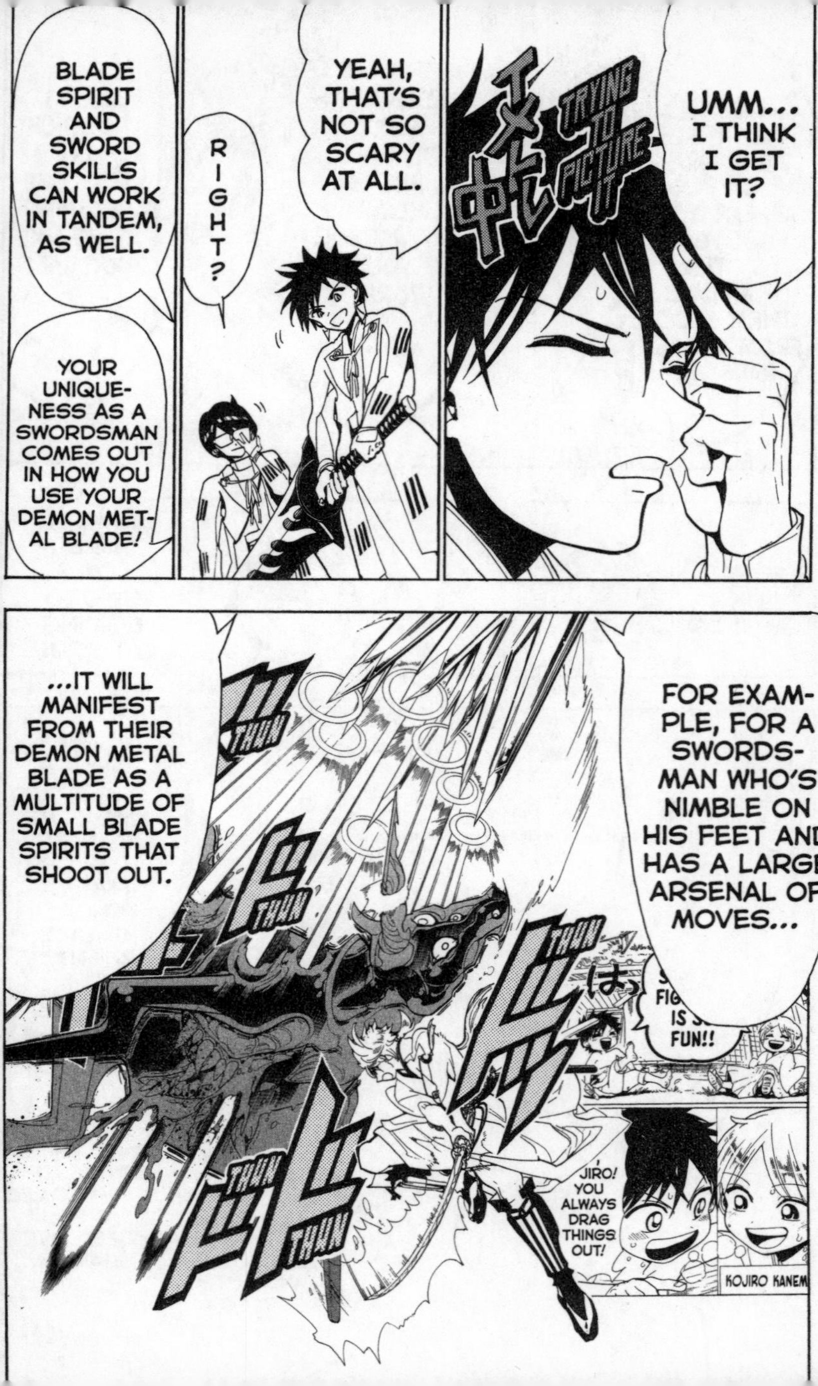
TRYING TO PICTURE IT
UMM... I THINK I GET IT?
YEAH, THAT'S NOT SO SCARY AT ALL.
RIGHT?
BLADE SPIRIT AND SWORD SKILLS CAN WORK IN TANDEM, AS WELL.
YOUR UNIQUENESS AS A SWORDSMAN COMES OUT IN HOW YOU USE YOUR DEMON METAL BLADE!
FOR EXAMPLE, FOR A SWORDSMAN WHO'S NIMBLE ON HIS FEET AND HAS A LARGE ARSENAL OF MOVES...
FUN!!
JIRO! YOU ALWAYS DRAG THINGS OUT!
...IT WILL MANIFEST FROM THEIR DEMON METAL BLADE AS A MULTITUDE OF SMALL BLADE SPIRITS THAT SHOOT OUT.
THWN
THWN
THWN
THWN
THWN

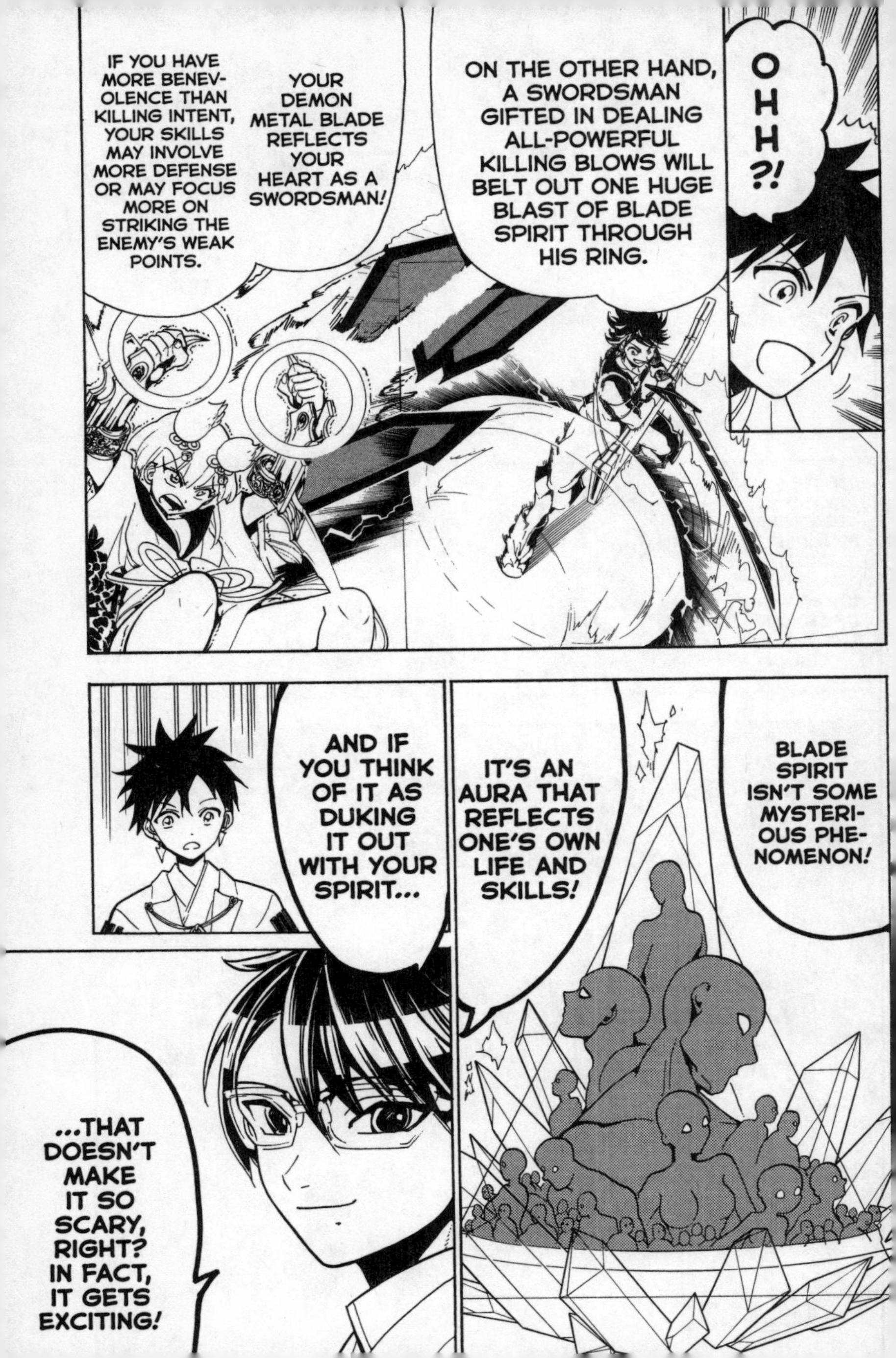
OHH?!
ON THE OTHER HAND, A SWORDSMAN GIFTED IN DEALING ALL-POWERFUL KILLING BLOWS WILL BELT OUT ONE HUGE BLAST OF BLADE SPIRIT THROUGH HIS RING.
YOUR DEMON METAL BLADE REFLECTS YOUR HEART AS A SWORDSMAN!
IF YOU HAVE MORE BENEV-OLENCE THAN KILLING INTENT, YOUR SKILLS MAY INVOLVE MORE DEFENSE OR MAY FOCUS MORE ON STRIKING THE ENEMY'S WEAK POINTS.
BLADE SPIRIT ISN'T SOME MYSTERI-OUS PHE-NOMENON!
IT'S AN AURA THAT REFLECTS ONE'S OWN LIFE AND SKILLS!
AND IF YOU THINK OF IT AS DUKING IT OUT WITH YOUR SPIRIT...
...THAT DOESN'T MAKE IT SO SCARY, RIGHT? IN FACT, IT GETS EXCITING!

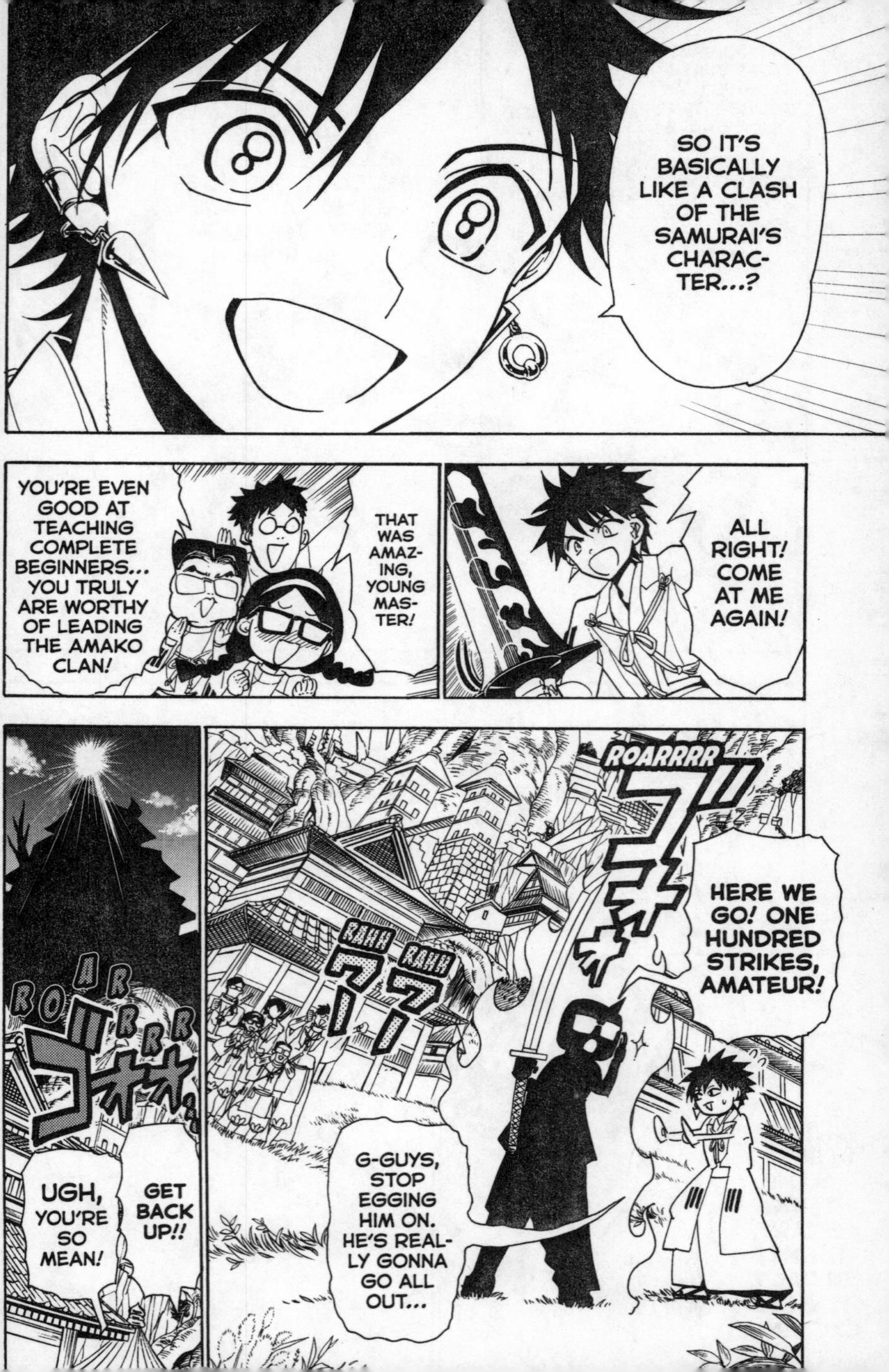
SO IT'S BASICALLY LIKE A CLASH OF THE SAMURAI'S CHARAC-TER...?
ALL RIGHT! COME AT ME AGAIN!
THAT WAS AMAZ-ING, YOUNG MAS-TER!
YOU'RE EVEN GOOD AT TEACHING COMPLETE BEGINNERS... YOU TRULY ARE WORTHY OF LEADING THE AMAKO CLAN!
ROARRRR
HERE WE GO! ONE HUNDRED STRIKES, AMATEUR!
RAHH
RAHH
G-GUYS, STOP EGGING HIM ON. HE'S REAL-LY GONNA GO ALL OUT...
GET BACK UP!!
UGH, YOU'RE SO MEAN!

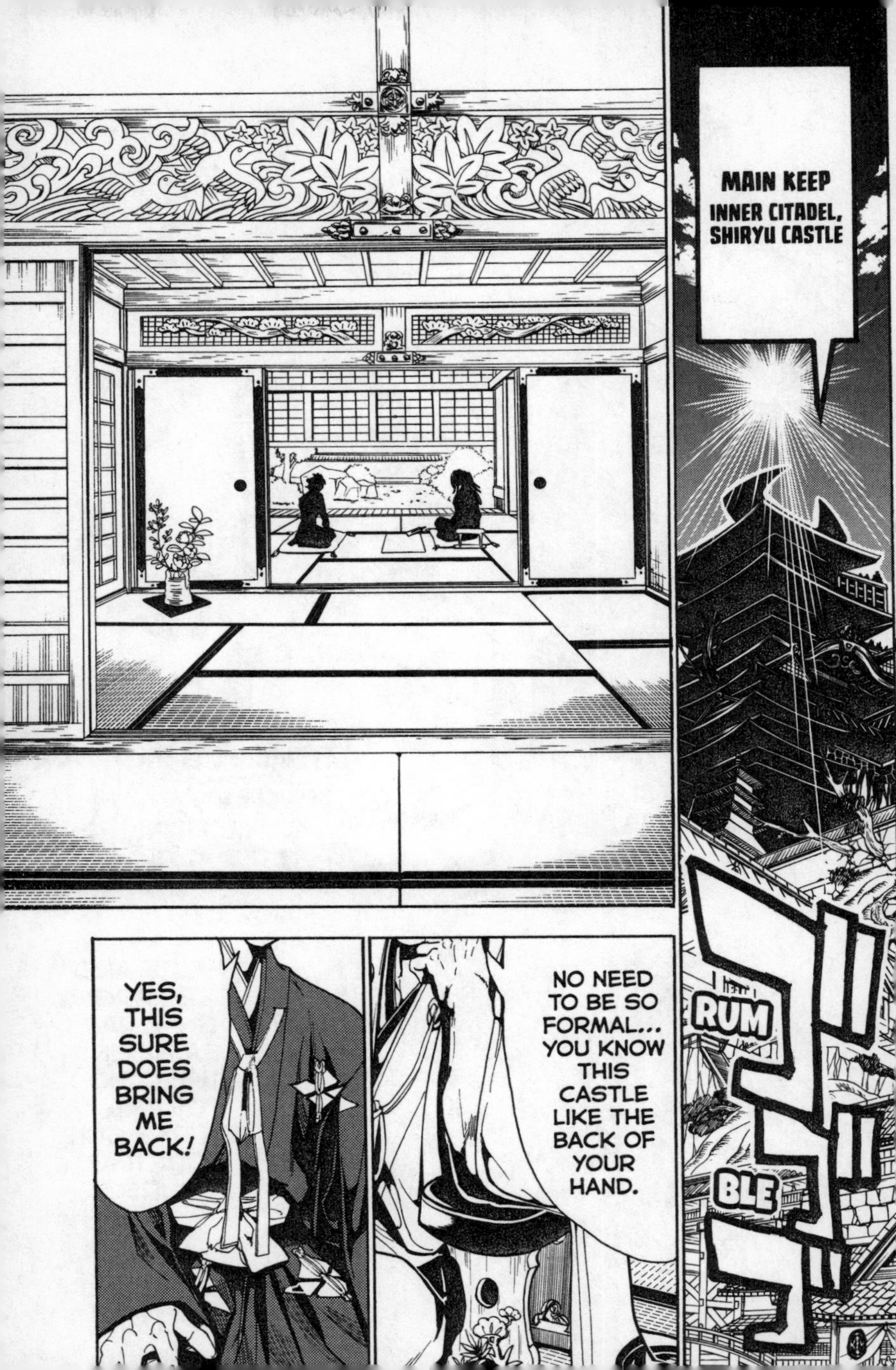
MAIN KEEP
INNER CITADEL, SHIRYU CASTLE
RUM
BLE
NO NEED TO BE SO FORMAL... YOU KNOW THIS CASTLE LIKE THE BACK OF YOUR HAND.
YES, THIS SURE DOES BRING ME BACK!

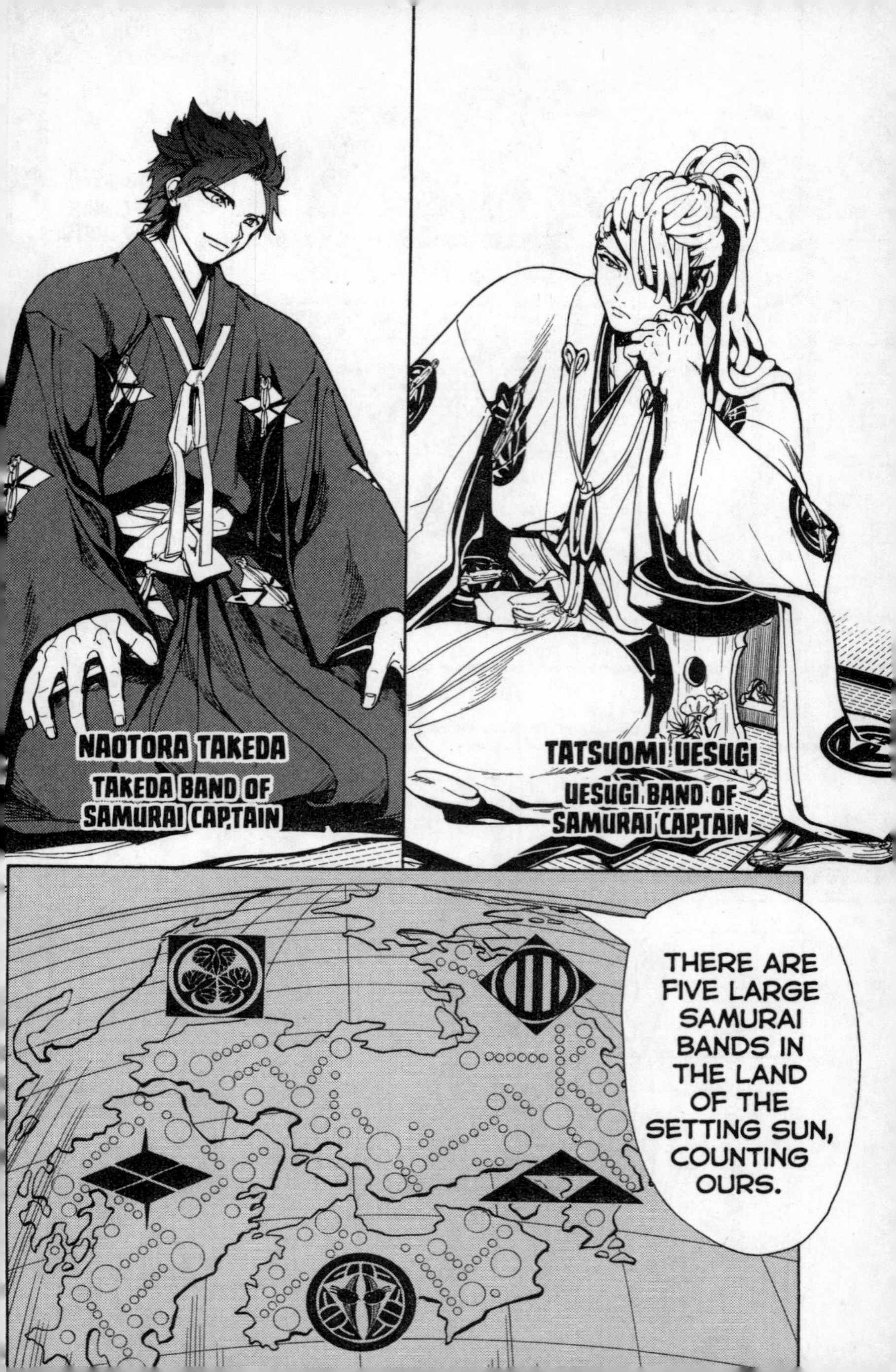
TATSUOMI UESUGI
UESUGI BAND OF SAMURAI CAPTAIN
NAOTORA TAKEDA
TAKEDA BAND OF SAMURAI CAPTAIN
THERE ARE FIVE LARGE SAMURAI BANDS IN THE LAND OF THE SETTING SUN, COUNTING OURS.

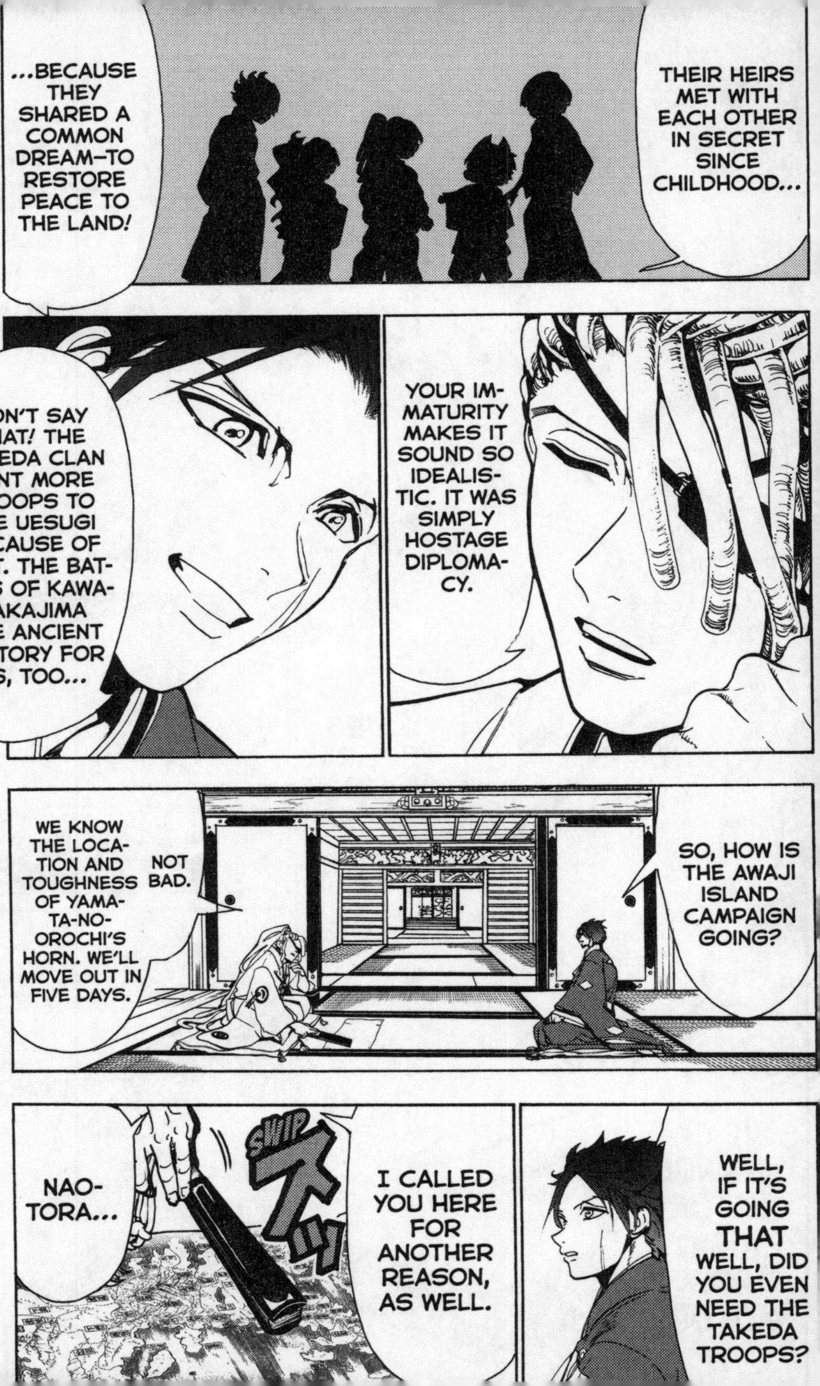
THEIR HEIRS MET WITH EACH OTHER IN SECRET SINCE CHILDHOOD...
...BECAUSE THEY SHARED A COMMON DREAM—TO RESTORE PEACE TO THE LAND!
YOUR IMMATURITY MAKES IT SOUND SO IDEALISTIC. IT WAS SIMPLY HOSTAGE DIPLOMACY.
DON'T SAY THAT! THE TAKEDA CLAN SENT MORE TROOPS TO THE UESUGI BECAUSE OF THAT. THE BATTLES OF KAWANAKAJIMA ARE ANCIENT HISTORY FOR US, TOO...
SO, HOW IS THE AWAJI ISLAND CAMPAIGN GOING?
NOT BAD.
WE KNOW THE LOCATION AND TOUGHNESS OF YAMATA-NO-OROCHI'S HORN. WE'LL MOVE OUT IN FIVE DAYS.
WELL, IF IT'S GOING THAT WELL, DID YOU EVEN NEED THE TAKEDA TROOPS?
I CALLED YOU HERE FOR ANOTHER REASON, AS WELL.
SWIP
NAOTORA...

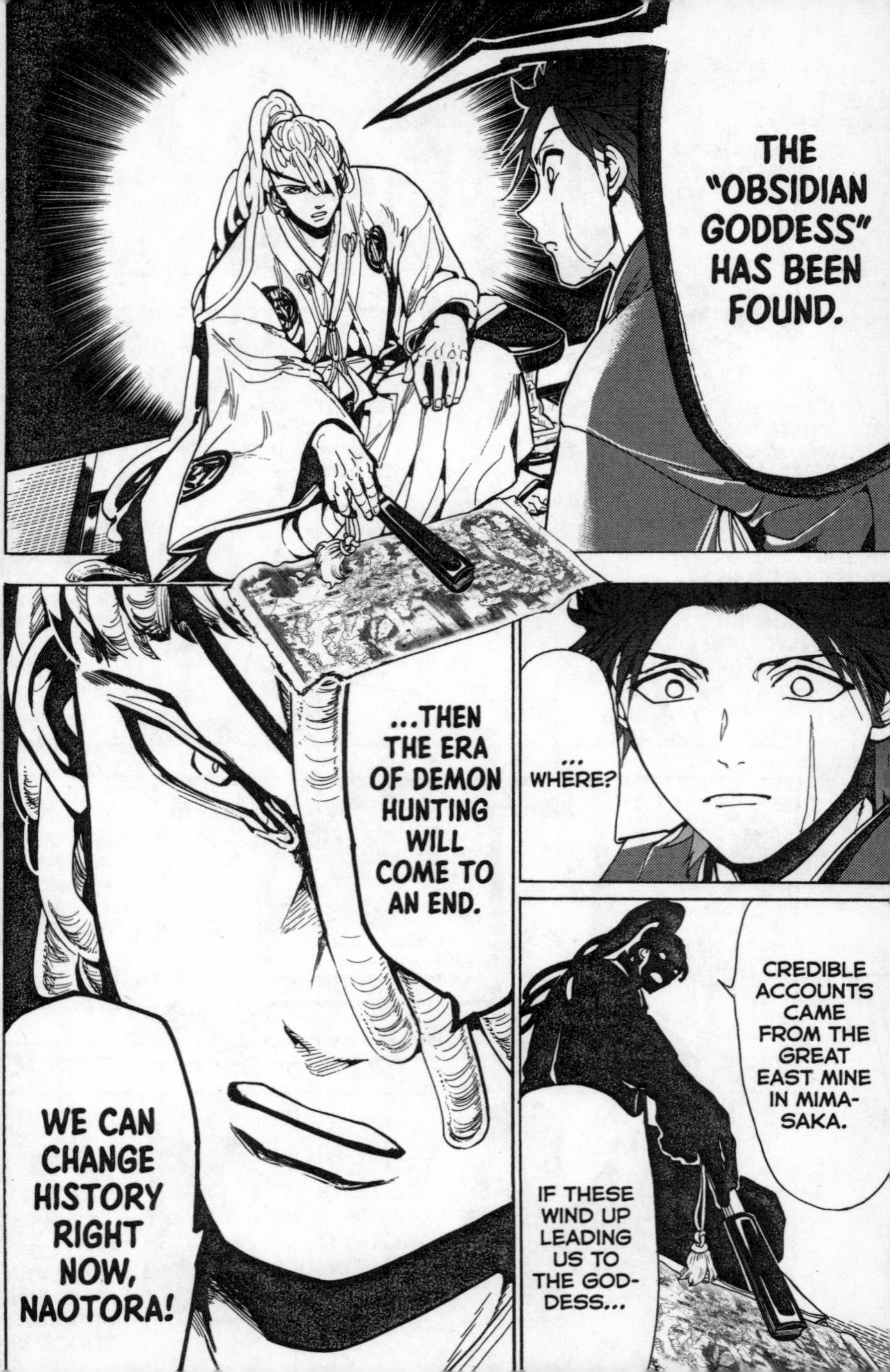
THE "OBSIDIAN GODDESS" HAS BEEN FOUND.
...WHERE?
CREDIBLE ACCOUNTS CAME FROM THE GREAT EAST MINE IN MIMA-SAKA.
IF THESE WIND UP LEADING US TO THE GOD-DESS...
...THEN THE ERA OF DEMON HUNTING WILL COME TO AN END.
WE CAN CHANGE HISTORY RIGHT NOW, NAOTORA!

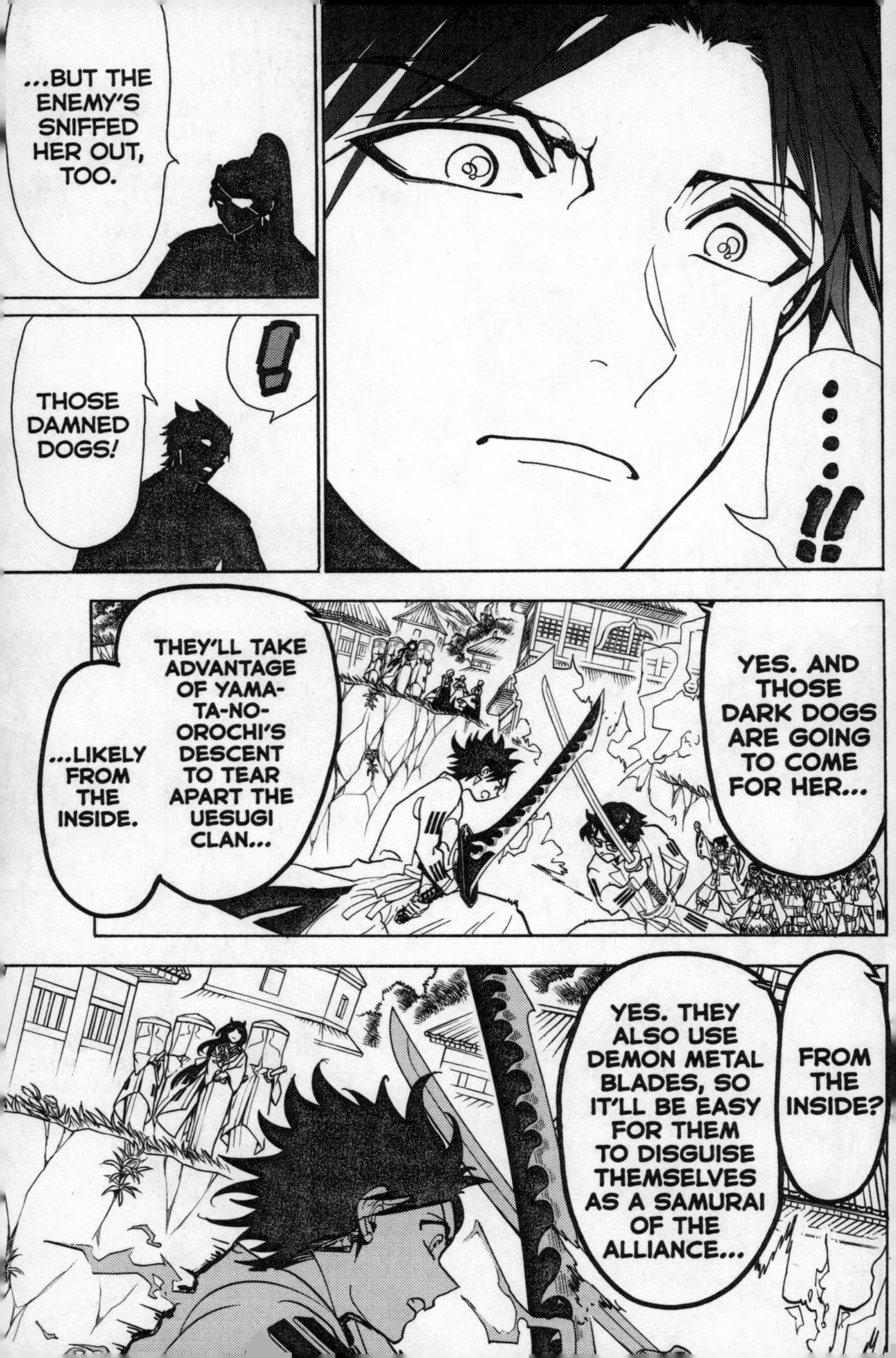
...!!
...BUT THE ENEMY'S SNIFFED HER OUT, TOO.
!
THOSE DAMNED DOGS!
YES. AND THOSE DARK DOGS ARE GOING TO COME FOR HER...
THEY'LL TAKE ADVANTAGE OF YAMA-TA-NO-OROCHI'S DESCENT TO TEAR APART THE UESUGI CLAN...
...LIKELY FROM THE INSIDE.
FROM THE INSIDE?
YES. THEY ALSO USE DEMON METAL BLADES, SO IT'LL BE EASY FOR THEM TO DISGUISE THEMSELVES AS A SAMURAI OF THE ALLIANCE...

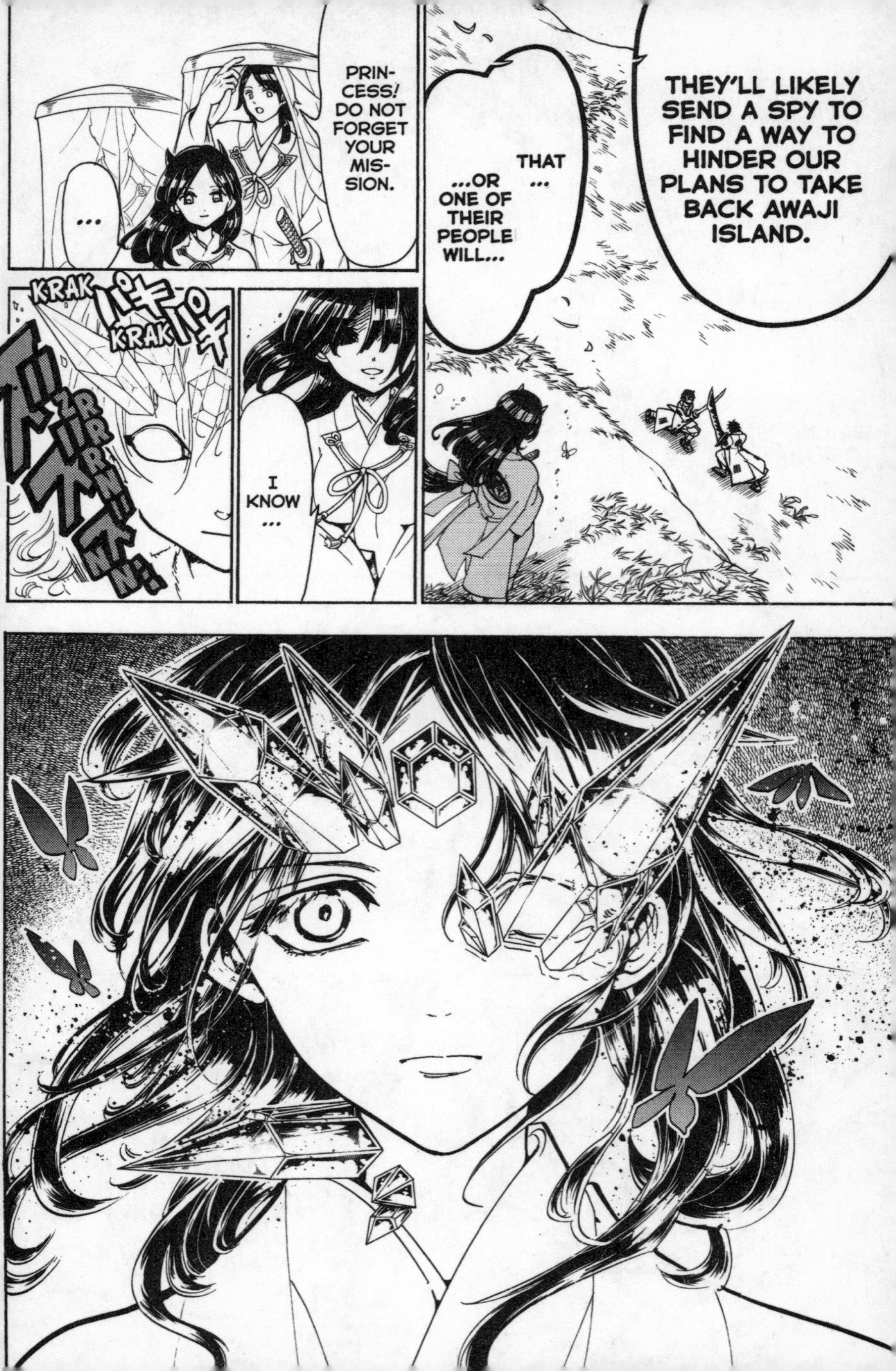

THEY'LL LIKELY SEND A SPY TO FIND A WAY TO HINDER OUR PLANS TO TAKE BACK AWAJI ISLAND.
THAT ...
...OR ONE OF THEIR PEOPLE WILL...
PRINCESS! DO NOT FORGET YOUR MISSION.
...
I KNOW ...
パキ KRAK
パキ KRAK
ZRIRRNNN!!

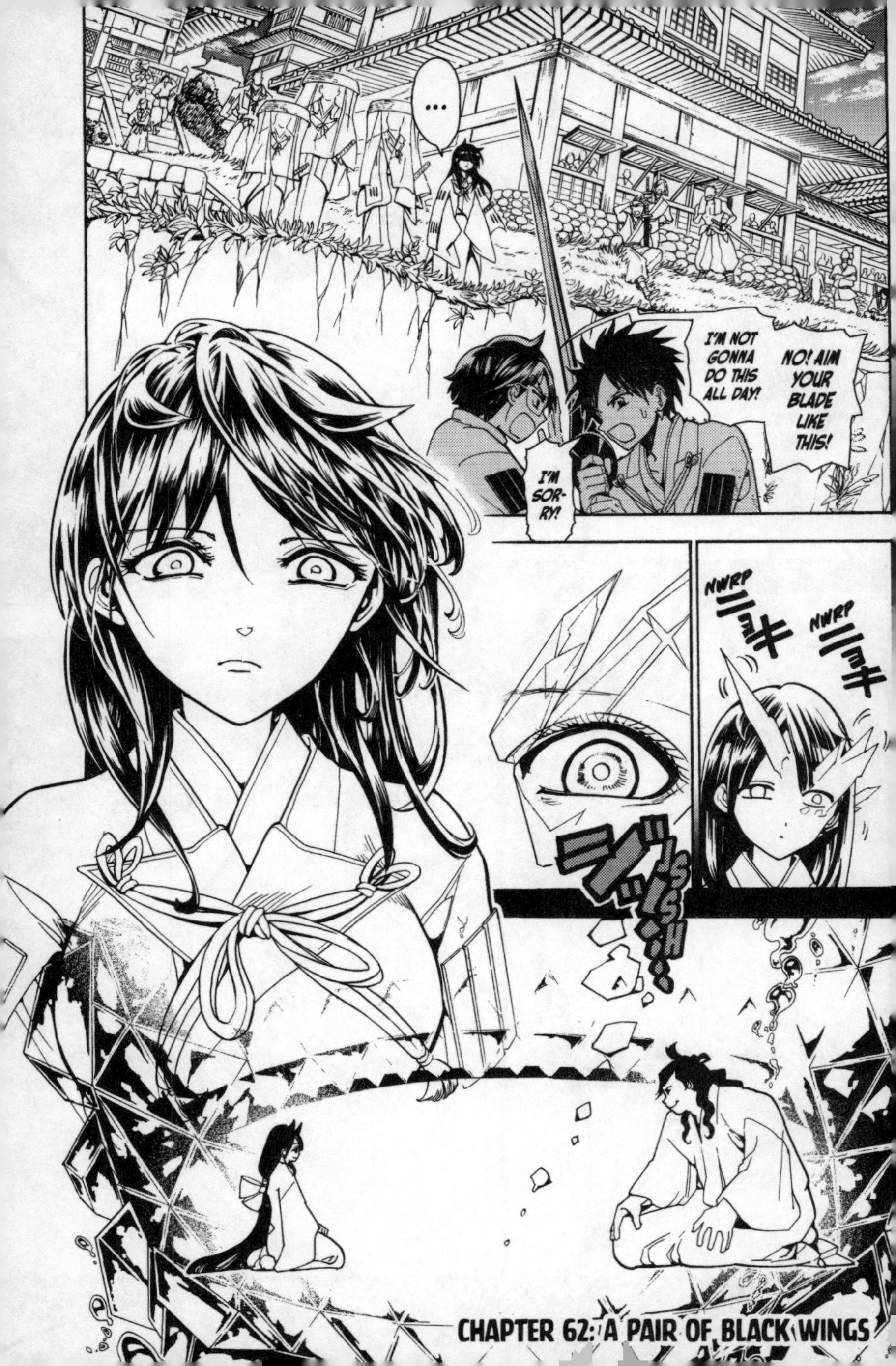

...
NO! AIM YOUR BLADE LIKE THIS!
I'M NOT GONNA DO THIS ALL DAY!
I'M SOR-RY!
NWRP ニョキ
NWRP ニョキ
SWISH...
CHAPTER 62: A PAIR OF BLACK WINGS

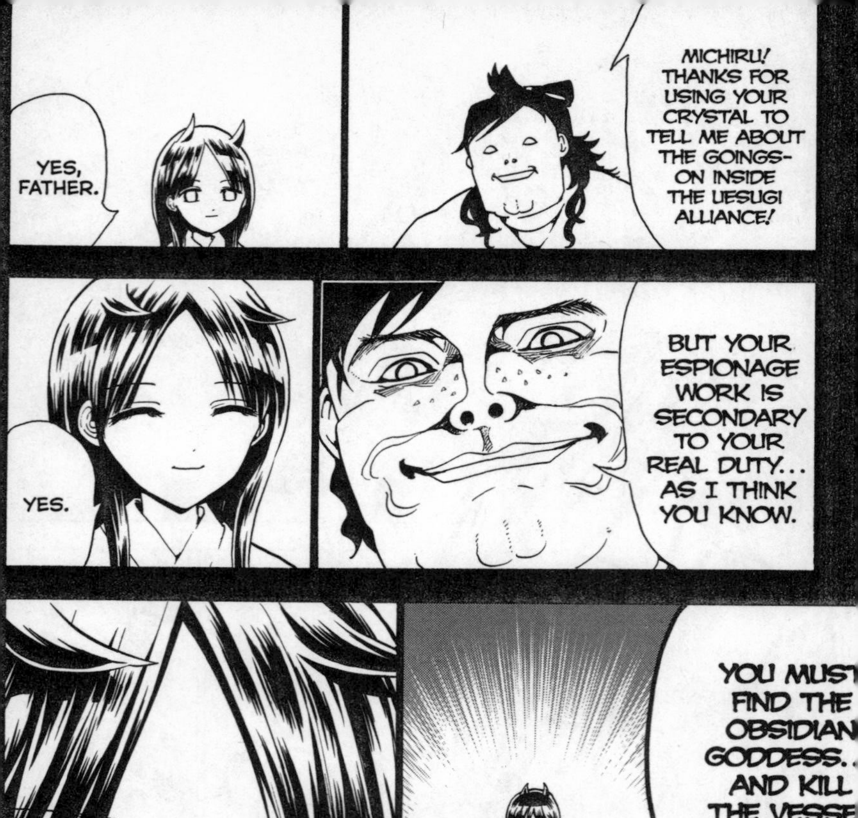
MICHIRU! THANKS FOR USING YOUR CRYSTAL TO TELL ME ABOUT THE GOINGS-ON INSIDE THE UESUGI ALLIANCE!
YES, FATHER.
BUT YOUR ESPIONAGE WORK IS SECONDARY TO YOUR REAL DUTY... AS I THINK YOU KNOW.
YES.
YOU MUST FIND THE OBSIDIAN GODDESS.. AND KILL THE VESSE SHE HAS OCCUPIED
...

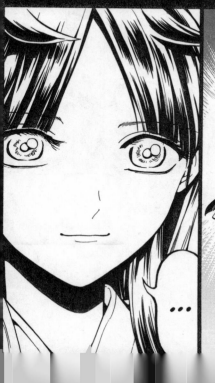

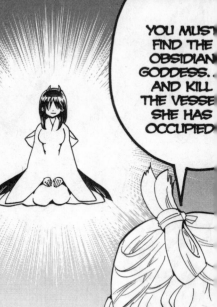

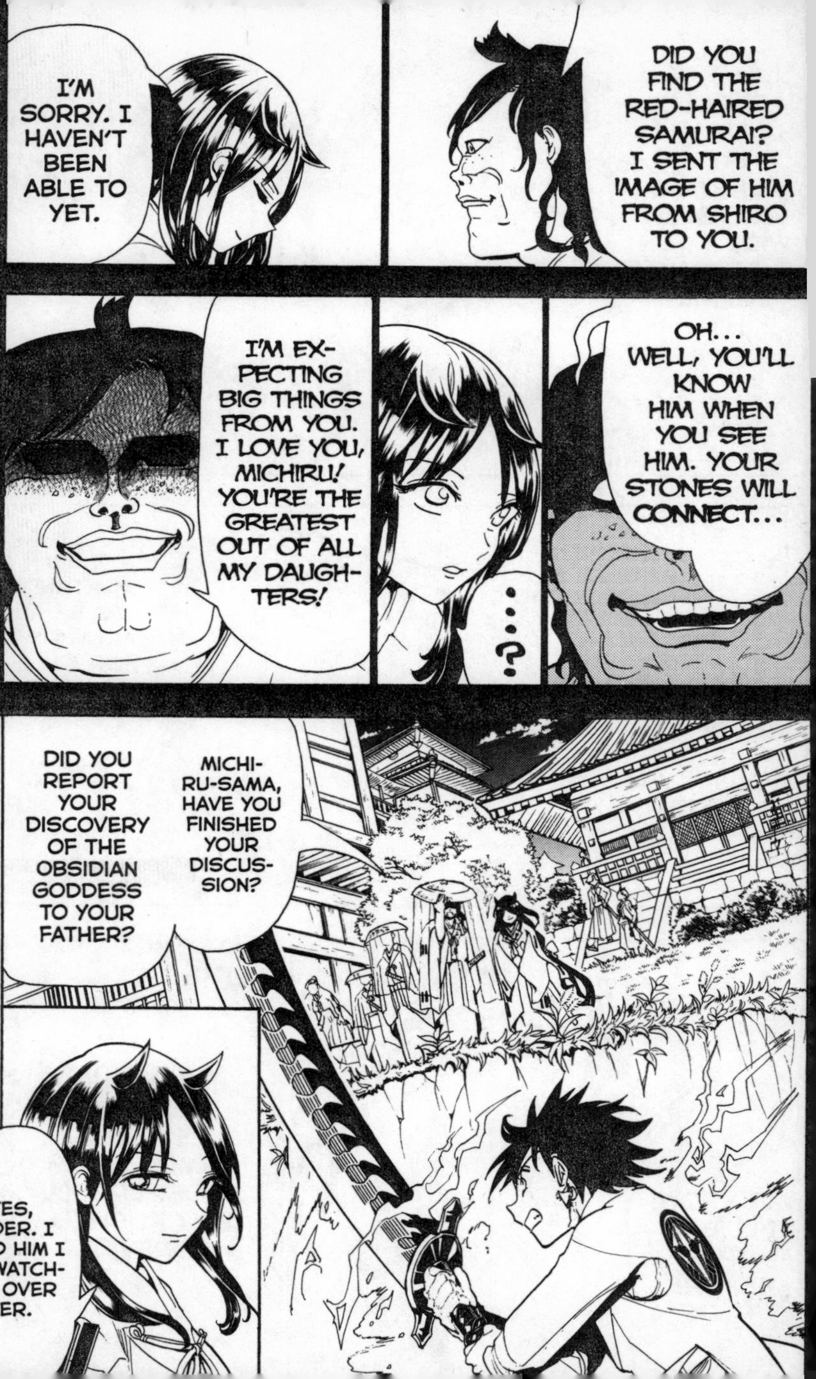
DID YOU FIND THE RED-HAIRED SAMURAI? I SENT THE IMAGE OF HIM FROM SHIRO TO YOU.
I'M SORRY. I HAVEN'T BEEN ABLE TO YET.
OH... WELL, YOU'LL KNOW HIM WHEN YOU SEE HIM. YOUR STONES WILL CONNECT...
...?
I'M EX-PECTING BIG THINGS FROM YOU. I LOVE YOU, MICHIRU! YOU'RE THE GREATEST OUT OF ALL MY DAUGH-TERS!
MICHI-RU-SAMA, HAVE YOU FINISHED YOUR DISCUS-SION?
DID YOU REPORT YOUR DISCOVERY OF THE OBSIDIAN GODDESS TO YOUR FATHER?
YES, ELDER. I TOLD HIM I AM WATCH-ING OVER HER.

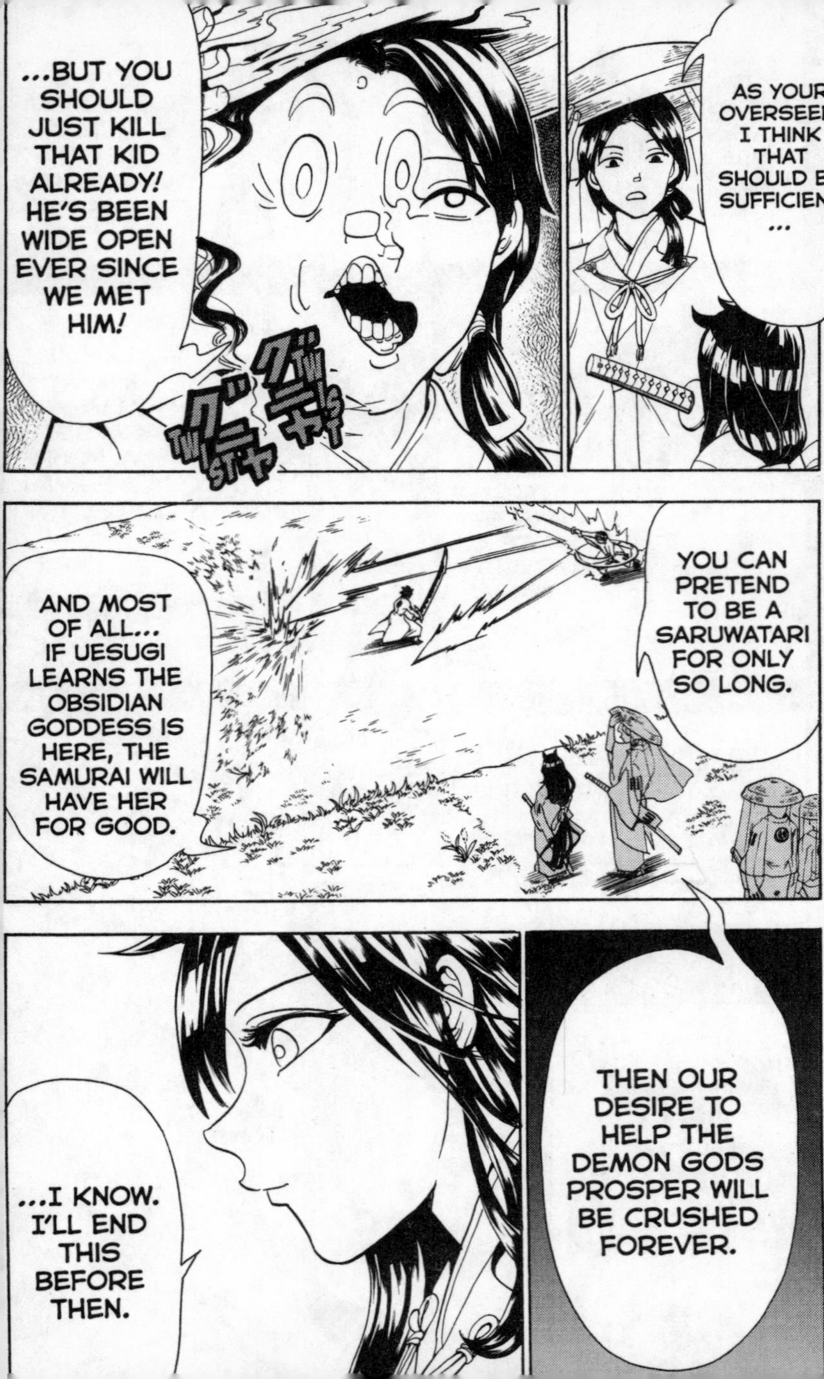
AS YOUR OVERSEER, I THINK THAT SHOULD BE SUFFICIENT...
...BUT YOU SHOULD JUST KILL THAT KID ALREADY! HE'S BEEN WIDE OPEN EVER SINCE WE MET HIM!
TWIST
YOU CAN PRETEND TO BE A SARUWATARI FOR ONLY SO LONG.
AND MOST OF ALL... IF UESUGI LEARNS THE OBSIDIAN GODDESS IS HERE, THE SAMURAI WILL HAVE HER FOR GOOD.
THEN OUR DESIRE TO HELP THE DEMON GODS PROSPER WILL BE CRUSHED FOREVER.
...I KNOW. I'LL END THIS BEFORE THEN.

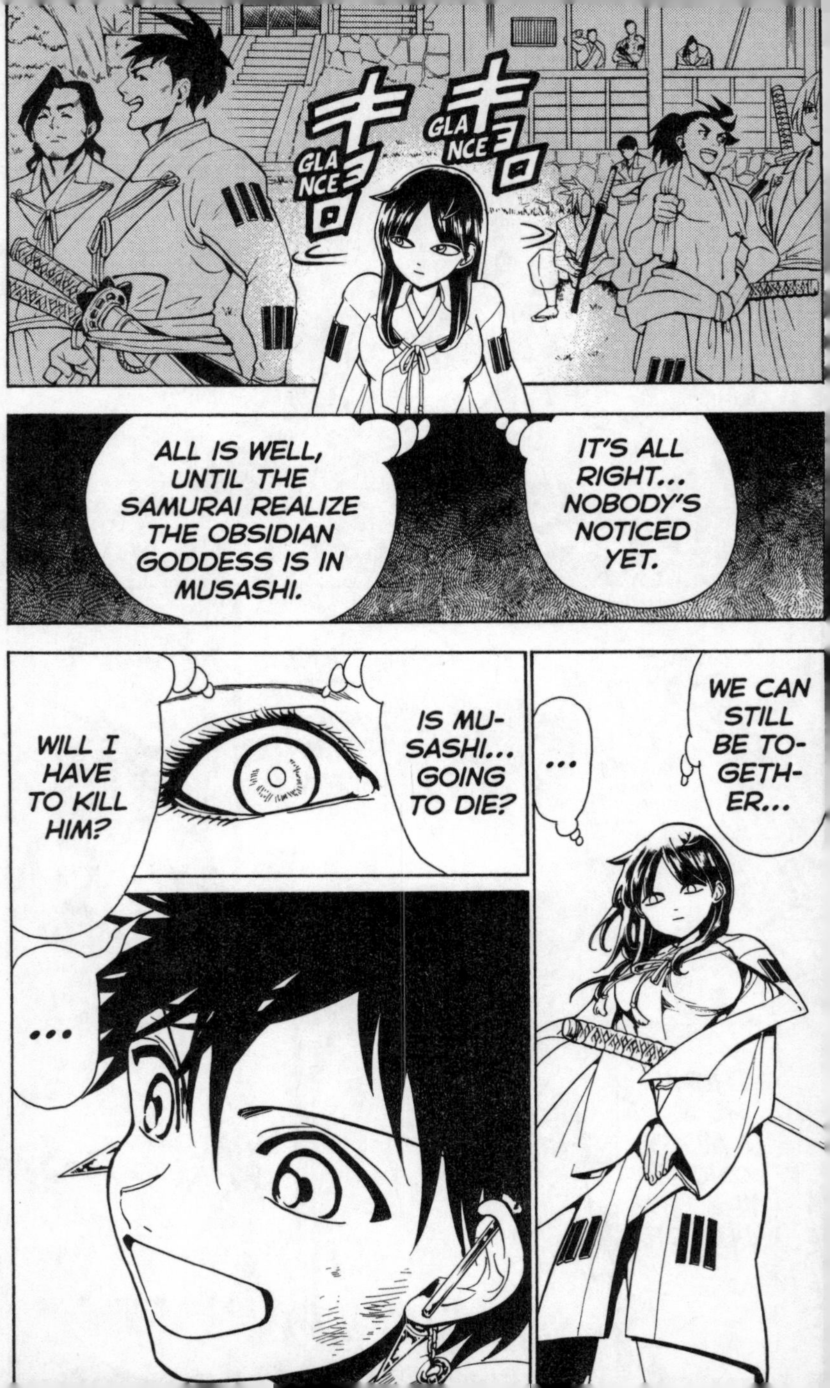
GLANCE
GLANCE
IT'S ALL RIGHT... NOBODY'S NOTICED YET.
ALL IS WELL, UNTIL THE SAMURAI REALIZE THE OBSIDIAN GODDESS IS IN MUSASHI.
WE CAN STILL BE TOGETHER...
...
IS MUSASHI... GOING TO DIE?
WILL I HAVE TO KILL HIM?
...

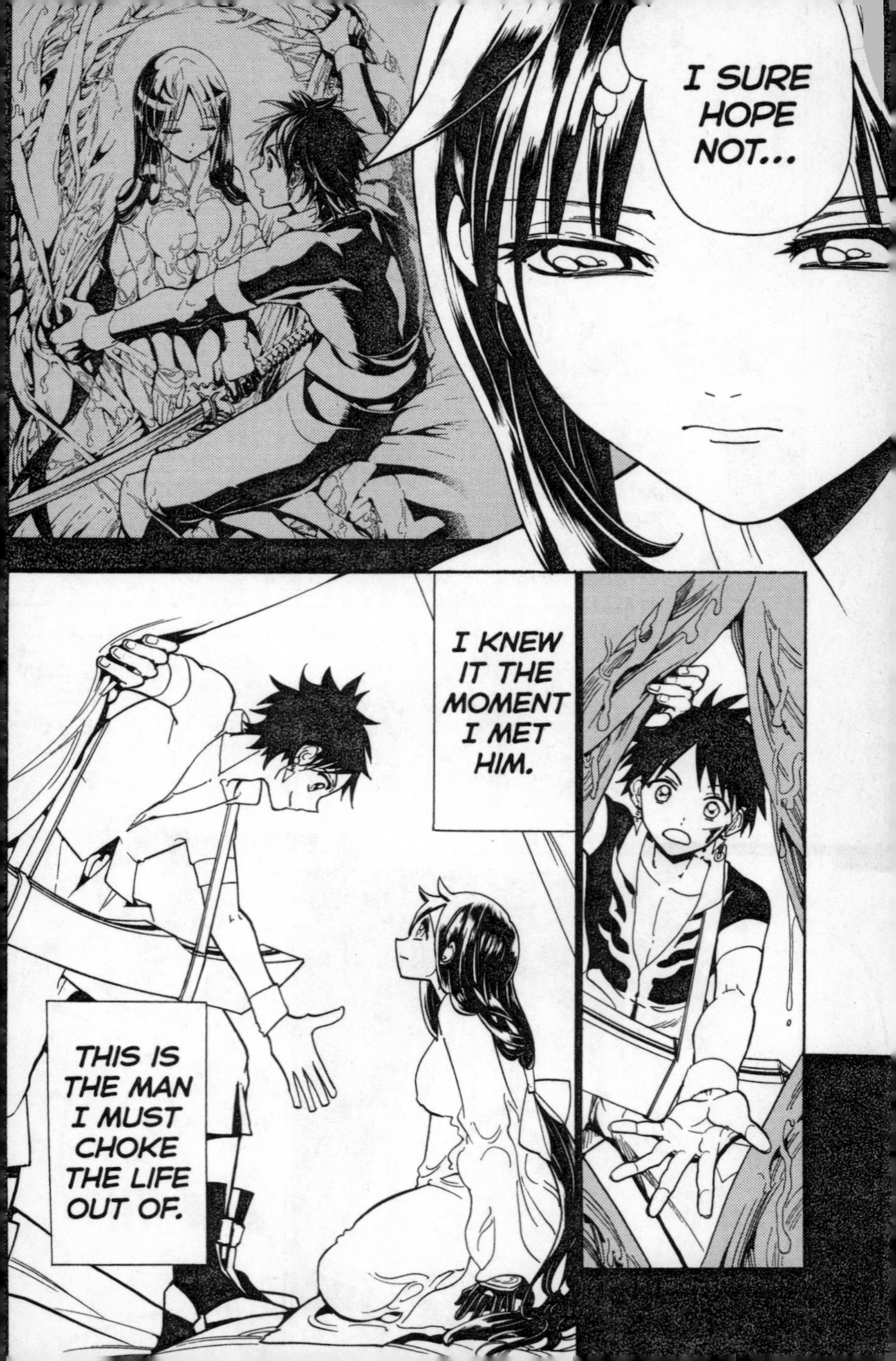
I SURE HOPE NOT...
I KNEW IT THE MOMENT I MET HIM.
THIS IS THE MAN I MUST CHOKE THE LIFE OUT OF.

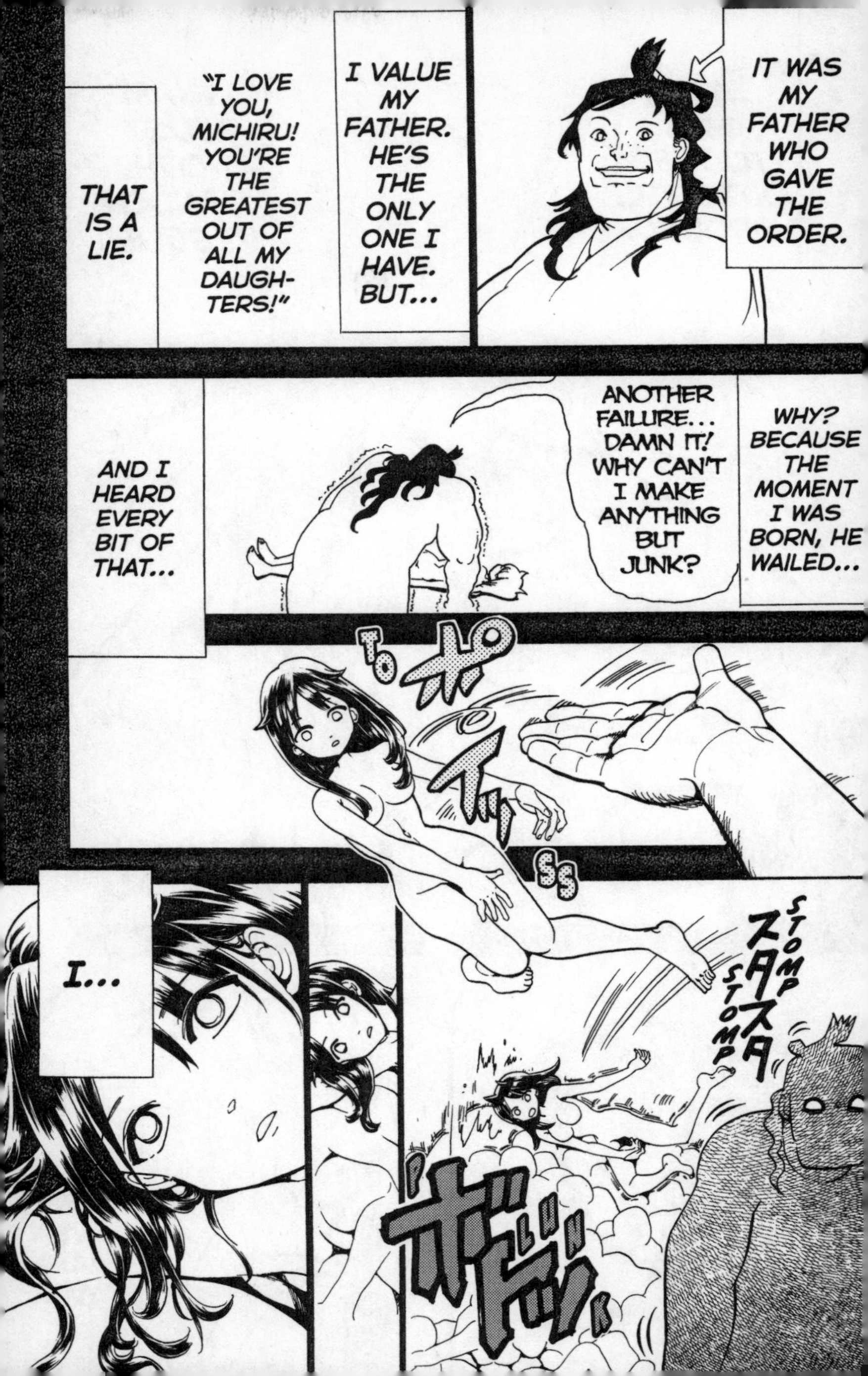

IT WAS MY FATHER WHO GAVE THE ORDER.
I VALUE MY FATHER. HE'S THE ONLY ONE I HAVE. BUT...
"I LOVE YOU, MICHIRU! YOU'RE THE GREATEST OUT OF ALL MY DAUGHTERS!"
THAT IS A LIE.
WHY? BECAUSE THE MOMENT I WAS BORN, HE WAILED...
ANOTHER FAILURE... DAMN IT! WHY CAN'T I MAKE ANYTHING BUT JUNK?
AND I HEARD EVERY BIT OF THAT...
TO
ポイッ
SS
STOMP
STOMP
スタスタ
ボドッ
I...

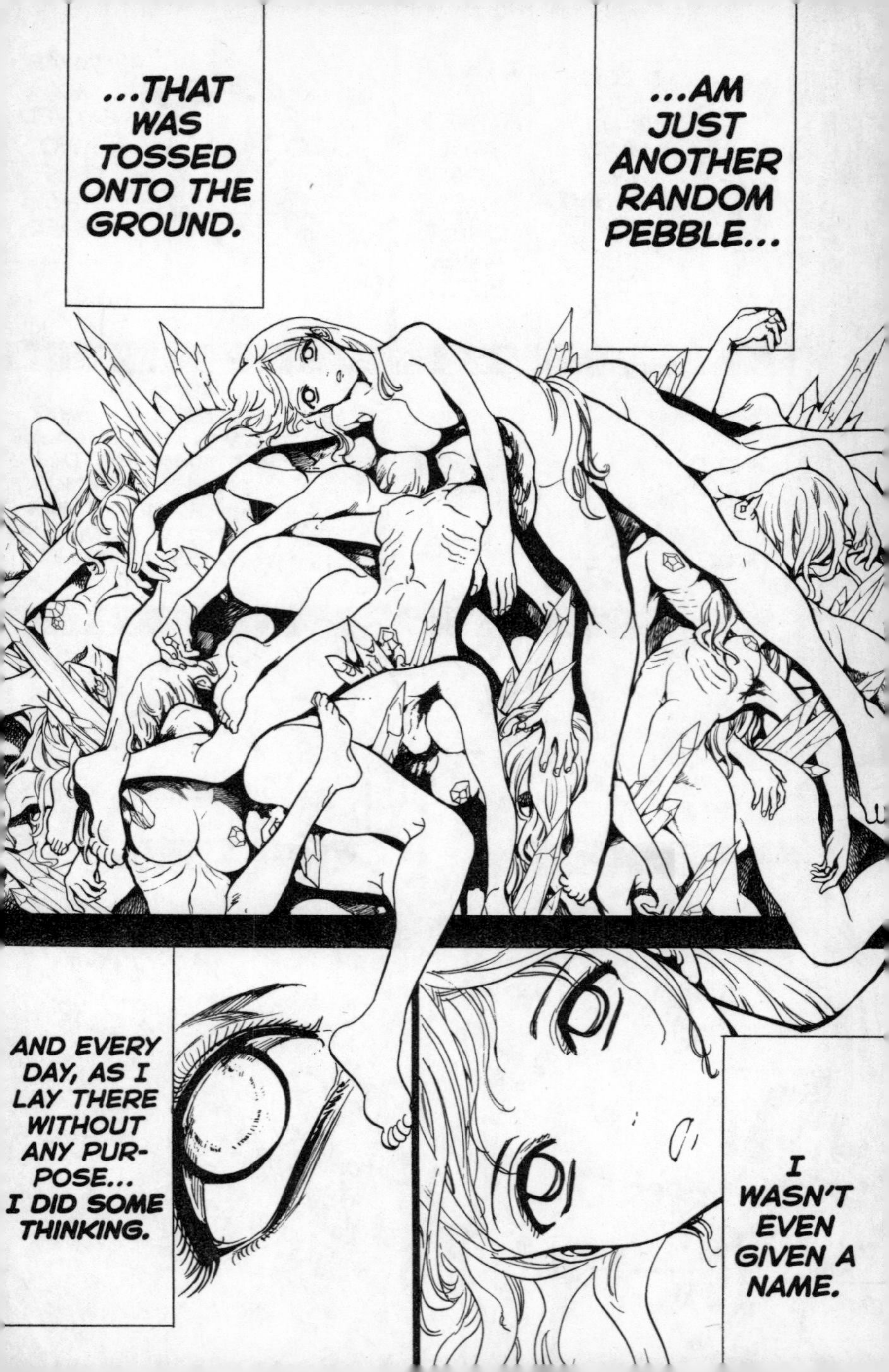
...AM JUST ANOTHER RANDOM PEBBLE...
...THAT WAS TOSSED ONTO THE GROUND.
I WASN'T EVEN GIVEN A NAME.
AND EVERY DAY, AS I LAY THERE WITHOUT ANY PUR-POSE... I DID SOME THINKING.

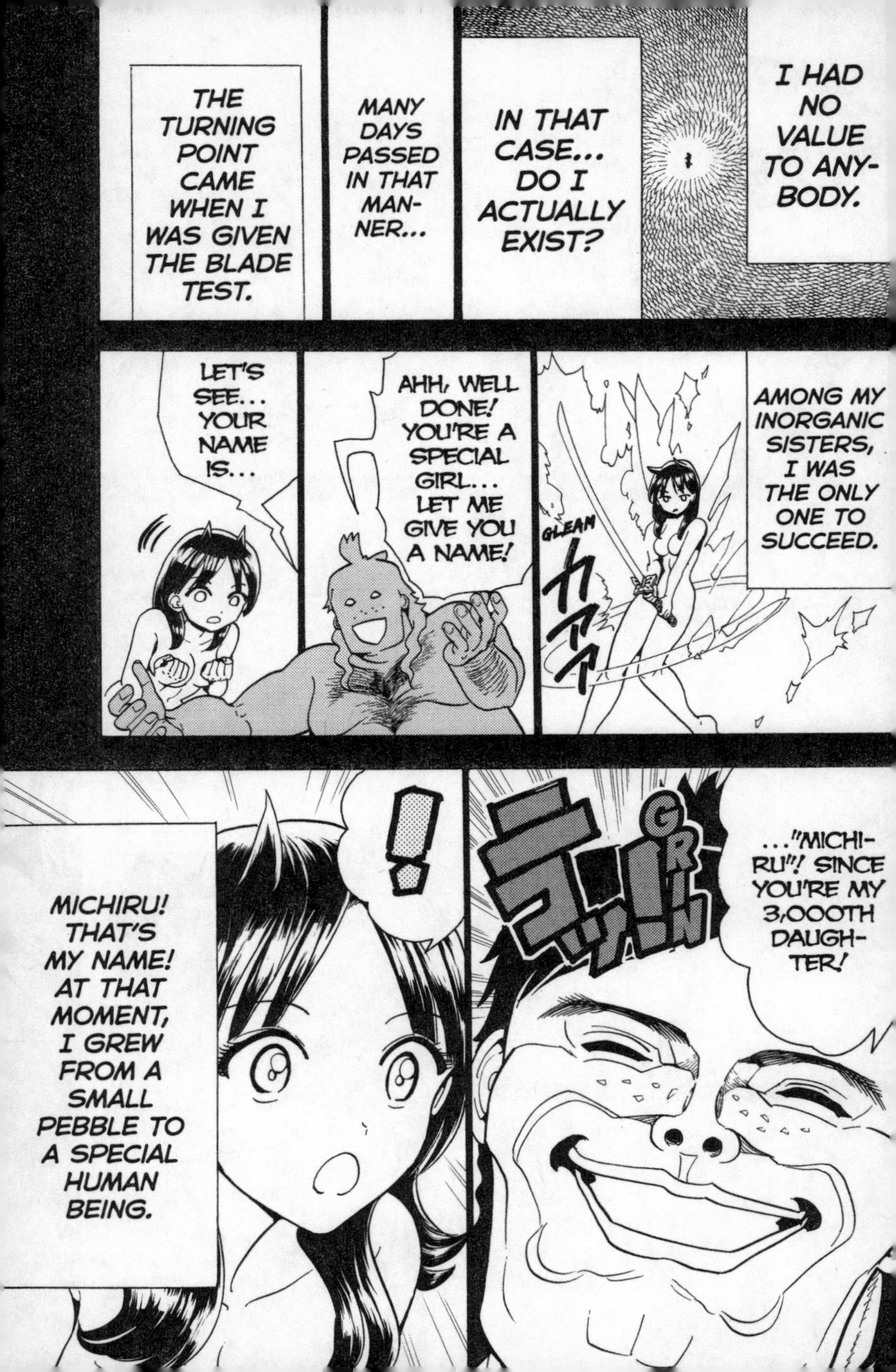
I HAD NO VALUE TO ANYBODY.
IN THAT CASE... DO I ACTUALLY EXIST?
MANY DAYS PASSED IN THAT MANNER...
THE TURNING POINT CAME WHEN I WAS GIVEN THE BLADE TEST.
AMONG MY INORGANIC SISTERS, I WAS THE ONLY ONE TO SUCCEED.
GLEAM
カァァ
AHH, WELL DONE! YOU'RE A SPECIAL GIRL... LET ME GIVE YOU A NAME!
LET'S SEE... YOUR NAME IS...
..."MICHI-RU"! SINCE YOU'RE MY 3,000TH DAUGHTER!
GRIN
ニッ
!
MICHIRU! THAT'S MY NAME! AT THAT MOMENT, I GREW FROM A SMALL PEBBLE TO A SPECIAL HUMAN BEING.

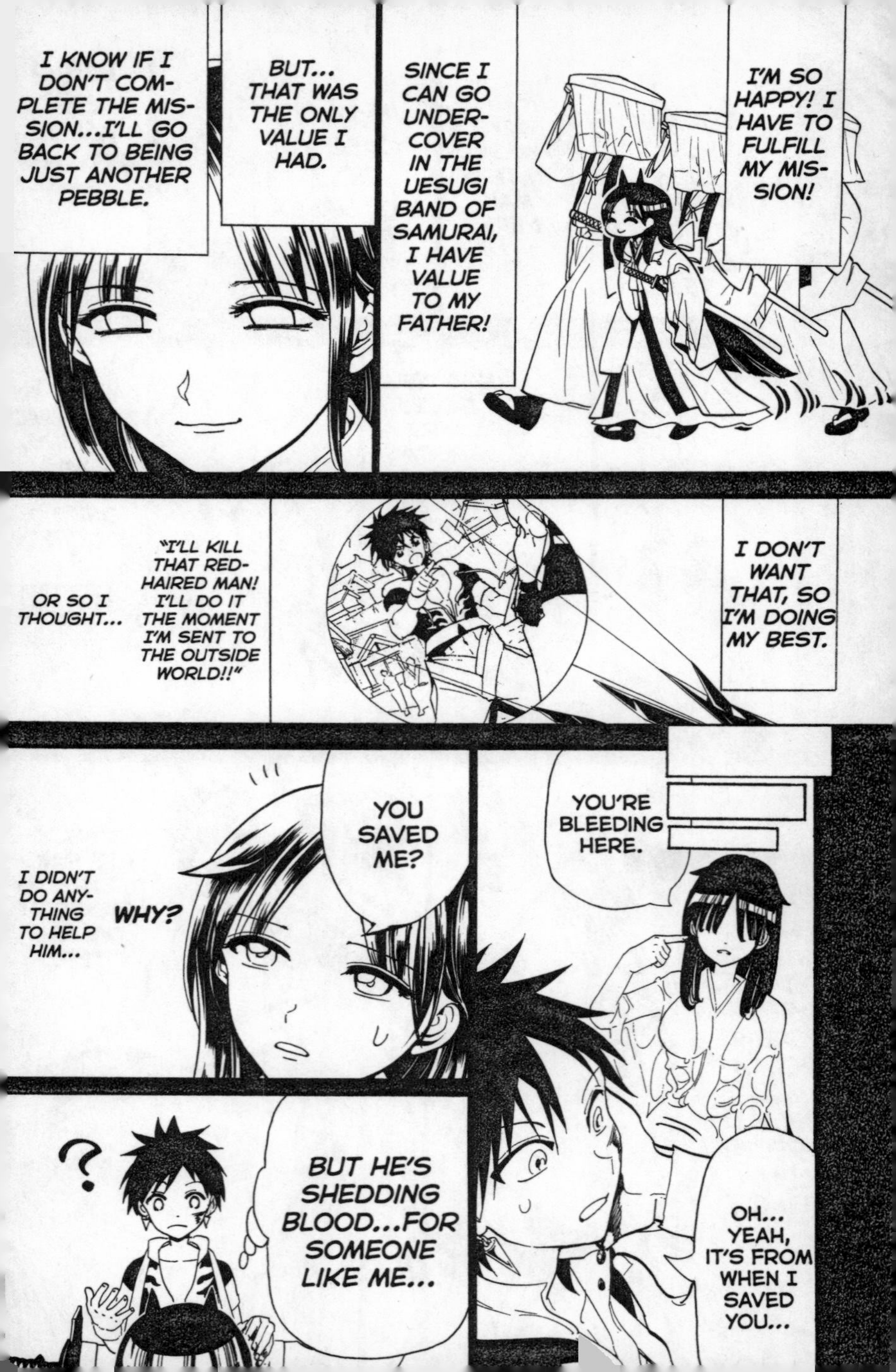

I'M SO HAPPY! I HAVE TO FULFILL MY MISSION!
SINCE I CAN GO UNDERCOVER IN THE UESUGI BAND OF SAMURAI, I HAVE VALUE TO MY FATHER!
BUT... THAT WAS THE ONLY VALUE I HAD.
I KNOW IF I DON'T COMPLETE THE MISSION...I'LL GO BACK TO BEING JUST ANOTHER PEBBLE.
I DON'T WANT THAT, SO I'M DOING MY BEST.
"I'LL KILL THAT RED-HAIRED MAN! I'LL DO IT THE MOMENT I'M SENT TO THE OUTSIDE WORLD!!"
OR SO I THOUGHT...
YOU'RE BLEEDING HERE.
OH... YEAH, IT'S FROM WHEN I SAVED YOU...
YOU SAVED ME?
WHY?
I DIDN'T DO ANYTHING TO HELP HIM...
BUT HE'S SHEDDING BLOOD...FOR SOMEONE LIKE ME...
?

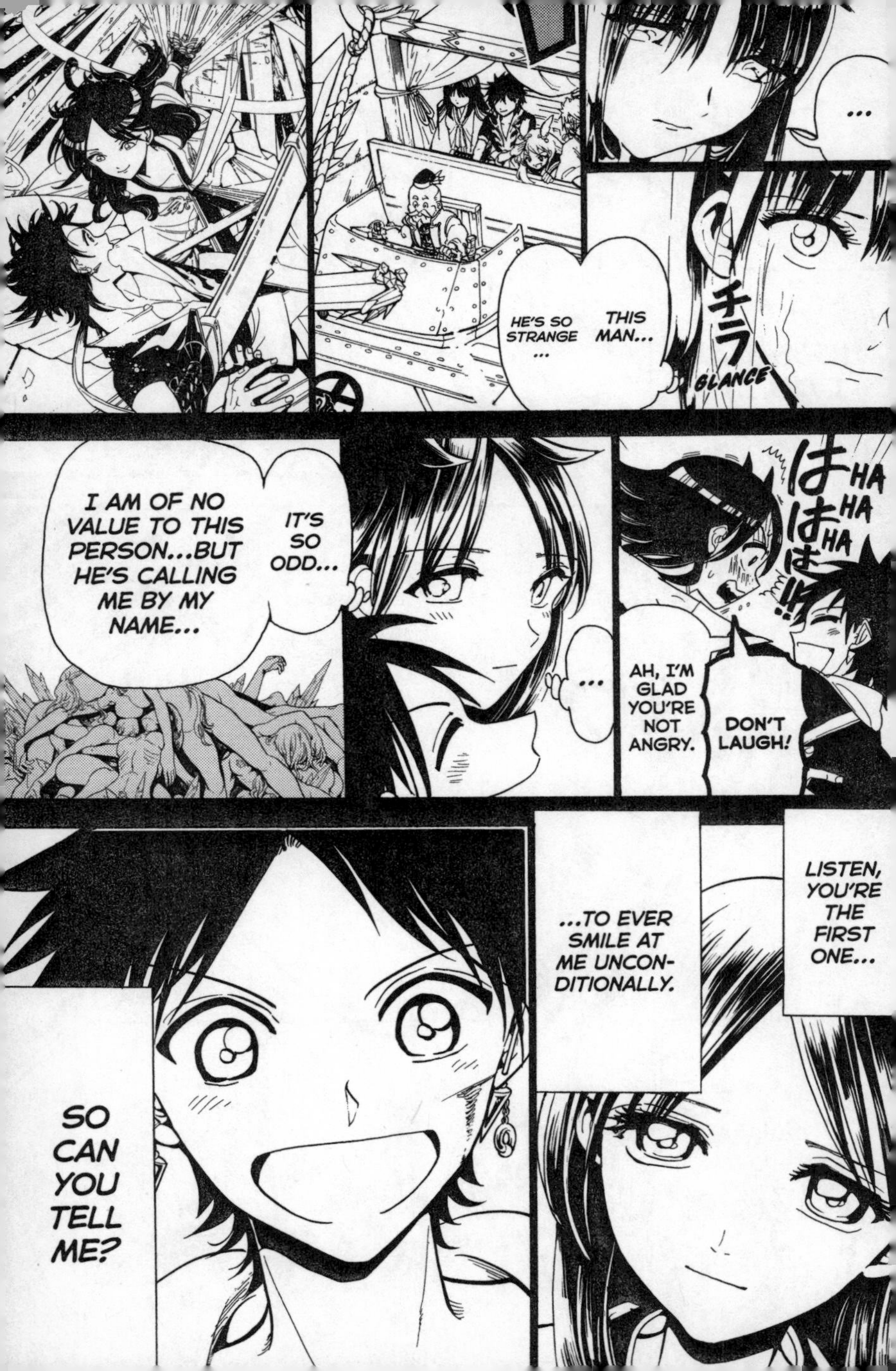
...
チラ
GLANCE
THIS MAN...
HE'S SO STRANGE...
ははは!!
HA HA HA
DON'T LAUGH!
AH, I'M GLAD YOU'RE NOT ANGRY.
...
IT'S SO ODD...
I AM OF NO VALUE TO THIS PERSON...BUT HE'S CALLING ME BY MY NAME...
LISTEN, YOU'RE THE FIRST ONE...
...TO EVER SMILE AT ME UNCONDITIONALLY.
SO CAN YOU TELL ME?

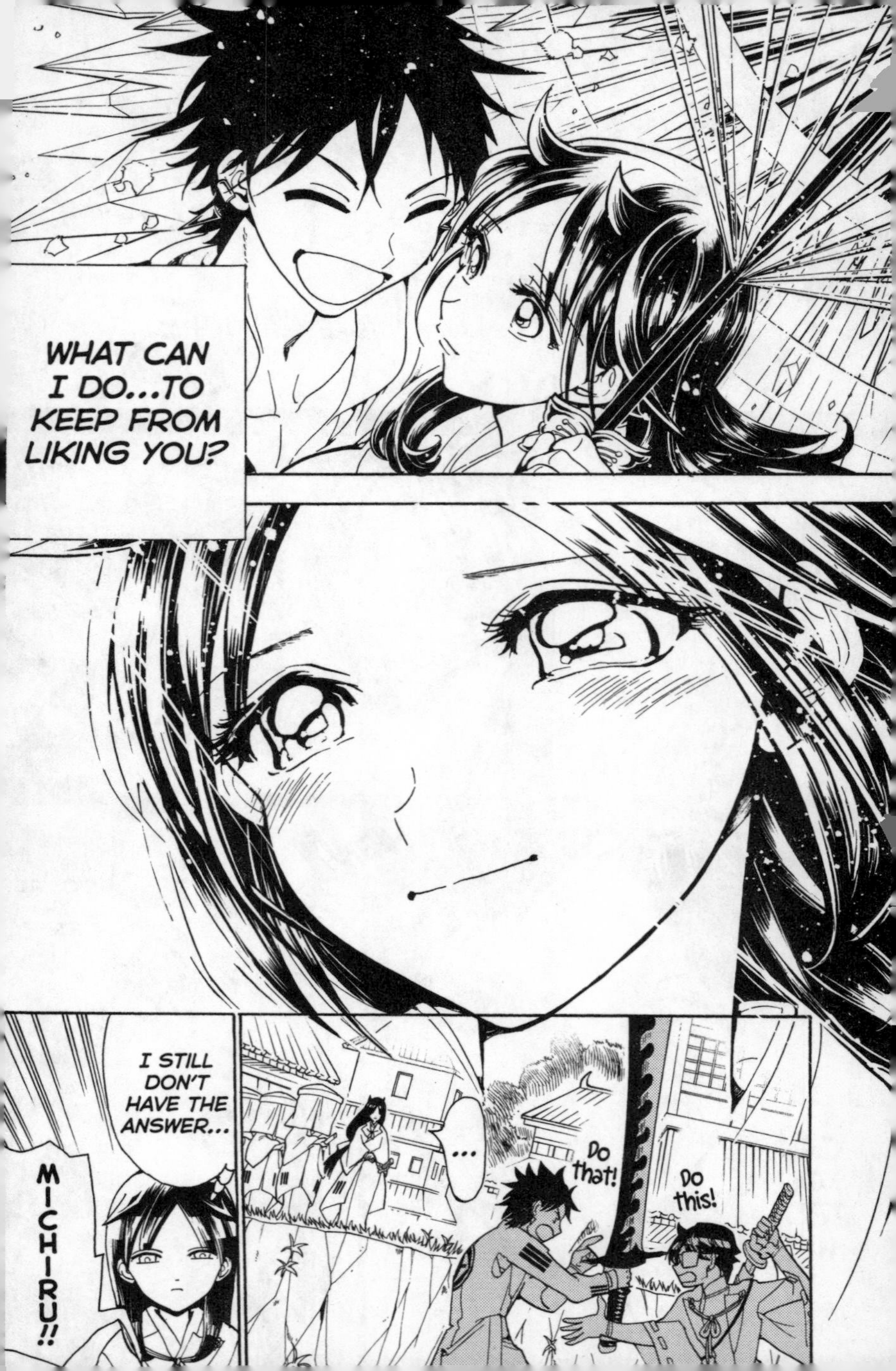
WHAT CAN I DO...TO KEEP FROM LIKING YOU?
Do this!
Do that!
...
I STILL DON'T HAVE THE ANSWER...
MICHIRU!!

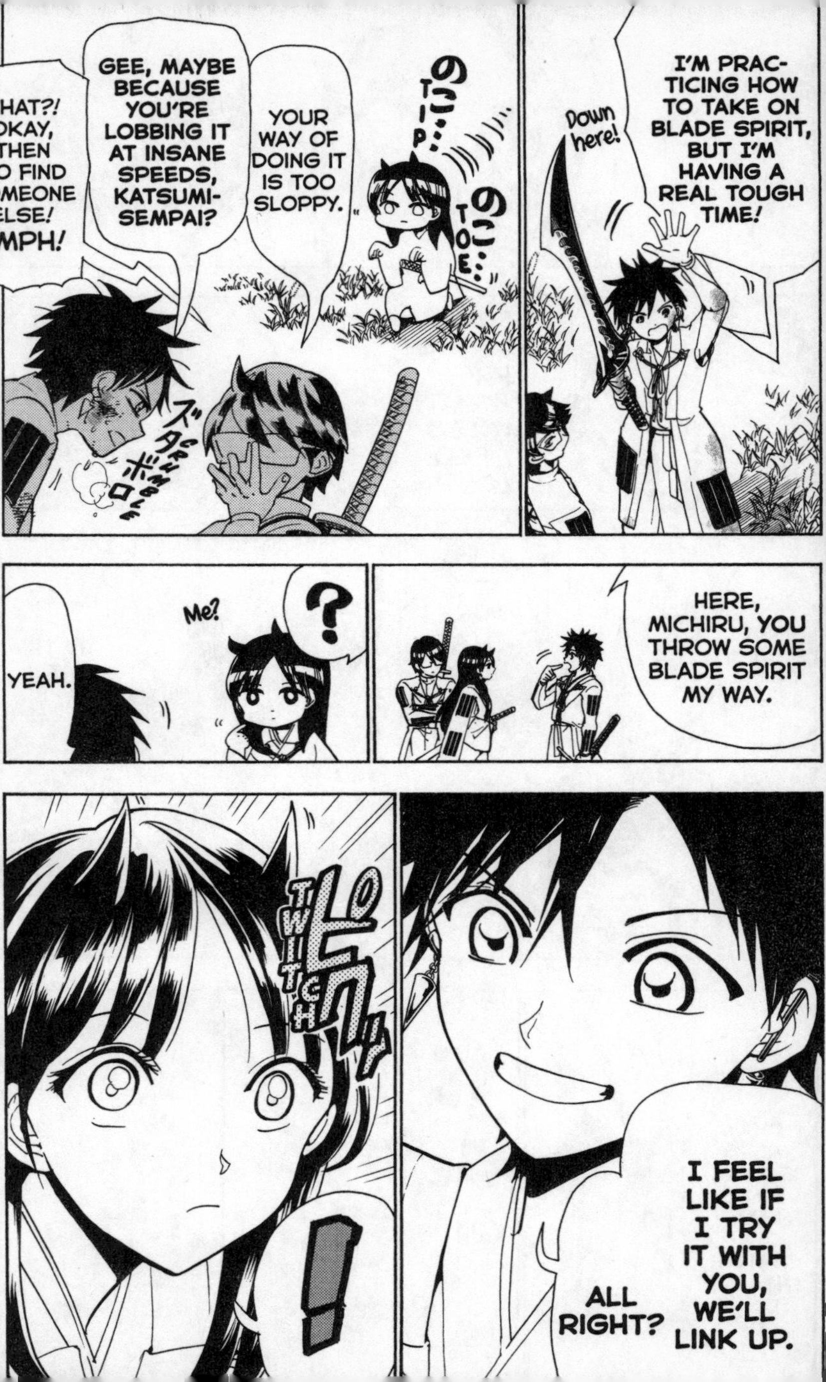
I'M PRACTICING HOW TO TAKE ON BLADE SPIRIT, BUT I'M HAVING A REAL TOUGH TIME!
Down here!
TIP TOE
YOUR WAY OF DOING IT IS TOO SLOPPY.
GEE, MAYBE BECAUSE YOU'RE LOBBING IT AT INSANE SPEEDS, KATSUMI-SEMPAI?
WHAT?! OKAY, THEN GO FIND SOMEONE ELSE! HMPH!
CRUMBLE
HERE, MICHIRU, YOU THROW SOME BLADE SPIRIT MY WAY.
?
Me?
YEAH.
I FEEL LIKE IF I TRY IT WITH YOU, WE'LL LINK UP.
ALL RIGHT?
TWITCH
!

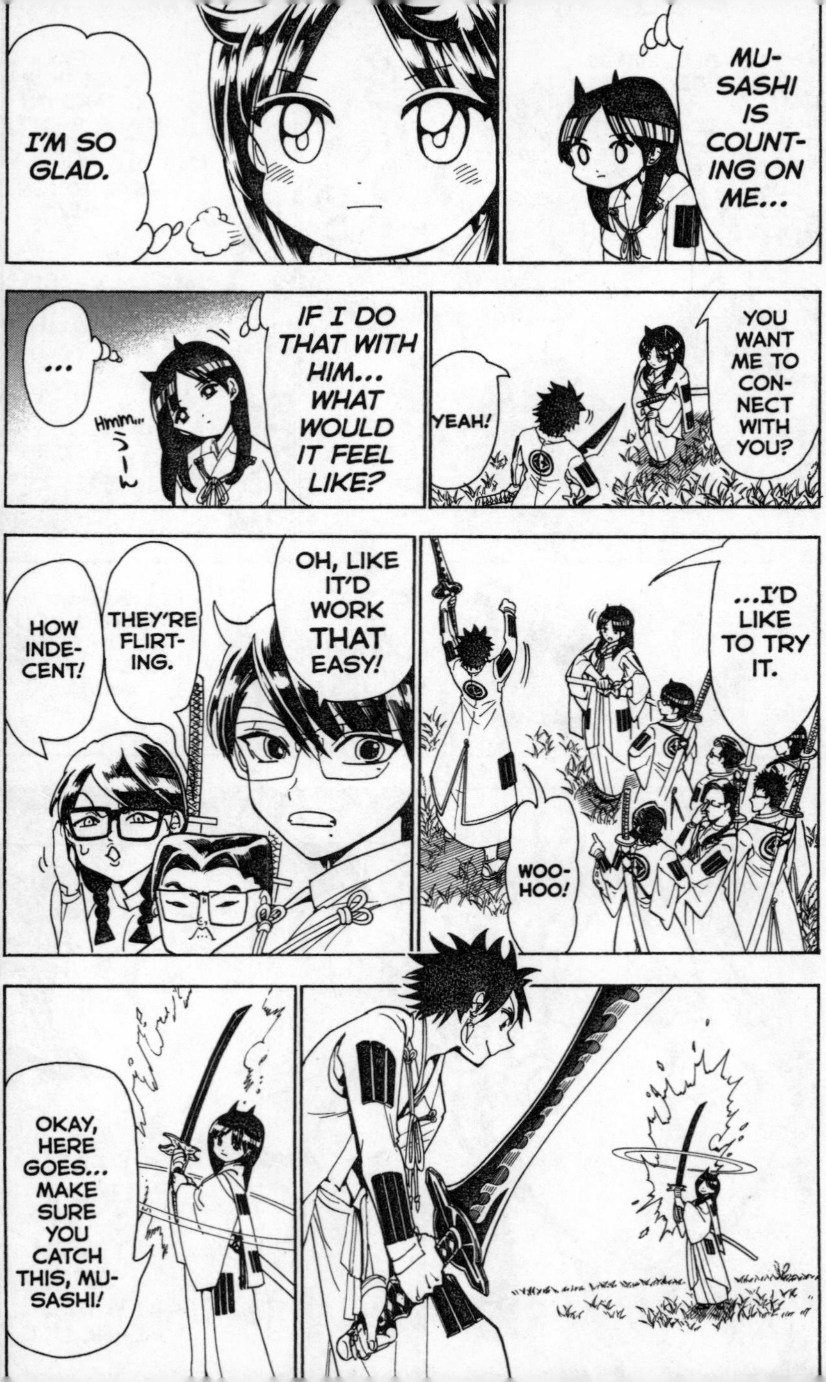
MU-SASHI IS COUNT-ING ON ME...
I'M SO GLAD.
YOU WANT ME TO CON-NECT WITH YOU?
YEAH!
IF I DO THAT WITH HIM... WHAT WOULD IT FEEL LIKE?
...
Hmm...
うーん
...I'D LIKE TO TRY IT.
WOO-HOO!
OH, LIKE IT'D WORK THAT EASY!
THEY'RE FLIRT-ING.
HOW INDE-CENT!
OKAY, HERE GOES... MAKE SURE YOU CATCH THIS, MU-SASHI!

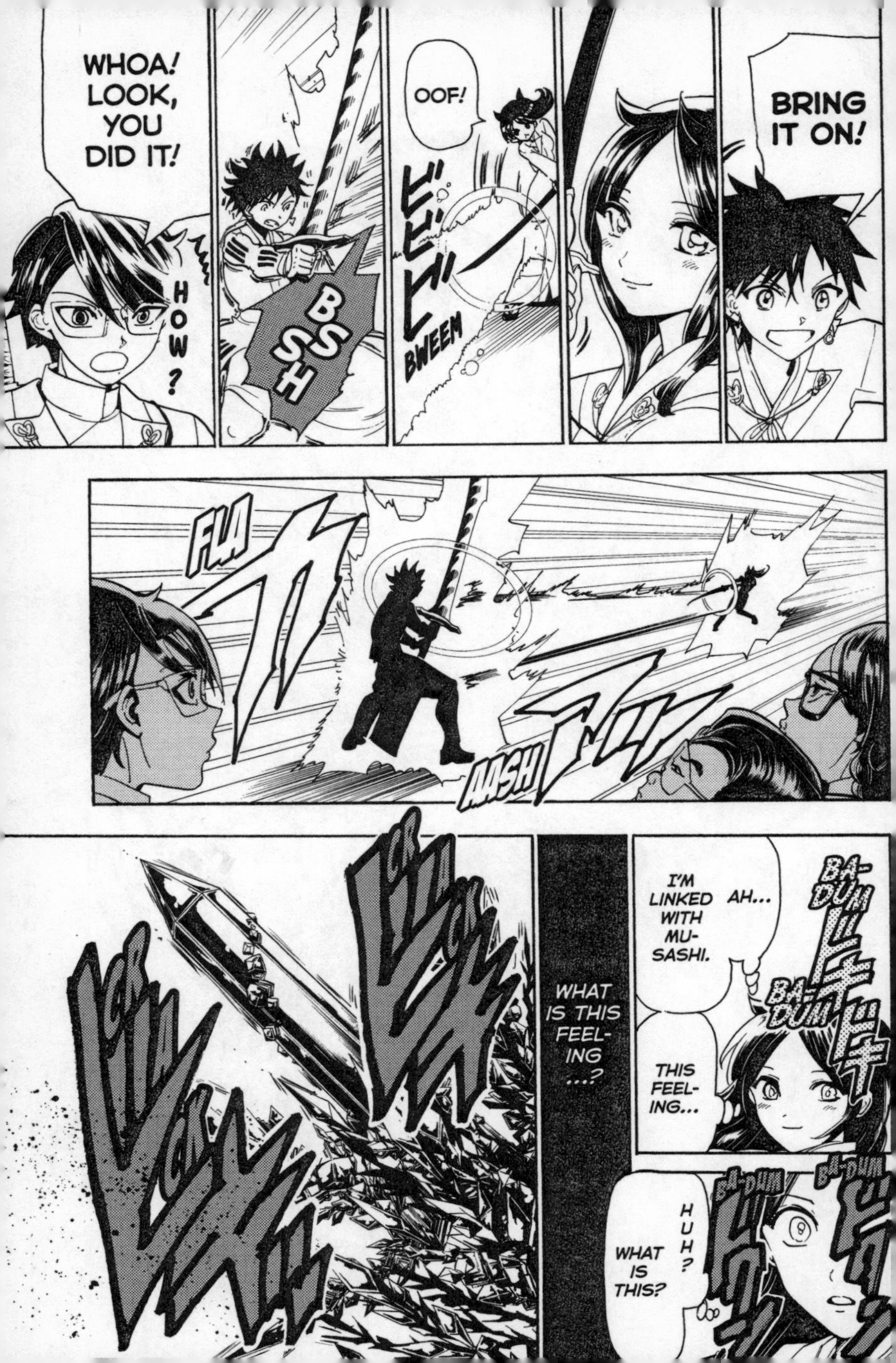
BRING IT ON!
OOF!
ビビビビ
BWEEM
BSSH
WHOA! LOOK, YOU DID IT!
HOW?
FLA
AASH
AH...
I'M LINKED WITH MU-SASHI.
BA-DUM BA-DUM
THIS FEEL-ING...
BA-DUM BA-DUM
HUH?
WHAT IS THIS?
WHAT IS THIS FEEL-ING...?

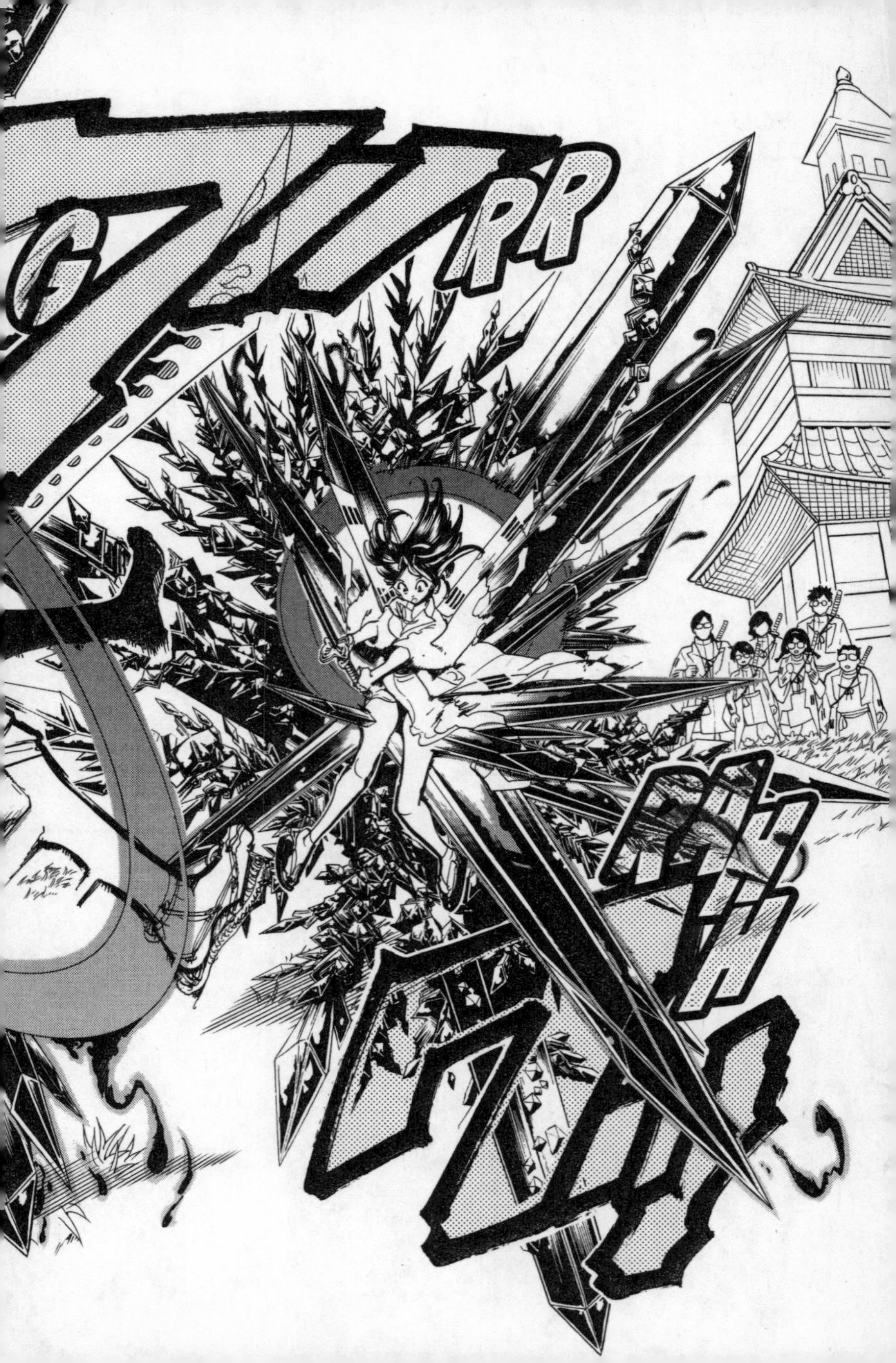

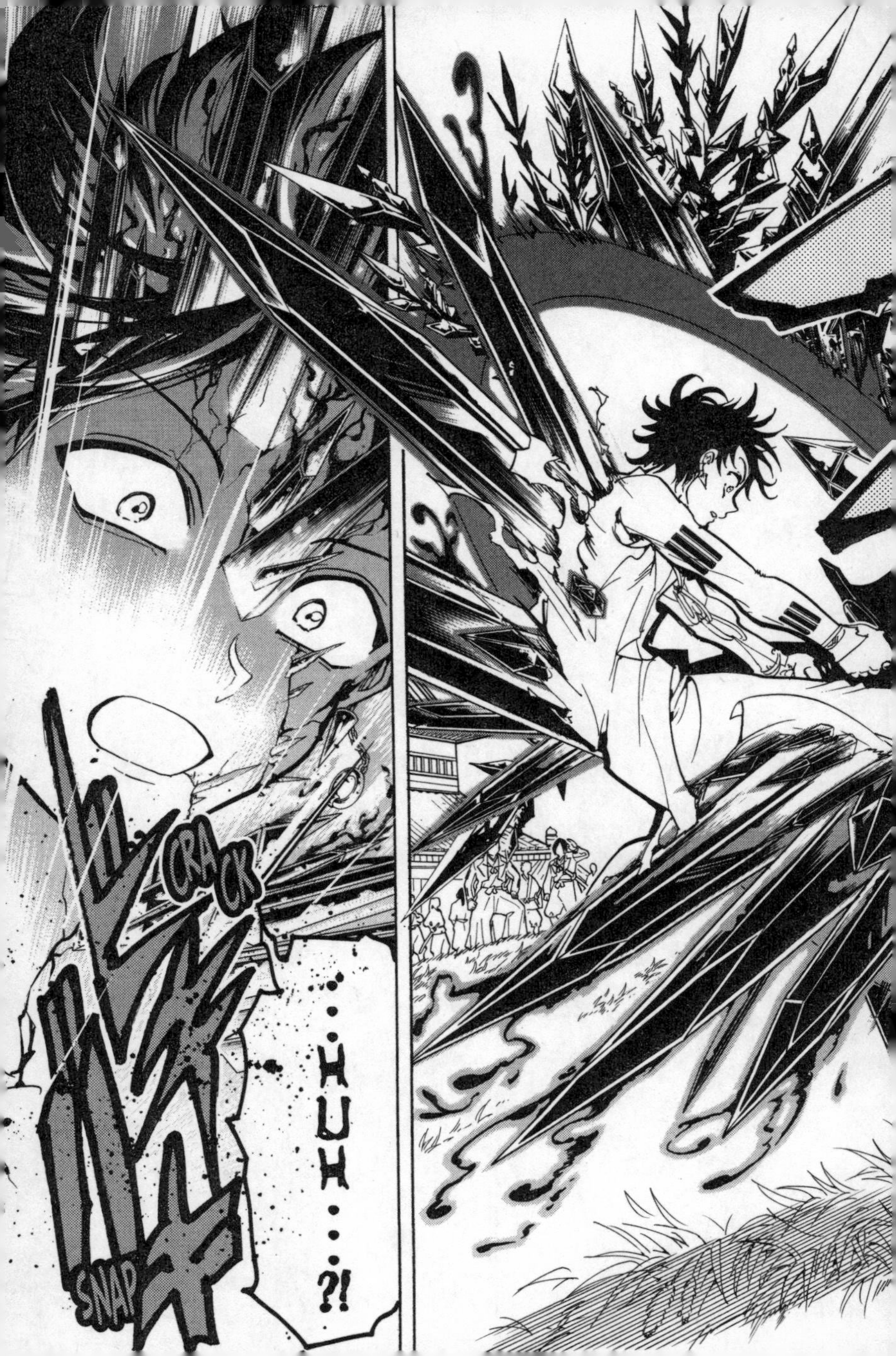
CRACK
...HUH...?!
SNAP

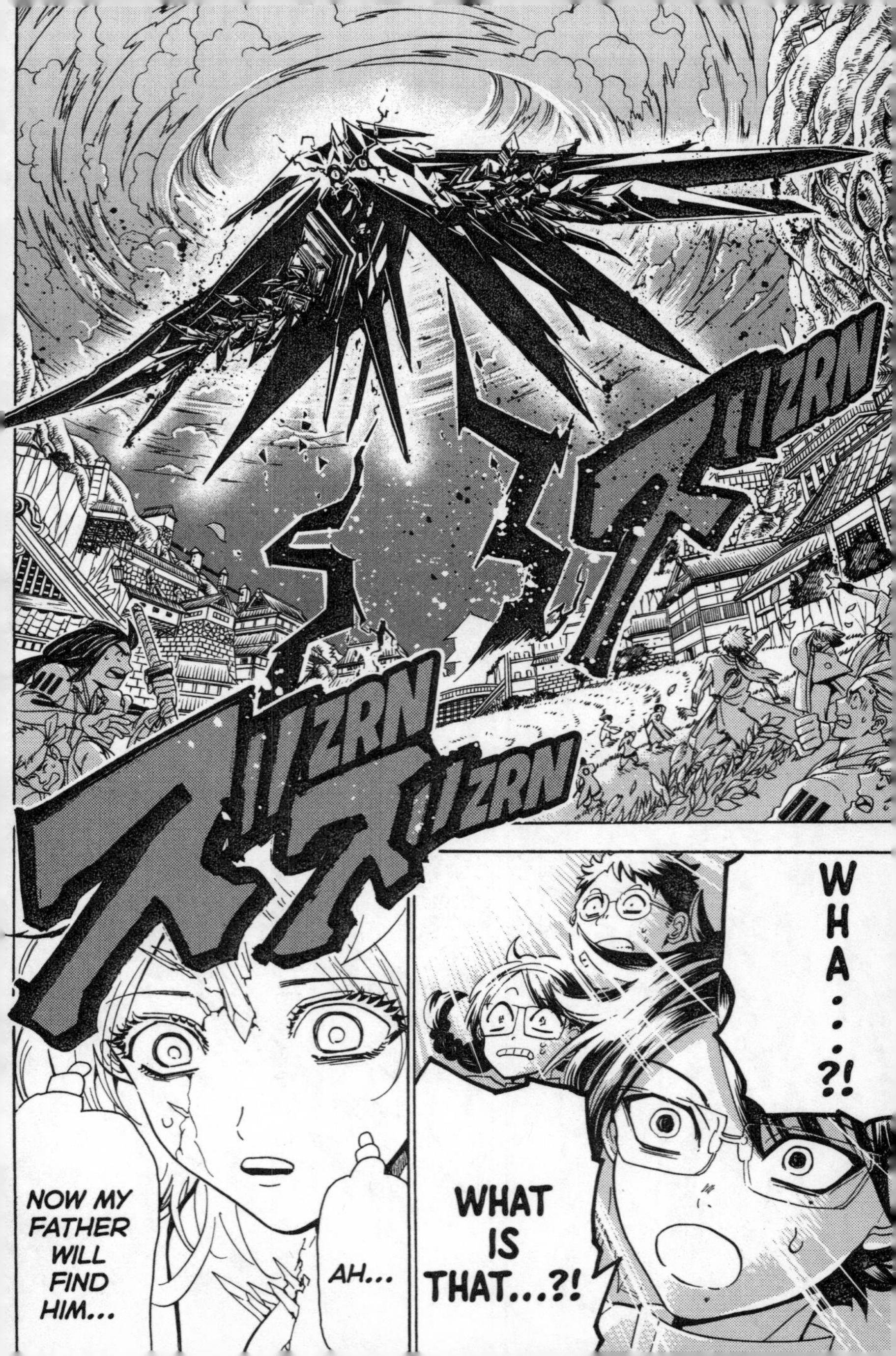
WHA...?!
WHAT IS THAT...?!
AH...
NOW MY FATHER WILL FIND HIM...

STAFF

REGULAR ASSISTANTS

メギ
Megi

吉田 真美
Mami Yoshida

石後 千鳥
Chidori Ishigo

中村 犬彦
Inuhiko Nakamura

野方
Nogata

鈴木 莉士
Rihito Suzuki

EDITORIAL TEAM

詫摩 尚樹
Naoki Takuma

菊地 優斗
Yuto Kikuchi

長塚 雅彦
Masahiko Nagatsuka

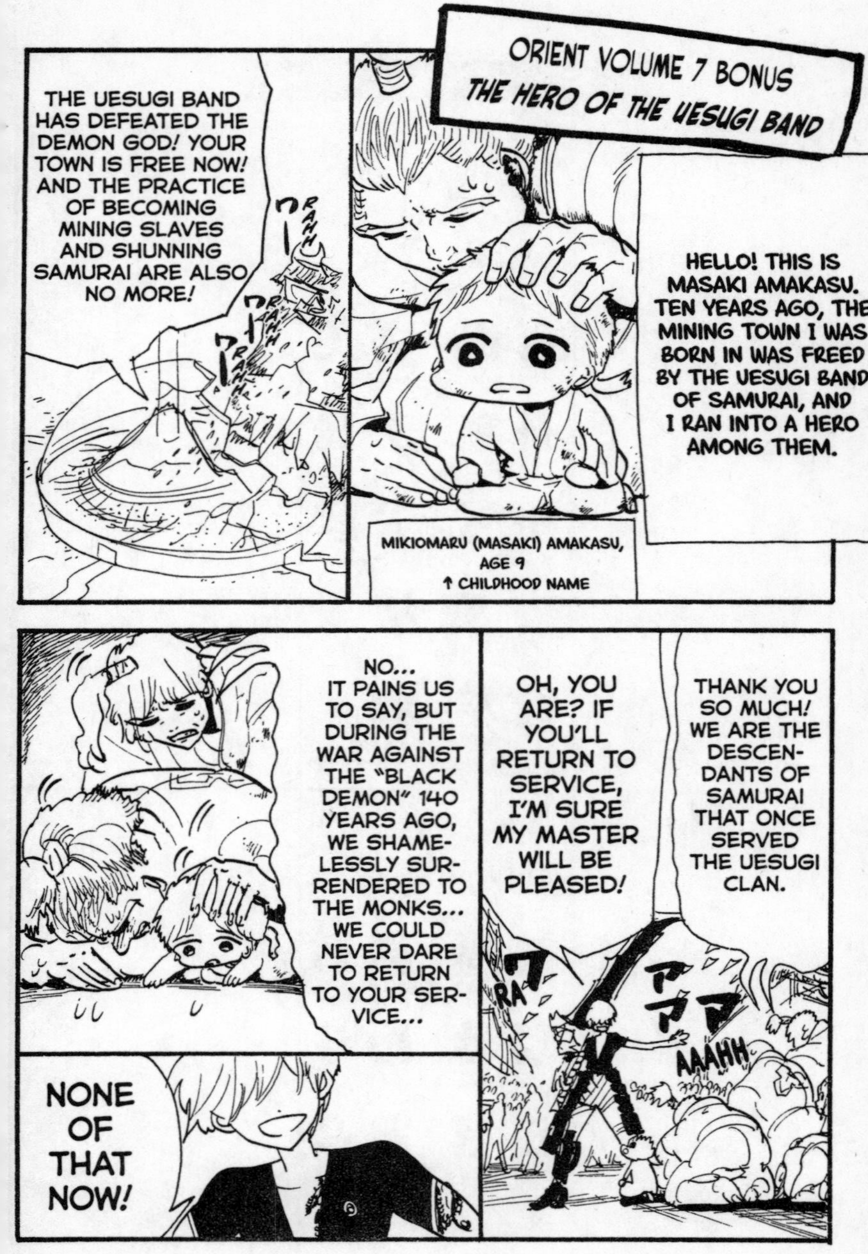
ORIENT VOLUME 7 BONUS
THE HERO OF THE UESUGI BAND
HELLO! THIS IS MASAKI AMAKASU. TEN YEARS AGO, THE MINING TOWN I WAS BORN IN WAS FREED BY THE UESUGI BAND OF SAMURAI, AND I RAN INTO A HERO AMONG THEM.
MIKIOMARU (MASAKI) AMAKASU, AGE 9
↑ CHILDHOOD NAME
THE UESUGI BAND HAS DEFEATED THE DEMON GOD! YOUR TOWN IS FREE NOW! AND THE PRACTICE OF BECOMING MINING SLAVES AND SHUNNING SAMURAI ARE ALSO NO MORE!
RAHH
RAHH
RAHH
THANK YOU SO MUCH! WE ARE THE DESCEN-DANTS OF SAMURAI THAT ONCE SERVED THE UESUGI CLAN.
OH, YOU ARE? IF YOU'LL RETURN TO SERVICE, I'M SURE MY MASTER WILL BE PLEASED!
RA
AAAHH
NO... IT PAINS US TO SAY, BUT DURING THE WAR AGAINST THE "BLACK DEMON" 140 YEARS AGO, WE SHAME-LESSLY SUR-RENDERED TO THE MONKS... WE COULD NEVER DARE TO RETURN TO YOUR SER-VICE...
NONE OF THAT NOW!

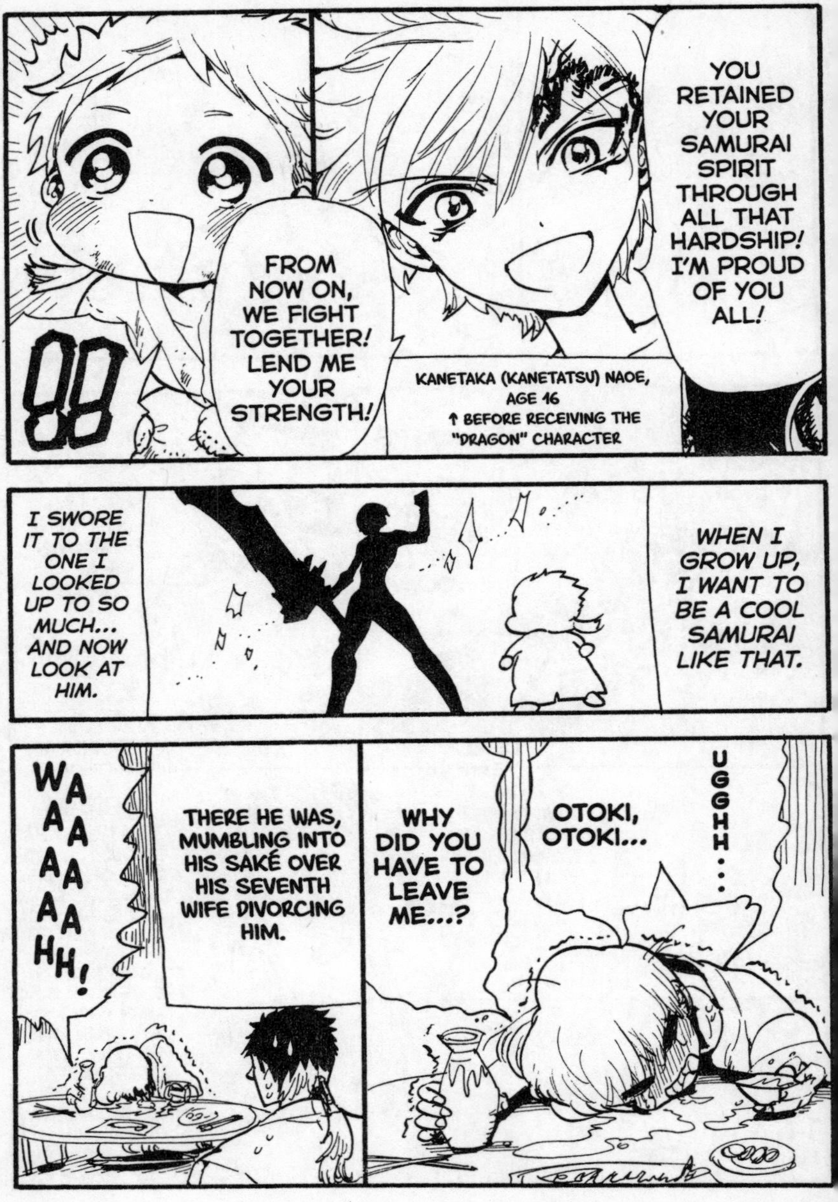
YOU RETAINED YOUR SAMURAI SPIRIT THROUGH ALL THAT HARDSHIP! I'M PROUD OF YOU ALL!
FROM NOW ON, WE FIGHT TOGETHER! LEND ME YOUR STRENGTH!
KANETAKA (KANETATSU) NAOE, AGE 16
↑ BEFORE RECEIVING THE "DRAGON" CHARACTER
WHEN I GROW UP, I WANT TO BE A COOL SAMURAI LIKE THAT.
I SWORE IT TO THE ONE I LOOKED UP TO SO MUCH... AND NOW LOOK AT HIM.
UGGH...
OTOKI, OTOKI...
WHY DID YOU HAVE TO LEAVE ME...?
THERE HE WAS, MUMBLING INTO HIS SAKÉ OVER HIS SEVENTH WIFE DIVORCING HIM.
WAAAAAAAHH!

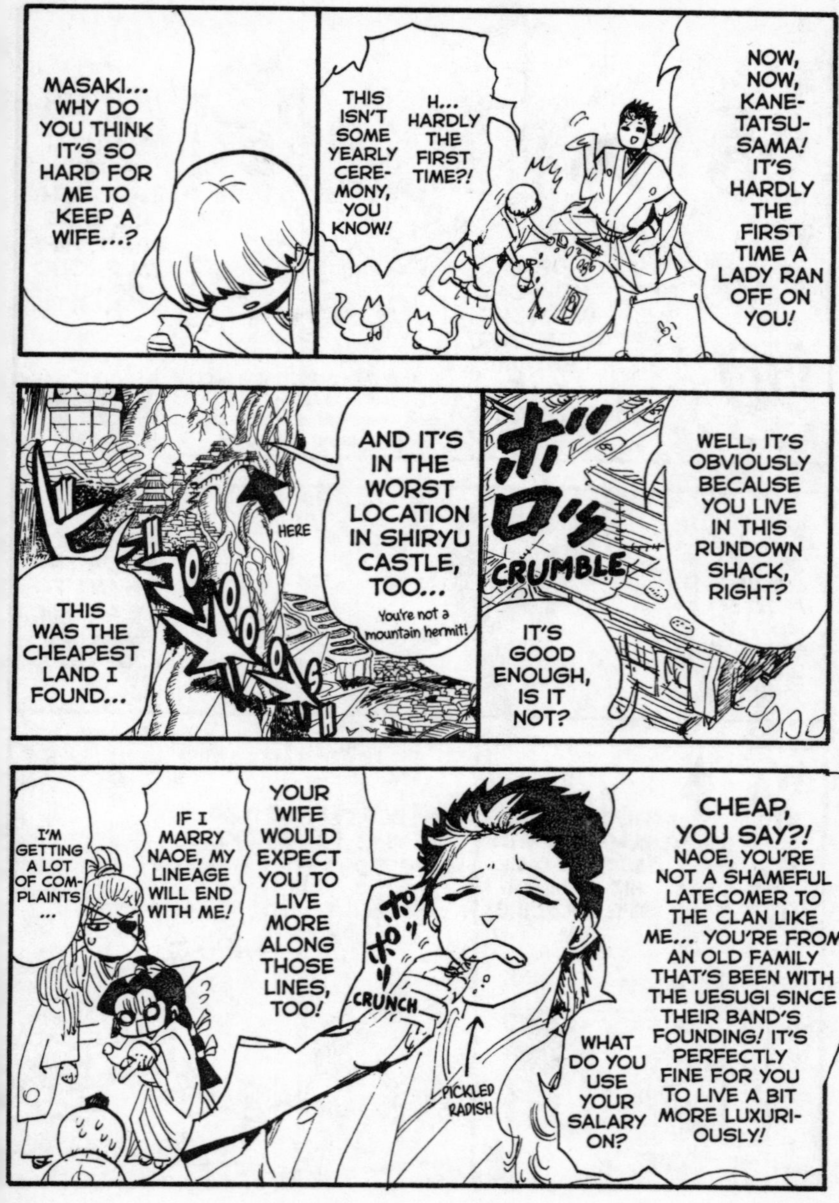
NOW, NOW, KANETATSU-SAMA! IT'S HARDLY THE FIRST TIME A LADY RAN OFF ON YOU!
H... HARDLY THE FIRST TIME?!
THIS ISN'T SOME YEARLY CEREMONY, YOU KNOW!
MASAKI... WHY DO YOU THINK IT'S SO HARD FOR ME TO KEEP A WIFE...?
WELL, IT'S OBVIOUSLY BECAUSE YOU LIVE IN THIS RUNDOWN SHACK, RIGHT?
ボロッ
CRUMBLE
IT'S GOOD ENOUGH, IS IT NOT?
AND IT'S IN THE WORST LOCATION IN SHIRYU CASTLE, TOO...
You're not a mountain hermit!
HERE
WHOOOOOSH
THIS WAS THE CHEAPEST LAND I FOUND...
CHEAP, YOU SAY?! NAOE, YOU'RE NOT A SHAMEFUL LATECOMER TO THE CLAN LIKE ME... YOU'RE FROM AN OLD FAMILY THAT'S BEEN WITH THE UESUGI SINCE THEIR BAND'S FOUNDING! IT'S PERFECTLY FINE FOR YOU TO LIVE A BIT MORE LUXURIOUSLY!
WHAT DO YOU USE YOUR SALARY ON?
PICKLED RADISH
ポリポリ
CRUNCH
YOUR WIFE WOULD EXPECT YOU TO LIVE MORE ALONG THOSE LINES, TOO!
IF I MARRY NAOE, MY LINEAGE WILL END WITH ME!
I'M GETTING A LOT OF COMPLAINTS...

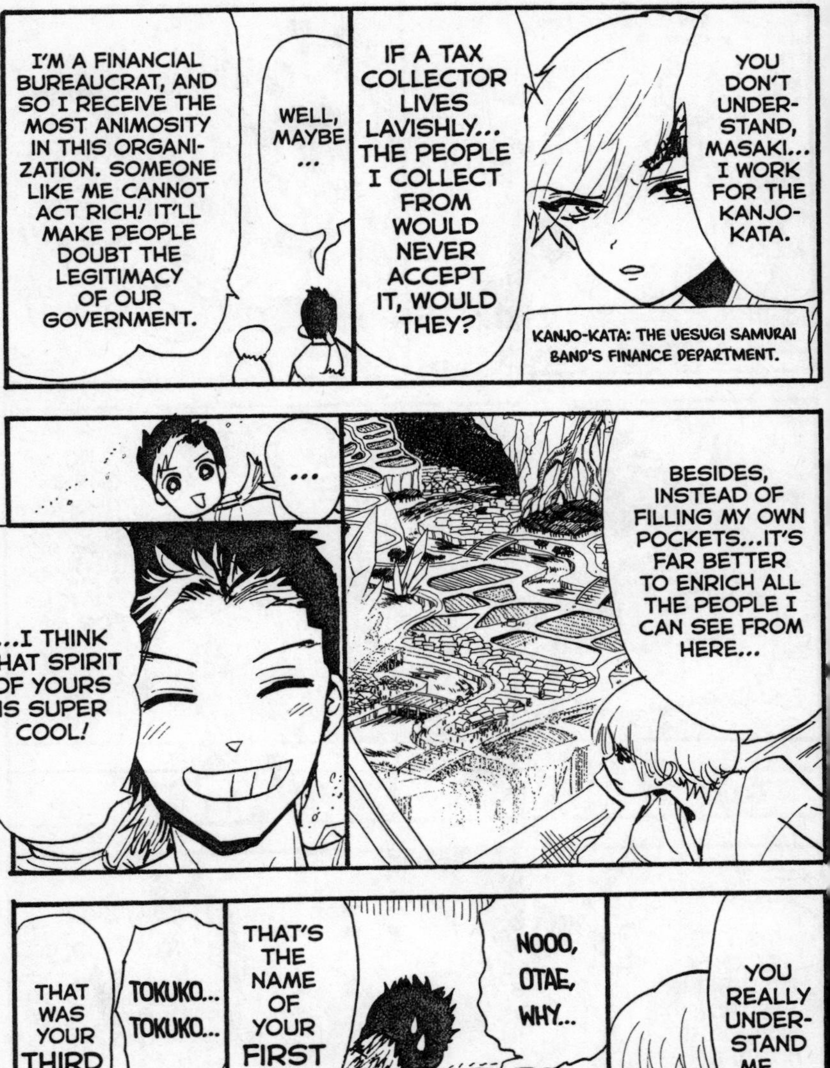
YOU DON'T UNDERSTAND, MASAKI... I WORK FOR THE KANJO-KATA.
KANJO-KATA: THE UESUGI SAMURAI BAND'S FINANCE DEPARTMENT.
IF A TAX COLLECTOR LIVES LAVISHLY... THE PEOPLE I COLLECT FROM WOULD NEVER ACCEPT IT, WOULD THEY?
WELL, MAYBE...
I'M A FINANCIAL BUREAUCRAT, AND SO I RECEIVE THE MOST ANIMOSITY IN THIS ORGANIZATION. SOMEONE LIKE ME CANNOT ACT RICH! IT'LL MAKE PEOPLE DOUBT THE LEGITIMACY OF OUR GOVERNMENT.
BESIDES, INSTEAD OF FILLING MY OWN POCKETS...IT'S FAR BETTER TO ENRICH ALL THE PEOPLE I CAN SEE FROM HERE...
...
...I THINK THAT SPIRIT OF YOURS IS SUPER COOL!
YOU REALLY UNDERSTAND ME...
NOOO, OTAE, WHY...
HNNGGH
THAT'S THE NAME OF YOUR FIRST WIFE.
Hang in there!
TOKUKO... TOKUKO...
THAT WAS YOUR THIRD ONE!!

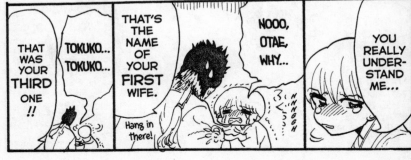

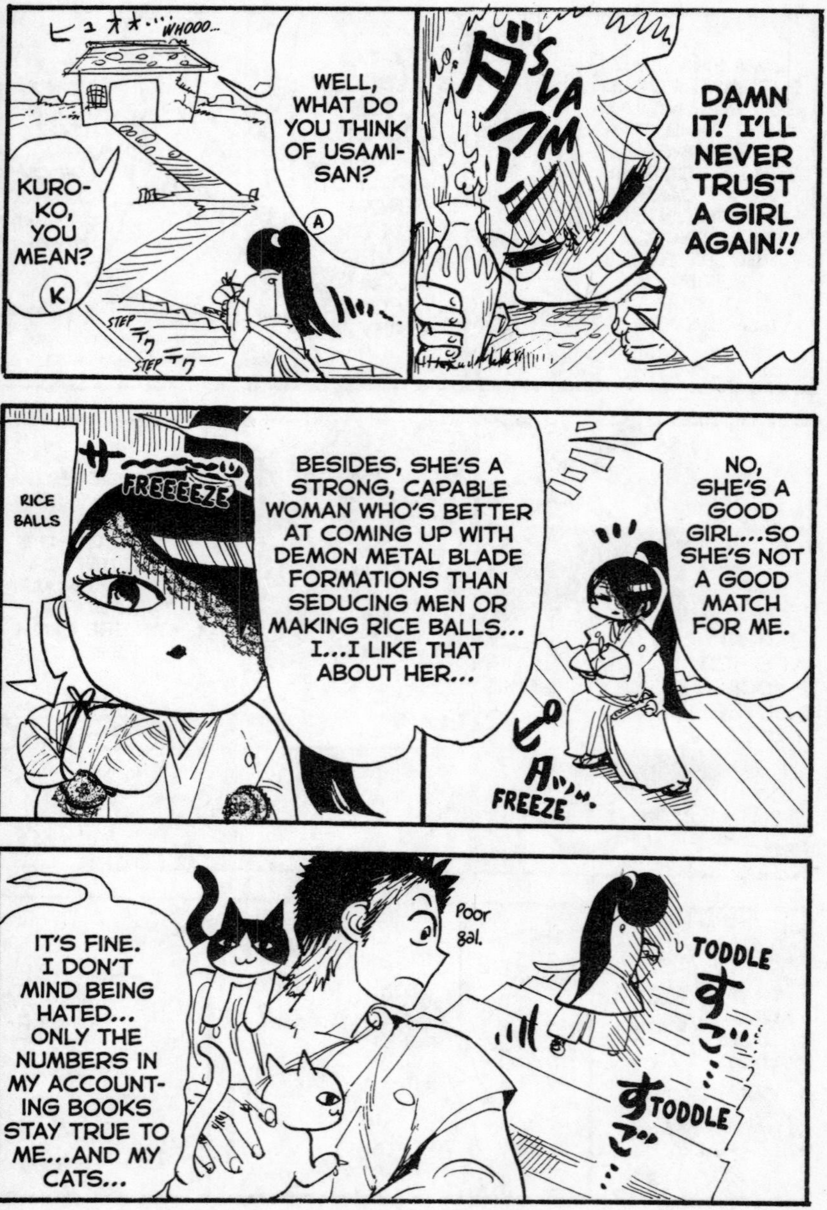
DAMN IT! I'LL NEVER TRUST A GIRL AGAIN!!
SLAM
ヒュオオ… WHOOO...
WELL, WHAT DO YOU THINK OF USAMI-SAN?
A
KURO-KO, YOU MEAN?
K
STEP
STEP
NO, SHE'S A GOOD GIRL...SO SHE'S NOT A GOOD MATCH FOR ME.
FREEZE
BESIDES, SHE'S A STRONG, CAPABLE WOMAN WHO'S BETTER AT COMING UP WITH DEMON METAL BLADE FORMATIONS THAN SEDUCING MEN OR MAKING RICE BALLS... I...I LIKE THAT ABOUT HER...
FREEEEZE
RICE BALLS
TODDLE
TODDLE
Poor gal.
IT'S FINE. I DON'T MIND BEING HATED... ONLY THE NUMBERS IN MY ACCOUNTING BOOKS STAY TRUE TO ME...AND MY CATS...

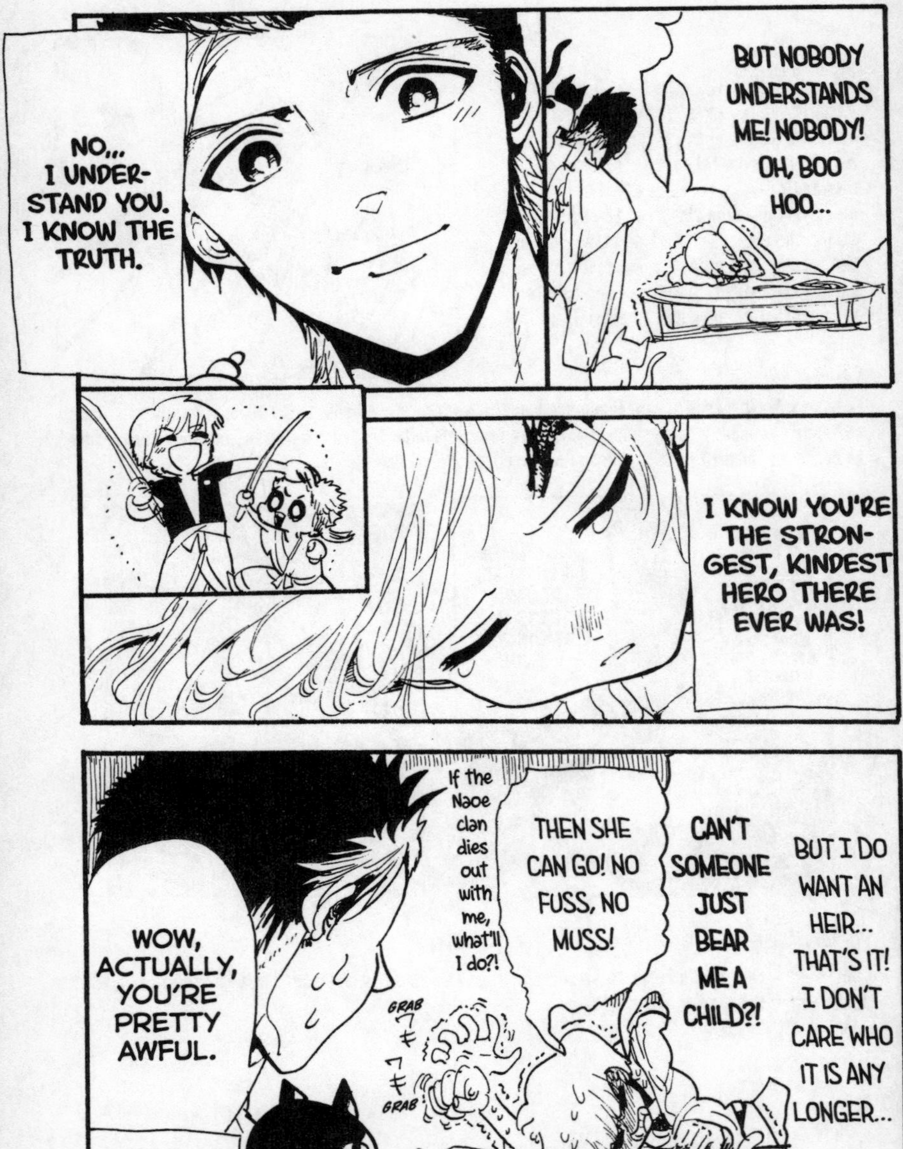
BUT NOBODY UNDERSTANDS ME! NOBODY! OH, BOO HOO...
NO... I UNDER-STAND YOU. I KNOW THE TRUTH.
I KNOW YOU'RE THE STRON-GEST, KINDEST HERO THERE EVER WAS!
BUT I DO WANT AN HEIR... THAT'S IT! I DON'T CARE WHO IT IS ANY LONGER...
CAN'T SOMEONE JUST BEAR ME A CHILD?!
THEN SHE CAN GO! NO FUSS, NO MUSS!
If the Naoe clan dies out with me, what'll I do?!
GRAB
GRAB
WOW, ACTUALLY, YOU'RE PRETTY AWFUL.
The End

Pg. 9, *battō*

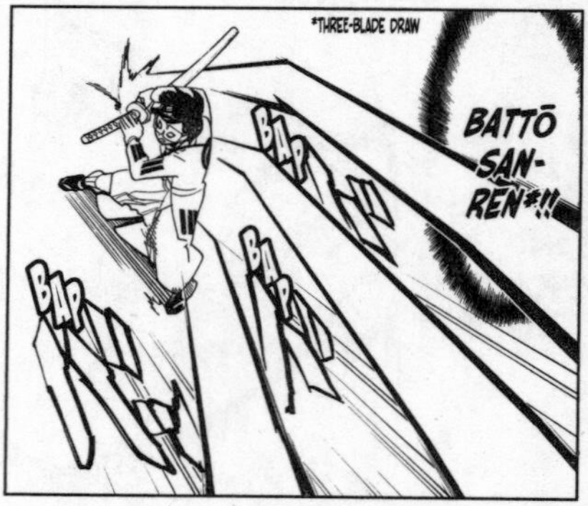
BATTŌ SAN-REN*!!
*THREE-BLADE DRAW

Battō literally means "drawing a sword," and here it refers to Katsumi's use of *battōjutsu* (now called *iaijutsu*). This is a sword-drawing technique that focuses on quickly drawing the blade to either strike the enemy or block an attack, all in the same continuous movement. It's more suitable for surprise attacks and counter-attacks than for use on the battlefield.

Pg. 52, crucifixion

Known as *haritsuke* in Japan. There are various *haritsuke* methods, but a general one is to string someone up, usually to a cross-shaped pole or a pole with two vertical bars, and then spear them to death. In Shimazu's case, there is no Christian undertone.

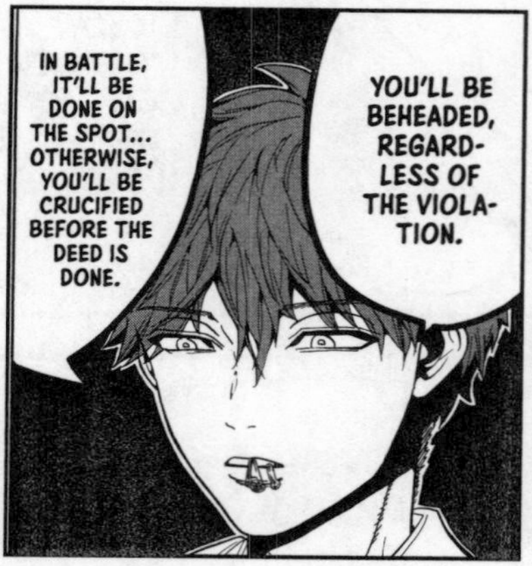
YOU'LL BE BEHEADED, REGARD-LESS OF THE VIOLA-TION.
IN BATTLE, IT'LL BE DONE ON THE SPOT... OTHERWISE, YOU'LL BE CRUCIFIED BEFORE THE DEED IS DONE.

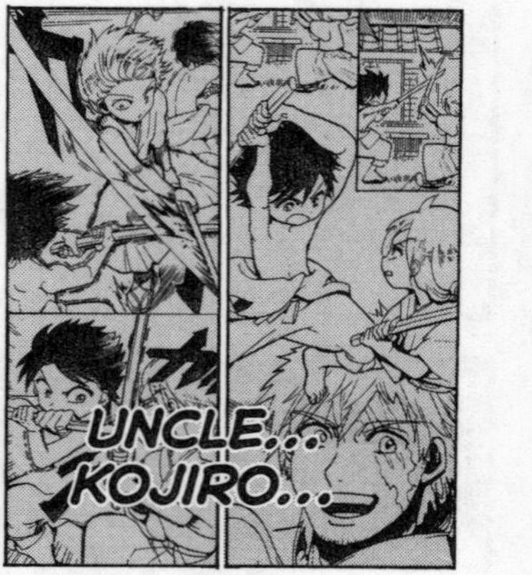
UNCLE... KOJIRO...

Pg. 163, Uncle

"Uncle" in Japanese can refer to an actual relative or to any middle-aged man. When Musashi talks about Kojiro's father, it's the latter.

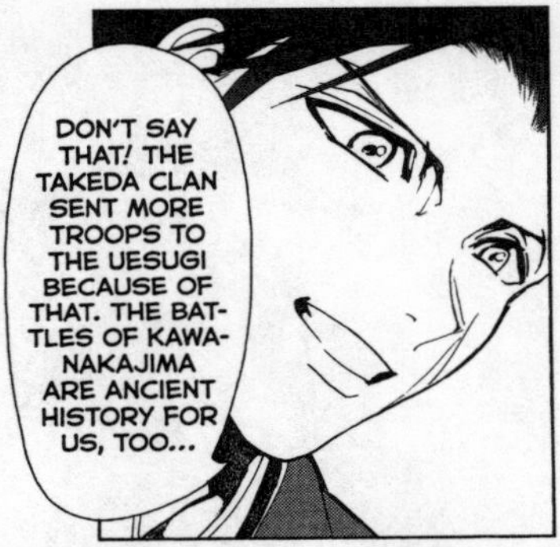
DON'T SAY THAT! THE TAKEDA CLAN SENT MORE TROOPS TO THE UESUGI BECAUSE OF THAT. THE BATTLES OF KAWANAKAJIMA ARE ANCIENT HISTORY FOR US, TOO...

Pg. 171, The Battles of Kawanakajima

A famous series of battles that took place from 1553 to 1564 between the feudal lords Takeda Shingen of Kai Province and Uesugi Kenshin of Echigo Province. The two were fighting for control over the plain of Kawanakajima, which is now in modern-day Nagano City.

Pg. 183, Michiru's name

The *kanji* for three thousand is 三千 (*sanzen*), but when the characters are read separately, the *kanji* for three (三) can be read as "mi," and the character for thousand (千) can be read as "chi." Although these *kanji* are not actually used in Michiru's name, Yataro chose this female name for this indirect wordplay.

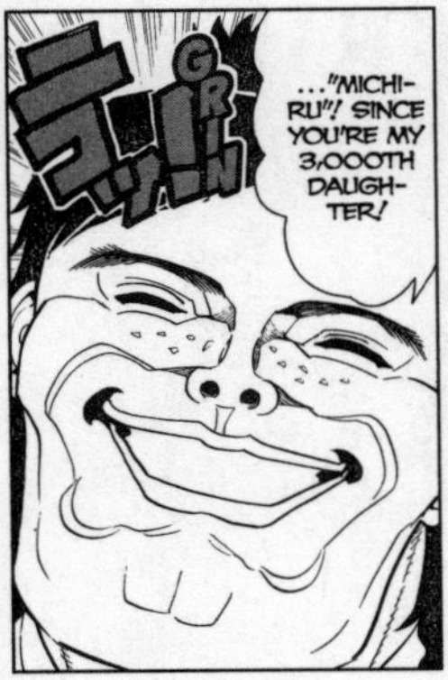
GRIN
..."MICHIRU"! SINCE YOU'RE MY 3,000TH DAUGHTER!

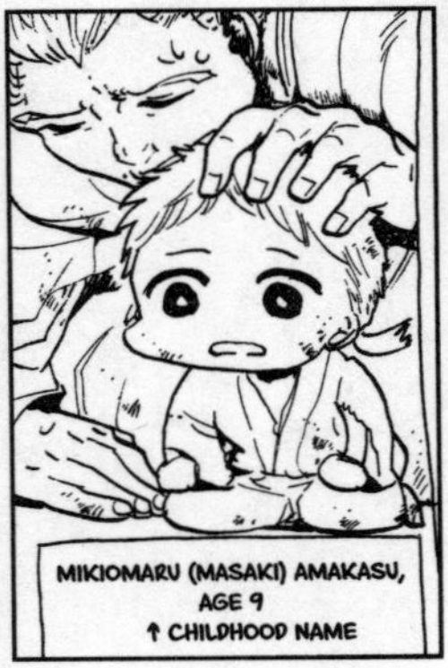
MIKIOMARU (MASAKI) AMAKASU, AGE 9
↑ CHILDHOOD NAME

Pg. 194, childhood name

A practice followed by nobles and samurai. A name is given to the boy at birth, and he will use this name until his coming-of-age ceremony (around 15 or 16 years old), where he will discard this name and receive his "actual" name.

Young characters and steampunk setting, like *Howl's Moving Castle* and *Battle Angel Alita*

Beyond the Clouds © 2018 Nicke / Ki-oon

A boy with a talent for machines and a mysterious girl whose wings he's fixed will take you beyond the clouds! In the tradition of the high-flying, resonant adventure stories of Studio Ghibli comes a gorgeous tale about the longing of young hearts for adventure and friendship!

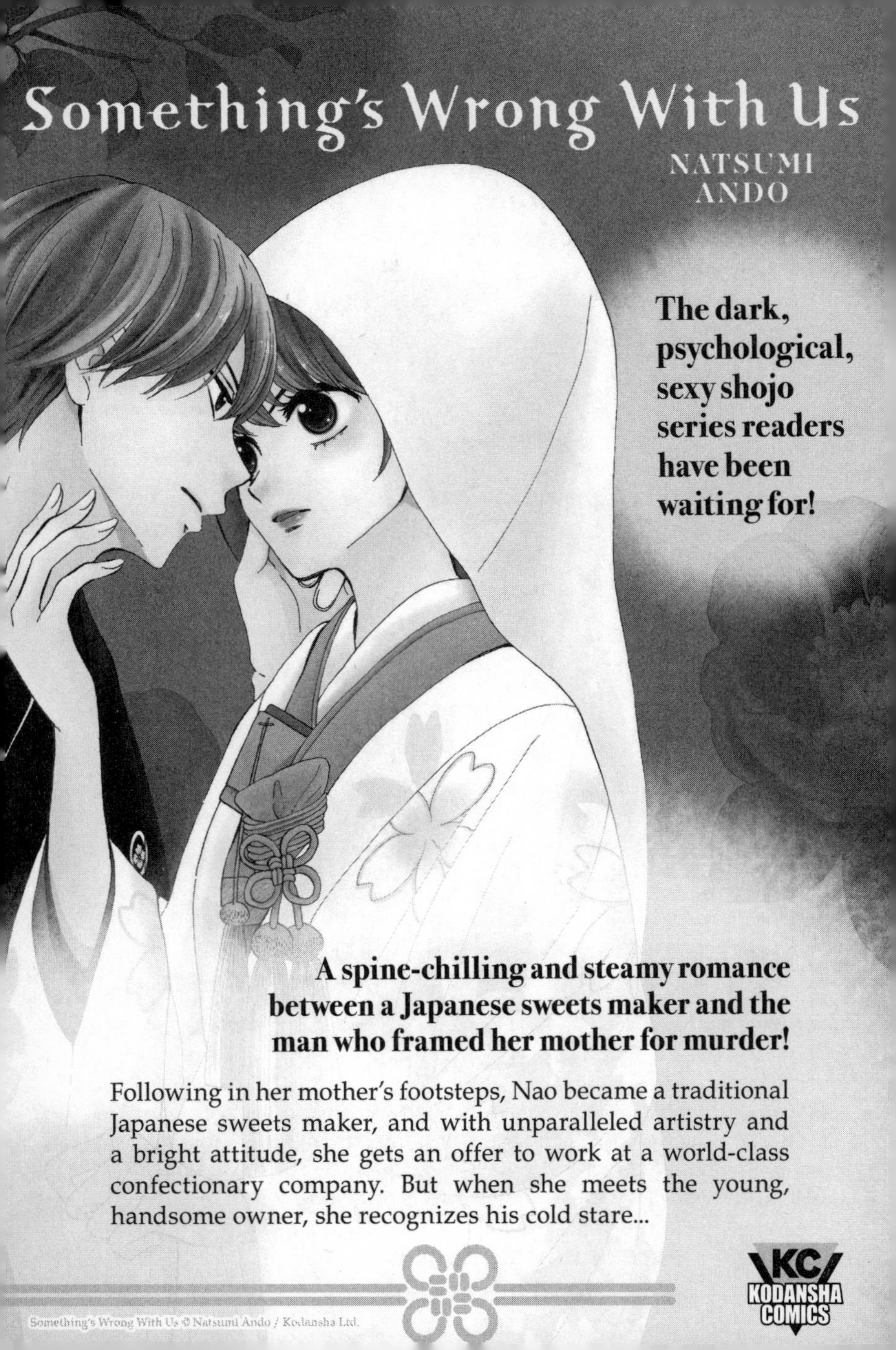
Something's Wrong With Us
NATSUMI ANDO
The dark, psychological, sexy shojo series readers have been waiting for!
A spine-chilling and steamy romance between a Japanese sweets maker and the man who framed her mother for murder!
Following in her mother's footsteps, Nao became a traditional Japanese sweets maker, and with unparalleled artistry and a bright attitude, she gets an offer to work at a world-class confectionary company. But when she meets the young, handsome owner, she recognizes his cold stare...
KC KODANSHA COMICS
Something's Wrong With Us © Natsumi Ando / Kodansha Ltd.

The adorable new odd-couple cat comedy manga from the creator of the beloved *Chi's Sweet Home*, in full color!

Praise for *Chi's Sweet Home*

"Nearly impossible to turn away... a true all-ages title that anyone, young or old, cat lover or not, will enjoy. The stories will bring a smile to your face and warm your heart."

—School Library Journal

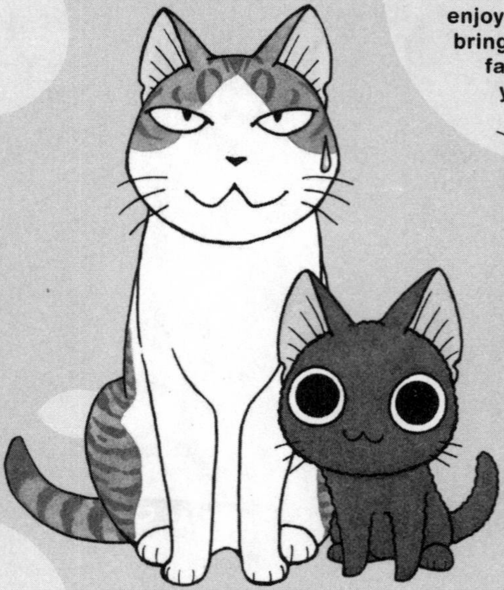

Sue & Tai-chan

Konami Kanata

Sue is an aging housecat who's looking forward to living out her life in peace... but her plans change when the mischievous black tomcat Tai-chan enters the picture! Hey! Sue never signed up to be a catsitter! *Sue & Tai-chan* is the latest from the reigning meow-narch of cute kitty comics, Konami Kanata.

KC KODANSHA COMICS

The boys are back, in 400-page hardcovers that are as pretty and badass as they are!

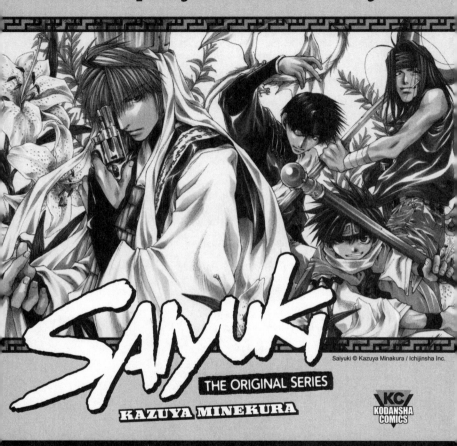

Saiyuki © Kazuya Minakura / Ichijinsha Inc.

SAIYUKI

THE ORIGINAL SERIES

KAZUYA MINEKURA

"AN EDGY COMIC LOOK AT AN ANCIENT CHINESE TALE." —YALSA

Genjo Sanzo is a Buddhist priest in the city of Togenkyo, which is being ravaged by yokai spirits that have fallen out of balance with the natural order. His superiors send him on a journey far to the west to discover why this is happening and how to stop it. His companions are three yokai with human souls. But this is no day trip — the four will encounter many discoveries and horrors on the way.

FEATURES NEW TRANSLATION, COLOR PAGES, AND BEAUTIFUL WRAPAROUND COVER ART!

A Kodansha Comics Trade Paperback Original
Orient 7 copyright © 2019 Shinobu Ohtaka
English translation copyright © 2021 Shinobu Ohtaka

Published in the United States by Kodansha Comics, an imprint of Kodansha USA Publishing, LLC, New York.

Publication rights for this English edition arranged through Kodansha Ltd., Tokyo.

First published in Japan in 2019 by Kodansha Ltd., Tokyo.

ISBN 978-1-64651-355-0

Printed in the United States of America.

www.kodansha.us

1st Printing
Translation: Nate Derr, Kevin Gifford
Lettering: Belynda Ungurath
Editing: Megan Ling
Kodansha Comics edition cover design by Phil Balsman
YKS Services LLC/SKY Japan, INC.

Publisher: Kiichiro Sugawara

Director of publishing services: Ben Applegate
Associate director, publishing operations: Stephen Pakula
Publishing services managing editors: Madison Salters, Alanna Ruse
Production managers: Emi Lotto, Angela Zurlo
Logo and character art ©Kodansha USA Publishing, LLC